Idleness Working

Idleness Working

The Discourse of Love's Labor from
Ovid through Chaucer and Gower

Gregory M. Sadlek

The Catholic University of America Press
Washington, D.C.

Library of Congress Cataloging-in-Publication Data

Sadlek, Gregory M., 1950–
 Idleness working : the discourse of love's labor from Ovid through Chaucer
and Gower / Gregory M. Sadlek.
     p. cm.
 Includes bibliographical references and index.
 ISBN 0-8132-1373-8 (alk. paper)

  1. Literature, Medieval—History and criticism. 2. Literature, Medieval—Roman influences. 3. Love in literature. 4. Work in literature. 5. Chaucer, Geoffrey, d. 1400—Criticism and interpretation. 6. Guillaume, de Lorris, fl. 1230.
Roman de la Rose. 7. Alanus, de Insulis, d. 1202. De planctu naturae. 8. An-
drâe, le chapelain. De amore et amoris remedio. 9. Gower, John, 1325?–408.
Confessio Amantis. 10. Ovid, 43 B.C.–17 or 18 A.D. Ars amatoria. 11. Ovid, 43
B.C.—17 or 18 A.D.—Influence. I. Title.
PN682.L68 S24 2004
809'.933543—dc22
2003018202

To Françoise, Jonathan, and Benjamin

Contents

Acknowledgments

All that matters is love and work.
—*Freud*

 Writing a book that conjoins two of the most fundamental areas of human experience has been a daunting challenge and a continuous pleasure. While it is not true that nothing matters beyond love and work, it would be difficult to find two more basic building blocks by which humans construct meaning and purpose for their lives. For an idealist and a romantic, love remains endlessly fascinating in its variety, its drama, its sweetness, and its ability to surprise. Love forms the towers and spires of life's castle—lifting us up to the heavens as high as we possibly can go. Humans often experience the onset of love as an unexplainable gift, an unmerited grace, the stuff of poetry. Work, on the other hand, forms the prosaic foundation upon which humans build their castles. Labor keeps us rooted to the earth. While it is one means by which we build our dreams, it is rarely poetic. Although work rewards us with a sense of accomplishment when our tasks are well done, the drudgery of work is not often inspirational. Work rhythms are the ticking metronome by which we keep time in our march through life.

These two crucial life experiences are so different that at first it seems wrong-headed to look for points of cross-fertilization, yet our poets and writers have been doing so for centuries. It began with the Roman poet Ovid, who, unlike his contemporaries, saw in love not madness but a project to be completed. Ovid declared that the qualities that went into a good worker were also those of a successful lover. Beyond a tender heart, Ovidian lovers needed a good head and a headstrong spirit. The ascending towers and spires of Ovidian love were built with laughter and high spirits on the prosaic foundation of effort and applied technique. Ovid left little to unmerited grace. The world of labor and the world of love merged to form a single coherent construct: love's labor, a concept that caught the attention of later writers and was lovingly developed over the course of the Middle Ages, a literary tradition that forms the focus of this study.

This book on the discourse of love's labor has been a labor of love for a good many years, and I owe debts of gratitude to many good friends and colleagues who have helped me along the way. The germ of the idea came during a graduate seminar on Geoffrey Chaucer's *Troilus and Criseyde* that I took under the late Joseph Milosh many years ago. The idea lay dormant for a number of years, however, until I had the good fortune to attend a National Endowment for the Humanities Summer Seminar organized by the late R. E. Kaske. Kaske was interested in my argument that the vice of *acedia* played an important part in the characterization of Troilus, and he encouraged me to continue my research and even expand it into a book-length study. Over the course of the next decade or so, I published several articles related to my overall project, and the project grew in terms of its scope and methodology. I was not able, however, to spend large amounts of time writing the book until 1998, when I was awarded a semester-long Periodic Professional Leave by the University of Nebraska at Omaha. Although it has taken me several more years to see the book into print, that semester was crucial in helping me turn an underdeveloped insight into a full, scholarly monograph. Indeed, my home institution has continuously provided generous support for the research on this book, including a number of grants and summer research fellowships from the University Committee on Research. In addition, Dean Shelton Hendricks and my department chairperson, Professor Michael Skau, offered me a generous subvention to aid in various last-minute expenses associated with publication of this book. Finally, I would like to acknowledge the Nebraska Humanities Council, which awarded me a summer fellowship to work on a book-related project in the summer of 1990.

It would be impossible to remember all of the individuals who offered advice and encouragement while I was writing the book. My discovery of M. M. Bakhtin and his writings on the ideological nature of discourse, critical to the central argument of the book, I owe to a faculty reading group on critical theory in which Susan Naramore Maher and Irvin Peckham played leading roles. Besides Bakhtin, there is Ovid. Classicists Thomas Rinkovich and Peter Aicher offered valuable insights into this Roman poet and his work. Indeed, Dr. Aicher not only offered helpful comments on an early draft of Chapter 2, but he also played quality control inspector with respect to my English translations of Ovid. Colleagues from the University of Nebraska at Omaha have offered generous help and support over the years. I am particularly grateful to Nora Bacon, Dr. Skau, Julia Garrett, and, again, Dr. Maher. None is a medievalist, but they all read parts of the manuscript and helped me hone my arguments and polish my rhetoric. The book is much stronger for their labors. Medievalists at other institutions also helped during the composition process. Juris Lidaka, Wendy Pfeffer, Thomas Coffey, R. F. Yeager, Winthrop Wetherbee, and my colleagues in the Medieval/Renaissance group at the University of Nebraska–Lincoln commented on various chapters. I am particularly in debt to the two superb readers who reviewed my manuscript for The Catholic University of America Press. The first remains anonymous, but the second is Heather Arden, whose insightful comments helped me improve not only my chapter on the *Roman de la rose* but, indeed, the entire book. Finally, I am grateful for the splendid assistance of David McGonagle, Susan Needham, Beth Benevides, Philip Holthaus, and other staff members of The Catholic University of America Press for the careful way they guided the book into print. Working with the press on this project has been a great pleasure. I should add, of course, that any errors that remain in the book are my own responsibility, not those of my friends and readers.

Finally, I want to thank my family, Françoise, Jonathan, and Benjamin, for their patience and continued support during the many long years this book was in process. While it may be true that, as John Donne writes, "The poor, the foul, the false, love can / Admit, but not the busied man," Donne was not thinking of familial love in that poem. Yet familial love has given the most help and comfort to this "busied man," who labored on a book about love and labor.

I am grateful to the following copyright holders for giving their permission to reprint excerpts from the referenced materials:

Centro Italiano di Studi Sull'alto Medioevo, for "De planctu naturae," edited by Nikolaus M. Häring, *Studi Medievali*, © 1978. Reproduced with permission.

Éditions du Cerf, for *Écrits*, St. Francis of Assisi, edited by Kajetan Esser, © 1981. Reproduced with permission.

Éditions Honoré Champion, for *Roman de la Rose*, edited by Félix Lecoy, © 1983. Reproduced with permission.

Gerald Duckworth and Company, Ltd., for *Andreas Capellanus on Love*, edited by P. G. Walsh, © 1982. Reproduced with permission.

Houghton Mifflin Company, for *The Riverside Chaucer*, edited by Larry Benson, © 1987. Reproduced with permission.

Les Belles Lettres, for *Poème au roi Robert*, edited by Claude Carozzi, © 1979. Reproduced with permission.

Oxford University Press, for *Amores, Medicamina faciei femineae, Ars amatoria, Remedia amoris*, Ovid, edited by E. J. Kenney, © 1961. Reproduced with permission.

Pegasus Press, for Gregory M. Sadlek, "John Gower's *Confessio Amantis*, Ideology, and the 'Labor' of 'Love's Labor,'" in *Re-visioning Gower*, edited by R. F. Yeager, © 1998. Reproduced with permission.

Penn State University Press, for Gregory M. Sadlek, "Love, Labor, and Sloth in Chaucer's *Troilus and Criseyde*," *The Chaucer Review*, Vol. 26, 350–68, © 1992. Reproduced with permission.

Pontifical Institute of Medieval Studies, for *The Plaint of Nature*, translated by James J. Sheridan, © 1980. Reproduced with permission.

Princeton University Press, for *The Romance of the Rose*, translated by Charles Dahlberg, © 1983. Reproduced with permission.

Book jacket: Illumination from Bodleian Library, University of Oxford, Ms. Douce 195, folio 155, recto. Reproduced with permission.

Idleness Working

CHAPTER I

The Discourse of Love's Labor and Its Cultural Contexts

What we call "white" is a rainbow of colored rays packed into a small space. The prism sets them free. Love is the white light of emotions. It includes many feelings which, out of laziness and confusion, we crowd into one simple word. Art is the prism that sets them free, then follows the gyrations of one or a few.

—*Diane Ackerman*

To see art whole, as humanist critics have long urged, must be to see it clearly as it has emerged from the generative conditions of its making, rather than envisioning it as some radical epiphany with no plausible principle of realization.

—*David Scott Kastan*

I

Erotic love has been a major theme in Western literature at least since the poetry of Sappho but at no time more so than in the Middle Ages. Although partially tied in complex ways to human biology, "love" is also in large part a cultural construct, which changes and evolves as it passes from culture to culture and epoch to epoch.[1] Its complexity resists simple foundational definitions, and artists have continuously played a role in the ongoing construction and deconstruction of models of erotic love, models constructed with language and motifs taken both from

---

1. A seminal treatment of the social construction of reality is found in Peter Berger and Thomas Luckmann, *The Social Construction of Reality* (New York: Doubleday, 1966). See especially their remarks on language (34–46), the origins of institutionalization (53–67), and roles (72–79). On the social construction of sexuality, see Alan Soble, *The Philosophy of Sex and Love* (St. Paul, Minn.: Paragon House, 1998) 14–19. For a psychoanalytic perspective on love as "culturally conditioned," see Lawrence Stone, "Passionate Attachments in the West in Historical Perspective," *Passionate Attachments: Thinking about Love*, ed. Willard Gaylin and Ethel Person (New York: Free Press, 1988) 15–26.

artistic predecessors and from experiences in other, often unrelated, areas of their contemporary cultures. Although the epigraph by Diane Ackerman implies an essentialist view of love and refers only to the emotion of love and not also to the cultural practices associated with it, it rightly brings to the fore the active role of artists in teasing out specific instantiations from the "white light" of love, a word whose definition, both as a noun and a verb, takes fifteen long columns in the *Oxford English Dictionary*.[2]

Love—the way we conceive it, the value we assign to it, and the way we practice it—has a history. In the fourteenth-century romance/novel *Troilus and Criseyde*, Geoffrey Chaucer is well aware that love and its ways change in various times and in various locations. To those who are tempted to criticize Troilus and his way of seeking love, for example, the poet argues that Troilus was simply following the customs of his times and that "Ecch contree hath his lawes" (Each country has its own laws).[3] In standard histories of love in the West, different sexual practices are noted, and various marriage customs observed.[4] Scholars call forth and examine the great lovers of history: Paris and Helen, Aeneas and Dido, Anthony and Cleopatra, Tristan and Iseult. They also lovingly scrutinize philosophical tracts on love (especially Platonic ones). Nevertheless, works of creative literature are among the greatest sources of information about the emotions and practices associated with various cultural models of love. The archaeology of love is, it seems, essentially tied to literature. The labor of love and the labor of writing are inextricably intertwined. As Lawrence Stone asks, "Did poetry invent love, or love poetry?"[5]

This study is, however, not primarily a history of love. It is a historically situated literary critical treatment of various classical and medieval amatory texts. Nevertheless, the history of these texts belongs to the history of love, for these writers too had a hand in the social construction of love. Indeed, they "refracted" a new color of love, a heretofore little-

2. "Love," *Oxford English Dictionary (OED)*, 1989 ed.

3. Geoffrey Chaucer, *Troilus and Criseyde, The Riverside Chaucer*, ed. Larry D. Benson, 3rd ed. (Boston: Houghton Mifflin, 1987) 2.42 (489). All quotations from Chaucer's works will be taken from this edition and cited in the text. Modern English translations are my own.

4. Some recent, helpful overviews of the history of love include Diane Ackerman, *A Natural History of Love* (New York: Random House, 1994); Martin S. Bergmann, *The Anatomy of Loving: The Story of Man's Quest to Know What Love Is* (New York: Columbia University Press, 1987); and Morton M. Hunt, *The Natural History of Love* (New York: Knopf, 1959).

5. Stone 16.

noticed tradition of constructing love as a form of labor. Love can be a work project even though it can also, and often at the same time, be experienced as a form of disease or of madness.

How can this be? Literature teaches us that love is more than complicated; it is paradoxical, a fact expressed particularly well in many a Renaissance sonnet. A particularly eloquent example is Francesco Petrarch's Sonnet 102, which was translated by Chaucer and appears in the *Troilus:*

> If no love is, O God, what fele I so?
> And if love is, what thing and which is he?
> If love be good, from whennes cometh my woo?
> If it be wikke, a wonder thinketh me,
> When every torment and adversite
> That cometh of hym may to me savory thinke,
> For ay thurst I, the more that ich it drynke.
>
> And if that at myn owen lust I brenne,
> From whennes cometh my waillynge and my pleynte?
> If harm agree me, wherto pleyne I thenne?
> I noot, ne whi unwery that I feynte.
> O quike deth, O swete harm so queynte,
> How may of the in me swich quantite
> But if that I consente that it be?

(1.400–413)

[If love does not exist, then what, in the name of God, am I feeling? And if love exists, what kind of thing is it? If love is good, why am I so unhappy? If it is wicked, I am truly amazed because I delight in its every torment and adversity. For the more that I drink of it, the more I thirst.

And if I burn at my own pleasure, why do I wail and moan? If harm is agreeable, why then do I complain? I know not why I faint although I am not weary. O living death, O sweet harm so strange. How can so much love be in me unless I consent for it to be there?]

The paradox is, of course, that love can be both hurtful and pleasurable, something for humans to avoid and yet something that humans desire. Love becomes a "living death," a "sweet harm," and its conflicting experiences drive Troilus into a state of total confusion. He later compares his state to being caught in a storm in a rudderless boat or to being in a "wondre maladie," a wondrous illness. In this, both Chaucer and Petrarch are recalling a tradition that goes back at least to the Greeks and perhaps even to the Egyptians before them.[6]

Love in the classical Greek tradition was certainly portrayed as a madness or passion.[7] The chorus in Sophocles' *Antigone*, for example, sings: "Love resistless in fight, all yield at a glance of thine eye / . . . Mad are thy subjects all, and even the wisest heart / Straight to folly will fall, at a touch of thy poisoned dart."[8] For Plato, *eros* was one of four different kinds of madness that are gifts from the gods. Love is

the fourth kind of madness, which causes [the lover] to be regarded as mad, who, when he sees the beauty on earth, remembering true beauty, feels his wings growing and longs to stretch them for an upward flight, but cannot do so, and, like a bird, gazes upward and neglects the things below.[9]

Roman writers also portrayed love as madness. In the *Georgics*, for example, Virgil describes love as a dangerous excess that weakens both men and animals.[10] In the *Aeneid*, Virgil presents Dido's love of Aeneas as a form of madness or illness. At the beginning of Book 4, he writes: "At regina gravi iamdudum saucia cura / volnus alit venis et caeco carpitur igni" (But the queen, long since smitten with a grievous love-pang, feeds the wound with her life-blood, and is wasted with fire unseen). Kindled by her sister Anna's encouraging words, the madness turns to frenzy: "uritur infelix Dido totaque vagatur / urbe furens, qualis coniecta cerva sagitta" (Unhappy Dido burns, and through the city wanders in a frenzy—even as a hind, smitten by an arrow).[11] The end result, of course, is her suicide over the loss of Aeneas. In another Roman classic, Ovid's *Metamorphoses*, Medea is struck with erotic madness at the sight of Jason.

6. I will concentrate on the Greek tradition below. However, Ackerman (13) argues that the malady of love is a theme even in early Egyptian poetry.

7. See A. W. Allen, "Elegy and the Classical Attitude toward Love: Propertius 1, 1," *Yale Classical Studies* 11 (1950): 264; R. I. Frank, "Catullus 51: *Otium* versus *Virtus*," *Transactions of the American Philological Association* 99 (1968): 233–36; E. R. Dodds, *The Greeks and the Irrational* (Berkeley and Los Angeles: University of California Press, 1966) 218; and P. G. Walsh, introduction, *Andreas Capellanus on Love* (London: Duckworth, 1982) 15–16. See also the comments of Molly Myerowitz, who compares love in the classical Greek tradition with the radically new idea of love presented by Ovid (*Ovid's Games of Love* [Detroit: Wayne State University Press, 1985] 32–33).

8. *Antigone: Sophocles*, ed. and trans. F. Storr, Loeb Classical Library (Cambridge, Mass.: Harvard University Press, 1981) 377.

9. *Phaedrus: Plato:* "*Euthyphro*," "*Apology*," "*Crito*," "*Phaedo*," "*Phaedrus*," ed. and trans. Harold North Fowler, Loeb Classical Library (Cambridge, Mass.: Harvard University Press, 1914) 483.

10. Virgil, *Georgics: Virgil*, ed. and trans. H. Rushton Fairclough, rev. ed., Loeb Classical Library (Cambridge, Mass.: Harvard University Press, 1986) 3.242–83.

11. Virgil, *Aeneid: Virgil*, ed. and trans. H. Rushton Fairclough, rev. ed., Loeb Classical Library (Cambridge: Harvard University Press, 1986) 4.1–2, 68–69 (1.396–99).

Ovid uses the term *furor*, which can mean madness, frenzy, or passionate desire.[12] Medea realizes that she suffers from love, but all her self-analysis and internal struggles cannot save her from her fate. The madness of love leads her to help the foreigner Jason, thereby betraying her father, and she flees with Jason back to Greece, with catastrophic results.

The Middle Ages also stood in awe of the passionate nature of love. The twelfth-century love theorist Andreas Capellanus defines love as *passio*, or suffering.[13] That love can cause intense suffering is thoroughly illustrated in the story of Abelard and Heloise, tragic twelfth-century French lovers.[14] That love is essentially tied to suffering is suggested by a fictional love story, the medieval tale of Tristan and Iseult. This story fashions love as suffering into a foundational myth of Western civilization, one that is thoroughly analyzed by Denis de Rougemont in one of the critical touchstones in the literature of love, *Love in the Western World*.[15] De Rougemont's book centers on love as passion—passion as "suffering, something undergone, the mastery of fate over a free and responsible person."[16] Such love is tragic by definition, and de Rougemont argues that the myth of Tristan and Iseult reveals at its core "the dark and unmentionable fact that passion is linked with death."[17] Overlooking the ancient history of love as madness, de Rougemont links the invention of passionate courtly love with the Cathar heresy that sprung up in southern France in the twelfth century.[18] In his interpretation, the literature of romantic love carries a coded message for a mystical belief system: the world is evil; the spirit alone is good; seek death to find the good. Romantic love becomes the equivalent of love of death. This, for de Rouge-

12. Ovid, *Metamorphoses: Ovid*, ed. and trans. Frank Justus Miller and G. P. Gould, 3rd ed., Loeb Classical Library (Cambridge, Mass.: Harvard University Press, 1984) 7.10.

13. Andreas Capellanus, *De amore: Andreas Capellanus on Love* 32. All subsequent quotations and translations from Andreas's text are taken from this edition and cited by page number. For a modern psychoanalytical analysis of passionate love, see Milton Viederman, "The Nature of Passionate Love," *Passionate Attachments* 1–14.

14. See Abelard's *Historia calamitatum* and the subsequent exchange of letters for a description of their passionate affair (*The Letters of Abelard and Heloise*, trans. Betty Radice [New York: Penguin Books, 1974]).

15. I take the phrase "critical touchstones to the literature of love" and several representative titles from his list from James J. Paxson, "The Medieval World of Desire, Discourse, Reception, and Writing: An Introduction," *Desiring Discourse: The Literature of Love, Ovid through Chaucer* (Selinsgrove, Pa.: Susquehanna University Press, 1998) 11.

16. Denis de Rougemont, *Love in the Western World*, trans. Montgomery Belgion (New York: Schocken Books, 1983) 50.

17. de Rougemont 21.

18. de Rougemont 75–91.

mont, is the sum total of the history of the discourse of love and sexuality in the West since the Middle Ages. For this reason, he argues that happy love in the West has no history.[19] Love, however, is constructed in many different ways in the West, and even happy love has a history.

Before leaving passionate love, however, I should also note that in the Middle Ages love could literally be an illness. For medieval physicians, *amor hereos* was a bona fide disease *(morbus),* and its treatment was prescribed in various medieval medical tracts like the one composed by Constantine the African.[20] In The Knight's Tale, Chaucer's Arcite suffers from the classical symptoms of *amor hereos* when he is forcefully separated from the sight of his love, Emelye:

> His slep, his mete, his drynke, is hym biraft,
> That lene he wex and drye as is a shaft;
> His eyen holwe and grisly to biholde,
> His hewe falow and pale as asshen colde.
>
> (1.1361–64)

[He was deprived of his sleep, his food, and his drink so that he grew lean and dry as a stick. His eyes were sunken and grisly to behold; his complexion was yellowish and pale as cold ashes.]

Arcite flees the company of other people and spends his nights weeping. The sounds of musical instruments make him especially melancholy. In short, he suffers what Chaucer understood to be "the loveris maladye / Of hereos" (the lover's malady of hereos; 1.1373–74), and thus lives in "cruel torment and . . . peyne and wo" (cruel torment and pain and woe; 1.1382). So deeply does he suffer that he risks death by returning to Athens to see Emelye in direct disobedience of the command of Theseus. There, disguised as a servant, Arcite again sees Emelye. He recovers somewhat, but his recovery is short-lived since it leads him into direct competition with Palamon for Emelye's hand. Only death brings an end to Arcite's torments, but medieval medical handbooks prescribed less drastic cures, such as wine, baths, good conversation, music, poetry, and, indeed, sexual intercourse.[21]

In contrast to this history of love as madness and disease, love can also

19. de Rougement 15.

20. Key medical tracts on "amor hereos" are collected, edited, translated, and analyzed in Mary Wack, *Lovesickness in the Middle Ages: The Viaticum and Its Commentaries* (Philadelphia: University of Pennsylvania Press, 1990). See also John L. Lowes, "The Loveres Maladye of Hereos," *Modern Philology* 11 (1913–1914): 491–546.

21. Wack 41–46.

be constructed as a form of work. While not every text in the tradition of love's labor presents love as happy, love in the tradition is generally not tragic nor linked with death. Love's "work" is often comic, presented in the form of a game played by a witty author. The writings of Ovid, who as a *praeceptor amoris*, or "teacher of love," wittily expounds upon love's labors for his fellow Roman citizens, offer one of the best examples. During the Middle Ages his works became the most influential model of this kind of discourse. Ovid's rakish persona often counsels dedicated labor to achieve one's amorous goals. In the *Ars amatoria*, for example, he treats love as a series of three labors *(labores)*: finding a lover, winning the lover, and making love endure.[22] Later, when he explains that the lover should try to win his beloved without gifts but with love letters, he exclaims: "Hoc opus, hic labor est" (Here is the task, here is the labor; 1.453). Not only Ovid's language and imagery but also his focus and attitude were influential. Characteristically, he does not spend much time analyzing emotions, dispositions, or feelings of attachment; rather, he concentrates on love's activities, from courtship through copulation, and presents them as "work." In addition, this representation is made with a wink and a nod. Indeed, the Ovidian discourse of love's labor is "rhetorical" in Richard Lanham's sense of the term: it is generally not to be taken as a serious description of the nature of love but as a playful analogy to life in the "real" world, where at least some men and some women have to labor in order to earn their livelihood.[23] In addition, the discourse is often dramatic, with characters acting "as if" love's activities were serious work.

Later writers, however, constructed a serious side to this discourse. When, for example, medieval writers added procreation to the menu of love's labor, the ensuing discourse assumed an urgent moral edge. For Alan of Lille, a twelfth-century writer, love's role in reproducing the species is deadly serious. Alan's Venus was created to be a worker god-

---

22. Ovid, *Ars amatoria: P. Ovidi Nasonis: "Amores," "Medicamina Faciei Femineae," "Ars Amatoria," "Remedia Amoris,"* ed. E. J. Kenney (Oxford, U.K.: Clarendon Press, 1961) 1.14–15. All subsequent quotations from the *Ars* will be taken from this edition and cited in the text. The English translations are my own. Reprinted with permission of Oxford University Press.

Ovid's text is an example of what Michel Foucault identifies as the ancient tradition of passing on sexual knowledge, the *ars erotica*, a compilation of sexual techniques intended as an initiation into sexual pleasure. The same cannot be said for Ovid's medieval imitator, Andreas Capellanus, in his *De amore*, which is a study of the discourse of seduction rather than of sexual pleasure itself. Foucault contrasts the *ars erotica* with *scientia sexualis*, the modern scientific discourse about sex (*The History of Sexuality*, trans. Robert Hurley, vol. 1 [New York: Vintage Books, 1990] 57–58).

23. Richard Lanham, *The Motives of Eloquence: Literary Rhetoric in the Renaissance* (New Haven, Conn.: Yale University Press, 1976) 3–5.

dess, a mistress of the mint, coining new human beings for the realm. Her child, Iocus, or sexual play, is simply an uncouth bastard. Alan's discourse influenced, in turn, the love poetry of Jean de Meun, John Gower, and Geoffrey Chaucer. In the writings of Jean de Meun and Chaucer, however, Alan's serious moral message was mixed with a playful Ovidian strain, creating a slippery mixture of earnestness and game.

II

What is true for love is also true for labor. Language and culture deeply condition the ways authors represent labor and its value.[24] How "labor" was conceived, the different values it stood for and the vices it opposed, and the different roles it was thought to play changed as one proceeded up the social ladder of imperial Rome and, later, of the feudal society of the Christian Middle Ages. "Labor" in this study is broader than just wage or even manual labor. It is not necessarily "physical exertion directed to the supply of the material wants of the community" or a reference to the "general body of laborers." Instead, "labor" or "work" denotes something more general: the "exertion of the faculties of the body or mind . . . directed to a definite end." This may or may not be a means of gaining one's livelihood.[25]

As to the history of this concept during the relevant periods, a few generalities can be noted in passing, while I leave the detailed exposition to later chapters.[26] Although the drudgery of heavy manual labor was associated with either Roman slaves or Roman wage laborers in imperial Rome, a strong ethic existed that condemned emasculating idleness among the Roman aristocracy. Indeed, Roman thinkers valued strenuous effort, especially the agricultural labors of an aristocratic landowner, as long as they were entered into freely and not forced by either physical or financial restraints. The labors of craftsmen, however, were considered beneath the dignity of free men.

Religious writings, traditional social models, and the difficult working conditions of the majority of laborers heavily influenced work ideologies in the Christian Middle Ages. The appreciation of the positive value of creative work, arising ultimately from the depiction of a "worker God" in

---

24. Patrick Joyce, "The Historical Meanings of Work: An Introduction," *The Historical Meanings of Work* (Cambridge, U.K.: Cambridge University Press, 1987) 1, 14.

25. "Labour" (1.a) and "Work" (4), *OED*.

26. Sources for this short history of the meaning of labor will be given in the notes of the extended discussions found in the following chapters.

Genesis, was overshadowed by an even more powerful contrasting belief in work as a punishment for original sin. The connotations of the medieval Latin word *labor* were negative. Starting from well before the advent of the three estates social model, medieval writers associated *labor* with the pain and drudgery of the rural peasant classes, while they associated *otium* (idleness or leisure) with the aristocracy. Yet while *labor* was constructed as the proper role of the third estate, each of the other two estates had its own proper *officium*, or duty. Neither was, in theory, completely free from the duty of strenuous effort.

The most developed medieval ideology of work sprang from the moral system of the Seven Deadly Sins and their characteristic antidotes. From as early as the fourth century, medieval moralists associated idleness with the sin of *acedia* (sloth). The value of work was thought to arise primarily from its status as an antidote to *acedia*. St. Benedict prized manual labor as a fitting and useful activity for his monks, and in his monastic rule he valorized labor as a form of prayer and prayer as a form of labor. Nevertheless, the fundamental value of these strenuous activities lay not in the material items they produced, but in the role they played in keeping Benedict's monks from idleness.

The urbanization of the twelfth century, when both Andreas Capellanus and Alan of Lille wrote, added new layers of complexity to the social construction of labor. A significant development was the increasing valorization of the skills of artisans. While agricultural labor was idealized and artisanal labor denigrated in imperial Rome, the relative positions of these two kinds of labor were reversed in the twelfth century. On the one hand, agricultural labor, associated exclusively with the nonprestigious working peasantry, was held in little regard. On the other hand, with the growth of the urban guilds, the work of artisans experienced a significant rise in prestige. Crafts began to be categorized in academic discussions of the arts.

The founding of the mendicant orders in the late twelfth century and the growth of the universities in the thirteenth added even more complexity to the question of labor ideology. Although St. Francis valued manual labor as an activity for his followers, he prized absolute freedom for evangelization even more. Franciscans were to have no monasteries and no regular routines of work and prayer. If his friars lacked day labor, they could return to the "table of the lord," begging. They, like the "lilies of the field" and the "birds of the air," were to trust in God to provide for their needs. In the thirteenth century, the nonproductivity of the mendicants came under attack by the secular masters of the University of Paris. With the writings of Guillaume de St. Amour, which had a critical influence on Jean de Meun, a tradition of antifraternal literature was born. The merits of "clerical work," "scholarship," and "manual labor" were thoroughly debated.

The late fourteenth century was another critical time in the history of labor and labor ideologies. The depopulation resulting from the Black Plague had an unsettling effect on the value, and thus the stability, of peasant labor. In England these conditions led to the enactment of the Statute of Laborers. This law attempted to stifle market forces, which were pushing workers' wages higher. In addition, old work rhythms changed and new conceptions of urban "work time" were born with the coming of the mechanical clock. Unhappiness with working conditions in England finally led to the Peasants' Revolt of 1381, the beginning of a decade during which Chaucer and Gower had extensive contacts with each other, a period when the *Troilus* and the *Confessio Amantis*, Gower's story collection on love, were written. Recent historical scholarship suggests that early states of a "work ethic," or "work ethics," were beginning to form at this time.[27] Indeed, during this period a developing belief in the dignity of work (as opposed to seeing the obligation to work as merely an effect of humankind's fall from grace), an intense concern with labor productivity, and the belief that time is a commodity to be spent wisely became a part of the ideological landscape. These are necessary but not sufficient elements of what would later be identified as a Protestant work ethic.

III

Against the backdrop of this evolution in labor ideology, this study treats the evolution of the discourse of love's labor, particularly the ideological flavor of the language by which it is expressed. In some ways, it complements de Rougemont's study of love as passion. Although love's labor may not always be joyous, it is always active rather than passive. Far from being a malady the lover suffers, love's labor demands exertion of the faculties of the mind and body to gain some goal. The canon of texts studied here begins in classical Rome and stops at the end of the Middle Ages. The texts are read using the methodological insights of M. M.

27. See, for example, Christopher Dyer, "Work Ethics in the Fourteenth Century," *The Problem of Labour in Fourteenth-Century England*, ed. James Bothwell et al. (York, U.K.: York Medieval Press, 2000) 21–41.

Bakhtin, who argues that utterance is never ideologically pure but reflects the beliefs of a particular profession, social group, age, and political
party. "Each word," he writes, "tastes of context and contexts in which it
has lived its socially charged life."[28] If, then, key ways of thinking about,
writing about, and valuing labor evolve over the history of a literary tradition, these changes should in some way be reflected in literary utterances about work, even when that work is the work of love.

   Although contemporary critical theory has splintered into a formida-
ble array of various schools and approaches, one of the clearest reorien-
tations of recent years is away from seeing literary texts as free-standing,
independent artifacts and toward seeing the interconnectedness of author, text, audience, and culture.[29] Characteristically, critics analyze a literary text not as a tranquil artifact but as a "site of action, a locus of complex agencies" in which social and literary forces "act on and modify each
other through sustained engagement."[30] Nevertheless, one need not jetti-
son the idea of the author to accept the idea that cultural forces are at
work in a literary text. On the contrary, literary texts are the products of
particular individuals with particular intentions, not simply "sites of action" in which social, political, or economic forces clash with each other
in a blind psychomachia.[31] While authors are not autonomous and are
subject to both conscious and unconscious constraints, constraints built
into the very nature of language, as Bakhtin has shown, they are not simply mediators of historical forces. An author is not simply "a hapless
scribe or 'reproducer' of ideology."[32] The relationship between authors
and cultures is dialogic; neither determines the other.[33]

   What follows is a historical analysis of the evolution of the discourse

----

28. M. M. Bakhtin, "Discourse in the Novel," *The Dialogic Imagination*, ed. Michael Holquist,
trans. Caryl Emerson and Michael Holquist (Austin: University of Texas Press, 1981) 293.

29. See, for example, Paul Strohm's comments on the interaction of the author and his culture in
the preface to his *Social Chaucer* ([Cambridge, Mass.: Harvard University Press, 1989] ix–xiii). See also
the comments of Stephen Greenblatt and Giles Gunn on the recent questioning of the archetypal
"scene of writing," which imagined an "individual author toiling in isolation from history and society" and the absolute separation of "text" and "context" (introduction, *Redrawing the Boundaries: The
Transformation of English and American Literary Studies* [New York: MLA, 1992] 3–4). See also Anne
Middleton's remarks on the convergence of literary studies and social history ("Medieval Studies,"
Redrawing the Boundaries 24–25).

30. Middleton 26.

31. See Lee Patterson, *Negotiating the Past: The Historical Understanding of Medieval Literature*
(Madison: University of Wisconsin Press, 1987) 73; and Middleton 26.

32. Strohm xii.

33. A sensitive treatment of determinism is undertaken by Raymond Williams, who rejects both
the strict Marxist doctrine of economic determinism and the bourgeois theory of the autonomous

of love's labor in select works of Ovid, Andreas Capellanus, Alan of Lille, Guillaume de Lorris, Jean de Meun, John Gower, and Geoffrey Chaucer. One chapter will be given over to each author, and the trajectory of all the chapters but the last is twofold. First, each highlights key elements in the work ideology of the culture in which the literary work was produced. Second, within these cultural contexts, each scrutinizes relevant diction and imagery to demonstrate not only how the culture's work ideology is either appropriated or subverted by the authors, but also how the literary tradition of working at love is refashioned anew within fresh ideological coordinates. In the words of David Scott Kastan, each text is analyzed "to see it clearly as it has emerged from the generative conditions of its making, rather than envisioning it as some radical epiphany with no plausible principle of realization."[34]

As David Wallace has written, the highest goal of literary-historiographical criticism is "to make visible relations and developments that would otherwise remain obscured or unconnected," and that is my intent.[35] Although portions of this canon of writers have already been the focus of such important works as C. S. Lewis's *Allegory of Love* and Peter Allen's *The Art of Love: Amatory Fiction from Ovid to "The Romance of the Rose,"* these studies approach the tradition from different perspectives and with different goals from mine. Lewis wrote what James J. Paxson calls "the most sweeping and powerful program of introduction to the literature of love."[36] He treats Ovid, Andreas Capellanus, Chrétien de Troyes, and Alan of Lille briefly before giving over entire chapters to the works of

---

individual free of social limits. What he proposes is to retain the idea of human agency but always to set it within concrete objective historical conditions that delimit the possible. He agrees with Engels, who said: "We make our history ourselves, but, in the first place, under definite assumptions and conditions" (*Marxism and Literature* [Oxford: Oxford University Press, 1977] 84–85).

34. "Shakespeare and the 'Element he Lived in,'" *A Companion to Shakespeare*, ed. David Scott Kastan (Oxford, U.K.: Blackwell, 1999) 5.

35. David Wallace, *Chaucerian Polity: Absolutist Lineages and Associational Forms in England and Italy* (Stanford, Calif.: Stanford University Press, 1997) xvii.

36. Paxson 21n. James Paxson and Cynthia Gravlee's anthology of essays, *Desiring Discourse: The Literature of Love, Ovid through Chaucer*, is another important contribution to the critical study of ancient and medieval love literature. Although the range of literature covered is similar to mine, the book is not a single, focused historical study of love, but rather a collection of essays on desire, specifically, "the interdependence of sexual desire, spiritual desire, and desire to make language itself" (12). The collection reflects the broad range of interests represented by those who attended a National Endowment for the Humanities summer seminar under the direction of Robert W. Hanning. Beside essays on Ovid and Chaucer, the collection contains essays on troubadour lyrics and the lais of Marie de France. A range of different critical methodologies is employed, but highlighted in the collection are works of feminist criticism, gender criticism, and reception criticism. All the studies center on the "problematic nature of *desire*—that is, on its psychological, phenomenological, and

Jean de Meun, Guillaume de Lorris, Chaucer, Gower, Thomas Usk, other medieval Chaucerians, and Edmund Spenser.[37] His focus is double: it is both thematic and stylistic. That is, he seeks to define courtly love and to show whence it came: "Ovid misunderstood." He then demonstrates how courtly love was incorporated into various medieval and Renaissance literary works. Treating the history of allegory, he also illustrates how the theme of courtly love and the methodology of allegory are inevitably intertwined. Courtly love is an important phenomenon, and the discourse of love's labor figures prominently in the literature of courtly love. Nevertheless, this discourse extends beyond the bounds of the courtly love canon and is not necessarily a defining feature of courtly love, whatever one believes the nature of that controversial topic to be.[38]

The scope of Allen's *The Art of Love* is narrower than that of Lewis. He begins with the *Ars amatoria* and continues with chapters on Andreas Capellanus's *De amore* and Jean de Meun's *Roman de la rose*. Allen contrasts arts of love with love poetry and emphasizes the deceptive quality of love in the arts. The arts of love, he claims, are works of literary theory rather than manuals on how to love. Allen writes that the *De amore* and the *Roman de la rose* are "essential to understanding love poetry of the Middle Ages, particularly of medieval France, and . . . they teach not the 'art of love' but the ways and means of amatory fiction—to be precise, how love becomes art."[39] To the extent that love's labor and the labor of

---

gendered bases" (11). Since the essays in this collection seek to highlight the ideological nature that underlies the ancient and medieval literature of desire, my study can be seen as allied to many of these projects, but with a focus on the ideology of labor, rather than on ideologies of gender.

37. C. S. Lewis, *The Allegory of Love* (1936; Oxford, U.K.: Oxford University Press, 1979).

38. Beyond Lewis's *Allegory of Love*, courtly love has been the focus of many other important studies of love in the Middle Ages. Alexander Denomy attempts to prove that courtly love was an outgrowth of the philosophy of the Latin Averroists in his book *The Heresy of Courtly Love* (New York: Declan X. McMullen, 1947). The essays by D. W. Robertson, Jr., John Benton, Charles Singleton, W. T. H. Jackson, and Theodore Silverstein in *The Meaning of Courtly Love* (ed. F. X. Newman [Albany: SUNY Press, 1968]) are crucial to understanding the debate on whether courtly love even existed. Roger Boase's *The Origin and Meaning of Courtly Love* (Totowa, N.J.: Rowman & Littlefield, 1977) is a learned and even-handed attempt to answer definitively the questions raised by such critics of courtly love as Robertson and Benton.

The history of the controversy over courtly love has been recently summarized by Robert R. Edwards and Stephen Spector, introduction, *The Olde Daunce: Love, Friendship, Sex, and Marriage in the Medieval World* (Albany: SUNY Press, 1991) 1–8.

Also recently C. Stephen Jaeger has excavated an even larger category of spiritualized love, called "ennobling love," to which courtly love is just a late addition. This category includes classical male-to-male friendship and is a public way of behaving, rather than a private way of feeling (*Ennobling Love: In Search of a Lost Sensibility* [Philadelphia: University of Pennsylvania Press, 1999]).

39. Peter Allen, *The Art of Love: Amatory Fiction from Ovid to the "Romance of the Rose"* (Philadelphia: University of Pennsylvania Press, 1992) 1–2.

writing love poetry are inextricably intertwined, Allen's study is an important reference point here. However, the literary texts from Ovid through Chaucer are not just examples of literary theory. They are also faithful to their self-presentation. They indeed teach the principles and the techniques of love and are constructed, in part, by means of ideological language from the world of labor and toil.

The target language here is thus the language of man's toil, which undergirds so much of the highly refined, aristocratic literature of love. Bakhtin's methodology can help to bring this little-noticed aspect to the fore. To be more precise, Bakhtin's interest is in "discourse" rather than in "language" or "rhetoric." By "discourse," he means "language in its concrete living totality," not "language" in the abstract, which he identifies as the proper object of linguistics. Discourse always is associated not only with a speaker but also with a social context or contexts.[40] In fact, he rejects what he calls "traditional stylistics" because they focus solely on the private craftsmanship of an individual author rather than on an author's social context. For Bakhtin, language is alive (i.e., is "discourse") only when it is in social circulation, only when it takes part in a dialogic relationship.[41]

Bakhtin found dialog not only in the give-and-take of two distinct speakers but also within the discourse of a single speaker and even within a single sentence or a single word.[42] The reason for this is that words carry ideological baggage. In his book on Dostoevsky, Bakhtin describes the circulation of words rather poetically:

The word is not a material thing but rather the eternally mobile, eternally fickle medium of dialogic interaction. It never gravitates toward a single consciousness or a single voice. The life of the word is contained in its transfer from one mouth to another, from one context to another context, from one social collective to another, from one generation to another generation. In this process the

40. Mikhail Bakhtin, *Problems of Dostoevsky's Poetics*, ed. and trans. Caryl Emerson (Minneapolis: University of Minnesota Press, 1984) 181, 184. Bakhtin's terminology, at least in the English translations, however, is often difficult to pin down. For example, he uses "language" in quotation marks and "social languages" to refer to specific instances of various kinds of discourse. In his essay "From the Prehistory of Novelistic Discourse," Bakhtin defines "language" as "a period-bound language associated with a particular world view," which is certainly different from the abstracted language studied by linguists (46). A better term for this instantiation of an ideological and hence period-bound "language" would be "social language," used in "Discourse in the Novel," which Bakhtin defines as "a concrete socio-linguistic belief system that defines a distinct identity for itself within the boundaries of a language" (356).

41. Bakhtin, *Dostoevsky's Poetics* 183.

42. Bakhtin, *Dostoevsky's Poetics* 184.

word does not forget its own path and cannot completely free itself from the power of these concrete contexts into which it has entered.

When a member of a speaking collective comes upon a word, it is not as a neutral word of language, not as a word free from the aspirations and evaluations of others, uninhabited by others' voices. No, he receives the word from another's voice and filled with that other voice. The word enters his context from another context, permeated with interpretations of others. His own thought finds the word already inhabited.[43]

Speakers or writers immediately set up a dialog between their own voices, their own "aspirations and evaluations," and those that they find clinging to the already-used words. This is what makes "dialog" possible even within the confines of the utterance of a single person. In his essay "Discourse in the Novel," Bakhtin puts the matter more directly:

There are no "neutral" words. All words have the "taste" of a profession, a genre, a tendency, a party, a particular work, a particular person, a generation, an age group. . . . Each word tastes of context and contexts in which it has lived its socially charged life.[44]

For Bakhtin, then, discourse is by its very nature "ideologically saturated."[45] The meaning of "ideology" here is broader than the traditional meaning, which is a coherent and rigidly held system of political ideas, something opposite to "pragmatism" or "common sense." Instead "ideology" includes a "rich 'system of representations,' . . . which helps form individuals into social subjects who 'freely' internalize an appropriate 'picture' of their social world and their place in it."[46] Not only political parties but all the other social groups in a society have ideologies, which help form members into good social citizens of that particular group. A full, historical understanding of a particular work of literature, Bakhtin argues, can only be obtained by becoming aware of the ideological content of an author's discourse. Some twentieth-century medievalists, the Exegetes in particular, have been keenly aware of the ideological baggage of the discourse of medieval authors.[47] They do not, however, consistently admit that authors can use the discourses of their source texts and

43. Bakhtin, *Dostoevsky's Poetics* 202.
44. Bakhtin, "Discourse in the Novel" 293.
45. Bakhtin, "Discourse in the Novel" 271.
46. James H. Kavanagh, "Ideology," *Critical Terms for Literary Study*, ed. Frank Lentricchia and Thomas McLaughlin, 2nd ed. (Chicago: University of Chicago Press, 1995) 310.
47. For an account of the Exegetes in their historical context, see Patterson, *Negotiating the Past* 26–39.

their cultures in a variety of sophisticated ways, some of which, like parody or satire, undermine rather than support the embedded ideologies (as opposed to the literal meaning of the text). Hence, critics must be aware not only of the discourse's ideology but also of the ways in which an author situates that discourse.

This kind of analysis can be difficult because of the historical or cultural distance of a text or because, in certain kinds of literature, authors tightly control their literary utterances, with the result that only one voice, the voice of the author, is heard. While multiple voices are present to a certain degree in all works, in some works language forces are tightly controlled, with the result that the author's discourse points only to his or her intended referential objects and does not acknowledge that it is composed of the speech of others.[48] These works Bakhtin calls "monologic," and the monologic voice Bakhtin argues is the quintessentially poetic voice; he also believes that all rhetorical forms are monologic as well.[49]

In other works, including stylizations, parodies, and dialog, however, the discourse serves a double duty: at one and the same time, it not only refers to the intended objects, but it also calls attention to itself as composed of the speech of others. That is, it foregrounds the centrifugal linguistic forces within it. Bakhtin calls this kind of discourse "double-voiced discourse" because in it one hears the voices of both the author and an earlier speaker.[50]

Within double-voiced discourse, Bakhtin makes a further distinction. In *passive* double-voiced discourse, the author's voice is clearly the authoritative voice and the second voice is subordinate. In parody, for example, one hears the voices of both the original author and the parodist, but it is clear that the voice of the parodist has the last word: the original author's distinctive voice becomes objectified, the butt of the joke.[51] If that were not the case, the parody would lose its humor. Another kind of double-voiced discourse exists, however, in which the various voices

48. Bakhtin, "Discourse in the Novel" 270. Bakhtin continues: "At any given moment of its historical existence, language is heteroglot from top to bottom: it represents the co-existence of socio-ideological contradictions between the present and the past, between differing epochs of the past, between different socio-ideological groups in the present, between tendencies, schools, circles and so forth, all given a bodily form. These 'languages' of heteroglossia intersect each other in a variety of ways, forming new socially typifying 'languages'" (291).
49. Bakhtin, *Dostoevsky's Poetics* 200; "Discourse in the Novel" 280.
50. Bakhtin, *Dostoevsky's Poetics* 185; "Discourse in the Novel" 272, 362–65.
51. Bakhtin, *Dostoevsky's Poetics* 195.

maintain parity. In this *active* double-voiced discourse, both voices retain equal power to influence the other.[52] Bakhtin identifies this kind of double-voiced discourse with "heteroglossia," which he defines as "another's speech in another's language." In heteroglossia the discourse serves the intentions of both author and character.[53] The fact of parity among the voices of heteroglossia is unsettling because readers experience a loss of a fixed, authoritative frame of reference.

Given Bakhtin's views on the nature of discourse, what, then, is the task of the critic? The task of the student of the novel, Bakhtin writes, is

uncovering all the available orchestrating languages [i.e., social languages] in the composition of the novel, grasping the precise degree of distancing that separates each language from its most immediate semantic instantiation in the work as a whole, and the varying angles of refraction of intentions within it, understanding dialogic interrelationships and—finally—if there *is* direct authorial discourse, determining the heteroglot background outside of the work that dialogizes it.[54]

Such an analysis, writes Bakhtin, forces the critic to determine the level of "artistic and ideological penetration" into the work. This is particularly difficult, writes Bakhtin, for texts written in other languages and in distant times. A study of the various "discourses" or "social languages" current at the time the works were written is necessary, as is a study of each language's "socio-ideological meaning."[55] To uncover *all* the underlying social languages found within the chosen works, however, would be a task going well beyond the scope of a single volume. Rather, one can highlight only those social languages and ideologies that pertain to a limited focus, such as labor. One can illuminate how these various social languages and ideologies are used by the authors, "grasping the precise degree of distancing that separates each language from its most immediate semantic instantiation in the work as a whole, and the varying angles of refraction of intentions within it." For the use of ideologically charged languages differs considerably among the authors in the tradition of love's labor.

---

52. Bakhtin, *Dostoevsky's Poetics* 195.
53. Bakhtin, "Discourse in the Novel" 323–24.
54. Bakhtin, "Discourse in the Novel" 417.
55. Bakhtin, "Discourse in the Novel" 417.

IV

Different social languages arise from different social classes or groups. Medieval love literature was clearly bound together with medieval ideologies of class and class privilege. Indeed, one of the striking ironies of the discourse of love's labor when found in medieval love literature is that "love" and "labor" seem to have formed a sort of cultural oxymoron because these two areas of life were assigned, at least according to the traditional social model, to different social classes. The courtly love code thus was constructed, at least at its inception, for the leisured classes. In the *Roman de la rose*, Guillaume de Lorris pointedly makes his character Idleness the gatekeeper to the Garden of Love.[56] At the same time, the dominant medieval social model, the model of the three estates, decreed that physical labor was to be the exclusive responsibility of the lower classes.[57] Although in several parts of the *De amore* Andreas Capellanus allows the possibility of love's labor being practiced by men on some different social levels, his comments in chapter 11 on the proper social spheres of labor and love are quite straightforward:

Dicimus enim vix contingere posse quod agricolae in amoris inveniantur curia militare, sed naturaliter sicut equus et mulus ad Veneris opera promoventur, quemadmodum impetus eis naturae demonstrat. Sufficit ergo agricultori labor assiduus et vomeris ligonisque continua sine intermissione solatia. (222–23)

[I maintain that farmers can scarcely ever be found serving in Love's court. They are impelled to acts of love in the natural way like a horse or mule, just as nature's pressure directs them. So for a farmer regular toil and the continuing uninterrupted consolations of plowshare and hoe are enough.]

Andreas concludes that, although one does occasionally find peasants who love, it is not appropriate to teach them love's doctrine because this kind of behavior is "naturaliter alienis" (naturally alien) to them. What is even worse from a traditional Christian ethical perspective, he counsels aristocratic men who fall in love with peasant women simply to take their pleasure by force. Although Andreas may have intended this pas-

---

56. Guillaume de Lorris and Jean de Meun, *Le Roman de la rose*, ed. Félix Lecoy (Paris: Honoré Champion, 1983) lines 522–92.

57. Adalbéron de Laon, *Poème au roi Robert*, ed. and trans. Claude Carozzi, Les Classiques de l'histoire de France au moyen âge (Paris: Les Belles Lettres, 1979). On Adalbero and the three estates model, see Georges Duby, *The Three Orders: Feudal Society Imagined*, trans. Arthur Goldhammer (Chicago: University of Chicago Press, 1980) 44–55.

sage as comic or ironic, it highlights attitudes that are often reflected in the love literature of the age. Andreas's contemporary Chrétien de Troyes, for example, who so thoroughly and wonderfully creates an elaborate world of love and refined manners, sets his romances exclusively in aristocratic social circles.

The discourse of love's labor, then, required from aristocratic writers a good measure of either playfulness or self-importance, for in this discourse "work" was required of a class whose self-definition was founded on the privilege of *not* working. Jacques LeGoff puts it succinctly:

La primauté du travail rural est un des héritages idéologiques du Moyen Age. Mais c'est surtout le primat de l'*otium* que l'intelligentsia médiévale retiendra longtemps de la pensée antique sur le travail. Les gens "bien" ne travaillent pas, un *otium* particulier étant bien entendu l'*otium cum dignitate.*[58]

[The primacy of rural work is one of the ideological heritages of the Middle Ages. But, above all, it's the primacy of *otium* that the medieval intelligentsia retained from classical thought on work. The "best" people do not work, this particular *otium* being, certainly, *otium with dignity.*]

Writers could portray aristocrats' work obligations seriously—as parallel to those of the monks, whose *otium cum dignitate* was required for the "work" of prayer—or they could portray them comically and ironically. Writers like Chaucer and Gower, among a professional class beginning to appreciate efficient work productivity, could use the discourse of love's labor satirically to reveal the shortcomings of the ruling class. One need only remember the magnificent and ultimately foolish inefficiencies with respect to love's labor of the aristocratic birds in Chaucer's *Parlement of Foules.* Thus, the traditional labor ideology of the Middle Ages, as it was crystallized in the three estates model, was built upon the base of social class distinctions. By the end of the Middle Ages, however, although the traditional three estates model was still evoked as a social ideal, the upper levels of the third estate were growing in power and prestige, and thus complicating the social picture.

---

58. Jacques LeGoff, "Le travail dans les systèmes de valeur de l'Occident médiéval," *Le travail au moyen âge: Une approche interdisciplinaire,* ed. Jacqueline Hamesse and Collette Muraille-Samaran (Louvain-la-Neuve: Institut d'études médiévales de l'Université Catholique de Louvain, 1990) 13. The English translation is my own. Peter Laslett notes that this tradition continued into the Renaissance. He writes that "[t]he primary characteristic of the [seventeenth-century English] gentleman was that he never worked with his hands on necessary, as opposed to leisurely, activities" (*The World We Have Lost* [New York: Charles Scribner's Sons, 1965] 29).

Max Weber associated the middle classes of the Reformation with a particular approach to labor.[59] His theory of the Protestant work ethic can be used as a convenient point of reference. According to this theory, Protestants value work in and of itself, as a dignified and essential component of successful living. Work is not a punishment for sin and is not simply an antidote to idleness. It is primarily valued for the riches it could produce, and those riches, in turn, are perceived as a sign of election. The medieval discourse of love's labor never pictures either courtship or the sex act as the results of original sin. In addition, the historical trajectory of the discourse of love's labor moves away not only from the traditional, medieval class ideology of the three estates, but also from the ideology of work as a remedy for *acedia*. It moves toward what might be described as a middle-class, "Protestant" work ethic. In this context, then, Chaucer's works might be taken as the logical end point of the "embourgeoisement de l'eros" (the making of love bourgeois).[60] Chaucer celebrates love's work as a healthy and essential component of life. Whether the subject is reproduction or courtship, love's work is valued in Chaucer because of what it can produce.

If love is constructed as a form of work, what is the effect upon readers and their society? The question of the social effects and significance of the discourse of sex is broached in Michel Foucault's *The History of Sexuality*. Although Foucault's book does not overlap with this study in terms of historical periods and although his focus is on sexuality rather than love, his book is a valuable resource because he analyzes *discourse*, not sexuality per se. In addition, some interesting parallels exist between the cultural work done by Foucault's texts and those in the tradition of love's labor. What he finds to be the third goal of the discourse of sexuality, socializing procreative behavior, is at times a direct goal of the discourse of love's labor. As Foucault writes:

All this garrulous attention which has us in a stew over sexuality, is it not motivated by one basic concern: to ensure population, to reproduce labor capacity, to perpetuate the form of social relations: in short, to constitute a sexuality that is economically useful and politically conservative?[61]

59. Max Weber, *The Protestant Work Ethic and the Spirit of Capitalism*, trans. Talcott Parsons (1930; New York: Charles Scribner's Sons, 1956).

60. The term is taken from Jean Charles Payen in his "*Le Roman de la rose* et la notion de carrefour idéologique" (*Romanistische Zeitschrift für Literaturgeschichte* 1 [1977]: 195, 197).

61. Foucault 36–37.

What is important to Foucault's analysis is that the discourse of sexuality is a way for power to be applied and for sexuality to be brought under social control, but something similar can be said about at least one branch of the tradition of love's labor. When love's labor turns to matters of reproduction, the intent of the discourse is always to underscore the importance of sex as economically and socially useful. The essential message of Alan of Lille's *De planctu naturae*, Jean de Meun's *Roman de la rose*, the *Confessio Amantis*, and Chaucer's *Parlement of Foules* is that love can be labor only to the extent that it produces new workers. The message is theologically (if not politically) conservative, at least from the perspective of the twentieth century, in that it is largely congruent with basic Thomist natural law ethics, in which sexual activity must be oriented primarily toward procreation rather than pleasure. Hence, Alan of Lille condemns homosexual love specifically because it cannot result in new children, and he aligns Venus with approved sexuality, assigning to Iocus, sport, the sponsorship of nonreproductive sex. In the *Confessio Amantis*, Amans's romantic activity is condemned because he is "too old" for acts of Venus and hence for reproduction. Similarly, approved sexuality in Jean de Meun's *Roman de la rose* is only that which can lead to reproduction. Here Pygmalion's story becomes the approved model of love because his desire moves from sterility to sexual productivity. (Jean de Meun, however, undermines this conservatism when he pushes the principle of reproductive love into unorthodox territory. He condemns not only homosexuality but also clerical celibacy because of its inability to reproduce.) In short, love is often constructed by these poets in a theologically approved fashion, and thus these poems become, in essence, medieval means of social control.

The tradition is also conservative in its gender orientation. The speaking subject in the discourse of love's labor is almost always male, and the discourse is generally aimed at a male audience. Ovid writes his handbook on love's labor basically for men; indeed, the section on labors for women is almost an addendum. Likewise, Andreas Capellanus's medieval art of love is written for men, and the narrator is an antifeminist male cleric to boot. Although in the *Roman de la rose* Jean de Meun gives the woman's perspective token attention in the discourses of Fair Welcoming and the Old Woman, most of the poem is centered on the thoughts of the male dreamer and his quest to deflower the rose. Gower's Amans is an elderly male, as is his main interlocutor, Genius. Moreover, the moral instruction in the collection is for Amans's benefit and for aging males like him. Chaucer's interest in and sensitivity toward women is well known, and in the *Troilus* he draws Criseyde's character with loving attention to detail. Nevertheless, male characters deliver the discourse of love's labor in the *Troilus*, and the central focus is on the labor expended by the men in pursuit of Criseyde's attentions. Love's labor is a predominantly male-oriented construct.

All aspects of the tradition, however, are not socially, politically, or theologically conservative. When love's labor becomes a code word for courtship rather than reproduction, the discourse becomes in some key ways subversive of the social order, as in Ovid's *Ars amatoria*. The *Ars* was, if anything, subversive vis-à-vis the conservative sexual morality upheld by Caesar Augustus. No one knows for sure why Ovid was banished from Rome, but it could well have been at least in part as a result of the popularity of the *Ars amatoria*, considered by many of his contemporaries to be a handbook for adultery. In addition, although the *De amore* is a self-contradictory text in many ways, to the extent that it functions as a manual for seduction it is subversive of the mainstream Christian morality. The *Troilus* is also a self-contradictory text. Its ending contains a repudiation of sexual love and an orthodox call to the love of Jesus. Nevertheless, the greater part of this romance/novel, particularly the first three books, presents a lovingly depicted narrative embracing the pursuit of erotic love. The poem's subversive labor discourse supports the work of productive courtship and sexual relations outside of marriage without any thought to reproduction. In the end, the reward for love's labors, Lady Mede/Criseyde, goes to Diomede, a "good" worker, rather than to the "slacker" Troilus.

Finally, to the extent that these works, taken together, present a strong endorsement of the dignity of labor, the ideology of these works is progressive. The traditional Christian labor ideology, which saw labor as the punishment for sin and transgression, is far removed from these texts. Over the course of this tradition these classical and medieval writers construct an increasingly vocal and self-conscious encomium to the dignity of human effort. The labor lexicon continuously improves to include words whose connotations do not carry the traditional associations of labor with back-breaking toil and sweat. In the end, love's labor evolves from *travail* to a dignified *occupacioun, servise, bysynesse,* or *emprise* (enterprise).

As David Wallace cautions, "Few people today would tie themselves to a model of history envisaging . . . 'a linear and necessary evolution,'

one positing that 'the only possible history is the one that in fact result-
ed.'"[62] The "embourgeoisement de l'eros" in the end does not represent a
linear progression through history. Moreover, with aspects of both orien-
tations, it can be classified as neither totally progressive nor totally conservative. On the contrary, it contains a fertile yet paradoxical mixture of
attitudes, a clash of ideologies in struggle, employed with a full range of
conflicting authorial agendas and creating new and exciting human possi-
bilities, an array of new colors from love's white light refracted via the
prisms of some of the greatest of ancient and medieval authors.

62. Wallace xvi.

CHAPTER 2

Labor Omnia Vincit

Roman Attitudes toward Work and Leisure and the Discourse of Love's Labor in Ovid's *Ars amatoria*

Labor omnia vicit / improbus.
[Persistent labor conquered all.]
—*Virgil*

Omnia vincit amor.
[Love conquers all.]
—*Virgil*

I

John Gower claims to have constructed his *Confessio Amantis* from two sources: the world "in olde dayes passed" and the world "which neweth everi dai." Most critics would agree that something similar could be said of Chaucer's love poetry, and their sources for the past were, of course, "olde bokes." As Chaucer writes:

Than mote we to bokes that we fynde,
Thurgh whiche that olde thinges ben in mynde,

...

And yf that olde bokes were aweye,
Yloren were of remembraunce the keye.[1]

---

1. John Gower, prologue, *The Confessio Amantis*, *The English Works of John Gower*, Early English Texts Society, ES, 81, 82 (Oxford, U.K.: Oxford University Press, 1900) 55, 59 (1.4). Geoffrey Chaucer, prologue, *The Legend of Good Women*, *The Riverside Chaucer*, ed. Larry D. Benson, 3rd ed. (Boston: Houghton Mifflin, 1987) F 17–18, 25–26. Modern English translations of Chaucer are my own.

[Then we must turn to books that we find, through which old things are brought to mind. . . . And if old books were taken away, the key of remembrance would be lost.]

Ovid's love poetry, whether taken directly or mediated through other medieval texts such as *Le Roman de la rose*, was certainly a vital "key of remembrance" for both English poets with respect to the discourse of love's labor. Thus, to appreciate fully the contributions made by these two poets to that discourse, one must be aware of how it sounded in Ovid.[2] Chaucer and Gower lived, as Gower himself noted, in a different world from Ovid's, a "world which neweth everi dai." Much the same could be said for the other medieval writers treated in this study. This meant, in part, that the medieval authors wrote in different languages, languages whose words carried, in some instances, different ideological connotations. While M. M. Bakhtin argues that discourse keeps its ideological coloring when passing from one speaker to another, I am not interested in proving that medieval writers were aware of the labor ideology in Ovid's discourse or that they consciously reacted to it one way or another. That ideology, in fact, may have been effaced by the ideology of the Christian scribes or commentators who made Ovid's texts available to writers in the Middle Ages. However, in order to understand fully how the discourse of love's labor in medieval love poetry differs from that

2. On Ovid's influence on medieval writers, see L. P. Wilkinson, "The Middle Ages: Venus' Clerk Ovyde," *Ovid Recalled* (Cambridge, U.K.: Cambridge University Press, 1955) 366–98; Dorothy M. Robathan, "Ovid in the Middle Ages," *Ovid*, ed. J. W. Binns (Boston: Routledge & Kegan Paul, 1973) 191–209; and Peter L. Allen, "From Rome to France: Under the Sign of Ovid," *The Art of Love: Amatory Fiction from Ovid to the "Romance of the Rose"* (Philadelphia: University of Pennsylvania Press, 1992) 38–58. Ovid's erotic poems were often used during the Middle Ages as Latin grammar texts. On the medieval reception of Ovid's erotic poems reconstructed through medieval teaching commentaries, see Ralph J. Hexter, *Ovid and Medieval Schooling: Studies in Medieval School Commentaries on Ovid's "Ars Amatoria," "Epistulae ex Ponto," and "Epistulae Heroidum"* (Munich: Arbeo-Gesellschaft, 1986).

On the specific debt of Gower to Ovid, see Bruce Harbert, "Lessons from a Great Clerk: Ovid and John Gower," *Ovid Renewed: Ovidian Influences on Literature and Art from the Middle Ages to the Twentieth Century*, ed. Charles Martindale (Cambridge, U.K.: Cambridge University Press, 1988) 83–97; and Götz Schmitz, "Gower, Chaucer, and the Classics: Back to the Textual Evidence," *John Gower: Recent Readings*, ed. R. F. Yeager (Kalamazoo, Mich.: Medieval Institute, 1989) 95–111.

On Chaucer's debt to Ovid, see Edgar Finley Shannon, *Chaucer and the Roman Poets* (Cambridge, Mass.: Harvard University Press, 1929); Richard Hoffman, *Ovid and "The Canterbury Tales"* (Philadelphia: University of Pennsylvania Press, 1966); John Fyler, *Chaucer and Ovid* (New Haven, Conn.: Yale University Press, 1979); Helen Cooper, "Chaucer and Ovid: A Question of Authority," *Ovid Renewed* 71–81; and Michael A. Calabrese, *Chaucer's Ovidian Arts of Love* (Gainesville: University Press of Florida, 1994). On Chaucer's approach to antiquity in general, see A. J. Minnis, *Chaucer and Pagan Antiquity* (Cambridge, U.K.: Brewer, 1982).

found in one of its most important sources, one needs to reconstruct the ideological resonances heard in each discourse.

Although Ovid does employ the discourse of passion in, for example, the *Amores*, the *Heroides*, and the *Remedia amoris*, his overall attitude toward love in the *Ars amatoria* is *not* best expressed by the well-known phrase that graced the broach of Chaucer's Prioress, "Amor Vincit Omnia" (Love conquers all), a verse that summarizes neatly the discourse of passion, of love's overwhelming power. This is particularly true given the phrase's context in Virgil's "Tenth Eclogue." In that eclogue, Virgil's lovesick Gallus says "non illum nostri possunt mutare labores" (Our labors cannot change that god) and concludes "et nos cedamus Amori" (let us, too, yield to Love).[3] Molly Myerowtiz has argued, rather, that Ovid's treatment of love in the *Ars* is best represented by the phrase "et mihi cedet Amor" (and to me Love shall yield), a phrase that plays off Gallus's opinion but reflects an active rather than a passive approach to love. In fact, a parallel phrase, adapted from Virgil, "Labor omnia vincit" (Labor conquers all), is an even better representation of Ovid's characteristic attitude in the *Ars*.[4] That is, he constructed love—courtship, the sex act itself, and even the writing of love poetry—as respectable work. For Ovid, love was skilled work that could be learned, practiced, and perfected by means of a set of rules under the tutelage of a *praeceptor amoris* (teacher of love; *Ars amatoria* [hereafter *Aa*] 1.17).

Ovid was not the first to employ the discourse of love's labor, but he is generally considered to be the first to place it in a didactic poem, hence,

3. Virgil, *Eclogues: Virgil*, ed. H. Rushton Fairclough, rev. ed., Loeb Classical Library (Cambridge, Mass.: Harvard University Press, 1986) 10.64.

4. Molly Myerowitz, *Ovid's Games of Love* (Detroit: Wayne State University Press, 1985) 33. Although she does not use the terminology of love's labor, Myerowitz does argue that love is a form of work in the *Ars*. She writes: "The simple satisfaction of a biological urge holds little appeal for the poet of the *Ars amatoria*. Love must be difficult, fraught with obstacles. To restrict love to simply biology or barter would be to eliminate play entirely and to leave no room for erotic culture. Ovid's elevation of courtship as an end in itself, while not rejecting the biological aspects of sexual desire, turns on the pleasure of human creativity" (33).

The quotation is from Ovid, *"Amores," "Medicamina Faciei Femineae," "Ars Amatoria," "Remedia Amoris,"* ed. E. J. Kenney (Oxford, U.K.: Clarendon Press, 1961) 1.21. All quotations from the *Ars*, the *Amores*, and the *Remedia amoris* will be taken from this edition and cited in the text by book and line number. English translations of Ovid are my own.

Although A. S. Hollis does not focus on the discourse of love's labor in the *Ars*, he points out that Ovid there presents love as a form of labor: "Ovid provocatively reverses the usual moral categories, presenting love as a worthy and strenuous occupation, like farming or hunting, in which all his fellow-citizens should be expert" ("The *Ars amatoria* and *Remedia amoris*," *Ovid*, ed. Binns 89).

The original quotation comes from the *Georgics: Virgil*, ed. Fairclough 1.145. The English translations are my own.

emphasizing courtship as a kind of occupation that can be learned and perfected via art.[5] One of the key texts that he is imitating is Virgil's *Georgics*, a didactic poem focusing on agricultural labor. Particularly in the *Ars amatoria* and in key poems in the *Amores*, Ovid's love poetry is often notably constructed with the discourse of love's labor. In the *Remedia amoris*, however, Ovid rejects the discourse of love's labor and takes up the discourse of passion. While in the *Remedia* he characteristically enjoins his reader to work, the work of the *praeceptor* becomes the work of the physician, that is, to cure the patient sick with love's madness.

It must be emphasized, however, that for Ovid, love's "work" is a self-conscious game. The *Ars* ends with the statement: "Lvsvs habet finem" (Our games are finished).[6] That is, while it is clear that he employs the discourse of labor to construct love, he does so ironically, or as Bakhtin might say, with "a sideways glance" at someone else's serious discourse about labor.[7] The discourse of labor in Ovid is always double-voiced, always self-consciously revealing the voices and ideologies of both Ovid and his source texts. Taking a cue from Richard Lanham, one might put it a different way: Ovid's treatment of labor in his love poetry is always rhetorical rather than serious. It is dramatic, it is ludic, it is marked by rhetorical virtuosity.[8]

What, however, was the ideological taste of those voices, voices like those of Cicero and Virgil, which made their way into Ovid's poetry? It is my task in this chapter to examine Ovid's discourse of love's labor in its cultural contexts, especially within the contexts of Roman attitudes toward labor in the Age of Augustus. After reviewing Roman attitudes toward labor during this period, I will examine both the language and the genre used by Ovid in the *Ars* to convey his witty lessons on love's labor.

<hr/>

5. Myerowitz 34. Wilkinson, *Ovid Recalled* (Cambridge, U.K.: Cambridge University Press, 1955) 120. On the characteristics of classical didactic poetry, see Hollis 90.

6. *Aa* 3.809. Allen notes that "lusus" carried the meanings of "game," "trickery," and "(nonmarital) sexual intercourse." He suggests that in the *Ars* all three denotations find a place (34).

7. Mikhail Bakhtin, *Problems of Dostoevsky's Poetics*, ed. and trans. Caryl Emerson (Minneapolis: University of Minnesota Press, 1984) 196.

8. Richard Lanham, "Fundamental Strategies: Plato and Ovid," *The Motives of Eloquence: Literary Rhetoric in the Renaissance* (New Haven, Conn: Yale University Press, 1976) 36–64. Myerowitz comments that "a central point of the *Ars amatoria* seems to me to be the deliberate confusion of the traditional categories of serious and unserious, real and unreal, important and unimportant" (11).

II

A survey of modern historians on Roman attitudes toward labor yields some areas of general agreement although notable exceptions exist. Often historians start with the statement that the ancients had contempt for labor and exalted leisure, but which ancients are they talking about, and what do they mean by "labor"?[9]

Paul Veyne and Moses Finley argue that there was no exact equivalent of the modern word "labor" in ancient Rome. Veyne's argument is that no abstract concept of labor (in the modern sense of the term) existed. Rather, an assessment of an activity was first based on the social status of the agent. Aristocrats, he argues, did not labor, no matter how strenuous their activity, whereas those in the lower classes did not have personal identities beyond their work. As for slaves, they did not work: they merely obeyed orders. Finley is of much the same opinion. He writes: "Neither in Greek nor in Latin was there a word with which to express the general notion of 'labour' or the concept of labour as a general social function."[10] These cautions are worthy of note, particularly if one associates "labor" with Marxist ideology or with a generalized social class of laborers over and against the ruling class of capitalists. It is more than likely that the ideological connotations of the Latin words for "strenuous activity" and/or "manual labor" were different from the connotations of corresponding English words.

As noted in the Introduction, what I will mean by "labor" here is broader than just wage or even manual labor. "Labor" and "work" will denote exertion of the faculties of the body and the mind directed to a definite end, exertions that may or may not be associated with gaining one's livelihood.

An authoritative passage illustrating the attitudes of the Roman elite

9. See, for example, the comments of Paul Veyne, *The Roman Empire*, trans. Arthur Goldhammer (Cambridge, Mass.: Belknap Press of Harvard University Press, 1997) 118. Herbert Applebaum sees the condescending attitude of the aristocracy toward the laboring classes as cutting across historical eras (*The Concept of Work: Ancient, Medieval, Modern* [Albany: SUNY Press, 1992] xiii). Dissenting opinions exist, however. Birgit van den Hoven argues against what she calls the traditional view of Roman attitudes toward labor. She contends that manual work, including both agricultural work and the work of urban craftsmen, was valued by various Roman Stoics (*Work in Ancient and Medieval Thought* [Amsterdam: Gieben, 1996] 1, 21–63). In the end, however, her argument is so nuanced and is limited to so few writers that she ends up conceding the general correctness of the traditional view. (See, e.g., van den Hoven 51–63.)

10. Veyne 124–29; and Moses Finley, *The Ancient Economy*, 2nd ed. (London: Hogarth Press, 1985) 81.

toward work is found in Cicero's *De officiis*. In his instructions to his son, Cicero makes clear that manual labor is not suitable for a free man. He writes:

Illiberales autem et sordidi quaestus mercennariorum omnium, quorum operae, non quorum artes emuntur; est enim in illis ipsa merces auctoramentum servitutis.

[However, the occupations of all hired workers, who are paid for physical labor and not for technical skill, are base and unworthy of freemen, for their very wage makes slaves of them.][11]

The passage makes two points. First, that a manual laborer sells only his physical labor, not a particular skill, makes his work unworthy of a free man. Second, when a laborer surrenders his time and free will to another, he draws himself closer to the condition of a slave. Following Cicero, Finley argues that a person's activities were clearly evaluated on the basis of whether he entered into them freely or with restraint. He contrasts the Greek terms *ploutos* and *penia*, the former referring to anyone who could live off the income of his properties and the latter referring to anyone who was not economically independent, including—but going beyond—slaves.[12] Later in the passage, however, Cicero does recognize a hierarchy of laborers and assigns a higher level to those whose work required a high degree of *prudentia*, that is, practical understanding or wisdom:[13]

Quibus autem artibus aut *prudentia maior inest* aut non mediocris utilitas quaeritur, ut medicina, ut architectura, ut doctrina rerum honestarum, eae sunt iis, quorum ordini conveniunt, honestae.

[However, those arts *requiring greater intelligence* or those which are greatly useful, such as medicine, architecture, or teaching of noble things, these are honorable for those whose social class is suitable.] (1.151; emphasis added)

Thus, the labor of those that need specialized training or those who exercise sophisticated levels of judgment is accorded a higher level of respect.

Going beyond this distinction, Cicero draws yet another, this time be-

---

11. Cicero, *De officiis*, ed. Walter Miller, Loeb Classical Library (Cambridge, Mass.: Harvard University Press, 1913) 1.150. The English translation is my own. All subsequent quotations from this work will be taken from this edition and cited in the text by book and section numbers. Finley vigorously defends this passage as reflecting the common Roman opinion of Cicero's time (41–61).

12. Finley 40–41.

13. "Prudentia" (1), *Oxford Latin Dictionary*, 1982 ed.

tween kinds of manual work. Among manual workers, those who labor
on the farms are accorded a much higher place than ordinary craftsmen.
"Omnium autem rerum," he writes, "ex quibus aliquid acquiritur, nihil
est agri cultura melius, nihil uberius, nihil dulcius, nihil homine libero
dignius" (But of all the occupations by which anything is acquired, none
is better than agriculture, none more productive, none more agreeable,
none worthier of a freeman; 1.151). If Cicero has nothing but praise for
the labor of the farmer, he shows little but contempt for labor in the mechanical arts: "Opificesque omnes in sordida arte versantur; nec enim
quicquam ingenuum habere potest officina" (And all artisans are engaged
in disgraceful trades, for no workshop can have anything worthy of a
freeman; 1.150).

In praising the labor of the farmer, Cicero is following what is a long
classical tradition.[14] After condemning trade and money lending, Cato
the Elder, for example, writes: "Et virum bonum quom laudabant, ita
laudabant, bonum agricolam bonumque colonum. Amplissime laudari
existimabatur qui ita laudabatur" (And when they praised a good man,
they praised him like this: They called him a good farmer, a good tiller of
the soil. Praised in this way, they thought themselves abundantly com-
mended).[15] Farming was also celebrated in Roman poetry. The *Georgics*
is, of course, one example.[16] One could also cite Horace's second epode:

> Beatvs ille qui procul negotiis,
>   ut prisca gens mortalium,
> paterna rura bobus exercet suis
>   solutus omni faenore,
> neque excitatur classico miles truci,
>   neque horret iratum mare,
> Forumque vitat et superba civium
>   potentiorum limina.[17]

[Happy the man who, far from business troubles, like the ancient race of mor-

14. See, for example, the comments of Applebaum xiii; van den Hoven 29–30; and J. P. V. D. Balsdon, *Life and Leisure in Ancient Rome* (New York: McGraw, 1969) 131.
15. Marcus Porcius Cato, "On Agriculture," *Marcus Porcius Cato "On Agriculture"; Marcus Terentius
Varro "On Agriculture,"* ed. and trans. William Davis Hooper and Harrison Boyd Ash, rev. ed., Loeb
Classical Library (Cambridge, Mass.: Harvard University Press, 1935) 2–3. The English translation is
adapted from Hooper and Ash's.
16. Specific praise of farm life is found in *Georgics* 2.458–74 and 2.490–540.
17. Horace, *Epodes, Odes and Epodes*, ed. C. E. Bennett, rev. ed., Loeb Classical Library (Cambridge, Mass.: Harvard University Press, 1927) 1–8. The English translation is my own.

tals, works with oxen on his family estate, free of all money lending, neither the soldier roused by the fierce trumpet, nor someone who fears the angry sea. He shuns the Forum and the proud dwellings of more powerful citizens.]

Here the life and labor of the country are praised as an ideal, not only for the lowest classes, but also for the aristocrat. Gary B. Miles, however, notes that the poem's last line deflates somewhat this idyllic picture. He argues that in the Age of Augustus the landed classes in fact had contradictory attitudes toward the countryside. On the one hand, the life of the country could indeed be a life of leisure and quiet restrained activities. As such, it offered an attractive alternative to the fast-paced and dangerous life of the cities. On the other hand, the agricultural life represented the best of the old Roman values and traditions, and these were being self-consciously revived during the Augustan period. Few if any aristocrats, however, actually worked the land themselves; that age had passed, writes Miles, by the second century B.C.E. Those that did work only dabbled at it in their spare time, time free from public responsibilities. Moreover, the actual life of the small farmer in the Age of Augustus was very difficult, with many straining under severe financial pressures.[18]

It is clear, then, that Veyne's statement that Romans condemned labor and praised idleness is correct only if understood in a limited fashion. First of all, the labor of farmers was not condemned. Second, the condemnation of manual labor was generally the opinion only of a certain class of people, the *ploutos*, those who were able to live off the income of their estates. These, of course, were the very people who had the time and means to write down their opinions. What the opinions of the actual working freemen, the *penia*, were toward their labor can only be ascertained indirectly. Historians, citing the epitaphs on the graves of working people, deduce that, far from despising their work, laborers took a great deal of pride in doing it well.[19] Also, when historians write that idleness was held up as an aristocratic ideal in imperial Rome, what they mean is that the ideal for Roman aristocrats was to gain one's income from one's property and not have to engage in wage labor.[20] Remarks in Cicero and in other Stoic sources make it clear that, at least on the level of ideology, most aristocratic Romans did not approve of unprofitable idleness. Ci-

18. Gary B. Miles, *Virgil's "Georgics": A New Interpretation* (Berkeley and Los Angeles: University of California Press, 1980) 1–63.

19. Balsdon 134ff.; Applebaum xiii; Veyne 131–34; and van den Hoven 21.

20. See similar comments in Balsdon 130; and Applebaum 93.

cero, for example, in the *De officiis*, cites a commonplace taunt aimed at people who lived such lives: "Salmacida, spolia sine sudore et sanguine" (Son of Salmacis, you win spoils without sweat and blood; 1.61). Salmacis, of course, was the nymph in whose pool the young Hermaphroditus was transformed into a hermaphrodite.[21] At least for the Stoics, strenuous effort and purposeful activity were, in fact, high ideals, and idle indolence was considered effeminate.[22]

In his study of Roman life, J. P. V. D. Balsdon argues that the "negotia publica," a combination of the practice of law, public oratory, military service, and government administration, was the highest form of aristocratic activity. These were generally not *paid* occupations. In his discussion of the work ideals of the Roman aristocracy, Balsdon makes a distinction between those who lived the "life in the sun" versus those who lived the "life in the shade." The "life in the sun" was a Stoic ideal, whereas the "life in the shade" was an ideal of the Epicureans.[23] Given what is the intensity of the Mediterranean sun, the phrase "life in the sun" did not suggest to the Romans what it might suggest to people living in northern climes, that is, the "good life." On the contrary, "the life in the sun" was the aristocratic ideal of public service, an exposed life of exertion and possibly danger, the life of an orator or soldier. Cicero speaks of this kind of life when he describes the virtues of the courageous man:

Altera est res, ut, cum ita sis affectus animo, ut supra dixi, res geras magnas illas quidem et maxime utiles, sed [ut] vehementer arduas plenasque laborum et periculorum cum vitae, tum multarum rerum, quae ad vitam pertinent.

[The other characteristic is that, when the soul is fashioned as described above, one should indeed perform great and useful deeds, extremely arduous deeds, deeds full of labor and dangers both to life and to many things that make life worth living.] (*De officiis* 1.66)

The other option was the easier life, the private life, the *vita umbratilis*. It was a life in pursuit of tranquillity and repose. Cicero believed that this kind of life was praiseworthy in retirement, but only if the time gained was employed for practical ends. He warned, however, that some men

---

21. The story is told in Ovid's *Metamorphoses* 4.285–388.

22. Catharine Edwards has described a nexus of qualities, including softness, sluggishness, timidity, and idleness, which were identified as effeminate and hence shameful qualities for free males in Augustan Rome (*The Politics of Immorality in Ancient Rome* [Cambridge: Cambridge University Press, 1993] 78–81).

23. Balsdon 130, 136–37.

retire from public life with high-sounding motives, "sed videntur labores et molestias, tum offensionum et repulsarum quasi quandam ignominiam timere et infamiam" (but they seem to fear labors and troubles and, then, perhaps, the disgrace and infamy of failures and rejections; *De officiis* 1.71). This, for Cicero, was an unacceptable motivation.

Not only Cicero but Romans in general made careful distinctions about different kinds of leisure. In fact, a key part of the Roman ideology of labor was constructed within the framework of discourse about *otium*.[24] *Otium* was an ambiguous term, carrying both positive and negative connotations. Synonyms for *otium* in the positive sense were *quies* (relief from toil, rest, repose), *requies* (rest from labor, a leisure occupation), and *tranquilitas* (tranquility, calm). Synonyms for *otium* in the negative sense were *desidia* (idleness, slackness), *inertia* (idleness, sloth, indolence), *ignavia* (idleness, sloth, faint-heartedness), and *luxuria* (indulgence, luxury, licentiousness).[25] One might assume that *otium* had always stood in opposition to one of the Latin words signifying work: *labor, opus, opera*, or *negotium*. The history of the concept, however, shows that this was not always true.

As J. M. André has argued, *otium* probably had its origins as a military term indicating the opposite not of labor but of war. The time for *otium* was the winter, when fighting was not possible. Any of the activities associated with the winter, then, such as tending to one's patrimony, were seen as the fruits of *otium*.[26] In at least one passage of the *Georgics*, for example, Virgil represents the life of the farmer as one of *otium*.[27] Active public life was also a form of *otium*. André argues, in fact, that *otium* in the positive sense continued to be associated in the minds of the Romans with joyous work. However, in its negative sense of idleness, *otium* was associated with the Greeks. Thus, the Romans carefully distinguished *otium negotiosum* (busy *otium*) from *otium Graecum*, or *otium otiosum*, an uncontrolled form of leisure.[28] A strong work ethic prevailed among the early Romans, and a dominant theme in the writings of Cato the Elder was the struggle against the wasting of time. For example, study for its own sake, study without a practical goal, was suspect. Manual labor, for

24. In the following discussion, I am heavily indebted to the magisterial study of J. M. André on *otium* in the history of Roman culture (*L'otium dans la vie morale et intellectuelle romaine des origines à l'époque augustéenne* [Paris: Presses Universitaires de France, 1966]). See also Jean Leclercq, "Otium," *Otia monastica: Études sur le vocabulaire de la contemplation au moyen âge* (Rome: Herder, 1963) 27–49.

25. André 9, 13.   26. André 12.

27. *Georgics* 2.467–68.   28. André 22, 42.

Cato, was the perfect antidote against *luxuria, deliciae* (pleasures, delights), *amoenitas* (comfort, luxury), *uoluptas* (pleasure, delight), *sumptus* (lavish or extravagant expenditure), and *libido* (desire, sexual appetite, lust).[29]

The bipolar opposition between *otium* and war eventually developed into a tripolar continuum: *bellum, otium,* and *negotium.* These three were thought to correspond to stages in a man's life.[30] While *negotium* came to be associated with life in the countryside (particularly the labor of the farm), *otium* came to be associated with the life of leisure in the city. Indeed, one of the moral messages of Roman comedy was to avoid the dangers of city *otium,* which was often associated with love and romance. One result of the Roman Civil Wars and the triumph of Julius Caesar, however, was that many fled from politics and neglected the *negotium publicum.* Thus, the private life became the focus of concern and the work subsequently praised was private work.[31] In fact, the definition of *otium* during Augustus's rule was resolutely apolitical; it meant the exercise of a profession, the management of one's patrimony (i.e., joyful work), or the activities of intellectual life.

In the Age of Augustus, then, *otium Graecum* was not an ideal. While the upper classes celebrated *otium* as a means of accomplishing great things, the urban poor, for whom there was not enough to do, identified it with wine, women, and circuses. In addition, the middle class, whence many of the age's great writers came, continued to distrust the *otium urbanum.*[32] In André's opinion, the whole complex of values associated with the term *otium*—exalted by the elegiac poets, contested by the historians, defended by Horace and Virgil—became the "point of confluence of idea-forces" for a whole generation.[33] Key tenets of the prevailing Roman labor ideology during the period in question revolved around the word *otium.*

Employing the discourse of love's labor, Ovid composed poetry in such a social and ideological context. Manual and wage labor were dis-

29. André 31, 39.

30. André (125–26) cites as characteristic a passage from the prologue of Terence's *Brothers,* in which the playwright admits he receives help from his friends: "qui vobis univorsis et populo placent, / quorum opera in bello, in otio, in negotio / suo quisque tempore usust sine superbia" (who are pleasing to all of you and to the people, men whose works in war, in leisure, and in business everyone has at time employed without arrogance; prologue, *The Brothers: Terence,* ed. John Sargeaunt, Loeb Classical Library [Cambridge, Mass.: Harvard University Press, 1965] 19–21).

31. André 396–97.   32. André 398–99.
33. André 403.

paraged by most of the upper classes as servile, but the life of *otium Grae-cum* or *otium otiosum* (and of poets who supported such a life) was sus-pect. The life of a lover, of course, was associated with *otium otiosum*, yet this life was being openly advocated by the elegiac poets.[34] It was a con-text in which *otium negotiosum*, joyous, independent labor was an ideal. Indeed, members of the administrative class (Ovid's class) would have been expected to contribute to the *negotium publicum* through military service, administration, or law. Ovid's father expected his son to take up such a life, but Ovid chafed under his expectations.[35] On the one hand, agricultural labor was considered a Roman ideal and praised as such; on the other hand, life in the country for the Roman aristocracy was often a luxurious life, filled with no more work than the overseeing of one's slaves.

III

The discourse of love's labor in the *Ars amatoria* reflects and subverts this cultural context. Although Ovid was a champion of city life, he artic-ulates a playful work ethic in the *Ars*. It is constructed using both the vo-cabulary of labor and tropes and figures from military and agricultural work. Generally this ethic seeks to convince would-be lovers to avoid the passivity of *otium Graecum* and to pursue the joyful work of love, whether that is courtship or the sex act itself. Ovid wants his readers to conquer love, not vice versa (*Aa* 1.17, 21). Ovid's discourse of love's labor is ironically double-voiced, however, because serious writers would have categorized his work of love as either *otium Graecum* or *otium otiosum*.

Love's labor in the *Ars* is presented as parallel and often identical to the work of the love poet. In the *Ars*, love's labor is not just any kind of labor. It is, to return to Cicero's distinction, a higher form of labor, one that de-mands a significant level of *prudentia*.[36] It is practiced by a craftsman, an *artifex*, and its precepts can be handed down from master to apprentice. The *Ars* is conceived as the handbook of this occupation, and Ovid creat-ed it using the *Georgics* as a model. Indeed, the *Ars* and the *Georgics* occu-py similar places in the literary careers of the two men. Their didactic po-

---

34. André 389.

35. For a short biography of Ovid with special focus on the composition of the erotic poetry, see Peter Green, introduction, *Ovid: The Erotic Poems* (New York: Penguin Books, 1982) 15–81.

36. See Myerowitz's comment: "The lover [in the *Ars*] is defined as one who brings intelligence to bear upon instinct, mind on material. In this view love becomes active, creative, and intellectually challenging—an assertion of self in the face of nature" (38).

ems, following collections of either elegies or pastoral poetry, appear before the authors' respective epics.[37] The close relationship of the *Ars* and the *Georgics* influences the discourse of love's labor in the *Ars* significantly, a point to which I must return below.

The *Ars* is divided in several ways. Most obviously, the work is divided into three books: the first two dealing with the work of love for men, the third dealing with the work of love for women. As Molly Myerowitz points out, the activities prescribed for men are "active" and go out into the world; those for women are mostly confined to the boudoir and involve the cultivation of the self.[38] Ovid makes yet another crucial division when he describes the structure of the first two books as treating a series of three *labors:* finding a woman, winning a woman, and making love endure:

> Principio, quod amare uelis, reperire *labora*,
>   qui noua nunc primum miles in arma uenis;
> proximus huic *labor* est placitam exorare puellam;
>   tertius, ut longo tempore duret amor.
>
> (Aa 1.35–38; emphasis added)

[First, for you who, as a soldier, come fresh into new arms, are the *labors* of finding someone to love; the next *labor* is to win the attractive girl; the third is to make love long endure.]

The key word here is the noun *labor* and its corresponding verb *laborare*, terms that Eleanor Leach signals as a particularly important borrowing from the discourse of the *Georgics*.[39] But what exactly do these two words denote?

At its origins, *labor* denoted an active and effective force. It also indicated a burden under which one might stagger. From there, its meaning passed to pain, suffering, and the fatigue one experiences in accomplishing a task.[40] *The Oxford Latin Dictionary* confirms that *labor* meant "physical stress," "hardship," "pain," and "distress," as well as "work" or "toil."[41] *Laborare* meant "to be distressed physically," "to be in trouble," "to suffer pain or disease," "to be anxious or worried," as well as "to exert oneself,"

37. Alison Sharrock, *Seduction and Repetition in Ovid's "Ars amatoria," 2* (Oxford, U.K.: Clarendon Press, 1994) 2.

38. Myerowitz 97, 127.

39. Eleanor Leach, "Georgic Imagery in the *Ars amatoria*," *Transactions of the American Philological Association* 95 (1964): 150.

40. "Labor," *Dictionnaire étymologique de la langue Latin: Histoire des mots*, 1959 ed.

41. "Labor" (1, 6, 7), *Oxford Latin Dictionary*.

"to perform physical work," and "to toil."[42] Both words carried, then, active and passive meanings: *labor* and *laborare* denoted both work and suffering.

At least Cicero, however, insisted that the word *labor* was to be reserved for the active senses of the word and that *dolor* should be used for the passive denotations. "Labor," Cicero writes, "est functio quaedam vel animi vel corporis gravioris operis et muneris, dolor autem motus asper in corpore, alienus a sensibus" (labor is a mental or physical execution of work or a duty of more than usual severity; pain, on the other hand, is sharp movement in the body, repugnant to the senses). He then criticizes the Greeks for having only a single word for both concepts and again insists that "Aliud . . . est enim dolere, aliud laborare" (It is one thing to suffer pain, another to labor).[43]

Although it is unlikely that Ovid's *labor* and *laborare* were free of any trace of the passive denotations, Cicero's definition of *labor*, "a mental or physical execution of work or duty of more than usual severity" is the *primary* denotation in this and other passages in the *Ars*. Love, for the *praeceptor amoris*, involves hard work, but it is a "joyful work" that can be learned and practiced by those who are willing to learn. In other words, the *praeceptor* is intent on presenting love as the fruit of *otium negotiosum*, not of *otium otiosum*.

Ovid uses *labor* eleven times in the *Ars*, although not all uses are directly relevant to the subject at hand. In many passages, however, *labor* is used to indicate that the activities associated with courtship or, in one case, even the sex act itself, call for determined effort (*Aa* 1.37, 1.453, 2.236, 2.538, 2.669). Three of these passages, all occurring in Book 2, are especially relevant. In the first, Ovid compares the life of a lover to that of a soldier. He writes:

> militiae species amor est: discedite, segnes;
>   non sunt haec timidis signa tuenda uiris.
> nox et hiems longaeque uiae saeuique dolores
>   mollibus his castris et labor omnis inest.
>
>   (*Aa* 2.233–36)

---

42. "Laboro" (1, 2, 4, 6, 7), *Oxford Latin Dictionary*.

43. Cicero, *Tusculan Disputations (Tusc.)*, ed. and trans. J. E. King, Loeb Classical Library (Cambridge, Mass.: Harvard University Press, 1927) 2.15.35. The English translations are adapted from King's.

[Love is a kind of warfare. Get lost, you slackers! These standards are not to be guarded by timid men. Night, winter, long marches, sharp pains and all kinds of labor are found in this soft camp.]

The strenuous demands of love's labor are here presented not only by means of a comparison to the labors of the military life but also by the direct denial that love is for the "slackers" and the "timid." As we shall see below, the ironic use of "mollibus" (soft, dainty) to refer to love's camp is significant as well. In this passage, the difficulties of love's labor are also reinforced by Ovid's pairing of *labor* with the sharp pains of military life.

This was not the first time, however, that Ovid compared the life of a lover with the hard life of a soldier. His elegy beginning "Militat omnis amans" (*Amores* 1.9) outlines in detail the similarities between the labor of the soldier and the labor of the lover. They both serve guard duty through the night; they both endure forced marches through unforgiving terrain; they both go out on scouting missions; and they both are called upon to attack while the enemy sleeps. The discourse of *militia amoris* in *Amores* 1.9 is important because, at the end of the poem, Ovid reveals the *reason* for this extended comparison. Here he wants to make the case that lovers are not the victims of *otium otiosum*. On the contrary, since lovers are like soldiers and since Roman soldiers had the reputation of being hard workers, lovers too must work strenuously.[44] Ovid comments in the poem: "ergo desidiam quicumque uocabat amorem, / desinat" (Therefore, let whomever called love an idleness cease doing so; *Amores* 1.9.31–32). In fact, if the truth be told, Ovid insists that the life of love can be used to reform someone who had previously fallen into the life of *otium otiosum*. He takes himself as a prime example:

---

44. The Roman soldier had a reputation for doing hard work. See the comments in André 20. Following his discussion of the contrast between *labor* and *dolor*, Cicero speaks somewhat of the toil of military life: "nostri exercitus primum unde nomen habeant vides, deinde qui labor quantus agminis, ferre plus dimidiati mensis cibaria, ferre si quid ad usum velint, ferre vallum, etc." (as for our army, you can see first whence it gets its name: the labor of the march; the load of more than half a month's provisions, the load of any requisite needed, the load of the stake for entrenchment, etc.; *Tusc.* 2.16.37–38).

On the perceived closeness of the labor of farmers and soldiers, Cato the Elder commented: "At ex agricolis et viri fortissimi et milites strenuissimi gignuntur, maximeque pius quaestus stabilissimusque consequitur minimeque invidiosus, minimeque male cogitantes sunt qui in eo studio occupati sunt" (On the other hand, it is from the farming class that the bravest men and the sturdiest soldiers come, their calling is most highly respected, their livelihood is most assured and is looked on with the least hostility, and those who are engaged in that pursuit are least inclined to be disaffected; "On Agriculture" 2–3).

See also the comments of van den Hoven 29.

ipse ego segnis eram discinctaque in otia natus;
   mollierant animos lectus et umbra meos;
inpulit ignauum formosae cura puellae,
   iussit et in castris aera merere suis.
inde uides agilem nocturnaque bella gerentem:
   qui nolet fieri desidiosus, amet.

(*Amores* 1.9.41–46)

[I myself was inactive and born into negligent *otium;* my bed and the shade had made my soul soft; love for a pretty girl destroyed my slothful ways and commanded me to take up arms in his camp. Thus, you see me agile and waging night war. Whoever wants to avoid sloth, let him love!]

Here we find two of the words identified by André as synonymous with *otium* in the pejorative sense: *ignavia* and *desidia*—or, to be more accurate, the adjective *desidiosus*. These, with the adjective *segnis* (slow, sluggish, torpid) are clear indications that the *otium* to which the poet alludes at the beginning of the passage is *otium otiosum*. In addition to these references, there is also the reference to shade in line 42, probably alluding to what Balsdon described as the disreputable "life in the shade." The persona, however, bore these qualities *before* he chose to love. Far from making him soft, love reformed him, and he now rejects his old, slothful self and has become a worker in the camp of Amor. By rejecting accusations that love makes one soft and effeminate, Ovid attempts to place the pursuit of love within the prevailing Stoic work ideology of Ovid's Rome. This may well be the source of the significant male orientation of the discourse of love's labor. In Rome, maleness was constructed as active, femininity as soft, passive, and idle. Hence, love's work was primarily oriented toward the male. This tradition will continue, as we shall see, into the Middle Ages.

Ovid is, of course, double voicing serious labor discourse in *Amores* 1.9, and therein lies the humor. The agenda is the same in the *Ars*. The call to work is made specifically to counter the charge that lovers are slothful. Beyond the direct reference to the "sluggards" in line 233, in line 229 the *praeceptor* argues that "Amor odit inertes" (Love hates the sluggish), the key word *inertes* being another of the Latin words synonymous with *otium otiosum*.

In the second passage, Ovid again uses the discourse of love's labor to affirm that love demands strenuous activity. This time, however, love's labor refers not to courtship but to the sex act itself. Here copulation is compared to the plowing of a field, and Ovid urges that men—again, the male—perform this labor while they are young and have the necessary strength:

> utilis, o iuuenes, aut haec, aut serior aetas:
> iste feret segetes, iste serendus ager.
> dum uires annique sinunt, tolerate labores:
> iam ueniet tacito curua senecta pede.
>
> (*Aa* 2.667–70)

[Profitable, O young men, are (aging women) or even a later age; that field will bear; that field must be sown. While vigor and years allow, endure the labor. Soon will come stooping old age with silent foot.]

From this passage, Ovid goes on specifically to compare the labor of sex to the labors of rowing a boat, plowing a field, or fighting in battle:

> aut mare remigiis, aut uomere findite terras
> aut fera belligeras addite in arma manus
> aut latus ct uires operamque adferte puellis:
> hoc quoque militia est, hoc quoque quaerit opes.
>
> (*Aa* 2.671–74)

[Cleave the sea with oars or the earth with the plow, apply your warlike hands to savage battle, or bring your flank and strength to the service of girls. This, too, is warfare; this, too, calls for strength.]

Sexual intercourse becomes an approved labor in the same category as idealized agricultural labor or the difficult labors of sailors and soldiers. This warning to young males against the waste of time and one's youth is paralleled, however, in Book 3 by a similar warning to females (*Aa* 3.65–68, 79–80). While the males risk losing their sexual powers, women risk loss of their beauty. Ovid's advice to both is to work while one can: "Carpite florem" (Pluck the flower; *Aa* 3.79).

In the third passage, Ovid deliberately conflates the labors of courtship with the labors of writing poetry. After a long passage describing the trials of lovers and strategies to combat them, Ovid pauses and asks himself why he is lingering over these "small things" when greater things call him forward. He continues: "ardua molimur, sed nulla, nisi ardua, virtus: / difficilis nostra poscitur arte labor" (We attempt an arduous task, but nothing is meritorious if not arduous. Hard work is demanded by my art; *Aa* 2.537–38). As we shall see below, Ovid uses the term *ars* with just about the complete range of denotations possible. Here, however, the *praeceptor amoris* seems deliberately to identify the art necessary to successful courtship and the art necessary to write successful love poetry. This is a pattern that is seen in many different passages in the *Ars*.

Another key labor term, *opus*, is used even more frequently—thirty times—in the *Ars* than *labor*, and Ovid uses it in very similar ways. *Opus* meant "that which needs to be done," a task, an occupation, one's business, a (strenuous) activity and, in particular, the product of one's work.[45] The close connection between "opus" and "labor" for Ovid is best seen in a section in which the *praeceptor amoris* discusses the goal of winning over one's lady without having to give her gifts. "Hoc opus, hic labor est," he writes, "primo sine munere iungi" (Here is the task; here is the labor: first to win her without gifts; *Aa* 1.453). Besides showing the semantic closeness of the two words, the passage is a particularly good example of Ovid's double voicing because the phrase "hoc opus, hic labor est" is a direct quotation taken from Book 6 of the *Aeneid*.[46] It comes at the point at which the Sibyl is explaining to Aeneas that the descent into the underworld is easy but that the climbing back to daylight is difficult. Ovid's borrowing is both double-voiced and parodic given the incongruity between the two contexts. After all, Aeneas's momentous labor is the descent to the underworld to see the shade of his father, and upon this *opus*, upon this *labor*, rests the future of Rome itself. For the *praeceptor amoris*, the labors are no more serious than trying to seduce a woman by writing a love letter rather than by sending her gifts, yet Ovid clearly wants Virgil's serious ideology of labor to linger in the phrase, for there is a serious point here for the lover to learn: perseverance. A good laborer, he writes, is not timid, nor does he surrender when faced with difficulties. Indeed, the *praeceptor* here compares the labor of love to agricultural labor, specifically the taming of horses or oxen, and the lesson to be drawn is to persevere: "Penelopen ipsam, persta modo, tempore uinces" (Provided that you persevere, in time you will conquer Penelope herself; *Aa* 1.477).

Ovid uses *opus* primarily in five senses, all of which are closely related. First, it is used to refer to the work of mythological craftsmen like Daedalus (*Aa* 2.46, 2.65, 2.78, 2.578). Second, it is used to refer to courtship or, in one instance, to the product of love's labor: the woman's face after applying makeup (*Aa* 1.409, 1.453, 2.502, 3.228, 3.370). Ovid uses *opus* for the work of courtship, for example, in a passage where he states

---

45. "Opus" (1, 2, 3, 4, 5, 9), *Oxford Latin Dictionary*. According to the *Dictionnaire étymologique*, the feminine "opera" carried the meaning of work "au sens abstrait."

46. Virgil, *Aeneid* 6.129.

that lovers should know the proper seasons for love's labor. If it is not the proper season, he warns, "differ opus" (put off the work; *Aa* 1.409). In Book 3, the *praeceptor amoris* speaks about the necessity for women to learn how to invent and play games in order to seduce a man. In fact, he argues, learning the games is the less difficult of the labors; the larger labor, the real *opus*, is for the woman to learn to control her emotions while playing the game. The passage reads:

> mille facesse iocos; turpe est nescire puellam
>   ludere: ludendo saepe paratur amor.
> sed minimus labor est sapienter iactibus uti;
>   maius opus mores composuisse suos.
>
> (*Aa* 3.367–70)

[Make up a thousand games; it is disgraceful for a girl not to know how to play. Often love is gained through games. But the smallest labor is to use your throws wisely. A greater work is self-control.]

Here Ovid mixes play and work in a witty reminder that love's labor in the *Ars* is never far removed from game.

Just as *labor* could refer to the sex act, so too could *opus* (*Aa* 2.480, 2.675, 2.730, 3.770). In Ovid's theogony of Book 2, for example, he treats the origin of love. In this context, the sex act is presented as an *opus*, albeit a natural work, which Venus herself taught to the animals (*Aa* 2.480). Ovid also uses *opus* to refer to the older woman's greater knowledge of the sexual technique (*Aa* 2.673–76). In addition, he adds: "hoc quoque militia est, hoc quoque quaerit opes" (This too is warfare, this too calls for labors; *Aa* 2.674). Just a few lines later, when Ovid describes some details of lovemaking, he adds that the work is best performed when there is leisure to do it right: "hic tibi seruandus tenor est, cum libera dantur / otia, furtiuum nec timor urget opus" (This is the course you must follow, when *otium* is plentiful, and no fear urges on the secret work; *Aa* 2.729–30). Finally, at the end of Book 3, before Ovid begins his suggestions on the proper sexual positions for various kinds of women, he identifies the sex act with Venus's *opus* (*Aa* 3.770).

Thus, courtship and the sexual act itself are presented using *opus* as part of the discourse of love's labor. Just as with *labor*, however, the *praeceptor* cannot help sliding back from the *opus* of the lover to his own work, both as a teacher of love and as a poet.[47] In these last two cate-

---

47. *Aa* 1.266, 2.162, 2.733, 3.747; *Aa* 1.29, 2.733, 3.206, 3.338, 3.346, 3.414, 3.747.

gories, we see the labors of the poet and the lover as parallel in the discourse of love's labor.[48] And why not? All three characters engage in the writing of letters and poems, and the work of all three is suspect in relation to the prevailing ideology of work.[49] In *Aa* 2.733 and 3.747, in fact, it is impossible to tell whether Ovid is referring to his work as the *praeceptor amoris* or as the poet. The status (in terms of the Roman work ethic) of these last two *opera* is similar to that of love's labor in that "serious" writers would see them as the fruits of *otium otiosum*. Indeed, in the third book of the *Ars*, Ovid complains specifically about how little honor is given to poets: "Nunc hederae sine honore iacent operataque doctis / cura uigil Musis nomen inertis habet" (Now the ivy lies without honor, and the laborious cultivation and sleepless care of the learned Muses is called idleness; *Aa* 3.411–12). Again we see Ovid employing *inertia*, a word related to *otium otiosum*. A passage from one of the *Amores* offers even deeper insight into Ovid's complaint. At the beginning of the fifteenth poem of Book 1, the persona bitterly asks:

> Qvid mihi, Liuor edax, ignauos obicis annos
>   ingeniique uocas carmen inertis opus,
> non me more patrum, dum strenua sustinet aetas,
>   praemia militiae puluerulenta sequi
> nec me uerbosas leges ediscere nec me
>   ingrato uocem prostituisse foro?

(Amores 1.15.1–6)

[Why, devouring Envy, do you reproach me with slothful years, and you call my song the work of an indolent character, just because the customs of the fathers were not for me? While youth sustained me, I did not pursue the dusty rewards of the military, nor did I study garrulous laws, nor prostitute my voice before the ungrateful Forum.]

Personified Envy in this passage essentially asks the persona why he is not pursuing the traditional occupations, those worthy of freemen. The language in line 3, in which Envy asks why the poet is not using the strength of his youth to better ends, is perhaps echoed in *Ars* 2.669–70, a

---

48. Note Myerowitz's comments: "Far more than has been assumed, it is Ovid's experience as a poet, rather than as a lover in the narrow sense, which is brought to bear on both the general topic and the explicit instructions of the *Ars amatoria*. . . . The cumulative effect of the cluster of identical images for poetry and for love is to subsume both the art of the lover and the art of the poet into the realm of *cultus*, a journey away from nature which is accomplished by means of *ars*" (77, 101).

49. For the *praeceptor*'s remarks on letter writing, see *Aa* 1.459–86. On poetry and eloquence, see *Aa* 2.107–76.

passage cited earlier, where the *praeceptor amoris* urges his male students to use the strength of their youth to make love. But in *Amores* 1.15, the answer is more traditional: "mortale est, quod quaeris, opus; mihi fama perennis / quaeritur" (The work you ask of me is mortal, but I seek everlasting fame; *Amores* 1.15.7–8). The problem is that none of the approved labors, even farm work, yields anything lasting beyond the present years: "ergo cum silices, cum dens patientis aratri / depereant aeuo, carmina morte carent" (therefore, although with time flint and the tooth of the patient plow go to ruin, song endures; *Amores* 1.15.31–32). For Ovid, the discourse of labor is fitting both for poetry and for love, although they both, given the prevailing work ethic, are suspect activities. Poetry, for Ovid, is a labor of love, but it is not synonymous with love's labor. The *Ars* focuses on love's labor proper even though Ovid intertwines the two labors continually throughout the work.[50]

A third, although less important, term in the discourse of love's labor is *officium*. Ovid uses it only four times for the labor of love. One's *officium* is one's work, a duty, an act of respect, or a helpful or beneficial act.[51] In the first two instances, Ovid uses it to refer to the fatuous activities of the lover—like flicking dust off the lady's skirt or gathering up her cloak—when he visits the Circus with his lady (*Aa* 1.152, 155). Ovid also uses the term to refer to the services a man can render to his mistress when she is sick (*Aa* 2.333). The double voicing of these passages stands out starkly when one remembers that Cicero devoted a serious treatise to *officia*. This is so because the actions covered by *officium* in *Ars* 1.52 and 1.55 are some of the most trivial in the entire *Ars*. Visiting the sick can be, of course, a useful activity, in many cases a real *officium*, except that in Ovid's hands even such noble actions become merely new stratagems to capture the beloved. Those ministrations that might hurt or be disagreeable, the *praeceptor* writes, are best left to one's rival (*Aa* 2.336).

The fourth example of Ovid's use of *officium* to denote love's labor is possibly the most interesting. Whereas the *praeceptor* has argued that both courtship and sex are work, he rejects women who engage in sex merely for the sake of duty: "quae datur officio, non est mihi grata

50. Peter L. Allen believes that the *Ars* is not a manual on the practice of love labor but rather a treatise on the construction of fictions about love (10, 20). It is a work of literary theory. While his argument is insightful, it may be too dogmatic. If, in fact, Ovid was aware that the meaning of his text needed to be constructed by his readers, as Allen argues (20), why is it not possible that some readers could have used it as a manual on the practice of love? Virgil may not have intended his *Georgics* to have been used as a farm manual, yet who is to say that some of his readers did not use it this way?

51. "Officium," *Dictionnaire étymologique;* "officium" (1), *Oxford Latin Dictionary.*

uoluptas: / officium faciat nulla puella mihi" (Pleasure given as a duty is not pleasing to me; let no girl perform an *officium* for me; *Aa* 2.687–88). Pleasure alone must be the appropriate motivation for such work. Even the discourse of love's labor has its limits, and although the *praeceptor* instructs his students to feign romantic feelings, the role playing must stop, apparently, when it comes to sexual pleasure.

Thus, Ovid uses *labor, opus*, and *officium* to denote the work of love, whether it is courtship, lovemaking, or writing love poetry. One would expect Ovid's discourse to contain at least one more term: *negotium*, a word coined as the negation of *otium*. However, Ovid does not use the term at all in the *Ars*, a fact that may be significant. Although *negotium* carried many of the same meanings of *labor* and *opus*, unlike those words it could also refer specifically to business dealings.[52] Was the term too closely tied to business affairs to be suitable for Ovid's rakish *praeceptor amoris*? Perhaps Ovid's ideal lover, like Horace's "happy man," is meant to be "procul negotiis," far away from business cares and blessedly given only to labors that echo those of the idealized farmer. Whatever the reason, this avoidance of the term for business dealings sharply distinguishes Ovid's treatment of love's labor from that of Chaucer and Gower, who freely use "bysynesse" when treating the subject. This, I will argue, is a significant shift for the later poets, and we will have occasion to return to this subject in later chapters.

I noted that Ovid defends the work of love as an antidote to the vices associated with *otium otiosum: desidia, inertia, ignavia*, and *luxuria*. Another word that one might expect but that does not appear in any significant way in the *Ars* is *servitium* (servitude, slavery). It occurs only once (*Ars* 3.488), where it is used to describe the situation in which a woman is put in a compromising situation because her love letters fell into the wrong hands. In addition, other hints that love's labors may be slavish can be found. One occurs in Book 2, when Ovid refers to a lover who is too available to his beloved and too willing to meet her every wish. He warns: "sunt quibus ingrate timida indulgentia seruit / et, si nulla subest aemula, languet amor" (Some women exist for whom timid indulgence

52. "Negotium," *Dictionnaire étymologique*. "Negotium" is defined as "quod not sit otium . . . S'emploie aussi par euphemism pour designer des choses ou des actes qu'on ne veut pas expressement nommer." See also "negotium" (6, 8), *Oxford Latin Dictionary*. An important study of the derivation of *negotium* from *otium* occurs in Emile Benveniste, *Le vocabulaire des institutions indo-européenes* (Paris: Éditions de Minuit, 1969) 1.139–47. *Negotium* does not appear as an entry in *A Concordance of Ovid*, ed. R. J. Deferrari, M. I. Barry, and M. R. P. McGuire (Washington, D.C.: The Catholic University of America Press, 1939).

slaves without reward, and if no rival exists, their love grows faint; *Aa* 2.435–36). Here the verb *servio* is employed to suggest a slavelike service. On the whole, however, the discourse of love's slavery does not play a significant role in the *Ars*.[53]

Although some Romans may not have perceived the activities of slaves as work, slaves were a crucial source of free labor in the time of Augustus. Cicero, for example, in *De officiis*, says that slaves must be required to work and that they must be given their due (1.41). If Ovid uses figures from military and agricultural labor in the *Ars*, why is *servitium amoris* largely absent from the work? The absence is even more noteworthy since *servitium amoris* had become a commonplace theme in the work of the other Roman elegiac poets.[54] It may be that *servitium amoris* did not carry the right ideological connotations. Although slaves certainly labored, *servitium amoris* belongs more to the discourse of passion than to the discourse of love's labor. In *servitium amoris*, the lover is passive, defeated. The lover descends into slavery as a result of an external force. Love's slaves find themselves in that position by the force of passion. Indeed, R. O. A. M. Lyne has argued that the function of this figure was to emphasize the lover's degradation at the hands of his beloved.[55] Ovid uses the figure for just this purpose in *Amores* 3.11, a poem in which he bemoans the wrongs he has endured and decides to give up his labors on behalf of a particularly ungrateful woman (*Amores* 3.11.12). The attitude expressed in this poem (revoked, however, in 3.11b) looks forward to Ovid's position in the *Remedia*, where Ovid returns to the discourse of passion. *Servitium amoris*, then, is not an attitude that would make sense in the *Ars* because, as I have tried to show, in that work Ovid employs a discourse whose ideology suggests that love's *labor* or *opus* is a purposeful and productive activity, an activity worthy of a freeman. Indeed, love is more dignified than common labor because it is a craft that can be codified and taught by a master craftsman. In that ideological context, it would be inconsistent to present love as either slavish or degrading.

53. Myerowitz notes the relative unimportance in the *Ars* of the metaphors of love as a disease, madness, or slavery, but she contrasts these metaphors with the theme of love as a journey, not with love as labor (79–80, 202n). Our readings of Ovid's portrayal of love as an active rather than a passive phenomenon accord with each other, however.

54. See F. O. Copley, "*Servitium amoris* in the Roman Elegists," *Transactions of the American Philological Association* 78 (1947): 285–300; R. O. A. M. Lynne, "Servitium amoris," *Classical Quarterly* n.s. 29 (1979): 117–27; and P. Murgatroyd, "*Servitium amoris* and the Roman Elegists," *Latomus* 40 (1981): 87–100.

55. Lynne 117–18. See also the comments of Hollis 95–96.

Indeed, in the *Ars amatoria*, love is more than *labor* and *opus;* it is a higher kind of work. As a result, it is able to be reduced to a system and taught by a master craftsman. Returning to the distinction made by Cicero in *De officiis*, one notes that love's labor is of a higher order because "prudentia maior inest," that is, it requires a higher degree of practical understanding or wisdom. The *Ars*, like the *Georgics*, is a didactic poem that claims to teach a master craftsman's skill. In fact, this is exactly how the *Ars* is described by Ovid as he looks back on the work from the perspective of the *Remedia amoris:* "quin etiam docui qua possis arte parari, / et, quod nunc ratio est, inpetus ante fuit" (Indeed, I taught by what art [love] can be obtained, and what is now a system, before was just instinct).[56]

Ovid uses the term *ars* fifty-seven times in the *Ars amatoria*, and the word carried a rich semantic load. First, it signified "a systematic body of knowledge and practical techniques," as well as "the rules and principles of an art." Closely allied to this was its sense of "a professional, artistic, or technical skill as something acquired and exercised in practice, skilled work, craftsmanship, and art."[57] The opening lines of the work strikingly display Ovid's use of *ars* in these senses:

> Si qvis in hoc artem populo non nouit amandi,
>   hoc legat et lecto carmine doctus amet.
> arte citae ueloque rates remoque mouentur,
>   arte leues currus: arte regendus Amor.
> curribus Automedon lentisque erat aptus habenis,
>   Tiphys in Haemonia puppe magister erat:
> me Venus artificem tenero praefecit Amori;
>   Tiphys et Automedon dicar Amoris ego.
>
> (*Aa* 1.1–8)

[If anyone among this people does not know the art of loving, let him read this poem, and having read it, let the well-instructed man love. By art swift ships are moved with sail and oar. By art nimble chariots are driven. Love, too, must be guided by art. Automedon was fit for chariots and pliant reins. Tiphys was the master of the Haemonian helm. Venus gave me command over delicate love as master craftsman. I shall be called the Tiphys and Automedon of love.]

---

56. *Remedia amoris (Ra)* 9–10. Note that while "ratio" here certainly means "theory" and "system" (as opposed to natural impulse), it could also mean "a plan of action," a meaning that accords even more closely to my reading of the active nature of Ovid's discourse of love's labor ("Ratio" [4.b, 10, 11], *Oxford Latin Dictionary*).

57. "Ars" (1, 5, 9), *Oxford Latin Dictionary*.

Tiphys and Automendon, of course, are two skilled craftsmen: one was the helmsman of the *Argo*, the other was Achilles' charioteer. Largely by means of the use of *ars*, then, Ovid immediately constructs the discourse of love as *skilled* labor, honorable labor that requires a large measure of *prudentia*. Love, therefore, is a fitting subject for a didactic poem, and Ovid, who styles himself an *artifex* of love, proposes to write such a poem. The word *artifex* denoted an expert practitioner of an art, a skilled craftsman.[58] Since an *ars* is "something acquired and exercised in practice," Ovid emphasizes that his skill, his body of professional knowledge, comes not from divine inspiration but from *usus*, experience.[59]

Ars, however, carried several more relevant meanings that Ovid employs in his poem. For example, *ars* could also signify human as opposed to natural ingenuity, that is, artificiality.[60] It could also denote a crafty action or stratagem.[61] When paired with the adjective "bona," as in "bonas artes," *ars* signified "cultural pursuits" or "liberal studies."[62] The word could also be used to refer to the product of skill: an artistic achievement, a work of art, an invention.[63] It could also mean a profession, occupation, or type of activity, including the occupation of a poet.[64] In fact, in all these senses, Ovid's use of *ars* to describe love's labor, the skills of love's labor, the labor and techniques of poetry continuously underscores his explicit argument that love's labor is an occupation that is dignified and worthy of respect because it demands a high level of *prudentia*.[65]

58. "Artifex" (2, 3), *Oxford Latin Dictionary*.

59. "Ars" (1), *Oxford Latin Dictionary. Aa* 1.7, 29. For other passages in the *Ars* in which Ovid uses the word in these senses, see *Aa* 2.12, 2.162*, 2.196, 2.512, 2.538*, 2.542, 3.208, 3.257*, 3.258, 3.291*; 1.12, 1.25, 1.265, 1.387, 1.692, 2.14, 2.76, 2.162*, 2.313*, 2.434, 2.506, 2.538*, 2.542*, 2.547*, 2.735, 3.25, 3.42, 3.291*, 3.301, 3.540* & 3.545* (art of poetry), 3.791. Those passages in which I felt the word may refer to two different denotations simultaneously, I have marked with an asterisk in this and subsequent notes.

60. "Ars" (2), *Oxford Latin Dictionary*. See *Aa* 1.106, 2.480, 3.155, 3.164, 3.200, 3.201, 3.210, 3.257*, 3.258.

61. "Ars" (3), *Oxford Latin Dictionary*. See *Aa* 1. 242, 1.266, 1.362, 1.419, 1.435, 1.612, 2.17, 2.313*, 2.542*, 2.547*, 2.592, 3.332, 3.594.

62. "Ars" (6) *Oxford Latin Dictionary*. See *Aa* 1.459, 2.121.

63. "Ars" (8) *Oxford Latin Dictionary*. See *Aa* 1.656, 2.48.

64. "Ars" (7) *Oxford Latin Dictionary*. See *Aa* 2.568, 3.540*, 3.545*.

65. The only exception to this rule is Ovid's use of *ars* to denote magic and the black arts. See *Aa* 2.99, 2.425. Nevertheless, just as Ovid implicitly rejects *servitium amoris* as unworthy, he also forbids lovers to resort to magic.

IV

Ovid's discourse of love's labor is constructed not only by means of such key words as *labor, opus,* and *ars,* but also by means of the poem's genre, for the *Ars* is neither elegiac nor pastoral but didactic poetry. Didactic poetry traced its roots back to Hesiod's *Works and Days* and sought to convey information on a "technical subject."[66] In the seminal study cited above, Leach demonstrates that the *Ars* was heavily indebted to a didactic poem about agriculture: the *Georgics.*[67] In that work, Virgil reviews and praises the labor of the farmer, the herdsman, the vine tender, and the beekeeper. Although his statements about work are not always consistent, in Book 1 Virgil presents agricultural work as Jupiter's innovation, a gift whose value arises, at least in part, from its potential as an antidote to idleness, for "ante Iovem nulli subigebant arva coloni" (before Jove no farmers worked the fields). For Virgil, the Golden Age of Saturn was an age of leisure, when the land gave forth its fruits without work. However, the Golden Age passed with the coming of Jupiter, and

> . . . pater ipse colendi
> haud facilem esse viam voluit, primusque per artem
> movit agros, curis acuens mortalia corda,
> nec torpere gravi passus sua regna veterno.

[The father himself wished the path of cultivation not to be easy. He first ordained that fields be cultivated by art, sharpening with cares mortal understanding, nor did he suffer his kingdom to slumber in heavy torpor.]

With the passing of the Golden Age, cultivation and civilization were made necessary. Hard work was required to subdue nature; hard work is part of man's patrimony; but hard work conquered all—"labor omnia vicit / improbus" (persistent labor conquered all).[68] While Miles has signaled the possible negative connotations of "improbus" as a description of work, it is probable, at least on one level, that in this passage Virgil sets up labor not only as the indispensable foundation for civilization but also as a god-given antidote to *torpor,* a word that carries many of the negative associations of *otium otiosum.*[69]

---

66. Hollis 89–90.

67. Leach 142–54. See also Myerowitz 109–12; and Hollis 91–93.

68. Virgil, *Georgics* 1.125, 121–24, 145.

69. Miles 84–85. Miles also argues that these passages designate "man's capacity for work and invention as his highest and most essential qualities" (74). L. P. Wilkinson writes that in the *Georgics*

In Books 1 and 2 Ovid continuously portrays the would-be lover as either a hunter or a farmer and the woman as an aspect of nature to be tamed or cultivated.[70] In line with Roman gender stereotypes, Ovid again suggests that males are active and females passive. Early in the *Ars*, for example, the labors of the male lover are compared to those of hunters, fowlers, and fisherman (*Aa* 1.45–50, 1.270). A second group of metaphors in the *Ars* links the care and cultivation of women and their love to the cultivation of crops and fields.[71] Just as Virgil teaches that farmers must know the correct places and seasons for each of their works, so Ovid's work is full of references to the correct times and places for various aspects of love's labor. *Ars* 1.399–418 is a particularly Virgilian passage.[72] It begins:

> tempora qui solis operosa colentibus arua,
> fallitur, et nautis aspicienda putat.
> nec semper credenda Ceres fallacibus aruis
> nec semper uiridi concaua puppis aquae,
> nec teneras semper tutum captare puellas:
> saepe dato melius tempore fiet idem.

[That person errs who thinks that seasons are to be considered only by sailors and those cultivating the toilsome fields. Not always should grain be committed to the uncertain fields. Not always the concave ship to the green waters. Nor is it always safe to chase young girls. That project often goes better during the proper season.]

The rest of the passage lists the seasons—particularly birthdays—when it is not safe to pursue women. The "seasons of love's labor" surely mimic references to the correct seasons for various agricultural chores that can be found throughout the *Georgics*.

In Book 3, Ovid's approach is only slightly different. Here Ovid instructs women on the doctrine of *cultus*. As the farmer must cultivate his fields or his vines, women must cultivate themselves in order to win their lovers.[73] Ovid's insistence on the importance of *cultus* is taken from Vir-

---

Virgil "proclaims a 'gospel of work'" (introduction, *The Georgics*, trans. L. P. Wilkinson [New York: Penguin Books, 1982] 15). See also *Oxford Latin Dictionary*, "torpor," defined as "absence of physical energy," "drowsiness," "lethargy," and "sloth" (2, 3).

70. Leach 142–46.

71. Leach 146. Leach rightly remarks on the antifeminist coloring of much of Ovid's work in the *Ars*.

72. Leach 150n.

73. Leach 147.

gil's recommendations to farmers on the necessity of cultivating trees.[74]

Ovid also owes a debt to the *Georgics* on the levels of style and vocabulary. Leach notes that Ovid incorporates such words and phrases as *quaere, nunc age, disce, adspicio, iubeo, labor,* and *opus* "which are important in creating the instructive tone of a didactic poem."[75] She demonstrates that "Ovid's amatory advice is couched in language that suggests an analogy between seduction and the common skills and practices by which man extends his dominion over nature" and that a full understanding of Ovid's "manner of expounding the amatory arts" cannot be achieved without comparing it to Virgil's teachings on the art of husbandry in the *Georgics.*[76] In conclusion, she writes:

The entire plan of the *Ars amatoria* seems contrived to bring Vergil repeatedly to mind. Through metaphor we see the lover undertaking the very tasks that the honest farmer performs. The virtues required of both are the same: natural intuition, patience, persistent care. As a teacher of these virtues, the *magister amoris* recalls the philosophical speaker of the *Georgics.*[77]

Ovid's ironic double voicing of labor discourse in the *Ars* extends, then, beyond the level of vocabulary, figures, and tropes onto the level of genre itself. The didactic genre as exemplified by the *Georgics* carried, at least on one level,[78] a positive labor ideology, and that positive labor ideology is certainly transferred to the labor of love by Ovid's use of the didactic genre.

V

One cannot complete a treatment of the discourse of love's labor in Ovid without considering his treatment of love in the *Remedia amoris*, which some believe to be the equivalent of a fourth book of the *Ars amatoria*. In this book, Ovid changes his mask and adopts a different discourse vis-à-vis love. Here he takes up the discourse of passion: love is an

---

74. *Georgics* 2.35–37; Leach 150.

75. On the level of vocabulary, Leach depends on the findings of E. J. Kenney, *"Nequitiae Poeta,"* *Ovidiana; Recherches sur Ovide publiés a l'occasion du bimillenaire de la naissance du poète,* ed. N. I. Herescu (Paris: Les Belles Lettres, 1958) 201–9.

76. Leach 149.

77. Leach 151.

78. Virgil's *Georgics* is, of course, a work of art in its own right. It is quite possible that Virgil's work includes an underlying double voicing of its own. To explore that double voicing, however, goes beyond the scope of this study. It is sufficient for my purposes simply to concede that one of Virgil's possible meanings in the *Georgics* is a sincere defense of the dignity of work.

illness, one that leads some to untimely death.[79] Indeed, the discourse of love as passion is indicated by the very title of the work. The work ethic of love's labor, enunciated in the *Ars* is, in the *Remedia*, turned on its head. No longer is love described as a task demanding strenuous activity, perseverance, and skill. It now becomes an illness that is fostered by *otium otiosum*. A key remedy, then, must be a return to "real" work. Hence, *Remedia* 135–68 is a crucial passage because Ovid here uses the term *otium* three times in relationship to love. He writes:

> ergo ubi uisus eris nostrae medicabilis arti,
> fac monitis *fugias otia* prima meis.
> haec ut ames faciunt; haec, ut fecere, tuentur;
> haec sunt iucundi causa cibusque mali.
> *otia si tollas, periere Cupidinis arcus*
> contemptaeque iacent et sine luce faces.
>
> (*Remedia amoris* [hereafter cited as *Ra*] 135–40; emphasis added)

[Therefore, when you would be found curable by my art, obey my counsels and first flee from *otium*. That causes you to love; that protects what it has done; that is the cause and food of the delightful evil. *If you take away otium, Cupid's bow is destroyed* and his torch lies despised and without light.]

He then becomes even more explicit: "tam Venus otia amat: qui finem quaeris amoris, / (cedit amor rebus) res age, tutus eris" (Venus loves *otium* so much: you who seek an end to love [love yields to business] be busy and you will be safe; *Ra* 143–44). Recall the three labors of love in the *Ars:* finding a lover, capturing a lover, and making love last. In this remarkable passage, Ovid states that *otium* is the sine qua non of at least two of the labors, and hence should be avoided. The rest of the passage makes clear that the *otium* to which Ovid refers here is *otium otiosum*, not *otium negotiosum*. Ovid speaks of *languor* (*Ra* 145) and too much sleep, dicing and too much drinking, and then he concludes: "desidiam puer ille sequi solet, odit agentes: / da uacuae menti, quo teneatur, opus" (That boy usually follows sloth; he hates active persons. Give the empty mind some work to occupy it; *Ra* 149–50). Whereas, in the *Ars*, love is *opus* and *labor*, in the *Remedia*, Ovid uses the discourse of *otium* in a more serious and conventional way: labor and love are binary opposites. Indeed, love is now aligned with terms either explicitly or implicitly linked to *otium otiosum: languor* and *desidia*. It is useless to try to make Ovid's discourses of

---

79. *Ra* 17–19. See the remarks of Hollis 110–11.

labor and *otium* consistent. Whereas these discourses are double-voiced in the *Ars*, in the *Remedia* there is no ironic space between the intentions of Ovid's sources and those of Ovid himself, at least in the key passages cited above.

What does Ovid here recommend for "serious" labor? He recommends two of the very occupations he rejected in *Amores* 1.15: the practice of law and military duty. He reinforces this point by citing the example of Aegisthus, who committed adultery with Clytemnestra. Aegisthus did so, according to Ovid, because he was "desidiosus," a sluggard (*Ra* 162). He did not bother to fight with the rest of the Greek soldiers in Troy. Hence, "quod potuit, ne nil illic ageretur, amauit" (What he could do, he did; lest he do nothing, he loved). Surprisingly, the discourse of love's labor sneaks in the back door of the *Remedia*. But love's labor here carries a pejorative connotation: Aegisthus took it up because he was not engaged in the real labor of fighting.

In the *Ars* and in the *Remedia*, Ovid defends contradictory positions on love, but the underlying work ethic is the same: get busy and work. In essence, he falls in line with what André has called the Augustan work ethic.[80] In other words, the motto "amor vincit omnia" of Virgil's "Tenth Eclogue" and of much Roman elegiac poetry is replaced by the more respectable "labor vincit omnia." The major difference between the two works is that Ovid neatly changes the definition of "labor" in the *Remedia*. In the *Ars*, Ovid uses the discourse of love's labor to associate all the positive qualities of skilled, determined work with the activities of love. Indeed, he co-opts the discourse of his critics and insists that courtship and the sex act itself are work activities. If André is correct when he states that the middle classes in the reign of Augustus distrusted *otium otiosum*, Ovid in his playful *Ars amatoria* uses the discourse of love's labor to pose as an ordinary, respectable citizen, who shares the values of his fellow citizens. André, who recognizes that Ovid presents leisure activities as forms of labor, sees this aspect of his poetry as a sign of a troubled conscience in the face of the old Roman ideals.[81] The discourse of love's labor in the *Ars*, however, is better seen as a joyous subversion and double voicing of conventional work ideologies. In contrast, Ovid employs the discourse of labor as a weapon against love, now portrayed as an illness, in the *Remedia*. In this sense, and perhaps only in this sense, the *Remedia* is a more serious work than the *Ars*.

80. André 396–97.
81. André 417–18.

In later chapters we will see how Ovid's practice of using prevailing labor ideologies in the discourse of love's labor for either serious or subversive ends was adapted by various poets in the Middle Ages. Writing with different cultural work ethics and with different social concerns, these writers constructed a sophisticated and nuanced series of discourses, sometimes "serious" and at other times "rhetorical," that play a major role in the amatory literature of the Middle Ages.

CHAPTER 3

Noble *Servitium*

Aspects of Labor Ideology in the Christian Middle Ages and Love's Labor in the *De amore* of Andreas Capellanus

The Romans and Greeks despised men who served anyone, especially a woman. Now we find service raised to an art form.

—Diane Ackerman

Est manifestum quod vobis servire solum est cunctis in hac vita regnare.

[I have the clear certainty that merely to serve you is to have universal kingship in this life.]

—Andreas Capellanus

I

The last chapter demonstrated that Ovid co-opted the Roman discourse of labor and incorporated it subversively to present the works of love as activities of *otium negotiosum* (busy leisure), not *otium otiosum* (unproductive idleness). He did this on several levels, borrowing key words, motifs, figures, and even a didactic genre from Roman labor discourse. Comparing courtship to the labor of soldiers and to the labor of farmers, two species of work that were highly respected in Roman society, Ovid treated the activities associated with finding a lover, winning a lover, and keeping a lover. Also included in these labors were the sex act itself and the writing of love poetry.

Ovid's writings were highly influential during the Middle Ages, particularly during the twelfth and thirteenth centuries, called the "aetas Ovidiana" by Ludwig Traube.[1] Because Ovid's writings on love were often

---

1. Traube is cited in Ralph J. Hexter, *Ovid and Medieval Schooling: Studies in Medieval School Commentaries on Ovid's "Ars Amatoria," "Epistulae ex Ponto," and "Epistulae Heroidum"* (Munich: Arbeo-

used as school texts, they became key sources for many medieval writers. Ovid's influence, for example, is thought to be particularly strong in the *De amore*, composed by Andreas Capellanus sometime during the middle of the 1180s.[2] Although little is known about the life of Andreas, it is probable that he was a cleric and possible that he was attached either to the royal court of France or to the court of Champagne.[3] *De amore* is written in three books, with the first two modeled roughly on the three books of the *Ars amatoria* and the third modeled on the *Remedia amoris*.[4] While Andreas discusses the labors of winning and keeping a lover, he does very little with the labor of finding a lover. Instead, he spends time defining what love is. Not only does Andreas borrow the general idea of using the didactic genre (at least in part of the *De amore*) to discuss love, but he also employs key terms used by Ovid in the *Ars*, such as *labor, opus,* and *militia amoris*. In place of *officium*, however, he adds such terms as *servitium* (service) and *obsequium* (act of service). The *De amore*, however, is not a slavish imitation of the *Ars* and *Remedia amoris*, for it is thoroughly imbued with the clerical and aristocratic cultures and with the labor ideology inherent in the three estates social model. Like other works in this tradition, however, it does not incorporate the primary labor ideology of the Bible, that is, labor as a result of mankind's sin.

The complexity of Andreas's treatise has spawned numerous debates over its self-contradictory treatments of love, its "real meaning," and its relationship with the possible practice of "courtly love."[5] The essentially

Gesellschaft, 1986) 2; and in Peter L. Allen, *The Art of Love: Amatory Fiction from Ovid to the "Romance of the Rose"* (Philadelphia: University of Pennsylvania Press, 1992) 47.

2. P. G. Walsh, introduction, *Andreas Capellanus on Love* (London: Duckworth, 1982) 1–2. All quotations and English translations from the *De amore* will be taken from this edition and cited in the text by page number. Walsh writes that there is no established manuscript tradition for the title of this work but that *De amore* "reflects most accurately the scope of the treatise" (1).

3. Walsh 2–3. See also John Benton, "The Court of Champagne as a Literary Center," *Speculum* 36 (1961): 578–82.

4. Walsh 12–13. On the one hand, Allen calls the split between Book 3 and the other two books "essentially and fundamentally Ovidian" (60–62). On the other hand, Michael Cherniss argues against any Ovidian influence on the *De amore* beyond the most general idea of making a mock didactic poem about love ("The Literary Comedy of Andreas Capellanus," *Modern Philology* 72 [1975]: 227). Cherniss believes that twelfth-century literature played a much more important formative role than Ovid's writings did. Allen, however, points out that forty-two references to Ovid exist in the *De amore*, most referring to either the *Ars* or the *Remedia*. Ovid, he claims, is Andreas's most cited secular source, and among all sources second only to the Bible (73). Don Monson agrees that Ovid is the most influential classical author, but he counts only fifteen Ovidian quotations and five allusions ("*Auctoritas* and Intertextuality in Andreas Capellanus' *De amore*," *Poetics of Love in the Middle Ages: Texts and Contexts*, ed. Moshe Lazar and Norris J. Lacy [Fairfax, Va.: George Mason University Press, 1989] 72).

5. Walsh 7–15. On the controversy over courtly love, see the essays in *The Meaning of Courtly Love,*

dialogic nature of the treatise is the source of this controversy. Beyond
the eight model dialogs in which Andreas sets out the discourse of love's
labor from a variety of different social positions, the *De amore* also contains the dialog of genre, in which he allows Christian moral teaching,
antifeminist diatribe, romance, allegory, and judgment literature all to
jostle with each other without letting any single genre become dominant.[6] Unable to settle on a single established genre for the work, P. G.
Walsh, for example, simply decides that *De amore* is sui generis.[7] Like
Ovid's *Ars amatoria*, the *De amore* is essentially a ludic text filled with a
plethora of different voices. By "ludic," however, I do not mean that it is
consistently "funny."[8] Although there are indeed funny passages, even
obscene punning in the *De amore*, much of the discourse has a serious flavor. The text is "ludic" in the sense that Andreas composed it playfully, incorporating many different viewpoints and styles of writing without ever
imposing a uniform, monologic voice or moral perspective.[9] One might

---

ed. F. X. Newman (Albany: SUNY Press, 1968); Roger Boase, *The Origin and Meaning of Courtly Love*
(Totowa, N.J.: Rowman & Littlefield, 1977); Robert R. Edwards and Stephen Spector, introduction,
The Olde Daunce: Love, Friendship, Sex, and Marriage in the Medieval World (Albany: SUNY Press, 1991)
1–8; and Paolo Cherchi, *Andreas and the Ambiguity of Courtly Love* (Toronto: University of Toronto
Press, 1994) 4–7.

For reviews of critical treatments of the self-contradictory nature of the *De amore*, see Cherniss
223, note 5; Bruno Roy, "À la recherche des lecteurs médiévaux du *De amore* d'André le Chapelain,"
Revue de l'université d'Ottawa 86.2 (1985): 46; and Toril Moi, "Desire in Language: Andreas Capellanus
and the Controversy of Courtly Love," *Medieval Literature: Criticism, Ideology, and History*, ed. David
Aers (New York: St. Martin's Press, 1986) 14. Roy's helpful formulation of nine critical approaches to
reconciling the treatment of love in Books 1 and 2 with that in Book 3 is recapitulated in Allen 71.

6. Monson reaches a similar conclusion. He writes: "The *De amore* is not only a speculative treatise on love, a practical manual on the art of loving, or a religious homily on the dangers of concu-
piscence. It is all these and more. . . . Hence the extreme complexity of Andreas' own discourse: very
much in the spirit of the times in which it was written, it is a multiple, dialectical, 'dialogic,' discourse interweaving all the medieval varieties of the discourse on love" (*"Auctoritas"* 77–78). See similar comments in his article "Andreas Capellanus and the Problem of Irony," *Speculum* 63.3 (1988):
572.

7. Walsh 12.

8. Cherniss, for example, calls *De amore* "a comic mock treatise, a *pastiche* of elements which Andreas found, or thought he found, not in the lives of his contemporaries, but in various kinds of literature in vogue in the late twelfth century" (224). Walsh believes that Andreas is "daringly and hu-
morously discussing in stylised play ideas of love and marriage which have no status in the real world
of twelfth-century society, but which challenge and criticise the prevailing mores of sex and marriage
imposed by feudal law and Christian precept" (6). On Andreas's obscene puns, see Betsy Bowden,
"The Art of Courtly Copulation," *Medievalia et Humanistica* 9 (1979): 67–85. Monson, however, believes that much of the punning critics find in *De amore* cannot hold up under scrutiny. For a thorough and critical review of critics who find humor in *De amore*, see Monson, "Problem of Irony"
555–58.

9. Among those most eager to find an ideological unity in the text is D. W. Robertson and those
critics who agree with his exegetical approach to medieval literature. Robertson constructs an ideological unity in *De amore* by finding the first two books to be ironic and the "real" meaning of the

also borrow Richard Lanham's distinction, described in Chapter 1, and argue that *De amore* is essentially "rhetorical" rather than "serious."[10] In the language of New Criticism, the text is complex but not unified. Indeed, Bruno Roy has shown that the medieval reception of *De amore* was often fragmentary, with scribes or translators passing on only those sections that supported their own preconceptions regarding the purpose of the treatise.[11]

Although the discourse of love as passion is more evident in *De amore* than in the *Ars amatoria*, several of the voices in the *De amore* also present love as a form of labor. They are voices filled not with the labor ideologies of Ovid's Rome, but with the labor ideologies of the Christian Middle Ages. Moreover, although the text's sexual morality and genres are dialogic, the labor ideology embedded in its discourse is fairly uniform: its presentation of labor is consistent with the labor views of Andreas's aristocratic patrons.

II

Making generalities about attitudes toward labor in the Middle Ages is just as perilous as making generalities about labor ideologies during the Roman Empire. One must always be aware that the medieval economy (and thus labor ideologies) evolved over the period's roughly thousand years. One must also be aware of social class variations in attitudes toward labor. As in the epoch of the Roman Empire, those with the education and the means to record their attitudes toward work were most often found in the classes whose very self-definition was based upon their freedom from manual labor. Again, as with Roman craftsmen, it is probable that medieval craftsmen had a much higher opinion of their work than did the clerics or the aristocrats. The evidence for their opinions, however, is scarce indeed.[12] Nevertheless, since this and all remaining chapters of this book focus on the writings of medieval authors, it will be

---

treatise only in the third book ("The Subject of the *De amore* of Andreas Capellanus," *Modern Philology* 50 [1952–1953]: 141–61, and *A Preface to Chaucer* [Princeton, N.J.: Princeton University Press, 1962] 394–448). Monson reviews and critiques Robertsonian readings of *De amore* ("Problem of Irony" 545–54).

10. Richard Lanham, *The Motives of Eloquence: Literary Rhetoric in the Renaissance* (New Haven, Conn.: Yale University Press, 1976) 3–5.

11. Roy 49–51.

12. George Ovitt, Jr., *The Restoration of Perfection: Labor and Technology in Medieval Culture* (New Brunswick, N.J.: Rutgers University Press, 1987) 135–36, 164–68; and Steven A. Epstein, *Wage Labor and Guilds in Medieval Europe* (Chapel Hill: University of North Carolina Press, 1991) 186–88.

helpful to begin to review some of the major points of difference between the medieval Christian attitudes toward labor and those of classical Rome. A review of medieval labor ideologies is a large field to plow,
and the completion of this project will be the work of several different
chapters in this book. My task in this chapter is merely to make a beginning by laying out some of the implications for labor ideology of the triumph of Christianity and of the social model of the three estates.[13]

One of the commonplaces about medieval Christianity is that it lifted
the status of manual labor and created a climate that fostered technological advance.[14] At the same time, however, one finds condescending attitudes toward manual, rural labor. Indeed, one of the defining attributes
of the medieval aristocracy was its freedom from manual or "servile" la-

13. While scholars sometimes complain about the lack of scholarship on medieval labor ideology (e.g., Brian Stock, "Activity, Contemplation, Work and Leisure between the Eleventh and the
Thirteenth Centuries," *Arbeit, Musse, Meditation: Betrachtungen zur "Vita Activa" und "Vita Contemplativa,"* ed. Brian Vickers [Zürich: Verlag der Fachvereine, 1985] 87), a significant number of attempts to
outline medieval work ideologies exist. Among those recent studies I have found most helpful are
the articles reprinted in Jacques Le Goff, *Time, Work, and Culture in the Middle Ages*, trans. Arthur
Goldhammer (Chicago: University of Chicago Press, 1980); and in Jacqueline Hamess and Collette
Muraille-Samaran, eds., *Le travail au moyen âge: Une approche interdisciplinaire* (Louvain-la-Neuve: Institut d'études médiévales de l'Université Catholique de Louvain, 1990). Le Goff's essay, "Le travail
dans les systèmes de valeur de l'Occident médiévale" (*Le travail au moyen âge* 7–21), is especially help-
ful. Other insightful treatments can be found in Keith Thomas, "Work and Leisure in Pre-Industrial
Society," *Past and Present* 29 (December 1964): 50–66; Stock 87–108; and Steven A. Epstein, "Guilds
and Labor in the Wider World," *Wage Labor and Guilds* 155–206. Also useful is George Ovitt, "Early
Christian Attitudes toward Manual Labor," *Technology and Culture* 27.3 (1986): 477–500 (reprinted in
The Work of Work: Servitude, Slavery, and Labor in Medieval England, ed. Allen J. Frantzen and Douglas
Moffat [Glasgow, U.K.: Cruithne Press, 1994] 71–94). In this chapter, I will be citing page numbers
from this reprint. Ovitt's *The Restoration of Perfection* has a fuller treatment. Finally, Birgit van den
Hoven, *Work in Ancient and Medieval Thought* (Amsterdam: J. C. Gieben, 1996), is another recent com-
prehensive study.

14. van den Hoven 1. See also Arthur T. Geoghegan, *The Attitude towards Labor in Early Christianity and Ancient Culture* (Washington, D.C.: The Catholic University of America Press, 1945) 229–32.

Interesting evidence corroborating this view comes from the depictions of the "Labors of the
Months," visual representations of the kinds of rural labor appropriate to the various seasons of the
year. James Carson Webster has found that medieval representations of the "Labors of the Months"
differ significantly from ancient representations. Ancient representations are essentially passive, that
is, they do not actually depict human labor but rather offer representations of various aspects of nature. Medieval "Labors of the Months" are essentially active: they depict a human activity actually
taking place. Over the course of the Middle Ages, the representations of these labors became more
and more detailed and country-specific. The exception to this general rule was the "labor" of April,
which was generally depicted as a "flower-bearer," a personification of the return of flowers (*The
Labors of the Months in Antique and Medieval Art* [Princeton, N.J.: Princeton University Press, 1936]
97–103). Jonathan Alexander argues, however, that while the images of the peasants in early medieval depictions of the "Labors of the Months" are neutral, those images become increasingly negative in the late Middle Ages because of social unrest ("*Labeur* and *Paresse*: Ideological Representations
of Medieval Peasant Labor," *Art Bulletin* 72 [1990]: 436).

bor. Jacques Le Goff argues that "work" for medieval men and women primarily meant rural work and that an essential part of the self-definition of the ruling classes was *otium*, the privilege of not working.[15] In fact, *otium* was a privilege of both the medieval aristocracy and the clergy, but one must be careful to define what is meant by "work" and "leisure." As a rule, *manual* labor was thought to be beneath medieval aristocrats and clergy—monks being the major exception to this rule. The aristocratic ideal was to live off one's property, one's *fief*, but the ideal did not include pure idleness. Medieval *otium cum dignitate* (dignified leisure), then, did not signify *otium otiosum* but *otium negotiosum*. From at least the eleventh century, each major social class had its assigned *officium*, or duty, and each was strenuously to work toward fulfilling that duty. Indeed, for Christians, work, defined as strenuous effort and purposeful activity directed at some goal, came to be valued above all as an antidote to idleness, which the Church judged to be a grave spiritual danger.[16]

In contrast to the work ideology in Ovid's Rome, the work ideology in the Christian Middle Ages was heavily influenced by Christian beliefs and by the treatment of work in the Bible. Le Goff insists, however, that the medieval Christian Church never developed a theology of work.[17] From the very beginning of the Middle Ages, the attitude of the Christian Church to labor was ambivalent. While Christianity was a religion for humble men, and thus never disdained manual labor, it also saw labor as the necessary result of original sin.[18]

The *locus classicus* for arguments concerning the nature of work was the Bible, and, in particular, the Book of Genesis.[19] It opens with a work-

15. Le Goff, "Le travail dans les systèmes" 13.

16. John Cassian, for example, writes that "Multa enim mala docuit otiositas" (For indeed idleness teaches many evils) and "operantem monachum daemone uno pulsari, otiosum uero innumeris spiritibus deuastari" (the monk who works is tempted by a single demon, but the idle monk is the victim of innumerable spirits). See *Institutions cénobitiques*, ed. Jean-Claude Guy (Paris: Les éditions du Cerf, 1965) 420, 422.

17. Le Goff, "Le travail dans les systèmes" 11–12. Le Goff's statement is supported by Epstein, who says he could find no medieval thinker "for whom work was a central preoccupation" (173).

18. Ovitt, "Early Christian Attitudes" 80. Note St. Augustine's comment that monks in his time came mostly from the class of freed slaves. He writes: "Nunc autem veniunt plerumque ad hanc professionem servitutis Dei et ex conditione servili, vel etiam liberti, vel propter hoc a dominis liberati sive liberandi, et ex vita rusticana, et ex opificum exercitatione et plebeio labore" (Now, however, those who present themselves for the service of God most often come from a servile condition. They are slaves whom their masters have set free, or to whom the masters have promised liberty so that they can go into the monastery. Their life is carried out in the fields, or in the artisan's workshop, or in the hard labors of the lower classes; *De opere monachorum*, *Oeuvres complètes de Saint Augustin*, ed. Péronne et al. [Paris: Librairie de Louis Vivès, 1870] 22.111).

19. Le Goff, "Le travail dans les systèmes" 11.

er God creating the universe in six days, resting on the seventh, and seeing that his work was good. Some have argued that the depiction of God
as a worker gave a de facto prestige to labor.[20] Later, this same worker
God assigns the task of cultivating the Garden of Eden to the first man,
Adam. In this passage, Jerome uses the Latin verbs *operari* and *custodire* to
describe Adam's prelapsarian duties.[21] According to the Bible, then, God
had planned for humans to work even in Paradise. When, however, God
expels Adam and Eve from the Garden of Eden, the obligation to work
takes on an ominous significance. God condemns the first couple to earn
their bread by the sweat of their brows when he says to Adam:

Quia audisti vocem uxoris tuae, et comedisti de ligno, ex quo praeceperam tibi
ne comederes, maledicta terra in opere tuo: in laboribus comedes ex ea cunctis
diebus vitae tuae. Spinas et tribulos germinabit tibi. . . . In sudore vultus tui
vesceris pane. (Genesis 3.17–19)

[Because you have listened to the voice of your wife and have eaten of the tree
from which I commanded you not to eat, cursed be the earth for your work:
with labor you shall eat from it all the days of your life. It shall sprout forth
thorns and thistles for you. . . . With the sweat of your face shall you eat bread.]

In this crucial passage, work (i.e., *opus* and *labor*) is clearly linked to sin
and punishment. Regarding this passage St. Augustine, for example, was
led to cry out:

Hos esse in terra labores humani generis, quis ignorat? Et quia non essent, si fe-
licitas, quae in paradiso fuerat, teneretur, non est utique dubitandum.[22]

[Who does not know these to be the earthly labors of the human race? Assured-
ly no one can doubt that they would not have existed if the happiness had been
held that man enjoyed in paradise.]

20. "Viditque Deus cuncta quae fecerat, et erant valde bona. . . . Igitur perfecti sunt caeli et terra,
et omnis ornatus eorum. Complevitque Deus die septimo opus suum quod fecerat: et requievit die
septimo ab universo opere quod patrarat" (And God saw all the things he had made, and they were
very good. . . . Thus, the heavens and earth were finished, and all their accoutrements. And on the
seventh day God completed the work which he had made. And he rested on the seventh day from all
the work which he had accomplished; *Biblia Sacra iuxta Vulgatam Clementinam: Nova Editio*, ed. Albert
Colunga and Laurence Turrado, 7th ed. [Madrid: Biblioteca de Auctores Christianos, 1985] Genesis
1.31–2.2). All quotations from the Bible will be taken from this edition. The English translations are
my own.
        A summary of the argument concerning the influence of Genesis's "worker God" on medieval
labor ideology can be found in Ovitt, "Early Christian Attitudes" 74–75.
        21. "Tulit ergo Dominus Deus hominem, et posuit eum in paradiso voluptatis, ut operaretur, et
custodiret illum" (The Lord God took man, and placed him in the paradise of pleasure, to work and
keep it; Genesis 2.15).
        22. St. Augustine, *De Genesi ad litteram: Libri duodecim, Oeuvres complètes de Saint Augustin* 7.332.

From this perspective, then, the condition of work is a direct result of man's fall. In another place, Augustine comments that the sentence of labor is one that no person escapes.[23] When medieval men and women spoke of work, their ideology was influenced heavily by this important passage.[24]

Nevertheless, Christian thinkers did not find in Jesus a consistent role model for workers. Rather, they found an itinerant preacher who preached insouciance toward the practical matters of earthly life by referring to the lilies of the field, which "non laborant, neque nent. Dico autem vobis, quoniam nec Salomon in omni gloria sua coopertus est sicut unum ex istis" (do not labor or spin. But I say to you that not even Solomon in all his glory was covered like one of these; Matthew 6.28–29). When Jesus instructs the first seventy-two disciples, he tells them that when they enter a house, they are allowed to eat and drink what is set before them, "dignus est enim operarius mercede sua" (for the laborer is worthy of his wages; Luke 10.7). The disciples are *operarii*, "wage laborers," and evangelization is thus "work." This kind of work, however, is not manual labor; it is the labor of preaching the gospel. Jesus' disciples are to do "spiritual work" and to "live off the Gospel."

In another seminal passage, Jesus prefers the contemplative Mary to her industrious sister Martha. In a visit to a certain village, Jesus stopped at the house of the two sisters. While one sister, Martha, spent her day attending to the tasks necessary for entertaining a guest, the other sister, Mary, spent her time listening to Jesus' words. Upon hearing Martha's complaint regarding her sister's inactivity, Jesus replies:

Martha, Martha, sollicita es, et turbaris erga plurima. Porro unum est necessarium. Maria optimam partem elegit, quae non auferetur ab ea. (Luke 10.41–42)

[Martha, Martha, you are agitated and confused about many things. But one thing is necessary. Mary chose the best part, which shall not be taken from her.]

In this passage, Jesus categorically affirms the superiority of properly directed *otium* over *labor*, contemplation over worldly work. At the same time, however, Jesus did not imply that Martha's role was *evil*; it was just inferior. In many ways, the story of medieval attitudes toward work could be written as a history of the ways various medieval thinkers managed to reconcile—or *not* to reconcile—the roles of Mary and Martha, the active life with the contemplative life.

---

23. *De Genesi contra Manichaeos, Oeuvres complètes de Saint Augustin* 3.479.
24. LeGoff, "Le travail dans les systèmes" 11–12.

Or to reconcile Jesus with St. Paul. St. Paul, unlike Jesus, clearly performed manual labor to support himself. In the Acts of the Apostles, Luke suggests that Paul's work was that of a tent maker (Acts 18.3) and that Paul was proud of the fact that he did not have to "live off the Gospel." Indeed, in a well-known warning to those who do not choose to work, St. Paul thundered "si quis non vult operari, nec manducet" (if anyone will not work, then let him not eat; 2 Thessalonians 3.10). This verse was perhaps the most influential New Testament passage regarding the Christian's obligation to work for a living.[25]

During the lifetime of St. Augustine, the apparent conflict between the work ideologies of Jesus and Paul came to a head in several Carthaginian monasteries and surrounding lay communities. A group of monks refused to perform manual labor, citing Jesus' teaching that Christians should not worry about food and clothing nor make plans for the future because God would provide (Matthew 6.25–34). Other monks, adhering more closely to the teachings of St. Paul, argued that performing manual labor was no impediment to the life of the gospel. The bishop of Carthage, Aurelius, troubled by the discord between the two groups, asked Augustine for his opinion in the matter. The conflict became the occasion of one of St. Augustine's most influential treatises, *De opere monachorum (On the Labor of Monks)*.

Citing 2 Thessalonians 3.10, Augustine took the side of St. Paul and insisted that all monks must perform manual work. He ridiculed the argument that this scriptural verse referred only to "spiritual work," not manual work.[26] Although he did not deny that "spiritual work" was worthy of being supported, he argued that Paul had set a higher standard for monks, who were expected to do both.[27] Monks, he wrote, should engage in "spiritual work" while supporting themselves with their hands. In fact, no conflict exists, according to Augustine, between working with one's hands and praying. In addition, those who refused to work and expected God to provide were guilty of tempting the Lord.[28]

An especially instructive passage occurs when Augustine considers the manual work that St. Paul performed. Ignoring the suggestion of Acts

25. Ovitt, *The Restoration of Perfection* 91. It was cited, for example, by John Cassian 404; St. Augustine, *De opere monachorum* 22.85, 86, 87, 89, etc.; and St. Jerome, *Lettres*, ed. Jérome Labourt (Paris: Les Belles Lettres, 1949) 52.

26. St. Augustine, *De opere monachorum* 22.86ff.

27. St. Augustine cites Matthew 10.10 twice, at 22.91 and 22.92. John Cassian also cited Paul's manual work as an inspiration for monks (402).

28. St. Augustine, *De opere monachorum* 22.107, 120–21.

18.3, Augustine writes that he does not know what work St. Paul engaged in. He does know, however, that whatever work it was, it was as innocent as it was honest.[29] Paul, he writes, would not have disdained agricultural work or the work of artisans. In fact, Augustine argues, "Quidquid ergo horum cum innocentia et sine fraude homines operantur, bonum est" (All work is good when one labors with innocence and without fraud).[30] He concludes this passage by citing Ephesians 4.28, in which Paul says that Christians should labor at useful occupations in order to be able to give to those in need.

Augustine's approval of useful work did not include, however, banking or trade. While simple artisans were able to keep their freedom of spirit, bankers, financiers, or merchants were deceivers and suffered from avarice. These people, argues Augustine, labor with their minds, but their goal is accumulation of personal wealth.[31] This theme is elaborated in Augustine's commentary on Psalm 70.[32] There he notes that businessmen are known to seek nothing but to accumulate wealth, and they lie about the value of their wares. Nevertheless, his treatment of business is even-handed in that he constructs a counterargument from the business man's point of view. Citing Luke 10.7, where Jesus says that the workman is worth his hire, he writes that the businessman's profit is only the "salary" he earns for transporting goods from one place to another, where they are needed. Moreover, even if some businessmen lie, the acts of a few do not soil the profession per se. Shoemakers lie and farmers curse the weather, but that does not make their professions evil. The same is true for businessmen. Why, then, does the Psalmist condemn business?[33] Citing the root of the word *negotiatio* as meaning "action" or "lack of repose" (i.e., from *negotium*), Augustine interprets the Psalmist's condemnation of *negotiatio* as being in reality not a condemnation of the profession but rather a condemnation of self-sufficiency, of those who take undue pride in their own work without trusting enough in the providence of God. Thus, Augustine stakes out a middle position between

29. "Sed innocenter et honeste quae apta sunt humanis usibus operabatur; sicut sese habent opera fabrorum, structorum, sutorum, rusticorum et his similia" (His work was as innocent as honest, concerning the objects of daily use, such as the work of smiths, builders, cobblers, rural laborers, and such like; *De opere monachorum* 22.101).

30. St. Augustine, *De opere monachorum* 22.101.

31. St. Augustine, *De opere monachorum* 22.102.

32. St. Augustine, *Enarrationes in Psalmos, Oeuvres complètes de Saint Augustin* 13.265–68.

33. The verse St. Augustine cites reads: "Tota die salutem tuam, quoniam non cognovi negotiationes" ([I shall celebrate] your salvation all the day because I did not know business affairs; Psalm 70.17, *Enarrationes in Psalmos* 13.265).

tempting God by giving up work altogether and making work the foundation of a proud self-reliance.

What is essential to grasp about the attitude of the medieval Church is that it was less concerned with *material* productivity than with the development of the spiritual self. In addition, an ethical incentive for improving work efficiency did not exist.[34] On the one hand, the Church insisted that "eos qui operari nolunt . . . otiositatis uitio inquietos semper exsistere" (those who refuse to work are always troubled with the vice of laziness).[35] On the other hand, it made no sense to invest too much time and effort in building the material world, for one never knew when Jesus would come a second time to bring that world to an end. In the meantime, however, the community had to meet its legitimate material needs. George Ovitt argues that the Church Fathers held a paradoxical attitude toward human labor. On the one hand, they praised otherworldly asceticism. On the other hand, they applauded the fact that the products of labor helped improve the quality of life for the Church while awaiting the Second Coming. Ovitt takes yet another of St. Augustine's remarks, this one in *De civitate Dei*, as typical. In a chapter entitled "De bonis quibus etiam hanc vitam damnationi obnoxiam Creator implevit" (Of the good things with which the Creator has filled even this condemned life), Augustine allows himself to marvel at the impressive results of man's labor in the earthly city. Fine clothing and buildings, advances in agriculture and hunting, new drugs to cure human ailments, new discoveries about the heavens, art, music, and literature—all are praised by Augustine as products of "industria humana."[36]

Along with *industria*, medieval writers had a full menu of Latin words (most used by classical writers) to refer to sustained effort and work: the nouns *labor, opus, servitium, negotium, ars*, and *officium*; the verbs *laborare* and *operari*. In Chapter 2, the classical meanings of these words were analyzed in detail, so in this chapter I will focus primarily on semantic development. Le Goff stresses that medieval Latin *labor* played a central role in the medieval concept of labor but that it carried with it, at least in the early Middle Ages, all of the negative connotations of its classical Latin cognate. The words *ars, artifex, opus, opera*, and *operari* were more closely

34. Ovitt, "The Early Christian Attitudes" 86–88.

35. Cassian 400.

36. Ovitt, "The Early Christian Attitudes" 82. St. Augustine, *The City of God against the Pagans*, ed. and trans. William M. Green, Loeb Classical Library (Cambridge, Mass.: Harvard University Press, 1972) 22.24 (7.328–29).

associated with the workshop and carried, claims Le Goff, a more favorable connotation.[37] Jacqueline Hamesse argues that the medieval Latin labor words had a certain semantic fuzziness. While *labor* carried a uniformly negative connotation, *industria* did not. In addition, she points out that Latin words referring to work often appeared with qualifying adjectives that make their denotations and connotations clearer—for example, *opus servile* (servile work), *labor corporalis* (bodily labor), and *labor manuum* (labor of the hands).[38]

Some of these basic Christian concepts, as we shall see, surely find their way into the medieval discourse of love's labor, either seriously or playfully. It is important to recognize, however, that one of the most fundamental of all Christian attitudes toward labor—that labor was the result of original sin—seems never to have been woven into the fabric of medieval amatory writings, at least not in the tradition that forms the focus of this study. Love may bring with it pains and difficulties, but these are never the direct result of some "sin." On the contrary, in some texts, the sin is in not undertaking the labor of love. Love's labor is always a positive value, and love's laborers earn their rewards through gritty, determined work. Thus, although some medieval lovers correspond to Mary, spending their days endlessly contemplating the joys and sorrows of love, the real heroes of the discourse of love's labor are the Marthas. The labor ideology of Paul, not Jesus, undergirds the entire tradition.

III

Beyond key biblical verses and the writings of the Church Fathers, the development of the characteristic medieval social model of the three estates helped to shape attitudes toward work and leisure during the High Middle Ages. According to Georges Duby, the theory behind this social model was first articulated in the eleventh century, and perhaps the most important of the early texts is Bishop Adalbéron de Laon's *Carmen ad Robertum regem*, composed somewhere between 1027 and 1031.[39] A dialog between a king and a bishop, Adalbéron's poem begins with a satirical description of a world turned upside-down: peasants suiting up for war, monks having pretty wives and children, knights spending their days in

37. Le Goff, "Le travail dans les systèmes" 13–14.

38. Jacqueline Hamesse, "Le travail chez les auteurs philosophiques du 12ᵉ et du 13ᵉ siècle," *Le travail au moyen âge* 117–19.

39. Georges Duby, *The Three Orders: Feudal Society Imagined*, trans. Arthur Goldhammer (Chicago: University of Chicago Press, 1980) 19.

prayer and fasting, and clergy plowing the fields.[40] In response to this chaos, the bishop explains to the king the divinely ordained order of things, the *ordo*, where specific functions, *officia*, are assigned to specific sectors of society. In the first place is the divine order of clerics, which is an order of complete equality (240–43). In order to keep themselves pure, clerics should neither fight nor perform manual labor. "Lex aeterna Dei," the bishop writes, "sic mundos precipit esse, / Iudicat expertes seruilis conditionis" (Thus, God's eternal law enjoins them to be pure; it would have them exempt from any servile condition; 254–55).

The strict equality of the heavenly order does not hold beyond the clergy, however. Hierarchy and distinctions characterize the social order on earth. For example, a strict division exists between the nobility and the peasantry, those who command and those who obey (276–77). Since those who command, however, are divided into clergy and lay aristocrats, the earthly order is, in fact, triple. In a key passage, the bishop explains:

> Triplex ergo Dei domus est quae creditur una.
> Nunc orant, alii pugnant aliique laborant.
> Quae tria sunt simul et scissuram non patiuntur:
> Vnius offitio sic stant operata duorum,
> Alternis uicibus cunctis solamina prebent.
>
> (295–99)

[The house of God, therefore, which seems one, is triple. Now some pray, while others fight, and still others labor. These three are together and cannot be separated. Thus the operations of the two stand in the service of one; each in turn provides comfort to the others.]

This passage makes two clear points about Adalbéron's attitude toward labor and about the labor ideology embedded within the three estates model. First, the verb *laborant* of line 296 refers clearly to performing *manual labor*, which Adalbéron adamantly restricts to those of the servile condition, that is, the third estate. For Adalbéron, manual labor of any kind is servile and sullies the purity of clerics (243–57). Nevertheless, Adalbéron also clearly indicates in this passage that the *otium* of the first and second estates is not unproductive idleness. On the contrary, each estate has an *officium*, a function, and this function is made possible only by

---

40. Adalbéron de Laon, *Poème au roi Robert*, ed. Claude Carozzi, Les Classiques de l'histoire de France au Moyen Age (Paris: Les Belles Lettres, 1979) 32–172. All subsequent references to this poem will be cited in the text by line numbers. English translations are my own.

the *operata*, the operations, of the other two. In the shorthand of line 296, the *officium* of the clergy is to pray (although in other parts of the poem the bishop alludes to teaching and learning as well), and the *officium* of the aristocracy is to defend the Church and the workers (278–84). At one point, Adalbéron even uses the term *labor*, here denoting strenuous fulfillment of Church-related duties, to describe the tasks of the clergy (124). Each estate must perform its own specialized work to build the peace: "Dum lex preualuit tunc mundus pace quieuit" (While this law prevails, then the world rests in peace; 301).

Although the aristocratic, military classes were not to dirty their hands in the fields, they were not given license to lead lives of unprofitable idleness either. This attitude is reflected in *Erec et Enide*, a romance composed by one of Andreas's contemporaries, Chrétien de Troyes. After marrying the maiden Enide, the knight Erec wishes to give himself totally to the joys of married bliss:

> Mes tant l'ama Erec d'amors
> que d'armes mes ne li chaloit,
> ne a tornoiemant n'aloit.[41]

[But Erec was so in love with her / that he cared no more for arms, / nor did he go to tournaments.]

Erec's retirement from the field of battle, however, is shown to be a serious concern to his aristocratic companions:

> Ce disoit trestoz li barnages
> que granz diax ert et granz domages,
> quant armes porter ne voloit
> tex ber com il estre soloit.
>
> (2421–24)

[All his lords said / that it was a great shame and sorrow, / when such a lord as he once was / no longer wanted to bear arms.]

It is only when Enide overhears the criticisms of Erec's companions that Erec leaves his "slothful" ways and pursues again his knightly *officium*. And what were these duties? Adalbéron deals with knightly duties quickly:

---

41. Chrétien de Troyes, *Erec and Enide*, ed. and trans. Carleton W. Carroll, Garland Library of Medieval Literature 25 (New York: Garland, 1987) lines 2396–98 (106–7). All quotations and translations from *Erec and Enide* will be taken from this edition and cited in the text by line numbers.

Hi bellatores, tutores aecclesiarum,
Defendunt uulgi maiores atque minores,
Cunctos et sese parili sic more tuentur.

(282–84)

[These are warriors, protectors of churches. They defend the laity, both the higher and lower. They, thus, equally protect everyone and their own persons.]

The knight took on his duties by becoming the "man" of a feudal lord. Marc Bloch argues that the technical term for a knight's duties was not *officium* but *servitium*, a word, he writes, that would have horrified free men in Ovid's day, for *servitium* in classical Latin meant "slavery."[42] Indeed, the long entry for *servitium* in Du Cange suggests significant semantic broadening and amelioration during the Middle Ages. Du Cange glosses *servitium* as the equivalent of *officium* (duty, obligation, function) or *ministerium* (function, service). Beyond this general gloss, the long entry suggests that the word was used for a wide range of activities appropriate to all three estates. What Hamesse noted as true for medieval labor words in general is true for *servitium*: shades of meaning were indicated by attaching different modifiers. The *servitium* of the serf, for example, was *servitium inhonestum*, *servitium servile*, or *servitium villanum*. Freemen, however, practiced a *servitium liberum*. Among the clergy, *servitium* by itself signified the *officium ecclesiasticum*, and the clergy sang the *servitium divinum*. Knights were sometimes obliged to fulfill the *servitium corporis*, the *servitium equi*, the *servitium socii*, or the *servitium militis*.[43] Unlike either slavery or serfdom, however, *servitium militis* carried with it great social prestige.[44]

Adalbéron's attitude toward manual labor and those who must do it is essentially aristocratic. In general, he has aristocratic contempt for manual labor as impure (254–55), and he is not above trotting out stereotypes of the lazy peasant (37). At the same time, however, one could argue that he does have some sympathy for the hard lot of the peasants. His character the bishop exclaims:

---

42. Marc Bloch, *Feudal Society*, trans. L. A. Manyon, 2 vols. (Chicago: University of Chicago Press, 1961) 1.150.

43. "Servitium," *Glossarium ad Scriptores Mediae et Infimae Latinitas*, 1883 ed.

44. Bloch 1.152–56.

Hoc genus afflictum nil possidet absque dolore.
Quis abaci signis numerando retexere possit
Seruorum studium, cursus tantosque labores?

(286–88)

[This afflicted race possesses nothing without sorrow. Who can count up on an
abacus the serfs' efforts, their lives, and so many labors?]

What is even more important for medieval labor ideology is that their
labors, their *officium*, although servile, play a crucial role in the proper
functioning of the state. Without food and the other material necessities
provided by the peasants, how could the clergy and aristocracy function?
The labors of the first and second estates thus were absolutely dependent
on the labor of the third.[45]

Such, at least, was Adalbéron's theory. Duby is skeptical of Adalbéron's sympathy for the poor and believes that the social reality differed
from Adalbéron's picture of harmonious cooperation among the
estates.[46] The economy of the eleventh century in France, he argues, was
one in which the principal aristocratic "mode of production" was an increased exploitation of the rural working classes under the threat of vio-
lence from the local lords and their henchmen. Duby's view is corrobo-
rated by Alan of Lille, a contemporary of Andreas Capellanus, in his
sermon "Ad milites." For Alan, despite Adalbéron's fine social theory,
knights were simply "fures" (thieves) and "raptores" (plunderers), and he
condemns them in no uncertain terms.[47] No doubt the efficiency of the
agrarian economy improved under this new order, but this, in Duby's

45. Cf. Otto Gerhard Oexle: "Par la simple juxtaposition de la fonction du travail, et des fonctions
de ceux qui prient et de ceux qui combattent, le schéma exprime un intérêt pour le travail manuel
qui témoigne d'une valorisation remarquable" (By the simple juxtaposition of the work function
with the functions of those who pray and those who fight, the schema expresses an interest in manual labor that bears witness to a remarkable valorization; "Le travail au XIᵉ siècle: Réalités et mentalités," *Le travail au moyen âge* 52).

46. Duby, in fact, believes that Adalbéron's description of the *servi* in the *Carmen* was intended to
emphasize the humiliation of their rustic labors (160). While Oexle agrees that Adalbéron's description did not fit with the actual state of peoples' lives in feudalism, he does argue that the description
had a social reality by virtue of being an accepted social ideal (56–57).

47. The text reads: "Jam suum prostituunt militiam, militant ut lucrentur, arma capiunt ut prae-
dentur. Jam non sunt milites, sed fures et raptores; non defensores, sed invasores. In viscera matris
Ecclesiae accuunt gladios" (Now soldiers prostitute their military calling. They fight for money. They
take up arms so they can steal. These aren't soldiers any more. They are bandits and thieves. They
are not our defenders but our invaders. They thrust their blade into the womb of Mother Church;
"Ad milites," *Summa de arte praedicatoria, Patrologia Latina,* 210.186CD; translated in John M. Trout,
The Voyage of Prudence [Washington, D.C.: University Press of America, 1979] 160–61).

opinion, "accentuated the contrast between [aristocratic] leisure and [peasant] labor."[48]

Some historians argue that the effect of the creation of this new tripartite structure was to secularize manual labor, traditionally valorized primarily via the Christian monastic tradition, and thus to detach it from its spiritual moorings. Ovitt, for example, writes:

> The church came to recognize manual labor, craftsmanship, and technology as the proper sphere of the order of society called to them—the *laborantes*—and in so doing the church modified its millennium-old ideal of spiritualized, communal, and inner-directed labor.[49]

This, in turn, freed the other two classes from the obligation to work with their hands. The result of this division of labor is suggested by an incident recounted in the works of Gervase of Canterbury.[50] In 1174, the choir of Christ Church in Canterbury burned down. The confusion and depression of the monks lasted for five years. They then contracted with William of Sens to reconstruct the choir. The monks were skeptical that the choir could ever be rebuilt, but in eight years William and his cohort of workers rebuilt the choir, much to the astonishment of the monks. The working laity had accomplished what the sons of St. Benedict could no longer do. The division of workers and nonworkers, this separation of Mary from Martha, contradicted the spirit of Benedict's ideal of the laboring monk and led to renewed monastic debates on the place of manual labor in the monastery.

IV

The labor ideology of the three estates social model is deeply woven into the text of the *De amore*, yet a specific labor is reserved to the aristocracy: the service of women.

Like Ovid's *Ars amatoria*, the *De amore* is divided into three books, but the division is somewhat different from that in Ovid's work. The first two books in the *De amore* deal with winning a love and keeping a love. The labor of finding a love is passed over in silence. Like Ovid's narrator, An-

---

48. Duby 152–61.

49. Ovitt, *Restoration of Perfection* 163. Of this division, Ovitt writes, "The notion of the *ordo*, a division of society, was formulated in the twelfth century in recognition of the social pluralism of the age. By the thirteenth century, the concept of the *ordo* was fixed in church policy as a means of distinguishing among the occupations, powers, and responsibilities of Christian men and women" (160).

50. Quoted in Ovitt, *Restoration of Perfection* 165–66.

dreas's narrator is a *praeceptor amoris* and boasts of his vast experience with love.[51] Andreas's third book is roughly comparable to Ovid's *Remedia amoris* in that it seeks to discourage the audience from loving. Unlike the argument in the *Remedia*, however, the argument against love in *De amore* is based on Christian moral teachings and the most extreme form of antifeminist rhetoric. While Ovid ostensibly wrote for a cohort of both male and female lovers (although he emphasized the work of the male), Andreas addresses his work to a certain Gualterius, or Walter, a single male cleric. How Walter relates to Andreas's actual twelfth-century audience is a vexing question. The traditional view that Andreas wrote for the twelfth-century court of Champagne has come under criticism.[52] Alfred Karnein believes that the work came out of the chancellery of the king of France.[53] Walsh believes that Walter stands for a sophisticated audience of clerics in general, and his opinion was supported by Roy's reception study of the work from the thirteenth through the fifteenth centuries. Interestingly, Roy found only one thirteenth-century manuscript, but eight fourteenth-century manuscripts and twenty-six fifteenth-century manuscripts. This suggests to Roy that the *De amore* gained its greatest influence only well after its condemnation in 1277 by the bishop of Paris.[54] Don Monson is impressed with much of Karnein's data, but he points out that none of it tells us much about the original twelfth-century audience. Monson argues that the work's original audience was composed of both sophisticated clerics and courtiers.[55] While courtly women may have been interested in some aspects of Andreas's text (indeed, women served in the courts of love), with respect to love's labor the perspective of the text is consistently male-oriented. It is the labor of the male that is most consistently analyzed and advocated.

In addressing his audience, Andreas starts in the fashion of a medieval clerk: he begins by defining "love," and this definition is more indebted to

---

51. The narrator says, "Et quamvis multum credamur in amoris arte periti et amoris praedocti remedia, vix tamen eius novimus pestiferos laqueos evitare et sine carnis nos contagione removere" (Though considered abundantly experienced in the art of love, and well versed in love's remedies, only with difficulty could I avoid its baneful snares and withdraw without contamination of the flesh; 212).

52. Benton 578–82.

53. Alfred Karnein, "La réception du *De amore* d'André le Chapelain au XIIIe siècle," *Romania* 102 (1981): 324–51, 501–42.

54. Walsh 4–5; Roy 48–53, 64–65.

55. Monson, "Problem of Irony" 551.

the discourse of love as passion than with the discourse of love as labor.[56] The definition runs as follows:

Amor est passio quaedam *innata* procedens ex visione et immoderata cogitatione formae alterius sexus, ob quam aliquis super omnia cupit alterius potiri amplex- ibus et omnia de utriusque voluntate in ipsius amplexu amoris praecepta comp- leri. (32; emphasis added)

[*Love is an inborn suffering* which results from the sight of, and uncontrolled think- ing about, the beauty of the other sex. This feeling makes a man desire before all else the embraces of the other sex, and to achieve the utter fulfillment of the commands of love in the other's embrace by their common desire.]

Following this definition, we are told that the madness and suffering of love causes the greatest "angustia" (pain, discomfort) possible.[57] The pains arise from the overwhelming fears of the lovers. This discourse ulti- mately finds its roots in the classical Greek conception of love as a mad- ness or illness. However, it also fits very nicely with the more contempo- rary medical tradition of *amor hereos*, and Andreas returns to it frequently during the course of his treatise.[58]

Thus, the discourse of passion finds a prominent place in the *De amore*. In fact, it is even more prominent in Andreas's treatise than in Ovid's *Re- media amoris*. The *De amore*, however, even more consistently treats love as a strenuous occupation. Monson's comment on this matter is relevant: "If Andreas had kept to his original definition, 'Amor est passio' . . . he would not have had to ask how love may be acquired . . . for he had al- ready explained that it comes 'from the sight of and excessive meditation upon the beauty of the opposite sex.'"[59] While Andreas *defines* love as passion, he more often *presents* it as the reward for highly skilled and dis- ciplined effort.

56. Karnein supports the Robertsonian reading of *De amore* by narrowly focusing on the me- dieval reception of this single passage ("*Amor est Passio*: A Definition of Courtly Love?," *Court and Poet*, ed. Glyn S. Burgess [Liverpool, U.K.: Cairns, 1981] 215–21). Given the complex dialogics of the entire treatise, however, an argument based on such a small portion cannot be convincing.

57. Similar definitions of love occur later in the treatise. In the seventh dialogue, for example, the man of higher nobility defines love as "immoderata et furtivi et latentis amplexus concupiscibiliter percipiendi ambitio" (an uncontrolled desire to obtain the sensual gratification of a stealthy and se- cret embrace; 146). The noblewoman counters this definition with her own: "de aliquo habita im- moderata carnalis dilectionis ambitio, quam nil inter coniugatos contradicit haberi" (an uncontrolled desire of physical affection for someone, and there is no obstacle to a married couple experiencing this; 148).

58. Cherchi argues that this definition of love owes more to the medieval medical handbooks than to the Ovidian tradition of the *artes amandi* (28–29).

59. Monson, "Problem of Irony" 569.

Indeed, the discourse of love's labor is even embedded in Andreas's analysis of the definition of love, for when he answers the question of why lovers fear, he immediately declares that lovers fear that "in vanum suos labores emittat" (he may expend his toil to no purpose; 32). He develops this point in detail:

uterque namque timet amantium ne quod est multis laboribus acquisitum per alterius labores amittat, quod valde magis onerosum constat hominibus quam si spe frustrati nullum sibi suos fructum sentiant sibi afferre labores. (32)

[Both (lovers) are afraid that they may lose the fruit of much effort through the zeal of another, and this is much harder for people to bear than if they are cheated of their hope and realise that their efforts are winning them no reward.]

The multiple uses of Latin *labor* in this passage clearly imply that love is won through strenuous effort. Despite the disdain for rural labor that runs deep in the *De amore*, Andreas uses Latin *labor* or the verb *laborare* repeatedly in this treatise to denote the more genteel work of courtship.[60]

The passage also implies that hard *labor* should be rewarded by some kind of *fructum* (fruit of the labor), ultimately reflecting the influence of a key Gospel passage on work, cited earlier, "The laborer is worthy of his wages" (Luke 10.7). Andreas pointedly suggests that the fear of lovers is grounded in the fear of their being cheated of their just rewards. In fact, two important and complementary themes related to labor resurface continuously throughout the dialogs in *De amore*. One is that good things can be won only through hard work, and the second is that diligent labor of any kind deserves an appropriate reward. In the eighth dialog, for example, the man of higher nobility feels constrained to seek those things "quod sine gravi non possumus labore percipere" (that we cannot attain without stern effort; 164). He continues "nam post triste malum dulcior ipsa salus" (for salvation itself tastes sweeter after grim hardship; 164). The explicit connection between *labor* and *triste malum* is consistent with what Le Goff has claimed about the connotations of Latin *labor*, but it goes beyond the traditional association of *labor* with manual work. The obverse of this position is stated by the man of higher nobility in the seventh dialog: things won too easily are not held dear. He says: "Cunctis enim claret hominibus quod facilis rei optatae perceptio vilitatis parit originem" (It is clear to all mankind that to obtain what one desires without difficulty breeds a cheap relationship at the start; 144). This valoriza-

60. Walsh 32, 34, 42, 58, 64, 74, 102, 192, 194.

tion of all things, including love, by strenuous effort is finally enshrined in the fourteenth of Love's rules found at the end of Book 2: "Facilis perceptio contemptibilem reddit amorem, difficilis eum carum facit haberi" (An easy conquest makes love cheaply regarded, a difficult one causes it to be held dear; 282).

Both of these themes are well embedded in the closing lines of the first dialog, between the common man and the common woman. To bolster his case that the lady should choose someone who is still learning about love, the commoner cites the proverb "Absque labore gravi non possunt magna parari" (Prizes great cannot be won unless some heavy labour's done; 58). To this the woman replies:

Si absque gravi labore magna parari non possunt, quum id quod postulas sit de maioribus unum, multis te oportet laboribus fatigari, ut ad quesita munera valeas pervenire. (58)

[If no great prizes can be won unless some heavy labour's done, you must suffer the exhaustion of many toils to be able to attain the favours you seek, since what you ask for is a greater prize.]

If the common woman seeks to intimidate the commoner by these words, she fails, for he welcomes the challenge and adds: "Absit enim ut tantae probitatis feminae ego vel alius quilibet possit lucrari amorem nisi multis fuerit primo laboribus acquisitus" (God forbid that I or any other could win the love of so worthy a woman without first attaining it by many labours; 58). While the commoner embraces the opportunity to perform love's labors, he also uses the inherent labor ideology to issue a warning. If such labors are carried out, she would be unjust to withhold the appropriate wages: "A bonae videtur rationis ordine deviare, si non benefacta suis actoribus debita commoda ferant" (For it seems a departure from the order of right reason if fine deeds do not win the appropriate rewards for those who perform them; 58). What reason affirms here is given scriptural support in Luke 10.7.

Given the many efforts of knights on behalf of ladies in the romances of Chrétien de Troyes, it is not surprising that this "work ethic" is voiced not only by commoners but also by nobles in *De amore*. In the sixth dialog, for example, the man of higher nobility says to the common woman:

Sed tunc sine dubio infertur iniuria amanti, quum ipse bonus propter facta malorum suis meritis defraudatur, vel quum propter vanam suspicionem eius non potest capere dignum labor effectum. (126)

[But undoubtedly a wrong is done to a suitor when he is good and when he is cheated of his deserts through the working of wicked people, or when his hard work cannot win a worthy reward because he is suspected without good reason.]

Here the noble speaker uses a circumlocution: scriptural "mercedes" (reward) is replaced by both "suis meritis" (his deserts) and "dignum . . . effectum" (worthy effect), but the biblical idea is essentially left intact: work is deserving of an appropriate reward. Again, when in dialog seven the man of higher nobility addresses the noblewoman, he says that his labors on her behalf should in justice be rewarded: "ut exhibita pro vobis obsequia non diu valeant muneris viduitate gravari" (that the services I manifest on your behalf may not for long lie afflicted without the conferment of a kindness; 140). Although the Latin *munus* meant a "gift freely bestowed," the implication of the nobleman is that the lady's *munus* should be given in return for services performed. Clearly, then, in the world of the *De amore*, aristocrats as well as commoners believe that the laborer is due his just reward.

A specifically Christian slant to this theme, one far removed from any precedent in the Ovidian discourse of love's labor, is the promise of *otherworldly rewards* for the labor performed in this life. As serfs were consoled for their difficult servile labor by the promise of a reward in heaven, so too aristocrats in the *De amore*. One of Andreas's characters, the nobleman in the fifth dialog, whether in jest or earnest, enjoins the labor of love on a noblewoman by the promise of heavenly rewards for work well done. The threat of otherworldly punishment for those slackers who refuse love's labor is also made explicit. The context of these remarks is the noblewoman's characterization of love's labors as "slavery" *(servitudo)* and her refusal to submit to them (100, 102). The nobleman responds, first, by using different terminology for love's labors. Those engaged in such labors, he says, belong to the "amoris . . . militiae," an Ovidian characterization used frequently throughout the dialogs in Andreas's treatise.[61] Further, the nobleman argues that service in the army of love is obligatory, and to prove this he relates a vision he had of the afterlife. In the vision, the god of love "prout bene vel male gessit in vita, mirabiliter pro cuiusque retribuit meritis" (grants wondrous recompense to each individual according to their deserts, depending on whether their achievements in life have been good or evil; 108). Specifically, the knight sees

61. Walsh 60, 100, 116, 156, 176.

three classes of ladies: those who loved wisely, those who loved immoderately, and those who refused love altogether. Each receives her appropriate *mercedes* (108). Those who refuse the service of love have the worst punishment, eternal condemnation to a desertlike setting and torment with bundles of thorns (112). However, those who serve reasonably in love's army dwell in splendor within a wonderful garden. As the nobleman says, "qui amori elegerit beneplacita facere centuplicata illa retributione suscipiet" (he who chooses to perform deeds pleasing to Love will obtain them in repayment a hundredfold; 110). Thus, an echo of the Christian belief in otherworldly rewards for earthy travails resides in Andreas's discourse of love's labor. This kind of promise is not typical, however. In general, authors in this tradition keep their sights firmly on this world rather than on the next.

I have cited Andreas's dialogs several times. These eight dialogs, all found in Book 1, are the rhetorical center of the treatise, and certainly the part on which Andreas lavished his greatest care.[62] They are unlike anything found in Ovid. Andreas nowhere calls his book an "art of love," as does Ovid, and yet the *praeceptor* affirms that he is learned in "amoris arte" (212) and intends to teach Walter all he knows, even if he does so somewhat reluctantly (30). He does his most intense teaching in these dialogs.

Is the *De amore* an "art" of love in the Ovidian sense? As I noted earlier, the subject has been controversial and the evidence contradictory. The repudiations of love in the Preface and in Book 3 of *De amore* are certainly well known and are used to argue against this proposition. Since Ovid himself, however, wrote the *Remedia amoris* after having completed the *Ars amatoria*, the doctrines of Andreas's Book 3 cannot of themselves completely efface the positive discourse on love appearing in Books 1 and 2. Ironic self-contradiction, it would seem, is an integral part of the Ovidian tradition. What can be said for certain is that, in the Preface of his work, Andreas's *praeceptor* does propose to teach Walter "amoris . . . doctrina" (love's lore; 30). In addition, the phrase "in amoris arte instructam" (instructed in love's art) is used by the commoner in the third dialog to characterize the lady of higher nobility (80). Like Marie, Countess of Champagne, and other noble ladies cited in the judgments, the woman of higher nobility agrees to instruct the commoner in "amoris . . . disciplina" (80). When listing the kinds of behavior necessary for the success-

---

62. Cherchi agrees that this section is the most important of the treatise (31).

ful lover, she says "In amoris . . . gubernatione prudentia grandis exigitur, et omnium in ea requiritur industria artium" (Abundant sense is demanded in the conduct of a love affair, for which a careful application of all the arts is required; 82). Since the word *gubernatio* denoted direction or control, one finds here intimations of the Ovidian presentation of love not as disease but as an art form, with rules that can be learned and mastered through experience by a careful student. For this voice, as for Ovid, the practice of love is an art because, again to quote Cicero, "prudentia maior inest." It thus must be taught by a wise and experienced *praeceptor*. In the third dialog, that *praeceptor* is the lady of higher nobility, but, overall, the *praeceptor* in the *De amore* is Andreas's narrator. To this extent, then, the work presents itself as an Ovidian "art" of love.

Book 1, chapter 6, contains a partial list of what topics need to be mastered in this art. Reflecting the idea behind the second labor in Ovid's *Ars amatoria*, the chapter is entitled "Qualiter amor acquiratur et quot modis" (How love is won and in how many ways; 40). Another, less tidy, list of topics, loosely deriving from the third labor in Ovid's *Ars*, is found in Book 2, chapter 1, entitled "Qualiter status acquisiti amoris debeat conservari" (How to maintain unchanged the love one has won; 224). The details of how these methods work in practice are fleshed out in Book 1's eight dialogs and codified in two sets of commandments given by the god of love (116, 282–84). The commandments are unlike anything found in Ovid's discourse of love's labor and clearly reveal yet another Judeo-Christian influence on Andreas's discourse. While the first set of commandments consistently enjoins correct behaviors, the second offers a potpourri of both rules of behavior and personal qualities belonging to those in the army of love. In addition to the commandments of love, Andreas offers yet another innovation: the judgments, found in Book 2, chapter 7, regarding the appropriateness of the behavior of various lovers. These judgments are rendered by a court of ladies of the higher nobility. Again, if problems of lovers can be adjudicated by a panel of expert "judges," not "physicians," then love in large parts of the *De amore* is not a "disease" but rather an "art," which demands skilled and appropriate labor.

If one grants that Andreas is at least in part constructing an art, one must also admit that it is not as consistently put together as is Ovid's. For example, Andreas's second set of rules for love contains an inconsistent mix of commandments and characterizations. Another example of this lack of accord is found in the list of "methods" in Book 1, chapter 5: a handsome appearance, honesty of character, fluent and eloquent speech, abundant riches, and readiness to grant what the other seeks, that is, sex (40–42). Of these five, Andreas immediately disqualifies the last two methods as unworthy of his noble audience, and, unlike Ovid, he is not much interested in the first. Andreas claims that gaining a handsome appearance requires only slight effort and is, in any case, a proper method only for the simple lover. An attractive woman with a less than honest character will attract the kind of man who is appropriate, and a man who spends too much time on his looks is effeminate.

At first, the second method, "honesty of character," seems to be less a method than a description of what one looks for in a partner. However, a belief that one can work at honesty of character and that one ought to *demonstrate* probity of character—by performing good deeds—is an essential aspect of Andreas's art and runs throughout the *De amore*. What is remarkable about this method is that good character is both a cause and an effect of love. Honesty of character, if demonstrated, is an acceptable method of gaining love, but love, Andreas proclaims, is also the cause of virtue. "O quam mira res est amor," marvels the *praeceptor*, "qui tantis facit hominem fulgere virtutibus" (What a remarkable thing is love, for it invests a man with such shining virtues; 38).

The fifth method of winning love, clearly the most interesting to Andreas, is "copiosa sermonis facundia" (fluent and eloquent speech; 42) because "Sermonis facundia multotiens ad amandum non amantium corda compellit" (Eloquence of speech frequently impels the hearts of indifferent persons to love; 44). This proper eloquence of speech is taught by means of the eight dialogs between persons of various social ranks that follow this chapter. If the treatise were a personal document written only for the use of Walter, three dialogs would have been sufficient, one for a cleric's approach to a women from each of the three different social ranks. As it is, Andreas is clearly trying to reach an audience beyond Walter by expanding the range of male speakers beyond those just in the clergy.

The eight dialogs not only demonstrate this key labor of love but they also clearly reveal the influence of the three estates social model and the presence of its inherent labor ideology.[63] The anonymous voices that engage in these dialogs are identified only by their rank in society. Indeed,

---

63. See Moi 23. Monson notes that class consciousness was stronger in northern than in southern France at the time *De amore* was composed, and that the class consciousness found in the treatise was based on current social reality ("*Auctoritas*" 76).

the proper rhetoric of love is determined precisely by the relationship between the ranks of the two would-be lovers, as Andreas's narrator explains in detail (44–46). Thus, the first dialog presents the proper approach to be used by a common man who seeks the love of a common
woman; the second, the proper rhetoric for a common man to use when
he seeks the love of a noble lady; the third, the proper rhetoric for a common man to use when he seeks the love of a more noble lady; and so
forth.[64] The eighth dialog presents an exchange between a man of higher
nobility and a lady of higher nobility, and clerics are associated with the
rank of "higher nobility" (46).

One may not wish to call the kind of love described in these dialogs
"courtly," but it is clear that the treatise reserves this kind of refined love
to the upper classes.[65] Even the voices of commoners belong to the upper
levels of the third estate. This becomes apparent in the second dialog, in
which the noblewoman denigrates the work of the rich merchant who
would be her lover. Contempt drips from her language as she asks:

Quis ergo tu es, qui tanta munera petis? Tua mihi satis patet forma, ac genus est
manifestum. Sed ubi deprehendi maior audacia potest quam illius qui totius heb-
domadae tractu variis mercimonii lucris toto mentis intendit affectu, septima
suae quietis die quaerat amoris vacare muneribus eiusque dehonestare mandata
et ordines in hominibus ab antiquo statutos confundere? (62)

[Who are you, then, to ask for such large favours? Your appearance I can assess
and your social origin is clear. But where could one find a shamelessness greater
than his who concentrates his whole attention during all the week on the different forms of profitable trading, but on the seventh day appointed for his rest
seeks to devote his leisure to Love's tasks, thereby dishonouring Love's commands and confounding the classes established in society from ancient times?]

Here one sees the same prejudice against the work of merchants that
was evident in the writings of Augustine. Although the commoner argues that love does not recognize social status and that his own work is
both successful and honorable, the noble lady is not convinced (60, 66).

---

64. Andreas's eight dialogues are conceived as follows: (1) a commoner addresses a common
woman; (2) a commoner addresses a noble lady; (3) a commoner addresses a woman of the higher
nobility; (4) a nobleman addresses a common woman; (5) a nobleman addresses a noblewoman; (6) a
man of higher nobility addresses a common woman; (7) a man of higher nobility addresses a noblewoman; (8) a man of higher nobility addresses a lady of higher nobility.

65. Citing Bloch, Moi writes, "The function of chivalry and courtliness seems to have been to
provide the ruling feudal aristocracy with a legitimising ideology," distinguishing the artistocracy
from the third estate (17).

Her position is that social rank matters. Otherwise, she argues, any "hairy farm labourer" or "mendicant" could excite the love of a queen.

This, of course, is the opinion of just one voice in the treatise and may not represent Andreas's opinion at all. An even more illuminating passage occurs, however, when the *praeceptor* speaks to Walter about the love of peasants. Peasants do not "love"; they couple like beasts. Underscoring the distinction between the labor of courtship and the labor of the farm and directly reflecting the ideology of labor in the three estates model, the narrator adds: "Sufficit ergo agricultori labor assiduus et vomeris ligonisque continua sine intermissione solatia" (So for a farmer regular toil and the continuing uninterrupted consolations of ploughshare and hoe are enough; 222). Here, clearly, is the disdain for manual labor found in parts of Adalbéron's poem.[66] Moreover, just as manual labor would be inappropriate for Walter because, according to Adalbéron, it would sully Walter's purity, so too the refined labor of love is unsuitable for the peasant. In addition, Walter is told that if indeed he is attracted to a peasant woman, he need not waste his time with the labor of courtship, but rather simply take his pleasure by means of "violento . . . amplexu" (rough embraces; 222). This haughty disdain for the peasant woman is generalized in Book 3 into an extremely shrill and ugly denunciation of all women. Trying to unify this shameful rhetoric with the refined sentiments expressed in Book 1 is futile.

We saw that the ideology of manual labor in Ovid's Rome was largely constructed in opposition to the ideal of aristocratic *otium*, not the *otium* of the lazy and dissolute, but the *otium negotiosum* of the responsible free man. We also saw that one of Ovid's goals in his discourse of love's labor was playfully but subversively to present the pursuit of love *not* as an activity of *otium otiosum* but as a difficult and dignified labor. Ovid points out, for example, that the hardships encountered by lovers in the pursuit of their ladies are comparable to those endured by a Roman soldier. In this context, he argues that those who would not be lazy or slothful should love. This particular Ovidian worry, that as a lover one might be

---

66. Moi's comment on this passage is relevant: "This aversion to the natural life of peasants reveals the real function of courtly ideology. If, as Bloch (1940) has argued, courtly ideology can be seen as an effort to impose the more refined habits of the aristocratic ladies on the boorish feudal lords, the cultured noble lady becomes the arbiter of taste in courtly society; no wonder then that peasant women were considered their absolute antithesis. The whole point of the various courtly and chivalric exercises described in Andreas's and Chrétien's texts was to escape all comparisons with villains" (18–19).

considered slothful, did not, however, concern Andreas. As we have seen, Andreas's concerns lie elsewhere: the lover might be considered stricken with love's madness or trapped in serious sin, but the particular concern with idleness does not arise in the *De amore* as something that needs to be addressed. Indeed, Andreas does not use the word *otium* very often, and when he does, he uses it only in connection with the life of the clergy. As Jean Leclercq has shown, the cultivation of *otium* or *quies* for purposes of divine contemplation was an important part of monastic discourse, and Jesus himself preferred the contemplative Mary to the industrious Martha.[67]

Nevertheless, *otium* carried negative connotations for Andreas and his characters. The woman of higher nobility, for example, in rebuffing the proposition of the man of higher nobility (who becomes a cleric halfway through the eighth dialog) speaks of the need for clerics to keep themselves pure. She refers here to sexual purity, not the "cleanliness" to which Adalbéron refers in the *Carmen* (182). At the same time, however, she denigrates the *otium* of the clergy, contrasting it unfavorably with the "grinding toils of war" suffered by the warrior class.[68] A clergyman, she says with disapproval, "continuo reperitur otio deditus et ventris solummodo mancipatus obsequiis" (is known to devote himself to constant idleness, a slave to nothing other than his belly; 186). Similar sentiments are voiced by the *praeceptor* when he addresses the love of clerics in Book 1, chapter 7.[69] Thus, while the fundamental class and labor ideology of Adalbéron's poem runs through the heart of *De amore*, Andreas is not without his concerns regarding the privilege of clerical *otium*, which he seems to equate with *otium otiosum*. Unlike Ovid or Chrétien de Troyes, he is not concerned with the possibility that aristocratic lovers might be considered slothful.

In fact, Andreas, while clearly rejecting manual labor as servile, lards the *De amore* with words and phrases describing the strenuous efforts re-

---

67. Jean Leclercq, *Otia monastica: Études sur le vocabulaire de la contemplation au moyen âge* (Rome: Herder, 1963) 63–133.

68. Speaking of knights, she says it is appropriate for them "contra rebelles animosum et omnimoda in proelio strenuitate gaudentem et bellorum assiduo labori suppositum" (to show fierceness against those who war on him, delight at the varying strains of battle, and application to the grinding toil of wars; 186).

69. "Clericorum sit vita propter otia multa continua et ciborum abundantiam copiosam prae aliis hominibus universis naturaliter corporis tentationi supposita" (The life of the clergy is naturally exposed to the temptation of the body more than are all others because of their considerable and uninterrupted leisure, and because of the plentiful abundance of their eating; 210).

quired of the aristocrats who wish to serve in love's army. We have seen that Andreas frequently uses *labor* in the *De amore* in ways that go beyond its traditional denotations of the hard agricultural work of the peasant (222) and pain and suffering.[70] Just as Ovid uses *labor* for the activities of courtship, so Andreas uses *labor* for more refined exertions. In the first dialog, the commoner uses the word to refer to the efforts he would make to win his lady.[71] While Adalbéron uses *labor* to refer to the work of the clergy, Andreas uses the term to refer to the toils of the warriors, the *labori bellorum* (186), a phrase used by the woman of higher nobility in the eighth dialog. She claims that being ready to participate in these labors is a minimal qualification for lovers. Hence, clerics are not fit to love. In fact, the *labori bellorum* become part of the labors of love for Andreas. Going beyond Ovid's position, Andreas's treatise indicates that the labors associated with love extend beyond the acts of courtship or the sexual act itself (Andreas ignores writing love poetry); they include battle and other forms of generalized service. "*Obsequia*," writes the *praeceptor*, "cunctis amorosus multa consuevit decenter parare" (A person in love grows to the practice of performing numerous *services* becomingly to all; 38; emphasis added). *Obsequia*, acts of assiduous service, performed not only for the beloved but also for all people the lover meets, are a part of the labor demanded in Andreas's treatise.

How can this be? As I noted earlier with regard to the method of "honesty of character," Andreas is concerned that lovers *demonstrate* this quality to their potential lovers. In the world of the *De amore*, one does this by performing good deeds—*facta, benefacta, obsequia, ministeria*, or *servitia*—on behalf of the beloved. In consistently presenting good deeds, deeds ostensibly unrelated to love, as indications of good character, Andreas significantly modifies the discourse of love's labor as it is found in Ovid. While Ovid suggests to his readers that they should cultivate their minds by means of liberal studies, none of his labors are meant to demonstrate probity of character. In fact, as we saw in Chapter 2, Ovid's position is quite the opposite. Although Ovid's lover should concentrate

---

70. An example of the word used to refer to pain and suffering is found when the woman of higher nobility, in arguing that it is better for lovers to be close than to be far apart, states that lovers who are close can better assuage each other's pains: "alternatim sibi possunt esse remedia et in suis se compassionibus adiuvare et suum amorem mutuis vicibus ac laboribus enutrire" (They can aid each other in their sufferings, and nourish their love because of the fortunes and afflictions they share; 144). Nevertheless, it is more common for Andreas to reserve *labor* for strenuous effort and to use *poenae* and *angustiae* for the sufferings of love (100, 144, 162, 164, 196).

71. Walsh 58. See also the use of *labor* on 32, 42, 64, 74, 192, and 194.

on *acting* a predetermined dramatic role, the lover's true inner character
does not concern the Ovidian *praeceptor* in the least. Acting a part often
produces the best results, he argues, so why worry about more? Far from
Ovidian, then, this aspect of Andreas's discourse may suggest the influence of Christianity, which is chiefly concerned with the state of the inner person; of contemporary romance literature, in which knights regularly set off on quests to prove their worthiness; and even of the poetry
of the troubadours.[72]

The place of these good deeds within the discourse of love's labor is
explained by the man of higher nobility as he makes his case for love with
the common woman. His general argument is that the differences in
their social classes should not be an impediment to their love, and in
choosing her lover she must discern the truly noble at heart. However,
since God alone can judge the human heart completely, the wise woman
must be content to survey a potential lover's good deeds. He says: "*Factis
ergo et operibus exterioribus* a femina sapienti interior debet cogitatio deprehendi" (Accordingly the wise woman must gauge inner attitudes by *external deeds* and *actions;* 124; emphasis added). Hence, unlike anything in
Ovid, Andreas's lovers must work to prove their inner worth by means of
various services rendered not only to the ladies in question, but to hu-
manity in general.

The man of higher nobility does not use the word *servitium* to describe those services he intends to render. Nevertheless, earlier in this
chapter I noted the general semantic broadening and amelioration of
that Latin word, which came in part to denote the duties, the labors, of
the knight. *Servitium* appears in the *De amore* at least twice, both times
with positive connotations. In the fifth dialog, the noblewoman promises
to accept the *servitia* of the nobleman at the appropriate time and place
(98). In the eighth dialog, the woman of higher nobility, contrasting ap-

---

72. This criterion may also indicate the influence of what Michael Nerlich has termed the "ideology of adventure" upon Andreas's discourse of love's labor. Nerlich argues that such an ideology,
which developed during the second half of the twelfth century, was constructed as a defense strategy
by the knightly classes (with the help of the clergy) against the villeins and the newly powerful bourgeoisie. Its aim was to "ennoble" the activities of this heretofore "gang of unscrupulous fellows"
(*The Ideology of Adventure,* trans. Ruth Crowley [Minneapolis: University of Minnesota Press, 1987]
1.9–15). Nerlich considers *De amore* to be a milestone in the development of the ideology of adventure. He writes: "This work attempts to unite the courtly love ethos with a new noble ethic based on
moral and spiritual values" (14).

Cherchi believes the concept of love in the *De amore* is taken from that found in troubadour poetry (12–28).

propriate deeds to empty words, speaks approvingly of a lover who petitions love by means of *servitiis* alone (190).

Andreas uses the verb *servire*, however, even more frequently than the noun to refer to love's labor. When, in the third dialog, the commoner seeks the love of the woman of higher nobility, he seeks to prove both his nobility of spirit and the depth of his love by serving the lady:

Firma namque in meo corde et stabilita conceptio est, nedum vobis sed pro vobis obsequia omnibus exhibere et humili animo placitoque *servire*. Spem namque gero plenariam quod nunquam apud vos permanere posset meus animus sine fructus dulcedine labor. (74; emphasis added)

[It is the fixed, unwavering resolve of my heart to demonstrate my allegiance not only to you but also to all men on your behalf, and *to serve* you with mind humble and content; for I entertain the full hope that my efforts in your interest could never linger on without sweet reward.]

It is striking and significant that the commoner immediately associates this act of service with wage labor. He believes that the act of serving should invariably produce the appropriate "sweet fruit," again suggesting the influence of Luke 10:7 on Andreas's discourse of love's labor. This passage does not, however, prove the semantic amelioration of *servire*. After all, commoners were expected to serve their betters in imperial Rome as well. The semantic amelioration is, however, strongly suggested when the same verb falls from the mouth of a nobleman in the context of declaring his love.

This occurs in the fourth dialog, in which the nobleman seeks the love of a common woman. At the end of that dialog, the nobleman declares his intention to prove his worth and love using words that are very similar to those of the commoner: "Ego tamen tibi nunquam *servire* cessabo et pro te omnibus semper *obsequia* cuncta praestare" (But I shall never cease *to serve* you, and shall always proffer every *service* to every person on your behalf; 94; emphasis added). The Latin *obsequium*, a word not used by Ovid, literally means a "service" and appears often in the *De amore*.[73] The amelioration of *servire* becomes even clearer when the man of highest nobility equates service to his lady with "universal kingship in this life." He says:

73. For examples of the word *obsequium* used to denote services for the beloved or, indeed, for good deeds in general, see Walsh 74, 94, 121, 128, 150, and 192.

est manifestum quod vobis *servire* solum est cunctis in hac vita regnare, et sine ipso nihil posset ab aliquo in hoc saeculo dignum laudibus adimpleri. (132; emphasis added)

[I have the clear certainty that merely *to serve* you is to have universal kingship in this life, and aside from that service nothing praiseworthy could be achieved by anyone in this world.]

We saw in Chapter 2 that the figure of *servitium amoris* was used by the Roman elegists, including Ovid, to suggest the lover's degradation at the hands of his beloved. In Andreas's text, however, service to the beloved, which includes a greater range of activities than it does in Ovid, is something that brings honor, not degradation. It transforms a nobleman into a king, not into a slave or serf.

This is not to say that the idea of "love's slavery" in a clearly pejorative sense is missing from *De amore*. In the Preface to his treatise, Andreas cautions Walter concerning the "Veneris . . . servituti."[74] Later, the noblewoman in the fifth dialog claims that no amount of prayers or toils from her suitor could break her resolve never to submit to the "Veneris . . . servituti" (100). At least in Book 1, however, this pejorative sense is the minority viewpoint.

The pejorative sense of *servitus* seems to be conveyed by matching it with the modifier *Veneris*. Similarly, *opus* and *opera* take on a pejorative meaning when linked with *Veneris* in *De amore*. For Andreas, the *opus Veneris* simply refers to sexual acts, intercourse in particular. We have already seen, for example, that Andreas contemptuously refers to the sexual acts of peasants as "opera Veneris" (222). One may have expected him to use other terms when referring to the sexual acts of the aristocracy, but he does not. When defining who can serve in love's army, the *praeceptor* notes that "anyone of sound mind" who is capable of completing "Veneris opera" can serve. Immediately he develops this idea further by noting that age can be an impediment because, although older people can have sexual intercourse, they do not experience the sexual pleasure necessary to generate love (38). Later, the man of higher nobility will use the phrase "in extremo Veneris opere" to refer to sexual intercourse when he seeks to distinguish "chaste" and "compound" love (180). Finally, when speaking against loving a licentious woman, the *praeceptor* says

---

74. Walsh 30. "Servitus," *Glossarium ad Scriptores Mediae et Infimae Latinitas.* The word is defined as *ministerium, officium,* and *officium Ecclesiasticum.* However, "servitutes exactoriae" is defined as "operae serviles."

that such love should be avoided because it leads to frustration. Such women can never be satisfied, "nisi te in Veneris opere tam potentem agnoveris ut eius valeas libidinem saturare" (unless you regard yourself as so virile in Venus's work that you can satiate her lust; 220).

The same pejorative connotation occurs when "opus" is linked with "amoris." For example, when, in Book 1, the *praeceptor* says "clericus non debet amoris operibus deservire" (the cleric ought not to devote himself to labours of love), there is no doubt that "amoris operibus" carries a pejorative and sexual connotation here, for the *praeceptor* explains that clerics are supposed to avoid "delights of the flesh" and "bodily defilement" (210). Something similar occurs when the man of higher nobility accuses the lady of higher nobility of hypocrisy. She speaks of God's being alienated by talk of love, yet he notes that when men approach her, she smiles, engages them in courtly conversation, and "amoris eis opera suadetis" (encourage[s] them to perform deeds of love; 162). Although sexual intercourse is probably not denoted here, other kinds of sexual behaviors may very well be indicated. In any case, the context makes it clear that the man is not here offering a compliment.

Andreas's use of the word *opus* is somewhat unexpected when one recalls that Le Goff found that in general *opus*, like *ars* and *artifex*, carried a more positive connotation than *labor*. What may have been true in general is not true in *De amore*, where the word often carries a sexual denotation and a pejorative connotation.[75] At the same time, while it is true that Andreas uses such words as *obsequia, ministeria, benefacta*, and *servitia* to refer to the acts of love's labor, he also employs both *labor* and *laborare* to refer in a positive way to those same courtly deeds, and not to sexual intercourse. It may well be that *labor* has benefited from its use in the monastic setting, where it denoted not only manual labor but also spiritual "works," or it may simply be that Andreas read his Ovid carefully and noted that the word was used for the labor of love in the *Ars amatoria*. Whatever the reason, the *De amore* presents us with the word used with a much fuller range of both connotations and denotations than we might come to expect from reading modern labor historians. Clearly the *De amore* attests to the semantic roots of *labor*—pain, suffering, and backbreaking labor—but it is also clear that the semantic range of *labor* went well beyond these traditional denotations and connotations.

75. An exception to this rule occurs in a passage cited earlier, in which the man of higher nobility suggests that women can judge the heart only by means of a man's "operibus exterioribus" (external deeds; 124).

V

While the discourse of love's labor in *De amore* shows some signs of its Ovidian past, it is much more clearly imbued with the labor ideology of the medieval Christian Church and the three estates social model. As we have seen, Andreas's treatise does not, like Ovid's, overtly seek to defend aristocrats against the charge of wasting time in slothful activities. This stance would be accounted for if the original audience of the *De amore* were aristocrats themselves, like the Countess of Champagne. The treatise does teach the activities of courtship, that is, winning a lover and keeping a lover, as forms of intelligent work, and hence as techniques that can be taught as an art by an experienced *praeceptor*. However, both the content and the focus of love's labor in *De amore* are quite different from those in the *Ars amatoria*. While Ovid is indifferent to the "inner man" and his treatise teaches that lovers may reach their amorous goals by playing different roles, Andreas's treatise teaches the practice of performing good deeds in order to reveal the true character of the inner man. While Ovid appears hardly concerned with the effect of social class on matters of love, questions of social class are a near obsession in *De amore*. While Ovid's treatise presents strategies for action in sexual conquest (including the writing of love letters and poetry), Andreas's treatise presents a rhetoric of polite debate between potential lovers. While the labor in Ovid's treatise gains its goals through playful strategy and sometimes deceit, the labor in Andreas's treatise wins its reward as the repayment for services rendered, a quid pro quo. While sexual and cosmetic techniques are a part of the art of love in the *Ars amatoria*, these are generally ignored in *De amore*, except for the curious discussion of the difference between "pure" and "mixed" love.

A word missing from the lexicon of labor in both the *Ars amatoria* and the *De amore* is *negotium*. In Chapter 2, I noted that *negotium* did not appear in the corpus of Ovidian poetry, and I speculated that this may have been because *negotium* was too closely linked to the world of trade and business. Given the opinions of the noblewoman in Andreas's second dialog, a similar argument might be made with respect to Andreas. If he was to expand the boundaries of the lexicon of love's labor, he preferred to add words like *servitium, obsequium,* and *ministerium* that were clearly used in the aristocratic world of the court. While Ovid avoided comparing love's labor to that of the merchant, he freely compared love's labor to that of the rural farmer, for the labor ideology of imperial Rome, while denigrating most manual labor as servile, held agricultural labor to be the exception. This was not possible in Andreas's twelfth-century context, where agricultural labor was soiled beyond redemption by its exclusive connection with the peasant classes. For Andreas, the labor of love could have nothing to do with any kind of manual labor at all. It could only be a labor associated with the *officium* of the aristocracy, something that could be practiced by the "militia amoris" and adjudicated in the "curia amoris." If, however, this total disdain of all kinds of manual labor shows Andreas's deep ties to the French aristocracy, it also suggests that he was out of touch not only with the long monastic tradition of venerating the practice of manual labor but also with contemporary urban developments with respect to the labor of artisans. This is not true of the work of his contemporary, Alan of Lille, who composed a roughly contemporary but contrasting document in the history of the discourse of love's labor.

CHAPTER 4

Homo Artifex

Monastic Labor Ideologies, Urban Labor, and Love's Labor in Alan of Lille's *De planctu naturae*

The sin of lechery consists, as we have explained, in a person applying himself to sex pleasure not according to right reason. . . . It may conflict with right reason on two counts. First, when the act of its nature is incompatible with the purpose of the sex-act. In so far as generation is blocked, we have unnatural vice, which is any complete sex-act from which of its nature generation cannot follow.

—*St. Thomas Aquinas*

O man, why is it that other creatures devote themselves to their assigned duties . . . while you alone, stupefied by idleness, deviate from your own duties and deform the image of God in you?

—*Alan of Lille*

I

Alan of Lille's *De planctu naturae*, written around the years 1160 to 1170, is a significantly different work from either Ovid's *Ars amatoria* or Andreas Capellanus's *De amore*. Far from a handbook of love, the *De planctu* is a menippean satire, a moral work, written in alternating sections of prose and verse, in the tradition of Boethius's *Consolation of Philosophy.*[1] Although it was written before Andreas's *De amore*, the discourse of love's labor in the *De planctu* contains influences of twelfth-century medieval labor ideologies not found in Andreas's treatise, and it is not at all Ovidian. Hence, it is more conveniently treated after the *De amore*. In-

---

1. Nikolaus Häring, "Alan of Lille, 'De Planctu Naturae,'" *Studi Medievali*, 3rd ser., 19.2 (1978): 797. Quotations from the *De planctu* will be taken from this edition and cited in the text by section and line numbers. English translations will be taken from James J. Sheridan, *The Plaint of Nature* (Toronto: Pontifical Institute of Mediaeval Studies, 1980).

deed, Alan's discourse of love's labor in *De planctu* was not only up-to-date, but it also influenced later writers of amatory fiction, such as Jean de Meun, John Gower, and Geoffrey Chaucer.[2] Unlike either Ovid or Andreas, Alan ignores the activities of courtship and focuses his attention exclusively on the "labor" of the sexual act.[3] Unlike Andreas, he embraces *manual* labor as a fitting figure for love's labor, and unlike Ovid, he figures love's labor by means of the work of a skilled artisan or scribe, not that of a soldier or a farmer. For Alan, love's laborers are either smiths, hammering out new "coins" to keep the human race in existence, or monastic scribes, writing new life into existence with powerful pens and tablets of paper. Another new aspect of Alan's discourse is his interest in *material* productivity. Speaking through his major character Dame Nature, he judges the morality of the sex act solely on the basis of its potential to coin new human beings. That which is productive is "natural" and hence approved; that which can never be productive, such as a homosexual union, is "unnatural" and subject to harsh condemnation. As such, Alan's discourse of love's labor seems thoroughly imbued with a labor ideology that is both traditionally monastic and particularly revealing of his twelfth-century urban culture.

Although Alan was a celebrated writer and scholar and came to be known in academic circles as the *Doctor universalis*, few details about his life remain. He died in the monastery of Cîteaux in either 1202 or 1203, but scholars are uncertain as to how long he was a monk there. It is possible that he went there only at the end of his life to die. We do know that

2. For the influence of the *De planctu* on later medieval poetry, see Thomas Hatton, "Nature as Poet: Alanus de Insulis' *The Complaint of Nature* and the Medieval Concept of Artistic Creation," *Language and Style* 2 (1969): 85; and D. Poiron, "Alain de Lille et Jean de Meun," *Alain de Lille, Gautier de Chatillon, Jakemart Gielee et leur temps*, ed. Henri Roussel and F. Suard (Lille: Presses Universitaires de Lille, 1979) 135–51.

Other critical studies of the *De planctu* include those of Ernst Robert Curtius, *European Literature and the Latin Middle Ages*, trans. Willard R. Trask (New York: Harper & Row, 1953) 117–22; Richard Green, "Alan of Lille's *De Planctu Naturae*," *Speculum* 31 (1956): 649–74; Winthrop Wetherbee, "The Function of Poetry in the 'De Planctu Naturae,'" *Traditio* 25 (1969): 87–125, and "Nature and Grace: The Allegories of Alain de Lille," *Platonism and Poetry in the Twelfth Century* (Princeton, N.J.: Princeton University Press, 1972) 187–219; Alain Michel, "Rhétorique, poétique et nature chez Alain de Lille," *Alain de Lille, Gautier de Chatillon, Jakemart Gielee et leur temps* 113–24; Alexandre Leupin, "The Hermaphrodite: Alan of Lille's *De Planctu Naturae*," *Barbarolexis: Medieval Writing and Sexuality*, trans. Kate M. Cooper (Cambridge, Mass.: Harvard University Press, 1989) 59–78; and Larry Scanlon, "The Unspeakable Pleasures: Alain de Lille, Sexual Regulation and the Priesthood of Genius," *Romanic Review* 86.2 (1995): 213–42. G. Raynaud de Lage's *Alain de Lille: Poète du XIIe siècle* (Montreal: Institute d'Études Médiévales, 1951) is a full-length study of both the *De planctu* and of the *Anticlaudianus*.

3. Wetherbee sees influences of courtly love traditions in the *De planctu* (*Platonism and Poetry* 190, 198).

Alan taught in Paris and in Montpellier, and that his theological and
homiletic writings are consistent with advanced clerical training. His
work is often identified with the tradition of the School of Chartres.
While James J. Sheridan finds it hardly believable that *De planctu naturae*
could have been composed by a monk in good standing, other scholars,
like Richard Green, do not have the same reservations about the content
of *De planctu*, finding it a perfectly orthodox allegorical work.[4] Whether
Alan was a monk in good standing or not when he wrote the *De planctu*,
it is clear that monastic attitudes with respect to the dignity of manual labor play a significant part in his presentation of love's labor. Moreover,
unlike Andreas Capellanus, Alan seems to have consistently had a more
sympathetic connection to the working poor than to aristocratic knights,
whom he portrays as bandits in two of his sermons.[5] He certainly had a
healthy respect for the dignity of manual labor, a respect that has its roots
in the labor ideology of Christian monasticism, to which I now turn.

II

It is often argued that Benedict of Nursia and his monastic *Rule*, composed around 540 C.E., played a crucial role in carving out a positive role
for labor in the Christian culture of the early Middle Ages.[6] Max Weber,
for example, argues that Benedict's *Rule* played a crucial role in the evolution toward the Protestant work ethic, a position that has been criticized
or qualified by many late-twentieth-century labor historians.[7] By setting

4. Biographical details are taken from James J. Sheridan, introduction, *The Plaint of Nature* 1–11;
and J. M. Trout, *The Voyage of Prudence: The World View of Alan of Lille* (Washington, D.C.: University
Press of America, 1979) 1–40. See also Green 649.

5. Trout 6, 153–56, 160–61.

6. In this treatment of Benedict's *Rule* I am indebted not only to Ovitt's remarks in "Labor and
the Foundations of Monasticism," *The Restoration of Perfection: Labor and Technology in Medieval Culture* (New Brunswick, N.J.: Rutgers University Press, 1987) 88–106, but also to those of Birgit van den
Hoven, "Work in the Monastic World," *Work in Ancient and Medieval Thought* (Amsterdam: J. C.
Gieben, 1996) 113–58. Both believe that Benedict's *Rule* makes an important contribution to medieval labor ideology, but van den Hoven shows that Benedict's *Rule* derives from an earlier, anonymous *Regula magistri*, also of the sixth century (152–55). For a summary of modern historians who
believe that Benedict's *Rule* was a crucial document in the history of medieval labor, see van den
Hoven 113–16. Also helpful is Jean Leclercq, "Observances claustrales et travail," *Otia monastica:
Études sur le vocabulaire de la contemplation au moyen âge* (Rome: Herder, 1963) 92–95.

On the date of composition, see Rudoph Hanslik, introduction, *Benedicti Regula*, ed. Rudolph
Hanslik, Corpus Scriptorum Ecclesiasticorum Latinorum 75 (Vienna: Hoelder-Pichler-Tempsky,
1960) 12–13. All quotations from Benedict's *Rule* will be taken from this edition and cited in the text
by chapter number. The English translations will be taken from *The Rule of St. Benedict*, trans. Cardinal Gasquet (New York: Cooper Square Publishers, 1966).

7. Max Weber, *The Protestant Work Ethic and the Spirit of Capitalism*, trans. Talcott Parsons (1930;
New York: Charles Scribner's Sons, 1956) 118ff.

up a rigid schedule of prayer and work for his monks, Benedict attempted to unite prayer and contemplation with labor, Mary with Martha. To
Benedict, both were dignified activities. Brian Stock argues that Benedict
effected a "spiritualization of labor," and this seems to be true in two
equally valid ways. On the one hand, Benedict, like St. Augustine and
John Cassian, insisted that manual labor was an integral part of the spiritual lives of monks. On the other hand, Benedict regularly used the *discourse* of labor, particularly its lexicon, to describe spiritual qualities.
Stock notes that "[w]hen monastic writers speak of work, it is often not
clear whether they are referring to physical or to spiritual endeavors or to
both at once."[8] Benedict, for example, calls prayer the "opus Dei," the
work of God, and obedience the "oboedientiae labor," the labor of obedience (chap. 43; prologue). He also calls the monastery a spiritual "officina" (workshop) and a series of moral precepts on monastic life the "in-
strumenta artis spiritualis" (tools of our spiritual craft; chap. 4).

Indeed, Benedict strongly believed that his followers were truly monks
only when they lived by the labor of their hands: "quia tunc uere
monachi sunt, si labore manuum suarum uibunt" (chap. 48). He saw labor, however, primarily as an antidote to idleness. He writes, for example, that

Otiositas inimica est animae; et ideo certis temporibus occupari debent fratres in
labore manuum, certis iterum horis in lectione diuina. (chap. 48)

[Idleness is an enemy of the soul. Because this is so brethren ought to be occupied at specified times in manual labour, and at other fixed hours in holy reading.]

The "opus Dei," however, was as a general rule to hold precedence over
any other kind of work:

Ad horam diuini officii mox auditus fuerit signus, relictis omnibus, quaelibet
fuerint in manibus, summa cum festinatione curratur. . . . Ergo nihil operi dei
praeponatur. (chap. 43)

[As soon as the signal for the Divine Office shall be heard each one must lay aside
whatever work he may be engaged upon and hasten to it, with all speed. . . .
Nothing, therefore, shall be put before the Divine Office.]

8. Brian Stock, "Activity, Contemplation, Work, Leisure between the Eleventh and the Thirteenth Centuries," *Arbeit, Musse, Meditation: Betrachtungen zur "Vita Activa" und "Vita Contemplativa,"*
ed. Brian Vickers (Zürich: Verlag der Fachvereine, 1985) 89.

Benedict is characteristically moderate when it comes to describing the work requirements of his monks (see especially his advice to the abbot, in chap. 64) and emphasizes that no monks should be crushed under an unreasonable work load. Nevertheless, he also insists that

Si quis uero ita neglegens et desidiosus fuerit, ut non uellit aut non possit meditare aut legere, iniungatur ei opus, quod faciat, ut non uacet. (chap. 48)
[If, however, any one be so negligent and slothful as to be unwilling or unable to read or meditate, he must have some work given him, so as not to be idle.]

Although monks were to enjoy the leisure to read or meditate, they were to avoid being *neglegentes* and *desidiosi*. *Desidia*, as we saw in Chapter 2, was a term that for the Romans signified *otium otiosum*, unprofitable idleness.[9] Monastic *otium*, therefore, was to be productive, a means to accomplishing a spiritual task, the *opus Dei*, the *officia divina*.[10]

Spiritual productivity is one thing; *material* productivity quite another, however. A concern for material productivity does not figure into Benedict's *Rule*. In fact, the opposite is true. If a monk's skill or expertise at a certain task led to pride, then Benedict insists that that monk must be removed from his job:

Quod si aliquis ex eis extollitur pro scientia artis suae, . . . hic talis erigatur ab ipsa arte et denuo per eam non transeat, nisi forte humiliato ei iterum abbas iubeat. (chap. 57)
[If any be puffed up by his skill in his craft . . . such a one shall be shifted from his handicraft, and not attempt it again till such time as, having learnt a low opinion of himself, the abbot shall bid him resume.]

At the risk of belaboring the obvious, it should be underscored that Benedict's work ethic was significantly different from the Protestant work ethic.[11] George Ovitt nicely sums up the contrast between Benedict's attitude and that of Max Weber's capitalist:

9. J. M. André, *L'otium dans la vie morale et intellectuelle romaine des origines à l'époque augustéenne* (Paris: Presses Universitaires de France, 1966) 13. Michel Rouch's otherwise interesting attempt to trace the path from *otium* as a positive quality in Roman society to *otium* as a negative quality in Benedictine discourse is marred by a rather one-dimensional understanding of Roman *otium*, by which Rouch means *otium otiosum* ("Une révolutione mentale du Haut Moyen Age: Loisir et travail," *Horizons marins, itinéraires spirituels [V^e–XVIIIe siècles]*, ed. Henri Dubois et al. [Paris: La Sorbonne, 1987] 1.233–37).
10. See Leclercq 82–83, 92–95, 115–18.
11. van den Hoven, especially, argues against the opinion of such scholars as Lynn White, Jr., who, in her opinion, make too much of the impact of the *Rule* in forming new, positive attitudes toward manual labor (113–16). She denies that the *Rule* laid the foundations for Weber's Protestant work ethic.

The Weberian capitalist, like the medieval monk, was inspired by a religious ethic to work indirectly on himself by working in the world; but while the "virtue of the English gentleman" was restraint and self-effacement in the interest of achievement, the virtue of the monk was restraint and self-effacement in spite of achievement.[12]

Benedict saw labor primarily as an antidote to a dangerous human failing: idleness. Idle hands, as the proverb tells us, are the devil's workshop. Over the course of the Middle Ages, idleness would become a subcategory of one of the Seven Deadly Sins, *acedia*, and work would become a major antidote against that vice. This is a topic to which I shall return in a later chapter.

Jean Leclercq argues that the twelfth century, six hundred years after the time of Benedict, was a particularly important period in the history of medieval spirituality. One of the major debates in the spiritual literature of the century regarded the monastic balance between manual labor and spiritual activities, *labor* and *otium*.[13] In many ways this dispute was embodied in two different approaches to twelfth-century monasticism, those of the Cistercians and those of the Cluniacs. One especially clear text that deals with this dispute is the *Dialogus duorum monachorum*, written by a German monk, Idung, sometime after 1155.[14] In his work, Idung argues that the Carthusians had abandoned the strict adherence to the Benedictine *Rule*, for the Carthusians believed that their obligation to contemplation (which, in turn, necessitated *otium*) was significantly more important than their obligation to perform manual labor. Although they did perform such work as copying manuscripts, they freed themselves from any manual labor by incorporating the *conversi*, an order of "half-monks" taken from the peasant classes, into their ranks. To Idung and the Cistercians, this abandonment of the Benedictine ideal was offensive. The Cistercians continued to hold that all monks must work with their hands, and Idung ridicules the clerical labor of the Carthusians as "ociosa opera" and "inutile." Such labors as illuminating manuscripts, for example, are "idle," writes Idung, because "non pertinent ad necessarios usus" (they are not directed toward necessary and useful purposes). The agricultural labor of the Cistercians, in contrast, is better because it is pro-

12. Ovitt, *Restoration of Perfection* 106.
13. Leclercq 129. For a treatment of twelfth-century approaches to monastic *otium*, see Leclercq 84–133.
14. R. B. C. Huygens, "Le Moine Idung et ses deux ouvrages," *Studi Medievali*, 3rd ser., 13.1 (1972): 298. The edition of the "Dialogus" appears on 375–470.

ductive insofar as the Cistercians can support themselves with it. Alluding to Genesis 3.19, Idung also implies that it is "good" work because it is hard: "multociens in sudore vultus nostri, pane nostro vescimur" (often we feed ourselves our bread by the sweat of our brow).[15] Ovitt notes that the dialog between these two views of the relative merits of manual labor and contemplation continues in monastic circles throughout the twelfth century.

Indeed, an example of a more liberal approach to the question of clerical labor in general is found in the *Libellus de diversis ordinibus*, written perhaps by Reimbald of Liège between 1121 and 1161.[16] The twelfth-century author interpreted the influential 2 Thessalonians 3.10, "if anyone will not work, then let him not eat," in such a way that the passage's verb "to work" *(operari)* need not refer to *manual* labor. In this treatise, *operari* could also refer to the clerical labors of monks in the *scriptoria*. The author writes:

Si autem et hi qui in claustro sedent aliquid manibus operari uolunt, bonum hoc esse pronuntio, et otiositatem ab eis sicut a caeteris amputandam esse, iudico, dicens cum apostolo, "qui non uult operari, nec manducet." Hoc enim ita intelligo, quod hoc non solum de *laboribus manuum* dicatur, sed etiam de omni *opere* quod aecclesiasticis uiris congruit. (94, 96; emphasis added)

[If they who remain in the cloister also wish to do some work with their hands, I declare this to be good, and I consider that idleness should be denied to them as it is to others, saying with the apostle: "If any man will not work, neither let him eat." I understand that this was said not only of *manual labour* but of all *work* suitable for men of the Church.]

Thus, the monk does not have to soil his hands to work. Any occupation suitable for men of the Church is sufficient to earn one's daily bread. The author uses the Latin noun *opus* for those tasks suitable for monks but *labor* for manual labor. This supports Le Goff's contention that medieval Latin *labor* was associated with backbreaking rural labor and pain and, in contrast, *opus* carried a more positive connotation. However, in a later

---

15. 2.54. The Cistercian voice says: "Sicut verba quae non aedificant sunt ociosa, ita opera illa quae non pertinent ad necessarios usus recte dicuntur ociosa" (Just as words that are not constructive are idle, so works that are not directed toward necessary and useful purposes are rightly called idle; 2.51). See Ovitt's summary 152–54.

16. Giles Constable and B. Smith, introduction, *Libellus de diversis ordinibus et professionibus qui sunt in aecclesia*, ed. and trans. Giles Constable and B. Smith (Oxford, U.K.: Oxford University Press, 1972) xv. All quotations from the *Libellus* and the corresponding English translations will be taken from this edition and cited in the text by page number. See Ovitt's remarks in *Restoration of Perfection* 157–58.

passage, in which the author forbids those canons who do manual labor
from feeling superior to other canons who work at their desks, he does
not maintain this distinction because he employs the Latin noun *labor* for
both activities.[17] When one remembers that St. Benedict himself used *labor* to refer to spiritual activities, this semantic fuzziness hardly seems an
innovation. In any case, between the position of Idung and that of the
author of the *Libellus*, we see an important clerical struggle taking place
over the definition of labor: the former taking the traditional position of
equating labor only with the hard, backbreaking toil of the fields, the latter casting his definition in much broader terms. For both authors, however, *labor* and *opus* signified activities worthy of men of the Church.

Monastic traditions regarding manual labor, then, played an important
role in the development of medieval labor ideologies. Beyond the confines of the twelfth-century monastery, however, other important developments were taking place that would affect those ideologies just as
deeply. Indeed, many historians identify the twelfth century as a crucial
epoch in the history of labor.[18]

A change took place, for example, in the overall economy, with a
movement from a more or less purely agricultural economy to a mixed
economy that included a strong urban component of trade and manufacturing as well as the traditional agricultural production. As a result of
these changes, Georges Duby sees a significant shift in attitudes toward
the material world during this century. He characterizes the change as a
turning away from the late-eleventh-century orientation of *contemptus*

17. "Nec ille qui laborat manibus iactet se super eum qui sedendo laborat, quia in utroque *laborem* inesse" (And let not him who works with his hands vaunt himself above the man who works
seated, since there is *labour* in both; *Libellus* 96; emphasis added).

18. Jacques Le Goff, for example, sees in the twelfth century the creation of a new spirituality of
labor in which the idea of labor as a punishment for sin was supplanted by an appreciation of labor
as a positive means to salvation ("Trades and Professions as Represented in Medieval Confessors'
Manuals," *Time, Work, and Culture in the Middle Ages*, trans. Arthur Goldhammer [Chicago: University
of Chicago Press, 1980] 115–17). Stock depicts the twelfth century as a crucial time in the articulation
of new attitudes toward work and leisure (87, 102–4). P. Boissonnade writes that between 1100 and
1340 "[a] few centuries of freedom and prosperity sufficed to bring [a] new world to birth in Western
towns. For the first time labour took a leading place in society, and made its power recognized. . . .
Not only had the working masses succeeded in the conquest of civil and political liberties, but they
had also, by the voluntary discipline which they had imposed upon themselves in their associations,
created a tradition of the honesty and dignity of labour" (*Life and Work in Medieval Europe*, trans.
Eileen Power [1927; Evanston, Ill.: Harper & Row, 1964] 224).

However, van den Hoven is skeptical. At least with respect to the characteristic attitude toward
the mechanical arts, she finds no movement at all in the twelfth century (171–77, 253). In fact, she
finds nothing radically different in medieval attitudes toward labor from those expressed in antiquity
(254–55).

mundi to a new, progressive belief in the positive value of *operatio* and man's ability to dominate nature. Interestingly, Duby argues that twelfth-century men were "opening their eyes, comprehending that man worked in God's employ, and that *procreation and manual labor* were less degrading than had been said." As a result, the status of the manual laborer was raised "slightly higher in the hierarchy of social functions."[19] Marie Chenu agrees. She sees in the twelfth century a technological revolution, and thus a new appreciation of man's ability to control nature. In philosophy and theology, she argues, man is conceived as *homo artifex*, skillful man, who is above all an imitation of the divine creator God.[20]

Changes in the traditional three estates model also began to develop. In large part due to a return of an adequate money supply, a new social category came to be distinguished from both the rural workers and the knights. These were the ministers, "specialized underlings, charged with those tasks, those occupations *(ministeria)* that had acquired a certain distinctive individuality within the staff of the great aristocratic houses." The new class of people came to be referred to in official documents as the "bourgeoisie," the city-dwellers, a term that highlighted the new importance of the city over against that of the countryside.[21] The bourgeoisie were initially identified solely with the merchant class, but in the twelfth century artisans also began to be more closely identified with the cities than with the countryside.[22] Indeed, these new urban artisans began to form confraternities, the guilds, to support both their spiritual and their economic welfare. Steven Epstein notes that the twelfth century witnessed the appearance and rapid growth of guilds in Western Europe.[23] Carlo Cippola argues that the triumph of the guilds was a real

19. Georges Duby, *The Three Orders: Feudal Society Imagined*, trans. Arthur Goldhammer (Chicago: University of Chicago Press, 1980) 211–12 (emphasis added). See also Stock 87.

20. Marie Dominique Chenu, "Man as Master of Nature: Art and Nature," *Nature, Man, and Society in the Twelfth Century: Essays on New Theological Perspectives in the Latin West*, ed. and trans. Jerome Taylor and Lester K. Little (Chicago: University of Chicago Press, 1968) 37–48.

21. Duby 112–13. "Ministeria," *Glossarium ad Scriptores Mediae et Infimae Latinitas*, 1883 ed. Among its other denotations, the word meant "officia majora et minora." Boissonnade argues that at the end of the eleventh century *the trader* was the new member added to the traditional tripartite structure (160–61). He goes on to underscore the transformative power that increased trade—especially in the trade fairs—and a larger money supply had on labor in twelfth-century Europe. Among the transformations experienced were increased consumption, a new interest in producing goods for export, and the growth of urban centers (177, 191).

22. Jean Alter, *Les origines de la satire anti-bourgeoise en France: Moyen âge–XVIᵉ siècle* (Geneva: Droz, 1966) 52–53.

23. Steven A. Epstein, *Wage Labor and Guilds in Medieval Europe* (Chapel Hill: University of North Carolina Press, 1991) 3, 98, 157. See also Boissonnade 206–11.

turning point in the history of labor. "The guilds," he writes, "played a more important role in giving their members a feeling of political importance, a socio-political bargaining power and a social status that as individuals they most certainly did not enjoy in the feudal world."[24] One might infer that growing sociopolitical power and social status would cause an increased appreciation of the value of the mechanical arts. Epstein reminds us, however, that little is known about the attitudes toward labor of the working classes. "Merchants, professionals, master artisans, and their employees," he writes, "have left behind no sure guide to their own thoughts."[25]

Twelfth-century scholars, however, did leave evidence of the growing influence of the bourgeoisie, especially the urban artisans. For the first time, twelfth-century scholars found a place for the mechanical arts within their traditional schemata of human knowledge. Whether this is in itself evidence of a new respect for the labor involved in the mechanical arts has been debated.[26] The best known and most influential of these twelfth-century classifications is found in Hugh of St. Victor's *Didascalicon*, written around 1120.[27] While in the *Didascalicon* the mechanical arts are consciously subordinated to the seven liberal arts, the fact that they were treated at all, placed, as it were, within the company of philosophy and the other liberal arts, implies a certainly legitimacy. Indeed, the mechanical arts, which are said to arise from human need, are defined, after all, as "arts" (1.9). Again, to recall a phrase from Cicero, they are "arts" because "prudentia maior inest," that is, they require intelligence and training. In art, writes Hugh, human practice is reduced to rules (1.11). Nevertheless, what Hugh means by "mechanical arts" varies somewhat. At times, he uses the term to indicate all kinds of human work, the *opus humanum* (1.9), and his list of the seven mechanical arts includes agriculture, hunting, commerce, medicine, and theatrics as well as the making

---

24. Carlo Cipolla, *Clocks and Culture, 1300–1700* (London: Collins, 1967) 19.

25. Epstein 184. In fact, Epstein believes that attitudes toward labor varied depending on one's level in the guild, that is, whether one was a master, a journeyman, or an apprentice (188–90).

26. Ovitt 117–20; van den Hoven 159–77. Both scholars, but especially van den Hoven, are skeptical about whether the inclusion of the mechanical arts in Hugh of St. Victor's schema of knowledge can be taken to indicate a more positive evaluation about mechanical labor in the twelfth century.

27. Jerome Taylor, introduction, *Didascalicon: A Medieval Guide to the Arts*, trans. Jerome Taylor (New York: Columbia University Press, 1961) 3. I will use Taylor's English translation in this discussion. The original Latin text will be taken from *Hugonis de Sancto Victore Didascalicon de studio legendi: A Critical Text*, ed. Charles Henry Buttimer, Studies in Medieval and Renaissance Latin 10 (Washington, D.C.: The Catholic University of America Press, 1939), and cited by book and chapter numbers.

of armaments and fabrics (2.20). At other times, however, he seems to use "mechanical arts" to refer only to the work of artificers, as when he compares human work to the works of God and nature. Here he writes that "opus artificis est disgregata coniungere vel coniuncta segregare" (the work of the artificer is to put together things disjoined or to disjoin those put together; 1.9).

Some argue that Hugh denigrates the mechanical arts because he calls them "adulterinum," adulterate, merely imitating, as they do, the works of nature.[28] Hugh also notes that *in antiquity* the mechanical arts were associated with the lowest classes, "plebei . . . et ignobilium filii" (the populace and the sons of men not free), while the liberal arts were associated with the upper classes, "liberi . . . id est, nobiles" (the free men . . . that is, the nobles; 2.20). A division of labor by social class is certainly a significant continuation of traditional Roman work ideology. At the same time, however, it is significant that in the passage quoted earlier, in which Hugh identifies the work of the artificer as putting things together and taking them apart, he uses the more positive word *opus*, not *labor*, to indicate not only the work of the artisan but also the works of God and of nature: "Sunt etenim tria opera, id est, opus Dei, opus naturae, opus artificis imitantis naturam" (Now there are three works—the work of God, the work of nature, and the work of the artificer, who imitates nature; 1.9). Given these somewhat contradictory indications, it is quite probable that Hugh's text shows an ideology in process, one that is groping its way toward a new positive assessment of the value of manual labor without being quite able to forget the traditional identification of manual labor with humiliation and pain.

In sum, the monastic tradition, in contrast to the ideology of labor found in the three estates model, continuously stressed not only the dignity of manual labor but also the necessity for monks to spend part of their days performing it. In addition, the discourse of manual labor was spiritualized, so that spiritual acts were described by St. Benedict in terms normally reserved for the tasks of manual labor. In the twelfth century, however, various monastic communities debated the necessity for monks to perform manual labor, and some historians believe that the ideological moorings of manual labor became detached from the monastery and secularized. As a result of a changing economy and the rise of guilds, the manual labor of artisans came to be valorized, particularly to the extent

28. 1.9; van den Hoven 172–73.

that it was seen to be an imitation of the work of the Divine Creator. As we will see, many of these trends underlie key aspects of Alan of Lille's discourse in the *De planctu naturae*, a discourse that is strikingly different from those in the *Ars amatoria* or even in the *De amore*.

III

The work opens with Alan's narrator, like Boethius in the *Consolation of Philosophy*, sorrowing, confused, and in need of supernatural guidance. At first, Alan's narrator grieves primarily over the widespread practice of homosexual sodomy. The practice of sodomy, however, is a model of all the "unnatural" acts that comprise sin, and thus the poem is about the fallen nature of man and the world as a whole. Winthrop Wetherbee, for example, argues that Alan "makes healthy sexuality his central metaphor for human perfection."[29] Instead of Lady Philosophy, a personification of nature appears to Alan's narrator. Alan's text is homophobic, but it deserves notice here because Nature's argument against sodomy is the springboard for Alan's use of the discourse of love's labor.[30] While Ovid and Andreas use the discourse of love's labor to describe the actions of courtship as well as the sexual act, Alan uses it to treat only the sexual act, particularly its reproductive aspects. For Alan, sex is "natural" only if it is (re)productive labor. In this he goes well beyond the Benedictine work ethic, which valued labor primarily as an antidote to idleness.

The focus on reproduction, of course, suggests that Alan's treatise falls in line with natural law ethics, the belief that unless sexual acts are in accord with natural law (and, hence, eternal law), they are sinful. According to St. Thomas Aquinas, sexual acts must be guided by "right reason," and reason commands that sex be oriented toward the common good of mankind.[31] Specifically, sexual acts must be judged by their ends, and the

29. Wetherbee, *Platonism and Poetry* 189. See also Green 651, 654, 666; Wetherbee, "Function" 101; and Scanlon 218.

30. De Lage divides the poem into three parts: (1) the coming and description of Nature, (2) the moral dialog between the narrator and Nature, and (3) the conclusion where new allegorical characters are introduced, including Genius (44). The discourse of love's labor in *De planctu* occurs mainly in the second portion, which de Lage believes is the heart of the poem (81).

31. This view is nicely summarized in the first epigraph of this chapter, taken from the *Summa theologica* 2a.2ae.154.1. (*Summa theologiae*, ed. Thomas Gilby, 60 vols. [New York: Blackfriars Press, 1963].) For scholarly summaries of Thomist natural law ethics, see Alan Soble, *The Philosophy of Sex and Love* (St. Paul, Minn.: Paragon House, 1998) 28–32; and Martin Rhonheimer, "The Concept of Natural Law in Thomas Aquinas," *Natural Law and Practical Reason: A Thomist View of Moral Autonomy*, trans. Gerald Malsbary (New York: Fordham University Press, 2000) 58–175.

final end of sex is reproduction and the raising of children.[32] Sexual acts that cannot by their very nature lead to reproduction constitute, then, by definition "vitium contra naturam" (unnatural vice).[33] In the *Summa theologica*, Thomas devotes an entire question to the analysis of the unnatural vices. While Alan keeps his focus on homosexuality, Thomas identifies four different sexual activities that qualify as "unnatural": masturbation, bestiality, homosexuality, and heterosexual sex that does not follow the "natural style" or use proper organs.[34] The "vitum contra naturam" is, for Thomas as for Alan, the worst kind of lust possible. Although from the perspective of the twenty-first century, this approach is morally conservative, one must keep in mind that Alan's treatment of natural sex antedates the writings of Thomas Aquinas by about one hundred years, and thus, in his own context, is forward-looking. It is also true, however, that whether one considers it progressive or conservative, Alan's doctrine is an attempt to exert social control over sexuality. To recall the words of Foucault, it is a way "to ensure population, to reproduce labor capacity, to perpetuate the form of social relations, [and] . . . to constitute a sexuality that is economically useful."[35] This agenda is another reason that Alan's text is different from the *Ars amatoria*, which in its own time was an attempt to *loosen* social controls over sexuality. As such, the *De planctu* initiates a new and influential strain of the discourse of love's labor. It is a strain that will resurface in the work of Jean de Meun, John Gower, and Geoffrey Chaucer.

Twentieth-century critics have often noted the highly ornate quality of Alan's writing.[36] Douglas Moffat comments on the "wonderful wild flowers of metaphor" that spring up in the *De planctu*.[37] Larry Scanlon notes that the poem is a tour de force because the cleverness of his conceits allows Alan to speak about sexual acts without ever having specifically to name them. He is able to condemn "unspeakable acts" without having to "speak" them.[38] Among the most important of Alan's conceits are the

---

32. *Summa contra gentiles*, trans. Vernon J. Bourke et al., 5 vols. (South Bend, Ind.: University of Notre Dame Press, 1975) 3.2.122 (4.143).

33. *Summa contra gentiles* 3.2.122.

34. *Summa theologica* 2a.2ae.154.11.

35. *The History of Sexuality*, trans. Robert Hurley, vol. 1 (New York: Vintage Books, 1978) 36–37.

36. On Alan's style, see especially de Lage 131–54. On Alan's ornate style and its relation to his theology, see Michel 113–15ff.

37. Quoted in Hatton 85. De Lage calls Alan's metaphors "à la fois audacieuses et pédantes" (audacious and pedantic at the same time; 47).

38. Scanlon 219.

likening of sex to a hammer striking an anvil and to a pen writing on pa-
per.³⁹ In Alan's discourse of love's labor, love is likened to the work of
smiths and scribes. Their work, in turn, is modeled after the work of the
greatest of all artisans, God himself. In one particularly striking passage,
Nature describes the work of God in the following terms:

Cum deus ab ydeali interne preconceptionis thalamo mundialis palatii fabricam
foras uoluit euocare et mentale uerbum . . . reali eiusdem existentia uelut mate-
riali uerbo depingere, tanquam mundi elegans architectus, tanquam auree fab-
rice faber aurarius, uelut stupendi artificii artificiosus artifex, uelut admirandi
operis operarius opifex, . . . mundialis regie ammirabilem speciem fabricauit.
(8.199–207)

[When God willed to call forth the fabric of the palace of the Universe from the
"ideal" bridal bed within which it had been preconceived and to give expression
to the idea of its creation . . . by giving it real existence by, so to speak, a material
word, as the choice architect of the universe, as the golden constructor of gold-
en construction, the skilled artisan of an amazing work of art, as the operative
producer of an admirable work, . . . He constructed the marvellous form of the
kingdom of the world.]

In this noteworthy and rhetorically ornate passage, which certainly recalls the creator God in Genesis, God is a mechanical worker par excellence: he is *architectus* (architect), *faber* (builder), *artifex* (artisan), and
opifex (craftsman).⁴⁰ He himself sets the pattern for all earthly work, including sexual reproduction, for he "preconceives" the idea of the universe in the "perfect bridal bed," the *thalamus*. In the *De planctu*, creative,
productive work, it seems, is modeled upon the deepest reality of all. Although one passage refers to work as the punishment for original sin,
overall the *De planctu* reflects the Benedictine position that manual work

39. De Lage notes these metaphors but does not find them realistic enough to be moving: "Il est
vrai encore que certaines métaphores reviennent constamment chez lui, images simples empruntées
à la vie familière: *mendicare, monetare, signare, sigillare, fabricare,* évoquant à l'origine les mendiants, la
frappe, les sceaux, la forge—mais devenues ici matière littéraire dans un emploi toujours figuré,
dépouillées alors leur saveur concrète, usées même au point d'être des clichés scolaires" (It is also
true that certain metaphors constantly return to him, simple images borrowed from everyday life:
begging, coining, marking, sealing, forging, evoking originally beggars, a stamp, seals, the forge—
but here becoming literary matter always used figuratively, stripped of their concrete zest, used up to
the point of their becoming scholarly clichés; 152).
    The poem's grammatical metaphors for sexual union usually gain more attention from critics
and are widely discussed elsewhere. See, for example, de Lage 45; Hatton 85–87; and Wetherbee, *Platonism and Poetry* 189.
    40. Beyond twelfth-century work ideology, the image of God as *opifex* may be derived from Pla-
to's *Timaeus* and from medieval commentaries on it. See Wetherbee, "Function" 92; and Chenu 40ff.

is valuable and dignified.[41] Indeed, in a passage that antedates similar passages in the *De amore*, Nature herself affirms that strenuous work sweetens the rewards that it wins:

Munera enim empta laboribus iocundius omnibus clarescunt gratuitis. Maioris enim laudis meretur preconia qui laborando munus recipit quam qui reperit ociando. Labor enim antecedens, quandam consequenti premio infundens dulcedinem, maiori fauore premiat laborantem. (6.69–74)

[Rewards purchased by toil bring more honor and delight than all gifts given gratis. The one who receives a reward for labour merits higher praise and commendation than he who obtains it while enjoying leisure. For the work that goes before, infusing a kind of sweetness into the reward that follows, brings a more pleasing recompense to the labourer.]

As purposeful labor is a gift of Jupiter in Virgil's *Georgics*, so too the Christian God in *De planctu* shares the gift of creative labor with his creation.[42] First, God delegates the work of reproduction to Nature. She, in turn, delegates a part of her reproductive duty to Venus, who represents the particularly human act of reproduction. Once an excellent worker, Venus, however, has become a slack worker, an idler, as a result of boring, repetitive work (10.115–26). From Nature's point of view, her major transgression has been to allow nonproductive play into the arena of sexual reproduction.

In a key description of her reproductive work, Nature describes the tools she gave to Venus in order that the work of reproduction be accomplished:

Et ut instrumentorum fidelitas praue operationis fermentum excluderet, ei duos legitimos malleos assignaui, quibus et Parcharum inaniret insidias resque multimodas essentie presentaret. (10.24–26)

[To ensure that the reliability of the instruments should preclude confused and defective workmanship, I assigned her (Venus) two approved hammers with

---

41. The only passage in the *De planctu* that contradicts Alan's generally upbeat assessment of manual labor is found in the lament over the fallen condition of humankind in section 14: "Heu, homini unde iste fastus, ista superbia? cuius erumpnosa natiuitas, cuius uitam laboriosa demolitur penalitas, cuius penalitatem penalior mortis concludit necessitas, cui esse momentum, uita naufragium, mundus exilium" (Alas! What is the basis for this haughtiness, this pride in man? His birth is attended by pain, the penalty of toil lays waste his life, the greater penalty of inevitable death rounds off his punishment. His existence is the matter of a moment, his life is a shipwreck, his world is a place of exile; 14.41–43).

42. Virgil, *Georgics: Virgil*, ed. and trans. H. Rushton Fairclough, rev. ed., 2 vols., Loeb Classical Library (Cambridge, Mass.: Harvard University Press, 1986) 1.125, 121–24, 145.

which to nullify the snares of the Fates and also make a variety of things ready for existence.]

The hammers, the *mallei*, represent the male sexual organs. Whether there are two because they represent the testicles or because, as Sheridan argues, they stand for the specifically human male as well as maleness in general is not crucial to my argument.[43] What is crucial is that the sexual organs are represented as *tools* for doing indispensable work. If the work is not done, the Fates conquer mankind (10.138–42).

Hammers need anvils to accomplish their productive work, and Nature supplied the other necessary tool as well:

Incudum etiam nobiles officinas eiusdem artificio deputaui precipiens, ut eisdem eosdem malleos adaptando rerum effigiationi fideliter indulgeret, ne ab incudibus malleos aliqua exorbitatione peregrinare permitteret. (10.27–30)

[I also set aside outstanding workshops with anvils in which to do this work, giving instructions that she (Venus) should apply these same hammers to these same anvils and faithfully devote herself to the production of things and not allow the hammers to stray away from their anvils in any form of deviation.]

To be productive, however, hammers must strike fitting *incudi* (anvils), which represent the female sexual organs.[44] The work of production is done in *nobilibus officinis* (noble workshops). In an earlier passage, this work is described as the minting of new coins, and Nature calls herself the *monetaria*, "mistress of the mint."[45] In this passage especially, love's labor is presented as a kind of mechanical art, the smith's art, which Hugh of St. Victor would have classified under *armatura*.[46]

Nature (and Alan's narrator) analyze the problem of homosexual sex-

---

43. Sheridan 155n.

44. Scanlon treats the hammer-and-anvil image in *De planctu* at length (227–30). He believes that Alan here retains some vestiges of classical Roman sexual morality, where sexual partners were categorized not according to their maleness or femaleness but rather by their activity or passivity. What is not classical in Alan's schema, he argues, is that the activity of the male is linked not only to his superior social position but also to his ability to reproduce. "In one respect," he writes, "this shift actually broadens access to the power of the phallus, which becomes a source of superiority common to all males irrespective of the particular class position" (229).

On the *incudus*, he writes: "The term literally means 'the struck against': thus, in this metaphor, the penis becomes that which strikes and any body part it contacts can be simply subsumed into the single category of that which is struck" (229).

45. 8.224–28. Alan's treatment of the personified Nature in both the *De planctu* and the *Anticlaudianus* has been called his most original contribution to poetry (de Lage 10).

46. Hugh's definition of the "mechanical arts" runs as follows: "mechanica est scientia ad quam fabricam omnium rerum concurrere dicunt" (mechanics is that science to which they declare the

uality by using the metaphor of sex as a mechanical art. The homosexual act is "unnatural" because it can never be productive. In a passage with mixed metaphors but whose meaning is fairly clear, the narrator says that the homosexual:

> Cudit in incude que semina nulla monetat.
> Horret et incudem malleus ipse suam.
> Nullam materiem matricis signat idea
> Sed magis in sterili litore uomer arat.
>
> (1.27–30)

[hammers on an anvil which issues no seeds. The very hammer itself shudders in horror of its anvil. He imprints on no matter the stamp of a parent-stem: rather his ploughshare scores a barren strand.]

The issue is the lack of material productivity, and Alan's treatment of it is similar to the Cistercian's attitude in Idung's *Dialogus*, where the Cistercian accuses the Carthusian of idle work (*ociosus* and *inutilis*) because the works of the Carthusian "are not directed toward necessary and useful purposes." In this passage, the homosexual's hammer strikes an anvil that has been converted from a hammer, which "semina nulla monetat" ("coins" no seed).[47] It is idle work because it cannot be materially productive. It is also a false "coining." The use of the medieval Latin verb *monetare* clearly sets this practice in opposition to that of Nature, who, as we just noted, identifies herself as a "monetaria."[48]

The second relevant, but less developed, metaphor found in Alan's discourse of love's labor is scribal writing. In this conceit, Nature compares the male sexual organ to a pen and the female sexual organs to a suitable page on which to write. Nature says:

---

manufacture of all articles to belong; *Didascalicon* 2.20). Hugh defines *armatura* as the general category containing all work related to fashioning things out of stone, wood, or metal. It is not restricted to armament making (*Didascalicon* 2.22).

There is only one passage in the *De planctu* that seems to call Alan's respect for the mechanical arts into question. In describing the effects of Venus's adultery with Antigenius, Nature says: "suique adulterii suggestionibus irretita letiferis liberale opus in mechanicum, regulare in anomalum, ciuile in rusticum inciuiliter immutauit" (Trapped by the deadly suggestions arising from her own adultery, she barbarously turned a noble work into a craft, a work governed by rule into something ruleless, a work of refinement into something boorish; 10.133–35). Thus, procreative sex becomes a "liberale opus" and homosexual union is a ruleless, mechanical art. Here we see Alan's preference for the liberal arts, but this passage contradicts the others in which the mechanical arts are presented as worthy imitations of divine creativity.

47. 8.79–80. Scanlon finds this to be Alan's most daring image (227).

48. "Monet/a," *Revised Medieval Latin Word-List*, 1965 ed. It is interesting that in the thirteenth century, the noun "moneta" became a medical term for a part of the womb.

Ad officium etiam scripture calamum prepotentem eidem fueram elargita, ut in competentibus cedulis eiusdem calami scripturam poscentibus quarum mee largitionis beneficio fuerat conpotita iuxta mee orthographie normulam rerum genera figuraret. (10.30–34)

[I had also bestowed on her (Venus) an unusually powerful writing-pen for her work so that she might trace the classes of things, according to the rules of my orthography, on suitable pages which called for writing by this same pen and which through my kind gift she had in her possession.]

The pen, of course, is a transparent phallic symbol, and the page, like the anvil, obviously represents the female sexual organs. By figuring reproductive sex as scribal writing, Alan reveals his own stand in one of the great ideological controversies of his age: whether manual labor could include such clerical activities as copying and illuminating manuscripts. While Alan agrees with Idung's position that real work must be materially productive, he disagrees with his argument that the clerical work of scribes is unproductive and idle. Nature's position is that scribal work need not be "ociosus" and "inutilis" if the proper writing surface is employed. It does become unproductive, however, if one writes on the wrong tablet, and so the work of the homosexual "scribe" can never be productive.

This conceit of love's labor as scribal writing is elaborated within a larger context in section 18 of the *De planctu*, when Genius, who represents the force of generation, arrives. While describing his appearance, the narrator explains that he spent his time in writing:

Ille uero calamum papiree fragilitatis germanum numquam a sue inscriptionis ministerio feriantem, manu gerebat in dextera: in sinistra uero morticini pellem nouacule demorsione pilorum cesarie denudatam, in qua stili obsequentis subsidio imagines rerum ab umbra picture ad ueritatem sue essentie transmigrantes, uita sui generis munerabat. Quibus delectionis morte sopitis, noue natiuitatis ortu alias reuocabat in uitam. (18.68–74).

[In his right hand he held a pen, close kin of the fragile papyrus, which never rested from its task of enfacement. In his left hand, he held the pelt of a dead animal, shorn clear of its fur of hair by the razor's bite. On this, with the help of the obedient pen, he endowed with the life of their species images of things that kept changing from the shadowy outline of a picture to the realism of their actual being. As these were laid to rest in the annihilation of death, he called others to life in a new birth and beginning.]

Here the natural cycle of life and death of all living things, not only humankind—life rising from dying material, only to die itself after giving birth to new life—is presented as the productive work of a monastic scribe, who writes living images onto the flesh of a dead animal, that is, parchment or vellum. This scribal work is productive as long as Genius continues to write with his right hand. His work becomes idle and perversely productive, however, only when the pen shifts to his left hand:

Post huius inscriptionis sollempnitatem dextere manui, continue depictionis defatigate laboribus, sinistra manus, tanquam sorori fesse subueniens, picturandi officium usurpabat, manu dextera pugillaris latione potita. (18.81–84).

[After this solemn process of enfacement, his left hand, as if it were helping a weary sister, came to the aid of his right which had grown tired from the toil of continuous painting and the left took over the work of portrayal while the right took possession of the tablets and held them.]

The results of this switching of hands are unnatural and monstrous creatures, perhaps the monsters or grotesque figures drawn in the margins of certain medieval manuscripts.[49] Although an authority figure of some weight, Genius, like Venus, can apparently produce corrupt work. While Alan does not develop this image at any length, it is clear that Genius's writing with the left hand is analogous to writing on the wrong kind of parchment. It is a labor that is not productive, and hence wrong.

I have already noted that, while the discourse of love's labor in both the *Ars amatoria* and the *De amore* concern both courtship and the sex act, the discourse of love's labor in *De planctu* focuses solely on the sex act. This, however, is only the beginning of the striking contrasts among the discourses of love's labor in the three works. Alan's discourse is so different from either of the two other texts that one is tempted to call it "anti-Ovidian." While it, like that of Andreas, contains particularly twelfth-century work ideologies, the labor ideologies of the two contemporaries could not be more distinct. In the *De amore*, we see the world of the aristocratic lords and ladies, who are well contented to perform *servitia, obsequia*, or *ministeria*, but who believe that manual labor is to be reserved for the unclean peasantry, who mate like animals. The peasants, they believe, should keep to the labor of farming and avoid the refined labor of love. Alan Frantzen may well have been thinking of the characters in the *De amore* when he wrote: "Slaves of love and servants of God were not, in

49. This idea was suggested to me by Winthrop Wetherbee in private correspondence.

most cases, also physical laborers. Labors of love, even Herculean labors, were different from the hard physical labor that was routine for most people in the Middle Ages."[50] Indeed, such an identification is the last thing that Andreas and his aristocrats would want. Matters are quite different in *De planctu naturae*, however. Alan's workers get their hands dirty. "In sudore," they coin new human beings in wondrous workshops or create new images with their pens and parchment in Nature's scriptoria.

They do not, however, till the fecund earth. One of the striking aspects of Alan's discourse is that he takes his images for love's labor from the workshop or the scriptorium, not from the farm. In contrast, the discourse of love's labor in Ovid is replete with farming images, and, indeed, we saw that the *Ars amatoria* was heavily influenced by the images of agricultural work found in the *Georgics*. The discourse of love's labor in *De planctu* is centered in the city. It is true that in a few introductory passages Alan toys with the agricultural metaphor. In the passage cited above, he compares homosexual intercourse to a plow scoring a barren land. In another passage, he compares the lips of maidens to fields that are not being harvested: "Virginis in labiis cur basia tanta quiescunt, / Cum reditus in eis sumere nemo uelit?" (Why do so many kisses lie fallow on maidens' lips while no one wishes to harvest a crop from them?; 1.43–44). Alan does not, however, develop these opening suggestions into what could have been a powerful image of worker productivity. Yet it is not too difficult to imagine how he could have done so, if he had wanted to. Nature could have returned to those maidens' lips; natural plows could have furrowed the earth, creating abundant harvests of new humans. Alan could have followed Ovid's lead, but he did not. Instead, the female body in *De planctu* becomes a workshop in which (re)productive work is carried out. One explanation for this difference, I suggest, is that while farm work was honored as an ideal labor in imperial Rome (at least in theory), the twelfth century was a period of increased interest in and respect for the mechanical arts. The *De planctu*, I would argue, reflects this difference. Alan was, after all, not trying to denigrate but to praise reproductive sex when he compared it to the work of smiths or scribes.

Another of the differences among the discourses of love's labor in Ovid, Andreas, and Alan is Alan's insistence on the ultimate seriousness

---

50. Alan J. Frantzen, "The Work of Work: Servitude, Slavery, and Labor in Medieval England," *The Work of Work: Servitude, Slavery, and Labor in Medieval England*, ed. Alan J. Frantzen and Douglas Moffat (Glasgow, U.K.: Cruithne Press, 1994) 2.

of love's labor. In the *Ars amatoria*, the teachings of the *praeceptor amoris* were ultimately revealed as a "lusus," a game. Ovid's discourse of love's labor in the *Ars amatoria* is self-consciously a veneer meant to repackage activities that moralists would have described as being the fruits of *otium otiosum*. Moreover, although Andreas never overtly characterizes his dialogs or the love judgments of his courtly ladies as "games," I have argued that his text is essentially ludic as well; it is certainly as self-contradictory as Ovid's text is. While the style of the *De planctu* may in fact be ludic, Alan's message is essentially moral and serious.[51] In Alan's discourse, reproduction is presented as a labor through which the human race is kept in existence. Activity that is not, or cannot be, productive is merely "sport," and as such is unnatural or monstrous. This position comes out overtly in Alan's personifications of the two sons of Venus.

Venus's son by her true husband, Hymenaeus, is Cupid, or Desire. When she rejects her lawful husband, however, Venus bears a son to her corrupt lover, Antigenius. That son, "Iocus," jest or sport, represents any nonproductive sexual activities, including but not limited to homosexual unions. Iocus is a contemptible figure in *De planctu*. While in Ovid playing the game of love's labor is presented as urbane and polished, Alan depicts Iocus as quite the contrary, a rustic boor. Comparing Cupid to Iocus, Nature states: "In illo paterne ciuilitatis elucescit urbanitas. In isto paterne suburbanitatis tenebrescit rusticitas" (In the former there shines the urbanity of his father's courteousness; the boorishness of his father's provincialism denigrates the latter; 10.156–57). In this passage and others, one sees the reason why the agricultural metaphor just would not work in the *De planctu;* it would have made reproductive sex too rustic. Thus, while Alan has the highest respect for the urban artisan, that respect did not extend to the "boorish" peasant, laboring in the fields.

About the only thing that the discourses of love's labor in Ovid, An-

51. Alan's style may not be as serious as his message. De Lage, for example, writes: "La métaphore est dans le *De planctu Naturae* d'une abondance incommensurable, quoique réglée; ingénieuse et quelquefois hermétique, elle n'est jamais échevelée, mais offre tant de fantaisie parfois qu'on se doute qu'elle n'est pas prise au sérieux par l'auteur qui la propose" (There is an immeasurable abundance of metaphor in *De planctu naturae*, although well regulated; ingenious and sometimes obscure, it is never extravagant, yet sometimes it is so fantastic that one wonders whether the author himself takes it seriously; 149–50).

Marc Pelen offers an ironic reading of *De planctu* in which Nature is an unreliable authority in comparison with Boethius's Lady Philosophy ("Boethian Themes in the Humor of the *De Planctu Naturae*," *Latin Poetic Irony in the "Roman de la Rose"* [Liverpool, U.K.: Francis Cairns, 1987] 75–106). Given the playfulness of Alan's rhetoric, this is a possibility. However, the whole work seems to make more coherent sense and it fits its genre better if Nature is a reliable authority figure.

dreas, and Alan have in common is at least a surface disdain for *otium*, and yet even in this they differ in the particulars. In the *Ars amatoria*, Ovid's disdain of *otium otiosum* is merely a pose, a way of ennobling his game by presenting the work of the lover as strenuous effort. It is only in the *Remedia amoris* that Ovid clearly rejects the play of love and recommends real work as an antidote to love: "Otia si tollas, periere Cupidinis arcus." Andreas does not concern himself much with *otium*, but when he does mention it, he aligns it with the self-serving leisure of the clergy and contrasts it specifically with the strenuous *labor* of knightly battle undertaken by the aristocrats. In this matter, Alan of Lille aligns himself with the Ovid of the *Remedia* but not for the purposes of renouncing love's labor. Indeed, for Nature, it is *otium*, a word that she aligns with boredom and the resulting unproductive activity, that corrupts Venus's work.

In section 10, Nature explains in detail that Venus was once a good worker, who, using her "tools . . . with labor and sweat," continued the reproduction of the human species and saved the species from extinction (10.115–18). The work becomes monotonous, however, and soon Venus became distracted from her important work (10.120–23). Instead of devoting herself to work, she gave herself to *otium:*

Illa igitur magis appetens ociis effeminari sterilibus quam fructuosis exerceri laboribus, serialis operationis exercitatione negociali postposita, nimie ociositatis eneruata desidiis cepit infantiliter iuuenari. (10.124–26)

[Accordingly, desiring to live the soft life of barren ease rather than be harassed by fruitful labor, disliking the strain of her task with its continuous work, enervated by thoughts of slothfulness and excessive ease, she began to wanton with childish indiscretion.]

Otium, for Nature, is essentially barren, while true labor alone is fruitful. Moreover, if *otium* does happen to produce progeny, the progeny is corrupt and monstrous—like Iocus or like the grotesque drawings of Genius's left hand.[52] Clearly *otium* is presented as the root cause of all the unnatural behaviors condemned in *De planctu naturae*. This point is reinforced by Nature, when she concludes section 10 by stating "Iam mea oratio cartule tue mentis inscripsit qualiter ocii dampnosa pernicies Venerem educauit emphaticam" (Now my speech has inscribed on the

52. "Et quoniam apud quem desidie torpor castrametatur, ab eo omnis uirtutis milicia relegatur ociique sterilitas praue sobolis solet fecunditate pregnari" (For, whenever sluggishness bivouacs with any man, all military valour is cashiered by him and a barren ease is wont to become pregnant and fecund with an evil progeny; 10.126–28).

tablet of your mind an account of how the ruinous destruction of idleness took hold of forceful Venus; 10.165–66). The implication is that, if Nature's writing is to be productive, the narrator (and reader) will avoid the dangers of *otium*.

The *otium* that Alan is condemning here is related to *otium otiosum*, also condemned (in a playfully subversive way) in the *Ars amatoria*. It is clearly not the productive *otium negotiosum* enjoyed by medieval clerics and monks, who fulfilled the duties of their offices, even though those duties may not have included manual labor. *Otium*, for Alan, was the opposite of working at one's *officium*, one's duty. In the three estates model, each estate had a specialized *officium* to fulfill. In *De plantu naturae*, the *officium* of mankind in general is to perform Venus's work, which is specifically presented as an *officium* in section 10. Earlier in the text, Nature had complained that while all creation fulfilled their divinely ordained *officia*, only man was perverse enough to reject nature's proper work and follow his own willful promptings (8.10–80). In section 10 we learn that man rejects his duty because of *otium*, which, as Alan defines it, is understood to be in the more general moral category of *acedia*, about which Alan composed a sermon.

In that sermon, entitled "Contra acediam," which may well have been addressed to a congregation of monks, humankind's assigned *officium* is achieving moral excellence, not reproduction. The sermon's argument, however, sounds very much like that in the *De planctu*. At one point Alan asks, in a passage appearing as this chapter's second epigraph, why man of all creatures deviates from the divine tasks assigned to him. The question is rhetorical, but the answer is clearly implied: idleness and *acedia* keep humans from fulfilling their duties. Rather than analyzing *acedia*, the sermon seeks to shame the congregation by citing the hard work, the "industria," of the lowly ant, "quae in aestate magna sollicitudine grana colligit quibus vivat cum hiemis austeritas ingruerit" (who gathers grain with great and anxious care during the summer, by which she would live when the austerity of winter will have descended). To those who heed the example of the strenuous labor of the ant, the sermon finally enjoins: "Surgite a terra in coelum, ab otio ad exercitium, a pernicioso torpore ad virtutis negotium, et occurrite ad judicium Salvatoris" (Rise up from the earth to the heavens, from sloth to exercise, from pernicious lethargy to the business of moral excellence, and hasten to the Lord's judgment).[53] In

---

53. "Contra acediam," *Summa de arte praedicatoria, Patrologiae cursus completus, sive bibliotheca universalis, Series Latina*, ed. J.-P. Migne (Paris, 1844–1864) 210.127.

the *De planctu*, a similar call, a call to rise up from the pernicious lethargy of "sport" and *otium* to the labor of reproduction, is expressed negatively by Genius's concluding ceremony of excommunication. Like Benedict, then, Alan enjoins productive work as a remedy against idleness, but his preoccupation with material productivity goes well beyond that found in Benedict's *Rule*. Alan's concern with productivity brings him much closer to that of his twelfth-century contemporary Idung. For Alan's Nature, just keeping busy to avoid sin is not enough. Like the ants, those who labor must produce something useful to the community, something to keep death at bay. Love's laborers have the most important labor of all, for they produce offspring to counteract the effects of death. For Alan, any other use of love's tools is worthless play.

CHAPTER 5

Repos Travaillant

The Discourse of Love's Labor in the *Roman de la rose*

> Yet marked I where the bolt of Cupid fell,
> It fell upon a little western flower—
> Before, milk-white; now purple with love's wound—
> And maidens call it love-in-idleness.
> —*Shakespeare's Oberon*

> 'Tis sweating labour / To bear such idleness.
> —*Shakespeare's Cleopatra*

I

The *Roman de la rose* is a comprehensive treatment of all aspects of love and includes a healthy dose of the discourse of love as passion. The discourse of love's labor, however, is at its very heart, for this long poem of nearly 22,000 lines presents the first and, to a much greater extent, the second labors of Ovid's *Ars amatoria* (finding and winning a lover) within a richly detailed allegorical dream narrative. In it, the Dreamer discovers where love is to be found, and once he arrives at the proper place, the Garden of Diversion, he is smitten by love of a young rose bud. Intent on capturing the rose, the Dreamer is thoroughly instructed by a host of *praeceptores amoris* on how to go about it. Weighing all advice, including that from Reason, who, like the *praeceptor* in Ovid's *Remedia amoris*, counsels him to reject erotic love, the Dreamer decides to pursue the work of love—courtship and, finally, procreative intercourse—with energy, strategy, and perseverance. The poem ends with his resounding success.

It is well known that the *Rose* was written by two different authors. Following the practice of Paul Zumthor, I will use *RI* and *RII* to refer to the

two parts.[1] Guillaume de Lorris, of whom we know almost nothing, began the poem in the early thirteenth century, probably between 1225 and
1230, but he never completed it, leaving a fragment of 4,028 lines. Forty
years after Guillaume's death, Jean de Meun took up his text, added the
remaining 17,722 lines, and brought the narrative to its literal and figura-
tive climax, in which the Dreamer captures the rose.[2] Félix Lecoy, a recent
editor of the work, believes that *RII* was composed sometime between
the years 1269 and 1278. Although we know that, besides composing *RII*,
Jean translated several Latin works, including *De re militari* of Vegetius,
the letters of Abelard and Heloise, and Boethius's *Consolation of Philosophy*, we do not know much about his education, his social situation, or his
métier.[3]

An immensely complex and popular poem, the *Roman de la rose* has
from at least the late fourteenth century, the time of the *Querelle de la
rose*, inspired controversy regarding its meaning, its levels of irony, its
artistic structure, and its unity (or lack of it). As Douglas Kelly writes,
"The *Roman de la rose* is still the once and future problem it has always
been in critical scholarship, a perpetual condundrum in the interpreta-

---

1. Paul Zumthor, "Narrative and Anti-Narrative: *Le Roman de la rose*," *Yale French Studies* 51
(1974): 185.

2. For a reading of *RI* as a complete work in itself, see David F. Hult, *Self-Fulfilling Prophecies:
Readership and Authority in the First "Roman de la Rose"* (Cambridge, U.K.: Cambridge University Press,
1986). Hult sees *RI* as a "prophetic prophecy of sexual fulfillment," which in itself is also an "instrument of seduction" (7–8).

For the argument that Guillaume de Lorris is a fictional creation of Jean de Meun, see Roger
Dragonetti, *Le mirage des sources: L'art du faux dans le roman médiéval* (Paris: Seuil, 1987) 200–225.
Sylvia Huot, however, writes that "the combined disciplines of textual and literary criticism allow us
to see that the two parts of the *Rose* do emanate from different authorial origins. And in the course
of their history, the poems of Guillaume and Jean passed through the hands of numerous scribes and
poets who produced the proliferating versions we know today" (*The "Romance of the Rose" and Its Medieval Readers: Interpretation, Reception, Manuscript Transmission* [Cambridge, U.K.: Cambridge University Press, 1993] 2).

3. Félix Lecoy, ed., introduction, *Le Roman de la rose*, 3 vols., Les Classiques français du moyen âge
(Paris: Honoré Champion, 1983) 1.v–x. Quotations from the *Rose* will be taken from this edition and
cited in the text by line number. The English translations will be taken from Charles Dahlberg,
trans., *The Romance of the rose* (Hanover, N.H.: University Press of New England, 1983).

On what is known of the lives of the two authors, see the remarks of Heather Arden, *"The Roman de la rose": An Annotated Bibliography* (New York: Garland, 1993) xiv–xvi. The critical passage in
which Jean's character, Love, comments on Guillaume de Lorris and notes that Jean will continue
Guillaume's poem forty years after the death of Guillaume occurs in lines 10496–650.

The question of the discourse of love's labor within the context of the full complexity of the
Rose's textual tradition, so thoroughly reviewed in Huot's *"The Romance of the rose" and Its Medieval
Readers*, is well beyond the scope of this study, which will concentrate on the discourse as it is found
in Lecoy's edition.

tion of medieval literature. . . . But some texts not only divide scholars, they invite divisiveness."[4]

Although some criticism, despite the dual authorship, defends the wholeness of the *Rose*, Zumthor notes that it is a commonplace to stress the differences between *RI* and *RII*.[5] As Sylvia Huot argues, much of the controversy is rooted in the *Rose*'s protean nature, its combination of widely divergent discourses—including erotic allegory, moral didacticism, political satire, and philosophical and theological discourse. She cogently argues that, because of its protean nature, the poem appealed to a wide range of audiences, reading for both pleasure and edification. The meaning of the poem thus depends "on the context in which it is read and the expectations with which it is approached."[6] Pierre-Yves Badel describes the discontinuous reading of the *Rose* during the fourteenth century and argues that readers were able to find support in it for whatever lessons on love they were looking for. My understanding of the *Rose*'s literary character, its polyphony of voices and meanings, is congruent with Huot's and Badel's. It is, therefore, not the purpose of this chapter to propose a grand theory of the meaning of the *Rose* or to reexamine all the key critical controversies. What I hope to demonstrate here is the significant presence of the discourse of love's labor in the *Rose* without claiming that this discourse exhausts the poem's entire meaning.

Alan M. F. Gunn has argued that the motif of work is one of the "three basic and interdependent motifs" of *RII*.[7] Indeed, *RII* contains more direct discussion of labor in general than any of the other amatory works discussed in this study. This chapter, then, will expand upon Gunn's insight regarding *RII* but go further to highlight the discourse of

4. Douglas Kelly, *Internal Difference and Meanings in the "Roman de la rose"* (Madison: University of Wisconsin Press, 1995) 3. Scholarship on the *Rose* is voluminous. Summaries of scholarship include Susan Ramsey, "État présent du *Roman de la rose*," *Chimères* 4 (Summer 1975): 14–28; and Arden xiv–xxv. Arden's bibliography of secondary criticism covers the years 1850 to 1992. Documents from the famous *querelle* are collected and edited in Eric Hicks, ed., *Le Débat sur le Roman de la rose*, Bibliothèque du XVᵉ siècle 43 (Paris: Honoré Champion, 1977).

5. Zumthor 185.

6. Huot 18–19. Compare with Pierre-Yves Badel's statement: "Car 'Art d'amours' ou 'Mirouer aus amoureus', le *Roman de la rose* est une autorité en matière amoureuse où chacun a puisé l'enseignement qui lui convenait" (Since "Art of Love" or "Lovers' Mirror," the *Romance of the rose* is an authority on love matters where each person could fetch the teaching that suited him; *Le Roman de la rose au XIVᵉ siècle* [Geneva: Droz, 1980] 143). Kelly, who argues that the poem imposes no single ethical view, agrees. The poem's meanings arise only in the responses of readers. Hence, the *Rose* acts as a mirror to its readers (10, 148).

7. Alan M. F. Gunn, *The Mirror of Love: A Reinterpretation of "The Romance of the Rose"* (Lubbock: Texas Tech Press, 1952) 271–72.

love's labor in *RI* as well. It will also demonstrate the significant differences in the lexicon and figures employed to construct those discourses in *RI* and *RII*. Steeped in the labor ideology of the medieval aristocracy, where *fin amors* is the exclusive domain of the landed and leisured aristocracy and noble *servise* is the model for all strenuous efforts on love's behalf, the discourse of love's labor in *RI* follows in a direct line from Ovid through Andreas's *De amore*. In contrast, the discourse of love's labor in *RII*, while also heavily influenced by Ovid's didactic works on love, is grounded not only in the ideology of (re)productive labor found in Alan of Lille's *De planctu naturae* but also in the midcentury controversies between the mendicants and their university critics over the universal obligation to perform manual labor. Key labor terms used in *RII* include the French nouns *euvre*, *labor*, and *travail*, as well as the French verbs *laborer* and *travailler*.

II

We begin, then, with a discussion of love's labor in *RI*. Like Ovid, Guillaume de Lorris identifies his work as a new art of love (38). Old French *art* typically referred to one of the seven liberal arts, but it also meant a *métier* or technique by which something is made via the application of rules.[8] The word recalls the Latin *ars* employed in both the *Ars amatoria* and the *De amore*. As we have seen, both authors style their didactic works as arts of love, that is, as works that set forth a systematic body of knowledge and practical techniques used in the performance of courtship.[9] Hence, love as a form of skilled labor lies at the center of Guillaume's conception of *RI*. Later in the work, however, Guillaume will boast that whoever reads the record of this dream will learn much

---

8. "Art," *Dictionnaire de l'ancienne langue française et de tous ses dialectes du IXe au XVe siècles*, 1895 ed. (Godefroy); "art" (1, 2), *Dictionnaire de l'ancien français*, 1968 ed. (Greimas).

9. On *RI* as an art of love, see Jean-Charles Payen, "L'art d'aimer chez Guillaume de Lorris," *Études sur Le Roman de la Rose de Guillaume de Lorris*, ed. Jean Durfournet (Geneva: Slatkine, 1984) 105–44. On the relationship of *RI* to Ovid's works, see Hult 134–35; H. Marshall Leicester, "Ovid Enclosed: Amors as *Magister Amoris* in the *Romance of the Rose* of Guillaume de Lorris," *Res Publica Litterarum* 2 (1984): 107–29; Marc M. Pelen, *Latin Poetic Irony in the "Roman de la Rose"* (Liverpool, U.K.: Francis Cairns, 1987); E. K. Rand, "The Metamorphosis of Ovid in *Le Roman de la Rose*," *Studies in the History of Culture*, ed. Percy Long (1942; Freeport, N.Y.: Books for Libraries, 1969) 103–21; and Eric M. Steinle, "Anti-Narcissus: Guillaume de Lorris as a Reader of Ovid," *Classical and Modern Literature* 6 (1986): 251–59.

On the relationship between the *De amore* and *RI*, see P. Demats, "D'Amoenitas à Deduit: André le Chapelain et Guillaume de Lorris," *Mélanges de langue et de littérature du Moyen Age et de la Renaissance, offerts à Jean Frappier*, 2 vols. (Geneva: Droz, 1970) 217–33.

about "des jeus d'Amors" (games of love; 2067). Like Ovid, then, Guillaume's conception of love's work includes a strong ludic element, where "work" is self-consciously fashioned from what others might consider idle activities. Unlike Ovid, however, Guillaume celebrates this paradox via the figure of Idleness, the gatekeeper of the garden.

At least one significant difference exists between *RI* and the amatory arts of both Ovid and Andreas Capellanus. Those earlier arts of love are clearly didactic works, long on precepts but short on story line. In contrast, the didactic lessons of *RI* are embedded in an allegorical dream narrative.[10] Here, instead of a single *praeceptor*'s voice, we hear the voices not only of multiple *praeceptores* but also of the Dreamer himself in pursuit of his beloved. The internal and external erotic experiences of both the lover and the loved one are dramatized by means of personifications.

It is certainly true that *RI* contains both the discourse of passion and the discourse of love's labor. In *RI* love is often portrayed as a disease or a kind of madness inflicted on unsuspecting lovers. Love is a "maladie mout cortoise," an aristocratic disease that both weeps and laughs (2167–76). Indeed, the God of Love describes the symptoms of this disease in full detail at another point (2253–520). In *RI*'s narrative, love's suffering is inflicted by an arrow wound from Love, which causes the Dreamer much pain (1679–1730). The personified Reason calls love a madness, a "folie" (3027), of which "La poine en est desmesuree, / et la joie a corte duree" (The pain of love is immeasurable and its joy of short duration; 3035–36). To leave this disease behind, says Reason, echoing the *praeceptor* of Ovid's *Remedia*, requires great skill (3045–46).

While love in *RI* is in one sense a disease inflicted on a passive victim, only members of the leisured classes are susceptible. In addition, once caught, love becomes, paradoxically, a labor and a quest, conducted under the rules of the art that *RI* proposes to teach. The Dreamer takes an active role in the pursuit of the loved one despite serious obstacles. The labor of *RI* is solely the labor of courtship, and it is presented primarily by means of the language of aristocratic and feudal *servise*.[11]

After shooting the Dreamer with his arrows, Love takes his man. The Dreamer is called "Vasaus," vassal, and becomes the servant of Love (1882–88). The Dreamer surrenders himself with courteous words, which move Love to take pity on him. Love says:

10. Zumthor sees an emphasis on narrative as a distinguishing characteristic of *RI* as opposed to *RII* (195).

11. For more on the knight's *officium* and his labor as a form of *servitium*, see Chapter 3 above.

Onques voir tex repons n'issi
D'ome vilain mal enseignié,
et si i as tant gaaignié
que je viel por ton avantage
que tu me faces tost homage.
Si me besseras en la bouche,
ou onques nus vilains ne touche.
Je n'i lesse mie touchier
chascun vilain, chascun porchier.

(1924–32)

[Such a reply truly never came from a lowborn fellow with poor training. More-over, you have won so much that, for your benefit, I want you to do homage to me from now on: You will kiss me on my mouth, which no base fellow touches. I do not allow any common man, any butcher, to touch it.]

The same class concerns that were so evident in the *De amore* are again present in *RI*. Three times Love denies that the Dreamer is a "vilain"; he is no butcher either. The work of *fin amors* in *RI* is not open to the de-spised working classes. Love's servants cannot be confused with servile workers. By means of actions modeled on the ceremony of feudal hom-age,[12] the Dreamer becomes the "man" of Love (1953–57). Although the duties of love are not servile, they are consistently presented as a form of noble *servise*.

Indeed, the noun *servise* and the verb *servir* are the key terms in the discourse of love's labor in *RI*.[13] While the Old French adjective *servile* and the noun *servitude* referred specifically to serfdom and slavery, the noun *servise*, like its medieval Latin analogue, carried more positive de-notations and connotations. Among them are service in general and "feudal service" in particular, including aid, support, and "service d'ost," "merit," and "likableness."[14] Much the same can be said of the adjective

12. For a description of this ceremony and its meaning, see Marc Bloch, "Vassal Homage," *Feudal Society*, trans. L. A. Manyon (Chicago: University of Chicago Press, 1961) 1.145–62.

13. The noun *servise* appears 15 times in *RI* (lines 661, 701, 1145, 1920, 2015, 2018, 2020, 2021, 2025, 2086, 2578, 2805, 2812, 3383, and 3707). Forms of the verb *servir* appear 12 times (lines 686, 693, 1029, 1844, 1942, 1951, 2039, 2116, 2130, 2405, 2823, and 2938).

14. "Servise" (1, 2, 3, 4), *Dictionnare de l'ancien français*. Godefroy has two entries, one for "servis" and another for "servise," both listed as masculine nouns. In Greimas, however, there is only a single entry, "servise," under which he gives definitions appropriate to both of Godefroy's entries. Similar-ly, in the concordance compiled by Joseph Danos (*A Concordance to the "Roman de la Rose" of Guil-laume de Lorris* [Chapel Hill: Department of Romance Languages, University of North Carolina, 1975]), there is only a single entry under "servise" (219). I will follow the practice of Greimas and

serviçable.[15] While the verb *servir* carried the negative denotation of being compelled by someone into servitude, it also carried a wide range of more positive meanings that touched the business of each social class. It, for example, could mean simply to be useful or to act, but it also could refer specifically to the work of the clergy, as in the phrase "servir à l'au-tel" (to serve at the altar). In addition, it denoted the work of the mer-chant since *servir* also signified the supplying of merchandise. Like the noun *servise*, however, it primarily referred to the fulfilling of the offices or duties of a vassal.[16] *Servise* in *RI* is like *servitium* in the *De amore*, an honorable activity, worthy of the aristocracy.

Love, for example, admits that serving him is difficult, but he adds that such service can only be accomplished by someone who is courteous and that it brings the servant great honor (1939–52). The Dreamer is fully in accord. In a key passage, he responds:

> Sire, . . . grant talant é
> de fere vostre volenté;
> mes *mon servise* recevez
> en gré, foi que vos me devez.
> Nou di pas par recreandise,
> que point ne dot *vostre servise*,
> mes sergenz en vain *se travaille*
> *de fere servise qui valle,*
> se *li servise* n'atalante
> au seignor cui l'en le presente.
> (2012–20; emphasis added)

[Sir, I have great capacity for doing what you wish. But, by the faith that you owe me, receive *my service* with thanks. I do not say so out of weakness, for I do not fear *your service* in any way, but because a sergeant *exerts himself* in vain *to perform worthy service* if it does not please the lord for whom he does it.]

Here Love's work is compared to the noble service of a knight. This *servise* is also, however, described using the reflexive verb *se travailler*. Al-though this verb did not denote manual work per se, it did denote the ex-pending of effort toward a goal,[17] which is the broader definition of

---

Danos. See also "servile" and "servitude," *Dictionnaire de l'ancienne langue française et de tous ses di-alectes du IXe au XVe siècles*.

   15. "Serviçable," *Dictionnaire de l'ancienne langue française et de tous ses dialectes du IXe au XVe siècles*.

   16. "Servir," *Dictionnaire de l'ancienne langue française et de tous ses dialectes du IXe au XVe siècles*; "servir" (1, 2, 3) *Dictionnaire de l'ancien français*.

   17. "Travaillier" (8), *Dictionnaire de l'ancien français*.

"work" I have chosen to use in this study. By employing this reflexive verb, Guillaume like Ovid emphasizes that knightly service (as well as love's labor) is work even though it is not the servile labor of the third estate.

After accepting the Dreamer as "his man," Love seeks to educate the Dreamer on the proper behavior of his vassals, and thus issues a set of commandments, or "work rules" as it were. Among the commandments of Love given by the god, for example, is the commandment to serve and labor for women. He commands: "Toutes fames *ser* et honore, / *en aus servir poine et labeure*" ([*Serve* and] honor all women and *exert yourself to serve them;* 2103–4; emphasis added). Other commandments are enumerated following this passage. Among the labors required by Love are dressing and acting elegantly, washing the body carefully, jumping, riding horses, playing viols and flutes, giving generously, avoiding the behaviors of the lower classes, and spending one's time thinking about a single loved one (2074a–252). These are clearly aristocratic pastimes, and Love is particularly careful to distinguish these activities from those of the peasants, who, paradoxically do not know true *servise*.[18] This is another attempt to distinguish the connotations of love's labor from the drudgery of peasants. The work here is clearly confined to aristocratic, leisure activities. No concern for productivity is shown in this work ethic, only a concern for self-cultivation. As in the third book of the *Ars amatoria*, it is not the soil but the self that is to be cultivated. Indeed, Love, while recounting the pains of love, goes so far as to affirm that the real métier of the aristocrat/lover is only to live well: "Et totes voies covient vivre / les amanz, qu'il lor est mestiers" (2594–95). While these lines could mean "In any case, it is fitting for lovers to live, for they *need* to live," Dahlberg's translation is particularly effective in underscoring the discourse of love's labor: "And in any case, lovers must live, for life is their occupation."[19] Thus, according to Love, the métier of an aristocrat is not to produce

---

18. In a key passage, Guillaume writes: "Vilenie premierement, / ce dist Amors, voel et conment / que tu gerpisses sanz reprendre, / se tu ne velz vers moi mesprendre. / Si maudi et escommenie / touz ceus qui aiment Vilenie. / Vilenie fait les vilains, / por ce n'est pas drois que je l'ains: / vilains est fel et sanz pitié, / sanz servise et sanz amitié" ("First of all," said Love, "I wish and command that, if you do not want to commit a wrong against me, you must abandon villainy forever. I curse and excommunicate all those who love villainy. Since villainy makes them base, it is not right that I love it. A villain is cruel and pitiless; he does not understand the idea of service or friendship"; 2074a–j).

19. Dahlberg 67. See "mestier" (1, 5), *Dictionnaire de l'ancien français*, defined as "besoin, nécessité," and "métier." See also "mestier," *Dictionnaire de l'ancienne langue française et de tous ses dialectes du IXe au XVe siècles.* A "bas mestier" meant "jeu d'amour," so there may be a subtle double meaning in these lines.

anything for the common good but merely to live well. In his view, *fin amors* is one of the central *officia* of this "good life."

Of course, Guillaume is not an innovator when he insists that *fin amors* is a job exclusively reserved for leisured aristocrats. As we have seen, Andreas Capellanus made a similar claim. However, unlike either Ovid or Andreas, who either ignored or condemned *otium otiosum* in their works while promoting its activities, Guillaume is more direct and honest with respect to the role of *otium otiosum* in the lives of aristocratic lovers: he openly embraces and even celebrates it. This is seen most clearly in the character of Idleness, the gatekeeper of the Garden of Love. Idleness is depicted as a beautiful young maiden, whose greatest effort for the day is to complete her own toilet (521–86). Beyond her beautiful looks, her most salient identifying characteristic is her complete freedom from productive activity of any kind. The Dreamer relates:

> Il paroit bien a son ator
> Qu'ele estoit poi enbesoignie.
> Quant ele s'estoit bien pigiie
> et bien paree et atornee,
> ele avoit feste sa jornee.
> Mout avoit bon tens et bon mai,
> Qu'el n'avoit sousi ne esmai
> de nule rien fors seulement
> de soi atorner noblement.
>
>   (564–72)

[It certainly seemed from her array that she was hardly busy. By the time that she had combed her hair carefully and prepared and adorned herself well, she had finished her day's work. She led a good and happy life, for she had no care nor trouble except only to turn herself out nobly.]

The Dreamer describes her as hardly *enbesoignie*, which, as Dahlberg's translation indicates, meant "occupied" or "busy."[20] However, since *enbesoignie* is ultimately derived from *besoing*, needs or necessity, it may have had stronger overtones than just "busy." Greimas defines *embesoignier* as "to be overloaded *with needs*" or "to be busy *with needs*."[21] Hence, the identifying characteristic of Idleness may not simply be that she is idle. Indeed, the Dreamer tells us that she was busy with activities related to

---

20. "Embesoignier," *Dictionnaire de l'ancienne langue française et de tous ses dialectes du IXe au XVe siècles.*

21. "Embesoignier," *Dictionnaire de l'ancien français.*

self-cultivation, which, after all, is an Ovidian labor for women. Rather, Idleness's distinguishing characteristic, which she shares with all courtly lovers, is that she is not busy providing for the needs of the community. Her activities do not produce food or shelter. She defends neither the Church nor the peasantry. Hence, even beyond leisure, nonproductivity is the hallmark of her character. This aspect of her character is under-scored again later in her description (569–72). The Dreamer states that Idleness has only "bon tens et bon mai," good times and pleasure.[22]

The Old French word *oiseuse* had a range of meanings including idle-ness, laziness, indolence, cowardice, baseness, uselessness, vain words, and futility.[23] Critical commentary has been divided as to whether Idle-ness should be interpreted as a neutral characteristic of the ruling classes (i.e., as leisure) or as a personal vice (i.e., unproductive laziness, idleness, narcissistic lethargy, or even lechery).[24] Sylvia Huot has argued that me-dieval readers of the *Rose* identified Idleness not only with the leisure time necessary for the pursuit of love but also with "the idleness of the mendicants and with the irresponsibility of those who fail to procre-ate."[25] We have seen that the Latin *otium* carried a range of both positive and negative connotations, and it seems reasonable to assume that Idle-ness carried both as well. Given her description, however, little in Idle-ness's character suggests *otium negotiosum, productive* leisure, such as that enjoyed by the monks.[26] On the contrary, Idleness at some level repre-

22. The word "mai" meant "green branches," "good times," "pleasure," or even "a party," but it also denoted, of course, the fifth month of the year, a month associated more with love and pleasure than with work ("Mai" [1, 3, 4], *Dictionnaire de l'ancien français*, and "mai," *Dictionnaire de l'ancienne langue française et de tous ses dialectes du IXe au XVe siècles*).

23. "Oiseuse," *Dictionnaire de l'ancienne langue française et de tous ses dialectes du IXe au XVe siècles*, defined as "oisiveté," "paresse," "lâcheté," "chose oiseuse," "inutile," "parole vaine," and "futilité."

24. The literature on Idleness is significant. See, for example, Carlos Alvar, "Oiseuse, Vénus, Lux-ure: Trois dames et un miroir," *Romania* 106 (1985): 108–17; John V. Fleming, "Further Reflections on Oiseuse's Mirror," *Zeitschrift für Romanische Philologie* 100 (1984): 26–40; Maria Powell Harley, "Narcis-sus, Hermaphroditus, and Attis: Ovidian Lovers at the Fontaine d'Amors in Guillaume de Lorris's *Roman de la rose*," *PMLA* 101 (1986): 324–37; E. Köhler, "Lea, Matelda und Oiseuse," *Zeitschrift für Ro-manische Philologie* 78 (1962): 464–69; H. Kolb, "Oiseuse, die Dame mit dem Spiegel," *Germanisch-Romanische Monatsschrift* 15 (1965): 139–49; Earl Jeffrey Richards, "Reflections on Oiseuse's Mirror: Iconographic Tradition, Luxuria and the *Roman de la Rose*," *Zeitschrift für Romanische Philologie* 98 (1982): 296–311, and "The Tradition of 'otium litteratum' and Oiseuse in *Le Roman de la rose*," *Studi francesi* 32 (1988): 271–73; Gregory M. Sadlek, "Interpreting Guillaume de Lorris' Oiseuse: Geoffrey Chaucer as Witness," *South Central Review* 10.1 (1993): 22–37; and Shigemi Sasaki, "Sur le personnage d'Oiseuse," *Études de langue et littérature* 32 (March 1978): 1–24.

25. Huot 323.

26. Jean Batany argues that Idleness represents the aristocratic claim to be a "leisured class," equivalent to the leisured monastic society. His argument is convincing to the extent that Diversion's garden is an enclosed world purposefully separated from the ordinary world of work ("Miniature,

sents *otium otiosum*, unproductive idleness. She is well connected (being a companion of Diversion), and she takes pride in her riches and her unproductive pursuit of "bon tens":

> Rice fame sui et poissanz,
> s'ai d'une chose mout bon tens
> que a nule rien je n'entens
> qu'a moi jouer et solacier
> et a moi pigner et trecier.
> Privee sui mout et acointe
> de Deduit le mignot, le cointe:
> ce est cil qui est cist jardins.
>
> (583–89)

[I am a rich and powerful lady, and I have a very good time, for I have no other purpose than to enjoy myself and make myself comfortable, to comb and braid my hair. I am the intimate acquaintance of Diversion, the elegant charmer who owns this garden.]

Besides specifying the activities undertaken to turn herself out, this passage advances our understanding of Idleness by underscoring her alliance with the character of Diversion, who, we are told, is matched with Joy (829–33). The formal description of Diversion does not go beyond the beauty of his body and the stylishness of his clothes (799–828), but the Dreamer also notes that he spends all his time directing the dancing of two young ladies (757–61). In addition, the reader is told that the *mestiers* of Joy is simply to sing (739–40).

Derived from the Old French verb *deduire* (to rejoice), *deduit* (diversion) signified "amusements," "amorous distractions," and "pleasure."[27] It must be noted that while amusements and the distractions of love are all activities, they are nonproductive activities, hence the fruits of *otium otiosum*. They are pastimes, activities undertaken to mask the passing of

---

allégorie, idéologie: 'Oiseuse' et la mystique monacale récupérée par la 'classe de loisir,'" *Études sur "Le Roman de la Rose" de Guillaume de Lorris*, ed. Jean Dufornet [Paris: Honoré Champion, 1984] 7–36). In addition, one could argue that aristocratic self-cultivation is in some senses parallel to monastic self-cultivation. The parallel cannot be taken too far, however. Monks, after all, were enjoined to work with their hands as well as to pray and meditate. In addition, there was a strongly communal orientation to monastic self-cultivation that is lacking in Idleness. Monastic *otium* was to be used for spiritual productivity, which benefitted the entire Church, and was definitely not meant to be the equivalent of *otium otiosum*.

27. "Deduit" (1, 2, 3), *Dictionnaire de l'ancien français*; "deduit" and "deduire," *Dictionnaire de l'ancienne langue française et de tous ses dialectes du IXᵉ au XVᵉ siècles*.

time. Jacqueline Cerquiglini notes that the word *passetemps* (pastime) did not enter the French lexicon until the fifteenth century, when she believes poets had a more keen sense of being owners of their own time. A "pastime" was meant to be an "activité douce," used to combat idleness and melancholy in place of real work.[28] Because he wrote in the thirteenth century, Guillaume could not specifically identify the activities of Diversion and his companions as "passetemps." However, their activities are surely consistent with Cerquiglini's definition.[29] The inhabitants of Diversion's garden must above all forget the power of time, noted in detail in the description of Old Age on the outside of the wall (361–92). Time, the reader is told, destroys or changes everything. It ages even kings and emperors, it brings senility, and it eventually brings death. But "bad time" is banished from Diversion's garden, locked securely outside with Old Age and Poverty. Only "bon tens" is allowed. Such, at least, is the illusion.

Although the labors described in the *Ars amatoria* are not socially productive, Ovid is not comfortable in highlighting the fact. On the contrary, as we have seen, he takes pains to disguise this reality by stressing the difficult nature of love's work and comparing it to the labors of farmers and soldiers. When Andreas Capellanus speaks of *otium*, he uses the word only to denounce the luxury and gluttony of clerics, not that of the aristocrats. From this perspective, then, Guillaume's treatment of the labor of courtship is indeed new in its honesty and directness regarding the nonproductivity of aristocratic labors of love (39). He squarely faces the paradox embedded within the Ovidian strain of the discourse of love's labor, which was only heightened by the class consciousness of the High Middle Ages. The courtship activities of the aristocracy are essentially the fruits of *otium otiosum* even though they can be represented as work. In this sense, they are well represented by the oxymoron, first suggested by Alan of Lille but then translated by Jean de Meun, of love as "repos travaillant," idleness working, which I took as the title of this study.[30] By means of Idleness, Guillaume puts the emphasis squarely on "repos,"

28. Jacqueline Cerquiglini, "Actendez, actendez," *Le nombre du temps: En hommage à Paul Zumthor* (Paris: Honoré Champion, 1988) 40–42. "Passetemps," *Dictionnaire de l'ancienne langue française et de tous ses dialectes du IXe au XVe siècles*, defined as "occupation légère et agréable" (a light and agreeable occupation).

29. Sarah Kay writes that Diversion's garden "is reserved for those whose conspicuous consumption of time denies them any occupation other than joining the dance of pleasure" (*The Romance of the Rose*, Critical Guide to French Texts [London: Grant & Cutler, 1995] 39).

30. Alan's phrase is "egra quies" (tiring rest). See Nickolaus Häring, "Alain of Lille, 'De Planctu Naturae,'" *Studi Medievali*, 3rd ser., 19.2 [1978]: 842. Love as "repos travaillant" occurs in *RII* 4296.

whereas Jean de Meun, as we shall see, shifts the emphasis to "travail-lant." Karl August Ott argues that this idealization of Idleness and her company, along with Guillaume's close attention paid to how much this life costs, is an indication that *RI* is a description of the aristocracy written by a member of the bourgeoisie, someone who would desperately like to be within the garden but who can only gaze at it from outside the walls.[31]

If this is true, Guillaume did not completely forget the work ideology of his own bourgeois origins, and, like Ovid, he was keenly aware of the nonaristocratic and moralistic voices that would condemn such a cele-bration of idleness. His character Reason strongly condemns Idleness and her company:

> Biaus amis, folie et enfance
> t'ont mis em poine et en esmoi.
> Mar veïs le bel tens de moi
> qui fist ton cuer trop agueer;
> mar t'alas onques ombreer
> ou vergier dont Oiseuse porte
> la clef, dont el t'ovri la porte.
> Fox est qui s'acointe d'Oiseuse;
> S'acointance est trop perilleuse.
> El t'a traï et deceü;
> Amors ne t'eüst ja veü
> S'Oiseuse ne t'eüst conduit
> ou biau vergier qui est Deduit.
>
> (2982–94)

[Fair friend, folly and childishness have brought you this suffering and dismay. It was an evil hour when you saw the beauty of May that gladdened your heart so much. It was an evil hour when you went to shelter in the cool shade of the gar-den where Idleness carries the key with which she opened the gate for you. He who acquaints himself with Idleness is a fool; acquaintance with her is very dan-gerous, for she has betrayed and deceived you. Love would never have seen you if Idleness had not led you into the fair garden of Diversion.]

Here, Reason double-voices the discourse of Idleness to her own ends. She condemns the life of unproductive activities. Idleness's "bon tens et

31. Karl Ott, "Pauvreté et richesse chez Guillaume de Lorris," *Romanistische Zeitschrift für Liter-aturgeschichte, Cahiers d'histoire des littératures romanes* 2 (1978): 236.

bon mai" are here described as dangerous because they gladden one's heart too much. They lead to the "folie" not only of *fin amors* but also of wasting one's time with unproductive diversions. Reason is not only the voice of the bourgeoisie but also of the *praeceptor* of the *Remedia amoris*. Like Ovid's *praeceptor*, she says it will take great skill to free oneself from love (3043–46). Guillaume reproduces these voices, however, only to allow the Dreamer to reject them in their own terms. It is Reason who is "idle," says the Dreamer. "Vos poriez bien gaster / en oiseuse vostre françois" (You could waste your French in idleness; 3072–73), for her words will not produce the desired effect.

Rejecting Reason, the Dreamer then goes off to seek out Friend, who can also teach him about the process of love. One of the innovations of Guillaume's poem is that he weaves sections corresponding to both the *Ars amatoria* and the *Remedia* together into a single narrative. While Reason corresponds to the voice of the *praeceptor* in the *Remedia*, Friend corresponds to the voice of Ovid's *praeceptor* in the *Ars amatoria*. Like the latter, for example, Friend brings crafty strategy to the pursuit of the beloved, which he characterizes as "vostre afere," your work, your business, or even your love affair.[32] Indeed, one of Friend's most important lessons is that patient and persevering work will be repaid (e.g., 3197–3200). When the Dreamer too quickly wishes to ask for a kiss, for example, Friend reminds him that one cannot cut down a tree with one stroke nor produce wine without struggling with a wine press. In the same way, one cannot succeed in love without patience and perseverance (3394–99). As we have seen, the *Ars amatoria* is heavily indebted to Virgil's *Georgics* in that Ovid compares love's labors to various kinds of agricultural labor, but the agricultural labor metaphor was largely ignored by Andreas Capellanus. Guillaume returns to this Ovidian tradition when he compares the patience and perseverance needed in courtship with those needed by woodcutters and wine makers.

He takes up this motif yet again to help express the Dreamer's frustrations when facing a severe setback to his love suit. When things do not work out, the Dreamer compares himself to a peasant, who sows good seed but then finds his crops ruined by the weather:

32. 3191–200. "Afaire," *Dictionnaire de l'ancienne langue française et de tous ses dialectes du IXe au XVe siècles*, defined as "ce qu'on a à faire d'une manière générale, travail, occupation, soin, devoir, fonction, transaction, marché, contestation, besoin, manière d'être," "relation sexuelle," or "besoins naturels."

Je resemble le païsant
qui giete a terre sa semance
et a joie grant ou comance
a estre bele et drue en herbe;
mes avant qu'il en cueille gerbe,
l'empire, tel eure est, et grieve
une male nue qui lieve
quant li espi doivent florir,
si fet le grain dedenz morir
et l'esperance au vilain tost,
qu'il avoit eüe trop tost.
Je criens ausi avoir perdue
et m'esperance et m'atendue.

(3932–44)

[I was like the peasant who casts his seed on the earth and rejoices when it begins to be fair and thick when it is in the blade; but before he collects a sheaf of it, the weather worsens and an evil cloud arises at the time when the ears should sprout and damages it by making the seed die within and robs the wretch of the hope that he had had too soon. I too fear that I had lost my hope and my expectation.]

The Dreamer here is frustrated by his own lack of productivity, but productivity in *RI* (as in the *Ars amatoria* and the *De amore*) is always success in courtship, never physical reproduction. Indeed, in some ways this is a curious passage in a poem that in general condemns the *vilains* and aligns itself with the aristocratic ideology of leisure. Love's labor in *RI* is consistantly feudal *servise*, not agricultural *travail*. One possible explanation is that this passage reflects the strong influence of the *Ars amatoria*, particularly the passage on the proper seasons for various projects in farming and in love.[33] The passage clearly indicates Friend's conviction that courtship is a long and risky labor in which the best work sometimes comes to naught.

The discourse of love's labor is clearly central to *RI*. For Guillaume, once the lover becomes smitten, love becomes a project for skilled workers, which can best be taught by means of an "art." The work ideology of *RI* is generally but not exclusively aligned with that in the *De amore*.

---

33. Ovid, *"Amores," "Medicamina Faciei Feminaeae," "Ars Amatoria," "Remedia Amoris,"* ed. J. E. Kenney (Oxford, U.K.: Clarendon Press, 1961) *Aa* 1.399–404. All quotations and citations of the *Ars* will be from this edition.

Love's labor in *RI* is expressed using the discourse of feudal *servise*. Like Andreas, Guillaume insists upon the social class requirements for this kind of *servise*. Unlike Andreas, however, Guillaume, using the figure of Idleness, underscores the paradox that this kind of *servise* is constructed from activities that are not socially productive and is made possible only by the precondition that the "worker" enjoys the privilege of aristocratic *otium otiosum*.

III

Jean-Charles Payen has argued that the *Roman de la rose* is a "carrefour idéologique," an ideological crossroads.[34] The *Rose*, argues Payen, is constructed using a certain number of ideological *ensembles*, and the *Rose* poets, particularly Jean de Meun, constructed a grand synthesis of the competing ideologies of various social classes in thirteenth-century France, the aristocrats, the clergy, and the bourgeoisie. In *RII* Payen sees a response to Guillaume de Lorris's aristocratic ideology by an ideological *ensemble* taken from the working bourgeoisie and Jean's clerical and university milieus.[35] Writing in response to this courtly ideology, *RII* accomplishes what Payen calls the "embourgeoisement de l'eros," among the elements of which is a strong respect for manual labor and a distrust of *otium*.[36] While I hope to demonstrate the truth of Payen's remarks, I will also show how the discourse on labor in general but also love's labor in *RII* was significantly borrowed from two clerics: Alan of Lille and Guillaume de Saint-Amour. That Jean de Meun owed a great debt to both writers is a commonplace in *Rose* criticism. What I hope to demonstrate is how the labor discourses of these two clerics came together in *RII* to produce a strong, coherent work ideology.

Indeed, with respect to the labor ideologies inherent in their discourses, passing from *RI* to *RII* is somewhat like turning from the pages of the

34. Jean Charles Payen, *"Le Roman de la rose* et la notion de carrefour idéologique," *Romanistische Zeitschrift für Literaturgeschichte* 1 (1977): 193.

35. Payen writes: "Jean de Meun exprime non pas une idéologie cléricale et bourgeoise, mais une *Weltanschauung* ou conception de la vie inspirée d'éléments idéologiques divers, qui tiennent à sa double appartenance au milieu universitaire et au milieu urbain" (Jean de Meun expresses neither a clerical nor a bourgeois ideology, but a world outlook or conception of life inspired by diverse ideological elements, due to his relation to both the university and urban environments; "Eléments idéologiques et revendications dans *Le Roman de la rose," Littérature et société au moyen âge*, Actes du Colloque des 5 et 6 mai d'Amiens 1978, ed. Danielle Buschinger [Amiens: Université de Picardie, 1979] 293).

36. Payen, "Carrefour idéologique" 195, 197. Jean Alter finds little antibourgeois satire in the *Rose* (*Les origines de la satire anti-bourgeoise en France: Moyen âge–XVI* siècle [Geneva: Droz, 1966] 148).

De amore to the *De planctu naturae*.[37] Whereas the "labor" in *RI* is confined solely to courtship and is modeled on the *servise* of a feudal vassal to his lord, the labor discourse in *RII* is largely *manual* work and is focused upon the material productivity necessary for the survival of the community. Rather than courtly *servise*, it characteristically depicts love in terms of manual *euvre*, *labeur*, and *travail*.

RII, however, is far more inclusive than *De planctu* in at least two ways. First, in the discourse of the Old Woman, Jean examines the question of the *monetary* value of labor, for economic exchange, money or gifts for sex, plays a key role in her lesson. Second, Jean figures love's labor by a wider range of strenuous activities than Alan does. While love is, at some times, the labor of blacksmiths and scribes, at others, it is also knightly *servise* and agricultural work.[38]

RII contains a polyphony of voices, no one of which can be identified with the authoritative voice of the author. Scholarship has long recognized that not all of the speakers in *RII* are trustworthy. Often scholars have imposed a unity of meaning on the text by not only accepting just one voice, such as that of Reason or Nature, as the voice of authority, but also rejecting the advice of all the others as ironic. However, others have come to argue that *all* the voices in the *RII* are untrustworthy to some extent.[39] With respect to the overall phenomenon of love, *RII* certainly produces a wide range of competing opinions, no one of which, finally, is given controlling authority. With respect to love, *RII* is disturbingly unruly and polyphonic. This is less true, however, with respect to labor ideology. While *RII* is not purely monologic regarding labor, the cumulative

37. That Jean de Meun is heavily indebted to the *De planctu* is a critical commonplace. See especially Winthrop Wetherbee, "The Literal and the Allegorical: Jean de Meun and the *De Planctu naturae*," *Medieval Studies* 33 (1971): 264–91.

38. Although the *labor* discourse in *RII* diverges from that in *De amore*, Peter Allen argues that *RII* has many features in common with Andreas's work: "[B]oth transpose the *Ars* and *Remedia* into a context of medieval literary forms, both are concerned with fantasy, and both address the conflict between secular, sexual, non-marital love and Christian morality and philosophy." Allen also notes that Jean de Meun is one of the few French writers who ever cite Andreas ("Through the Looking Glass: Jean de Meun's *Mirror for Lovers*," *The Art of Love: Amatory Fiction from Ovid to the "Romance of the Rose"* [Philadelphia: University of Pennsylvania Press, 1992] 79).

39. In general Robertsonian critics, especially John Fleming, find Reason to be the authoritative voice in the *Rose* (*Reason and the Lover* [Princeton, N.J.: Princeton University Press, 1984] 64). Zumthor sees Nature as the most authoritative voice (190). False Seeming has also come to the fore (Susan Stakel, *False Roses: Structures of Duality and Deceit in Jean de Meun's "Roman de la Rose"* [Saratoga, Calif.: ANMA Libri, 1991] 46–60). Allen writes that readers must interpret "the discourses of Jean's many speakers with insight and caution," and be willing to trust only themselves and to refute authority (83). Pelen, as well, argues that no particular character in the *Rose*, not even Reason or Nature, is to be trusted (157–66).

effect of the majority of the voices in *RII* produces an encomium to materially productive labor, whether it be the labor of the fields and workshop or the labor of the bedroom.[40] Payen, for example, takes the emphasis on productivity as a key aspect of Jean's "embourgeoisement de
l'eros."[41] Indeed, the defense of labor and the condemnation of those
aristocratic and clerical drones who refuse it is a motif that runs consistently through the often self-contradictory heteroglossia of *RII*.

Some of the voices in *RII* focus on the labor of courtship. Jean's
Friend, like Guillaume's character of the same name, playfully and subversively represents the activities of courtship as work, taking his cue directly from Books 1 and 2 of the *Ars amatoria*. For the Old Woman,
courtship is primarily a path to financial gain. Other voices, however, focus on the (re)productive aspects of love's labor. In the monologues of
Reason, Nature, and Genius, love's labor is not play but a duty, an *officium*. From the perspective of these last three characters, *RII* is not a continuation but a reversal of the labor ideology of *RI*. In certain respects,
RII is Jean's *Remedia amoris* vis-à-vis Guillaume's *Ars amatoria*, but it is a
Remedia in a different key. The remedy for *fin amors* is not to flee from
love but, à la Alan of Lille, to redirect one's efforts away from sterile
games and toward materially productive labor.

Unlike his predecessors, Jean de Meun incorporates a work ideology
both within the discourse of love's labor and within other sections devoted to labor issues in general. The work ideology found in both kinds of
text was influenced not only by Alan of Lille and Ovid, but also by general labor discourse generated within a powerful ideological dispute at the
University of Paris that occurred about fifteen to twenty-five years before
the composition of *RII*.

IV

The thirteenth century saw the birth of the mendicant orders, the Do-
minicans and the Franciscans, who, following Jesus' example literally, renounced all property and dedicated themselves to wandering throughout
the world preaching the gospel to the downtrodden, especially those in
the cities and towns.[42] The friars and their evangelical poverty were part

---

40. On the "modern" conception of labor and exchange in *RII*, see Payen, "Carrefour
idéologique" 194.

41. Payen calls Jean de Meun the "poète de ce productivisme" (poet of this productivity; "Carrefour idéologique" 197).

42. On the friars, see Rosalind Brooke, *The Coming of the Friars* (Oxford, U.K.: Allen & Unwin,

of a larger societal response to the growing dominance of the money economy in the High Middle Ages. Lester Little has shown that the growth in the use of money was tied with the growth of cities and was met, at least initially, with suspicion and resistance. In addition, during this epoch, avarice, the love of money, came to take the place of pride as the chief of the Seven Deadly Sins.[43] St. Francis of Assisi, for example, would have nothing to do with money. Although his followers were allowed to work and accept a material recompense for their work, their *Rule* forbid them ever to accept money.[44] Coins were to be treated like stones.

Indeed, Francis did not condemn manual labor—far from it. In both versions of his *Rule*, Francis wrote that those brothers who could work should work. In the first, the *Regula non bullata*, for example, Francis devotes all of chapter 7 to the manner in which the friars should work. He wrote:

Et fratres, qui *sciunt laborare, laborent* et *eandem artem exerceant*, quam noverint, si non fuerit contra salutatem animae et honeste poterit operari. (134; emphasis added)

[And let the friars who *know how to work, work*, and *exercise the same craft that they learned*, if it is not detrimental to the health of their soul and it can be engaged in honestly.]

Francis's position is clear: work, and indeed skilled work, should be part of the lives of the brothers. He then goes on to cite the usual scriptural passages in support of this position. When he preaches that the main value of work is that it keeps friars from idleness, Francis sounds much like earlier Christian writers (136).

However, the spirit of Francis's attitude toward manual labor is not as consistent as Benedict's. First of all, despite what he wrote in chapter 7 of

---

1975); William A. Hinnebusch, *The History of the Dominican Order* (Staten Island, N.Y.: Alba House, 1966); and John Moorman, *A History of the Franciscan Order: From Its Origins to the Year 1517* (Oxford, U.K.: Clarendon Press, 1968).

43. Two works by Lester Little are especially useful in charting the social and ethical consequences of urbanization and the coming of the profit economy: "Pride Goes before Avarice: Social Change and the Vices in Latin Christendom," *American Historical Review* 76 (1971): 16–49, and *Religious Poverty and the Profit Economy in Medieval Europe* (Ithaca, N.Y.: Cornell University Press, 1978). On the initial mistrust of money, see *Religious Poverty* 33–34. See also Jean Batany, *Approches du "Roman de la Rose"* (Paris: Bordas, 1973) 81–95.

44. Francis of Assisi, *Écrits*, ed. Kajetan Esser et al., Sources Chrétiennes (Paris: Editions du Cerf, 1981) 138. Quotations from Francis's writings will be taken from this edition and cited by page number in the text. English translations are my own.

the *Regula non bullata*, manual labor is not a sine qua non of Franciscan living. That is to say that the role of the friar minor was not founded in his commitment to manual labor. The core values for Francis were, rather, evangelical poverty and the itinerant life of preaching and service to the poor.[45] Second, far from advocating a communal self-sufficiency, Francis encouraged his friars to beg without shame. Alms are the inheritance of the poor, he writes:

Et eleemosyna est hereditas et iustitia, quae debetur pauperibus, quam nobis acquisivit Dominus noster Jesus Christus. Et fratres, qui eam acquirendo laborant, magnam mercedem habebunt et faciunt lucrari et acquirere tribuentes. (140)

[And alms are an inheritance and a right of the poor, which our Lord Jesus Christ acquired for us. The friars who labor begging alms will have a great reward, and cause the givers to be enriched and to acquire a reward.]

Upon reading the *Rule*, one is tempted to say that Francis's commitment to manual labor was perfunctory, that his real interest lay in preaching and what he understood to be evangelical poverty.

When it came time to write his *Testament*, however, Francis sharply refocused on the necessity of work for friars:

Et ego manibus meis laborabam, et volo laborare; et omnes alii fratres firmiter volo, quod laborent de laboritio, quod pertinet ad honestatem. Qui nesciunt, discant, non propter cupiditatem recipiendi pretium laboris, sed propter exemplum et ad repellendam otiositatem. (206)

[And I worked with my hands and I wish to work still; and I firmly want all the other brothers to labor in some kind of honorable toil. Let those learn who do not know how to work, not out of desire to receive labor's rewards, but to give good example and to avoid idleness.]

While Francis's ideas basically did not change, the tone of this passage is much more emphatic. Perhaps in response to charges of laziness in the Order, Francis here underscores the necessity of work, and he goes so far as to say that even those who do not know how to work must learn. They learned to work, writes Francis, not because of the rewards of hard

45. The first sentence of the first chapter of the *Regula non bullata* opens as follows: "Regula et vita istorum fratrum haec est, scilicet vivere in obedientia, in castitate et sine proprio, et Domini nostri Jesu Christi doctrinam et vestigia sequi, qui dicit, 'Si vis perfectus esse, vade et vende omnia quae habes, et da pauperibus et habebis thesaurum in caelo'" (The rule and life of these brothers is this: to live in obedience, in chastity and without property, and to follow the teachings and the footsteps of our Lord Jesus Christ who says, "If you will be perfect, go, sell what you have, and give it to the poor, and you will have treasure in heaven"; 122).

labor, but to combat idleness. It is only after this emphatic embracing of work that he mentions that friars may also "return to the table of the Lord," that is, to begging.

The labor ideologies of the mendicants were put to the test in Paris of the mid-1250s, when a significant controversy arose between the secular masters of the University of Paris and the upstart mendicants, who now had begun to work as rival university professors. The controversy was rooted in the question of the rights of the mendicants to perform this work.[46] The secular masters feared losing student fees to the mendicant masters and were scandalized by the willingness of the friars to flout the control of the local university authorities.[47] The dispute quickly degenerated, however, into an attack on the very nature of the mendicant orders themselves and whether they were good sons of the Church or, indeed, the incarnations of the Antichrist, harbingers of the end of the world.[48]

The leader of the secular masters was an outspoken scholar named Guillaume de Saint-Amour. It has long been recognized that Jean de Meun's portrait of False Seeming was heavily influenced by the writings of Guillaume, particularly his controversial treatise *De periculis novissimorum temporum (Concerning the Dangers of Present Times)*, which is one of the most important texts in the European tradition of antifraternal literature.[49] Lecoy has identified twenty-five passages in Faux Semblant's monologue that were either borrowed from or heavily influenced by parallel passages in the *De periculis*.[50]

---

46. Accounts of the dispute can be found in Hastings Radshall, *The Universities of Europe in the Middle Ages*, ed. F. M. Powicke and A. B. Emden, new ed. (Oxford, U.K.: Oxford University Press, 1936) 1.370–97; Moorman 123–31; and Penn R. Szittya, *The Antifraternal Tradition in Medieval Literature* (Princeton, N.J.: Princeton University Press, 1986) 11–17. The most complete account, however, is found in M.-M. Dufeil, *Guillaume de Saint-Amour et la polémique universitaire parisienne, 1250–1259* (Paris: J. Picard, 1972). For a fuller bibliography of scholarship on the quarrel, see Szittya 12, note 3.

47. Szittya 12–14.

48. The connection of the advent of the friars with apocalypse was first made not by the university masters but by a friar, Gerard of Borgo San Donnino, in the heretical *Introduction to the Eternal Gospel*. Gerard's positive assessment of what that meant was turned on its head by the university masters' identification of the friars as agents of the Antichrist. See Szittya 15–16 and Dufeil 118–31.

49. Szittya 17.

50. Batany 16. Also see Lecoy 2.282ff.

On the relationship between *RII* and the *De periculis*, see Szittya 184–90; and Daniel Poirion, "Jean de Meun et la querelle de l'université de Paris: Du libelle au livre," *Traditions polémiques*, Cahiers V. L. Saulnier (Paris: Centre V. L. Saulnier, Université de Paris-Sorbonne, 1984) 9–19.

Although it is clear from the treatise that the friars are Guillaume's target, Guillaume denies that the treatise was written against any particular group of people: "Protestamur autem ab initio, quòd omnia quae hic dicuntur ad cautelam & instructionem Ecclesiae universae, non circa personam aliquam, nec circa statum aliquem per Ecclesiam approbatum, sed circa peccata malorum, & pericula

One particular issue in this controversy is crucial to the ideological coloring of Jean's labor discourse, and in particular to his characterization of False Seeming.[51] The issue was the legitimacy of the mendicants' labor and their right to beg. Guillaume argued that the friars were false prophets, had no right to take alms for "spiritual work" such as preaching, and hence were required to perform manual labor. In the course of debating this issue, the nature of manual work and the proper *officium* of the friars came under close scrutiny by some of the greatest minds of the age. A quick review of Guillaume's position in *De periculis* and the responses of Bonaventure and Thomas Aquinas sets an important ideological context for labor and love's labor in *RII*.

For the purposes of this discussion, the key section of the *De periculis* is chapter 12. The general argument of the chapter, like that of the whole treatise, is ostensibly directed against the false prophets predicted for the last ages, but it is clear that Guillaume's friar contemporaries are his specific target. Guillaume accuses the friars of being lazy and robbing the poor via illicit begging. It is a learned but ultimately inconsistent argument based on quotations from the Scriptures and scriptural glosses. As M.-M. Dufeil wryly notes, "Le *De Periculis* dénonce, il ne prouve pas" (The *De periculis* denounces; it does not prove).[52]

Much like the problem treated by St. Augustine in *De opere monachorum*, the argument of chapter 12 circles around the question of licit versus illicit begging and the scriptural command to work.[53] Guillaume's premises are not controversial: all Christians have the obligation to work, but begging is sometimes permitted on a temporary basis to those who are infirm or do not have a trade to practice. Friars who are strong and

---

Ecclesiae universalis dicturi sumus: quae non ex inventione nostra, sed ex veritate Sacrae Scripturae collegimus" (From the start we publicly declare, however, that all which is said here provisionally and for the instruction of the whole Church, shall be said not against any person, or against any state approved by the Church, but against sins of the evil ones and the danger to the universal Church: which we collected not from our own imagination but from the truth of Sacred Scripture; "De Periculis Ecclesiae," *Fasciculum Rerum Expetendarum et Fugiendarum*, ed. Edward Brown [1690; Tucson, Ariz.: Audax Press, 1967] 2.19). All quotations from the *De periculis* will be taken from this edition and cited in the text by page number. The English translation is my own. For a summary and a structural analysis of the *De periculis*, see Dufeil 222–26.

51. For the opinion that the *De periculis* "is by far the most important subtext" for the speech of False Seeming, see Kevin Brownlee, "The Problem of Faux Semblant: Language, History, and Truth in the *Roman de la Rose*," *The New Medievalism*, ed. Marina S. Brownlee, Kevin Brownlee, and Stephen G. Nichols (Baltimore: Johns Hopkins University Press, 1991) 265.

52. Dufeil 227.

53. "La répétition est caractéristique du style de ce *De Periculis*" (repetition is characteristic of the style of *De periculis*; Dufeil 223).

healthy, however, ought not to beg but to work for their living. In fact, Guillaume subtly plays with the definitions of "work" and "begging" to indict the practices of the friars, who, as we saw earlier, renounced all their goods and proclaimed the right to beg *when necessary* in order to live the perfect Christian life. Guillaume argues, however, that, despite their claims to perfection, all friars who are not ordained clergy are obligated to do manual work.

Although Guillaume's definition of work is, in fact, much broader than just manual work, when he speaks of labor in general, he generally represents it by *manual* labor. Thus, when he quotes St. Paul on the necessity to work, "Operemini manibus vestris, sicut praecepimus vobis" (32; 1 Thessalonians 4.10–11), he specifically rejects the argument that "work" here could include spiritual work.[54] As we shall see, Guillaume's ideology, however, did indeed allow for the legitimacy of spiritual work performed by a carefully defined group of other Christians.

A central question of the chapter, then, is the status of making a living from spiritual work. As Guillaume concedes, Paul wrote that evangelists are allowed to make their living from the gospel: "Ita et Dominus ordinavit iis qui Evangelium annuntiant, de Evangelio vivere" (Thus, the Lord ordained that those who announce the gospel should live from the gospel; 1 Corinthians 9.14). In defense of paying for spiritual work with material rewards, Paul cites the examples of soldiers, farmers, and pastors. Who would do their work if they did not receive the appropriate rewards, here called *stipendium* or *fructu*?[55] For example, he argues: "Quis pascit gregem, et de lacte gregis non manducat?" (Who feeds the flock and does not drink the milk of the flock?).[56] The friars, in fact, could (and did) argue that their "begging" was no more than receiving their just reward for their evangelization, and Guillaume allows this argument with respect to Jesus himself (33). Jesus, he writes, "worked" as a pastor of souls, and there is no scriptural evidence that he ever begged (33).

Guillaume would not, however, accept a parallel argument for the fri-

---

54. Guillaume refers to *De opere monachorum* at this point: "sed superfluè cognoscant sibi & caeteris caliginem obducere, ut quod utiliter charitas monet, non solùm facere nolint, sed nec intelligere, cum in multis aliis locis Epistolarum suarum, quid hinc sentiat Apostolus, manifestissime doceat Christianos corporaliter operari, ne compellantur egestate necessaria petere" (However, they may admit that they and others are beclouded, so that what charity usefully advises, not only would they not want to do, they would also not want to understand, whereas in many other places in his epistles, the Apostle most clearly teaches what he feels on this topic: that Christians are to work with their hands lest they be compelled by poverty to ask for what is necessary; 32)

55. See 1 Corinthians 9.1–18.

56. 1 Corinthians 9.7, cited in *De periculis* 33.

ars. His chief argument against their "living off the gospel" was that they were not authorized by the Church to perform spiritual work. Quoting St. Augustine, he writes:

Si enim Evangelistae, si ministri altaris, si dispensatores Sacramentorum sunt, fateor habent. Si haec officia non habent, nec vivendi de Evangelio potestatem habent. (31)

[For if (they are) evangelists, if ministers of the altar, if dispensers of the sacraments, I concede that they have (the right to just reward). If they do not have these duties, they do not have the power to make their living by evangelizing.]

Guillaume adds: "Illis ergo solis debentur sumptus, qui praesunt in regimine animarum & officii dignitate" (Therefore, those alone who are charged with the care of souls and have the dignity of office ought to be supported; 31). For Guillaume, those who had the official responsibility for evangelization and the care of souls were only those ordained specifically for this work, that is, the secular clergy. Hence, spiritual labors could *not* be among the *officia* of friars not so ordained. When the friars take money or gifts for preaching, they are, then, not "working" but "begging." To further shame the friars, Guillaumes cites the epistles of Paul and the Acts of the Apostles to suggest that the apostles never took anything from their flocks, even though they were entitled to do so.[57]

From Guillaume's perspective, what makes the friars' begging especially sinful is that most of them are healthy men who could easily perform manual labor. What is worse, they often take donations from the sick and the needy. Guillaume thunders:

Ita videtur, quòd validus corpore, qui de labore suo vel aliunde vivere potest, si eleemosynas pauperum mendicorum recipit, sacrilegium committit. (33)

[Thus it seems that if someone strong of body, who is able to live from his own labor or from a different source, receives the handouts of the poor or needy, he commits a sacrilege.]

The thrust of much of Guillaume's portrayal, then, is that the friars prey on the weak and infirm to support an idle lifestyle. In essence, they are con artists. They are pseudoapostles because "illud onus indebitum importunè a plebibus exigebant" (they rudely place an undeserved burden

---

57. *De periculis* 32–33. Guillaume cites Peter's statement "Vado piscari" (I go to fish; John 21.3) to show that the apostles continued to labor with their hands even after Christ's resurrection (32). He also notes Paul's comment in Philippians 4.17, "Non quaero datum, sed fructum" (I seek not the gifts but the fruit [of my preaching]), quoted on 33.

on the people; 31). The solution, writes Guillaume, is that the ecclesiastical permissions for the friars to perform Church functions, which were
given by the pope and bishops in error, should be revoked (33).

In most of this chapter, Guillaume writes as if *none* of the friars ever
performed manual labor, and *all* of them continuously lived in idleness,
without producing anything of value for society. There is a section, however, in which he admits that the friars are active. However, when friars
do labor, they make things worse, for they seek to perform the work of
others, the "negotia aliena," a phrase that occurs three times in the space
of about a paragraph (31). Here the reader finds the core of what really
bothers Guillaume. As noted earlier, the conflict between the friars and
the secular masters arose from a turf battle. The secular masters, Guillaume among them, feared the loss of their own source of income from
the encroachments of the popular new mendicant scholars. In essence,
Guillaume is battling for the work privileges of his "union." When the
pope, bishops, and secular lords allowed the friars to perform "scab labor," Guillaume and the secular masters rebelled. Guillaume, then, argues that friars revealed their true nature not only by idleness but also by
being paid to perform the intellectual work rightly belonging to the secular masters. Here we see the influence of the new money economy on
Guillaume's labor discourse, for he equates the intellectual work of the
masters with "mere" wage labor, unworthy of real evangelists. Again, he
cites St. Paul to make his point: "Labora sicut bonus miles Christi Iesu.
Nemo militans Deo implicat se negotiis saecularibus" (Labor like a good
soldier of Jesus Christ. No one soldiering for God becomes entangled
with the labor of the world; 2 Timothy 2.4). But what are the labors of
the world? Quoting the *Glossa Ordinaria*, Guillaume writes: "Illa negotia
sunt secularia, cum quis occupatur colligendae cura pecuniae, sine labore
corporis" (Those labors are secular, when someone, collecting money, is
occupied with an office not demanding bodily labor; 31). In this passage,
then, the friars are shown to be busy, but in a perverse way. Their labors
are corrupted in two ways. First, they accept money for performing
them, but, second, they steal the *negotia* of others, those worldly, noncor-
poreal labors heretofore assigned by social contract to the secular clergy.

Thus, what seems on the surface to be a ringing declaration of the dignity and necessity of *manual* labor for all turns out to be something a little different, an argument for reserving certain types of nonmanual labor
for those with approved qualifications. With respect to the labor ideology
in *RII*, however, Guillaume's outspoken championship of the universal

obligation to perform manual labor had the greatest influence on Jean de Meun.

The friars did not sit idly by when they were attacked. Among those responding to Guillaume even before the publication of *De periculis* was the Franciscan master of theology St. Bonaventure. Indeed, Bonaventure and Guillaume engaged in public debate over the status of the friars, their way of life, and their right to beg.[58] Bonaventure's positions on manual labor in general and on the right of the friars to engage in other kinds of work appear in his treatise *De paupertate Christi: Contra Magistrum Guilelmum.*[59]

Bonaventure defends the work practices of his order in several ways. First, while admitting that humans are obliged to perform manual work (both because of human nature and because of original sin), Bonaventure carefully distinguishes between obligations of the race in general and those of individuals. Eating, for example, is an individual obligation because a person cannot have others eat for him. Manual work (and procreation too!), however, are obligations of the race in general and are not necessarily commanded for each individual (402, 406). As long as humankind as a whole can provide for its most basic needs, a specialization of labor can occur, and some kinds of labor are worthier than others. If this is so, Bonaventure argues that "membrum habens officium dignius non tenetur ad actum membri indignioris" (a member having a more worthy duty is not held [to perform] the act of an inferior member; 401). Citing the gospel passage on Mary and Martha (Luke 10.41–42), Bonaventure claims that spiritual work—and here he refers specifically to contemplation—is always superior to worldly work (401).

In one of the most important passages of this treatise, Bonaventure notes that if medieval society is divided into three parts, each part must have its own proper work:

Triplex genus operis est necessarium ad regnum Reipublicae et Ecclesiae militantis, scilicet opus artificiale, quod et manuale dicitur, quia manus est organum organorum, opus civile, et opus spirituale. (404)

---

58. Dufeil 174–87.

59. Bonaventure, *De Paupertate Christi: Contra Magistrum Guilelmum, Opera Omnia,* ed. A. C. Peltier, 15 vols. (Paris: Ludovicus Vives, 1868) 14.364–409. Bonaventure's treatment of labor occurs under question 2 (14.400–409). All quotations from the *De paupertate* will be taken from this edition and cited in the text by page number. The English translations are my own.

Christian Wenin undertakes a general review of Bonaventure's position on labor in "Saint Bonaventure et le travail manuel," *Le travail au moyen âge: Une approche interdisciplinaire,* ed. Jacque-

[Three kinds of work are necessary to the rule of the Republic and the church militant. That is, physical work—which is called "manual" because the hand is the instrument of all instruments—civil work, and spiritual work.]

Contrary to the impression given in *RI*, no estate has the right to idleness, but each has a specialized *officium*. Indeed, Bonaventure specifies the kinds of work falling under each category. Through manual work, man provides himself with food, shelter, clothing, and the works of diverse arts. Under civil labor, Bonaventure includes not only the work of the soldier, but also the work of the civil administration and, surprisingly, the work of the merchant (404). Finally, under spiritual labor, Bonaventure includes preaching, meditating, dispensing the sacraments, and sharing God's gifts, either worldly or spiritual (404). Bonaventure notes that if one argues that all men are bound to perform manual labor, and thus does not recognize an appropriate specialization of labor, then not only are the friars sinful, but so are soldiers and even secular clerics who teach in universities (402, 404). But this argument, claims Bonaventure, is absurd.

On the question of manual work for those in the mendicant orders, Bonaventure stakes out what he identifies as the middle ground. He rejects two extreme positions, both of which, he says, are heretical. The first extreme position is that *no* religious must perform manual labor because Christ said that Christians, like the birds, should not worry about what they will eat or wear.[60] The second extreme position, that of Guillaume, is that *all* strong poor men, including those in orders, must perform manual labor. Bonaventure's middle position is that *some* men who are strong but poor are obliged to perform manual labor, but for others labor is merely recommended but not enjoined. Finally, for a third group, manual labor is *not* recommended (405). Why? Because different humans have different gifts—"Unusquisque proprium donum habet ex Deo" (405)—and humans thus should choose their proper work according to their gifts and according to how they can best serve the common good. Those who are more gifted at manual work than spiritual work should perform that kind of labor. But those who are better at spiritual work should apply their talents where they can best serve:

---

line Hamesse and Collette Muraille-Samaran (Louvain-la-Neuve: Institut d'études médiévales de l'Université Catholique de Louvain, 1990) 141–55.

60. This is essentially the extreme position attacked by St. Augustine in *De opere monachorum*.

His autem qui maxime sunt idonei ad spiritualia opera praedicta, vel etiam ad civilia, et minime ad haec manualia, hujusmodi opera lucrativa et artificialia non sunt in praecepto, nec etiam in consilio, quia stultum esset, quod pro re modicae utilitatis commune bonum magnum incurreret detrimentum. (405)

[For those however who are most suited to spiritual works described above, or even to civil labor, and not at all suited to manual labor, profitable and artificial works of this kind are not required nor even recommended because it would be stupid—stupid in that for something of moderate utility the greater common good should incur detriment.]

Sending great minds to dig potatoes is not efficient use of God's gifts, nor does it yield the most benefits for society. Thus, he argues that communal productivity is an important criterion for judging the quality of work and, specifically, for the friars to continue to be supported for doing their spiritual labor.

A final argument against requiring all friars to work is that the benefits of manual labor can be obtained by doing other kinds of labor. What are the benefits of manual labor? Bonaventure writes:

labor corporalis valet ad corpus domandum, ad otium tollendum, ad victum honeste quaerendum, idem apostolus imponebat eis laborem, quasi in vitiorum istorum medicamentum. (406)

[labor of the body is valuable for subduing the body, for removing idleness, and for honestly seeking one's food. The apostle likewise commands labor for people as a kind of medicine against their vices.]

Labor here is a remedy against the vices; productivity is almost an after-thought. The apostolic command to manual labor (in 2 Thessalonians 3.11–12), then, is not given generally but is addressed specifically to those who are "sick," that is, restless, lazy, or curious, and to those who do not have any other means to earn their livelihood (406). What is most important here is that Bonaventure's labor ideology differs from Guillaume's in his emphasis on the division of labor. While he recognizes that manual labor is good, its good effects can be obtained in other ways. Society benefits more if the people follow their talents into the kinds of work that best suit them.

The reply of another great friar, Thomas Aquinas, on the same question is found in the *Quaestiones quodlibetales*, question 7, where he argues many of the same points found in Bonaventure's *De paupertate Christi*.[61]

61. St. Thomas Aquinas, *Quaestiones quodlibetales*, ed. Raymundi Spiazzi, 8th ed. (Rome: Marietti,

Thomas's major contribution to the argument is that he develops the defense of "spiritual work" in more detail and makes a distinction not found in Bonaventure. Like Bonaventure, he argues that as a general principle, spiritual work is more important than physical work, and thus those who do perform spiritual works should not be required to perform manual labor.[62]

However, Thomas makes a critical distinction when he divides spiritual work into two categories. The first is the spiritual work that is specifically directed toward the common good, like serving in ecclesiastical courts, preaching, singing the divine office for the good of the Church, and teaching the sacred Scriptures (153–54). Since these works directly contribute to the well-being of society, those who perform them are excused from manual labor (154). They are soldiers of Christ, and, like regular soldiers, they deserve to be supported in their ministry.[63] The second kind of spiritual work, however, is that intended primarily as private devotion and is not specifically directed to filling some need of the community (154). Examples of these kinds of spiritual works are private prayers and fasting. Thomas argues that while those who are supported by other means and who engage in private spiritual works are not required to perform manual labor, those who are poor and can only earn their bread by manual labor are indeed required to work with their hands, even when they engage in private spiritual works (154). The only exception to this

---

1949) 148–56. All quotations from this work will be taken from this edition and cited in the text by page number. The English translations are my own. Thomas treated this question again in the *Summa theologiae*, 2a.2ae.187.3, "utrum religiosi manibus operari teneantur" (*Summa theologiae*, ed. Thomas Gilby, 60 vols. [New York: Blackfriars Press, 1973] 47.152–63).

On Thomistic work ideology in general, see Philippe Delhaye, "Quelques aspects de la doctrine thomiste et néothomiste du travail," *Le travail au moyen âge* 157–75.

62. Thomas quotes the *Glossa Ordinaria* on Luke 9.60, "Dominus docet minora bona pro maioribus esse dimittenda" (The Lord teaches that lesser goods are to be allowed to pass in favor of greater goods; 158). He adds: "Sed opera spiritualia sunt maiora bona quam opera manualia. Ergo debet haec praetermittere propter illa" (But spiritual works are greater than manual works. Therefore, these ought to be passed over because of it).

63. Here Thomas, like Guillaume, cites 2 Timothy 2.4, "Nemo militans Deo implicat se negotiis saecularibus" (No one in the army of God involves himself with secular business). Like Guillaume, he cites the *Glossa Ordinaria* to define "secular business" as any business concerned with gathering money. In his conclusion, however, he quietly leaves out the exception cited by Guillaume—"occupatur colligendae cura pecuniae *sine labore corporis*," *without manual labor*—and thus turns Guillaume's conclusion on its head: "Sed qui operantur manibus, habent curam de colligenda pecunia. Ergo implicantur negotiis saecularibus" (But those who work with their hands are concerned with gathering money. Therefore, they are implicated with secular business; 153). At the end of the second article (156), however, Thomas again cites this gloss but reinstates the crucial qualification, and he thus warns the friars that they should not earn money as merchants.

rule would be someone who is called to give him- or herself wholly to contemplation, the "opus contemplationis" (154).

Reduced to their basic principles, then, the labor ideologies of the two friars are not substantially different from that of Guillaume. The differences, I would submit, are matters of emphasis. On the one hand, Guillaume emphasizes the universal requirement of humans to perform manual labor although he concedes that properly ordained clergy can make a living off the gospel. On the other, the friars recognize a universal obligation to manual labor, but they argue that this obligation is given to the entire human race, not necessarily to individuals. In addition, the friars are eager to highlight the legitimacy of a division of labor and to define all possible human activities, such as teaching, soldiering, and governing, that benefit the community as legitimate forms of work, deserving of material reward. Moreover, they wish to portray themselves as workers producing something of value for the community, something of even higher value than food and shelter. What they receive from begging is in reality a justified wage for their performance of spiritual work. Guillaume, as we have seen, agrees in principle that spiritual work should be supported, but he and his secular colleagues did not believe that the friars had any legitimate right to engage in the "negotia aliena," and hence never had any right to community support.

In a very real sense, what we see in this dispute is a replay of several earlier monastic work controversies. There is the controversy over whether evangelists or monks should perform manual labor at all, first addressed by Paul in his epistles, and then addressed by St. Augustine in *De opere monachorum*. In the twelfth century, such controversies broke out again over the nature of legitimate monastic work, whether such clerical activities as copying manuscripts could substitute for manual labor. In this thirteenth-century replay, Guillaume de Saint-Amour and his colleagues took the hard line on manual labor vis-à-vis the friars; the friars, on the other hand, sought a more liberal interpretation of the Christian requirement to work for one's bread. They grounded their arguments on the wisdom of work specialization for the common good. Regarding the universal nature of the call to *manual* labor, Jean de Meun takes his ideology more from Guillaume than from the friars. Regarding the obligation to perform productive work for the good of the species, however, Jean's ideology is closer to that of the friars than to that of Guillaume. That may in fact be why he found Alan of Lille's *De planctu* so attractive, for, congruent with natural law ethics, Alan continuously stresses that the work of love should produce something for the common good.

V

As noted above, Jean's treatment of the friars and their work claims is found in the discourse of False Seeming. Although False Seeming claims that he is found in all walks of life (11157–92), it is clear that Jean fashions his character with the friars in mind. Wearing a humble habit, he is in the religious orders that profess poverty (10981–86, 10997–11019, 11207–8). Apart from these references, Jean includes a long section on the controversy between the mendicants and the secular masters, with specific references to the theory of mendicancy and to the scandal of the publication of Gerard of Borgo San Donnino's *Introductorius ad Evangelium Aeternum*.[64]

At the command of Love, False Seeming, a personification of hypocrisy, is constrained to reveal everything about himself and his confreres (10957–72). On the whole, False Seeming is critical of the friars' position on manual labor and consistently echoes the labor ideology found in the *De periculis*. For example, False Seeming notes that although the friars claim to be living in perfect accord with the gospels, nowhere in the gospels does it say that Jesus himself begged for food. What's more, after Jesus' death, the apostles went back to manual labor in order to support themselves (11265–86). False Seeming then makes a statement of the general principle: No one should voluntarily make himself a beggar. Poverty is good, he admits, but poor men should live off the work of their hands (11287–302). Those who are fit to work but choose to devote themselves to contemplation should enter a monastery (11384–94). Those who remain out of the monasteries and beg are "oiseus" and "lobierres" (thieves; 11301–2).

False Seeming even outlines the rules that establish when begging is allowed.[65] Among those conditions that excuse a poor man from manual labor are ignorance of a trade, illness, old age, unemployment, and star-

64. Specific references to Guillaume de Saint-Amour and his banishment, the university masters, the controversy, the mendicants as agents of the Antichrist occur in the following passages: 11453–86 and 11761–866. For the opinion that False Seeming speaks as an avatar of Guillaume de Saint-Amour, see Brownlee 262. This article contains an excellent treatment of the dialogic nature of False Seeming's introduction to Love.

65. Lecoy 11395–460. These are taken from the *Responsiones* of Guillaume of Saint-Amour (Edmond Faral, ed., "Les *Responsiones* de Guillaume de Saint-Amour," *Archives d'Histoire et littéraire du moyen âge* 18 [1950–1951]: 337–94). See Lecoy 2.285.

vation wages. Also excluded from manual labor are the poor who want to take on some sort of "chevalerie" for the faith, whether that be deeds of arms or the cultivation of the mind. These are allowed to beg until they can work with their hands.

False Seeming is very specific on the nature of work, and his emphasis is taken directly from the *De periculis*. When he speaks of work, he means manual labor, not spiritual labor. He insists that the poor, whether religious or not, must work "non pas des mains esperitex, / mes des mains du cors proprement / sanz metre i double entendement" (not with spiritual hands but with the actual bodily hands, without putting any double meaning on them; 11450–52). In two manuscripts these lines are reinforced by illustrations of a bodily hand and a "spiritual hand," which looks something like a stylus.[66] True to his hypocritical nature, however, while False Seeming proclaims a hard line on the ethics of work (which, as we have seen, the friars did not do), his practice is completely at odds with what he preaches. In fact, one of the most characteristic features of False Seeming and his friends is that they detest manual labor. "Laborer ne me peut plere," he admits, "De laborer n'ai je que fere, / trop a grant paine en laborer" (Working can give me no pleasure: I have nothing to do with it, for there is too great difficulty in working; 11489–91). Here the utter disgust for manual labor is emphasized by the repetition of the infinitive *laborer* three times.

While the rejection of manual labor is clearly foremost among the characteristics of False Seeming, Jean, like Guillaume, recognizes that the friars are not completely idle. The work they perform, however, is illicit; it is work reserved for others. Throughout False Seeming's monologue, he reveals that while the friars avoid work with the poor, they are continuously busy chasing wealthy patrons and seeking handouts. They also engage in some secular clerical duties: undertaking brokerage commissions, drawing up agreements, arranging marriages, executing wills, acting as messengers, and even investing money (11649–54). University teaching is not mentioned in this passage, but all these other activities are illicit because they are "negotia aliena," the work of others. False Seeming specifically declares that the work of others is indeed a very pleasant occupation: "les autrui besoignes trestier, / ce m'est un trop plesant mestier" (To occupy myself with someone else's business is to me a very pleasant occupation; 11655–56).[67] Thus, False Seeming's criticism of the

66. See the description in Lecoy 2.285–86. These illustrations are reproduced in Dahlberg 201.

67. "Besoigne" (3), *Dictionnaire de l'ancien français*, defined as "work" as well as "needs."

friars' work attitudes is self-contradictory, but there is no doubt that it comes directly from Guillaume de Saint-Amour. Whether the reader can identify False Seeming's opinions with those of Jean de Meun is a question that comes up even more acutely when the character speaking represents hypocrisy and deceit.[68] As I hope to show, however, the ideology that False Seeming articulates (as opposed to the ideology and moral preferences that really guide his behavior) is consistent with the work ideologies of Jean's other main characters. It clearly reflects a rejection of idleness and a belief in the universal human obligation to earn one's living by means of manual and not spiritual labors.

While the monologue of False Seeming strongly reveals Jean de Meun's interest in labor issues, it is not the only passage in *RII* to do so. Other key passages are found in the monologues of Reason, Friend, and Genius. During the sermon of Genius, for example, Jean refers to the myth of the Golden Age found in the *Georgics*. As we have already seen, Ovid uses the *Georgics* as the generic model of his *Ars*, but he never treats Virgil's foundation myth directly. Jean does. Genius notes that in the Golden Age of Saturn, humankind did not work but lived communally without boundaries of any kind (20089–96). This passage develops, to some degree, the instruction of Friend, who first informs the Dreamer about the Golden Age, in which men did not have to work, but lived simply in ease and idleness (8325–424, esp. 8409–14). During the Golden Age, then, idleness was licit. Later, however, Friend returns to this theme and describes the "fallen" nature of the earth under Jupiter, in which social classes, servitude, fraud, poverty, and the lust to acquire possessions were first created (9463–649). In the Age of Jupiter, work is a sad, social necessity. On this point, Genius agrees with Jean's Friend. Quoting the *Georgics*, Genius argues that the end of the Saturnian Golden Age meant the end of licit leisure; the obligation to practice materially productive work is the unfortunate result of the change in divine regimes (20085–108). For man's survival, however, Jupiter created various new arts (20109–10). The arts are not necessarily gifts, but they do provide survival skills:

> Ainsinc sunt arz avant venues,
> *car toutes choses sunt vaincues*
> *par travaill, par povreté dure,*

68. Brownlee 263.

par quoi les genz sunt en grant cure;
car li mal les angins esmeuvent
par les angoisses qu'il i trevent.

...

Briefment Jupiter n'antandi,
quant a terre tenir tandi,
for muer l'estat de l'ampire
de bien an mal, de mal an pire.

(20145–50, 55–58; emphasis added)

[Thus have the arts sprung up, *for all things are conquered by labor and hard poverty;* through these things people exist in great care. For difficulties incite people's ingenuity because of the pain that they find in them. . . . In short, when Jupiter set out to take the earth, he intended nothing other than changing the state of the empire from good to ill and from ill to worse.]

Without bothering to cite Genesis, Friend and Genius evoke what Jacques LeGoff has called the dominant medieval interpretation of labor, that is, labor as the result of a fallen world.[69] Jupiter, says Genius, turned the state of the world from good to bad, and from bad to worse. He even cites Ovid to prove this point (20151–54). This foundation myth forms the basis for what seems to be the characteristic attitude in *RII* toward all the human arts, including the art of love: they are bodies of practical knowledge to help men perform the productive labor crucial to surviving in a fallen world.

If work is the universal human condition, how does one reconcile this with the fact that certain medieval social classes were not expected to perform manual labor? As we saw above, this was a central question analyzed by the mendicants as they sought to respond to Guillaume's charge that they were nonproductive drones. Both Thomas Aquinas and Bonaventure pointed out that the aristocracy and the clergy were not given any license to practice idle lives. Instead, they were performing other, specialized kinds of labor that ultimately were supposed to make a contribution to the common good.

This particular labor ideology, which, as we saw, was actually shared by Guillaume de Saint Amour, comes out strongly in the monologue of Nature, when she discusses the legitimacy of inherited class position. In essence, Nature critiques the shortcomings of an inherited class status

69. Jacques LeGoff, "Le travail dans les systèmes de valeur de l'Occident médiévale," *Le travail au moyen âge* 11–12.

and argues that nobility is justified only by its productive work.[70] In a surprising statement, she affirms that social status is a gift of Fortune. Indeed, except for what they contribute to society, all men enjoy equal dignity (18569–70). Despite the fact that labor is a by-product of a fallen world, nobles are *not* better than those who labor with their hands, she argues.[71] On the contrary, Nature affirms that to be a true noble, one must earn his high status with appropriate hard work:

> par quoi doit estre en li paranz
> la proece de ses paranz,
> qui la gentillece conquistrent
> par *les travauz* que *granz* i mistrent.
>
> (18593–96; emphasis added)

[For this reason a nobleman must display the prowess of his ancestors, who conquered their nobility by means of *the great labors* that they gave to it.]

Nature uses the words "les travauz . . . granz" to describe the great efforts of worthy aristocrats to earn their social status. The Old French *travail* denoted work and labor, but, like the Latin *labor*, it could also denote physical discomfort, suffering, and even fatigue.[72] Since the great works of these ancestors were demonstrations of their *proece*, in this passage *travail* carries the more active meaning of sustained, even laborious, effort, although clearly not manual labor. Later, Nature specifies the nature of these works as she continues her attack on aristocratic idleness. The work of the aristocrat is battle, the study of arms (18651–54). Nature then calls up the examples of Sir Gawain and Count Robert of Artois, who, she argues, were never satisfied with periods of idleness (18667–80).

Nature sums up her argument by specifically criticizing one of the most fundamental of Guillaume de Lorris's underlying assumptions: that aristocratic idleness is to be celebrated. Instead, Nature criticizes those who consider themselves noble, for example, Diversion and his companions, because they are so reputed and because they can waste time on idle

---

70. Norman Cohn argues that an egalitarian social doctrine was one of the "guiding ideas" of *RII* (*The World View of a Thirteenth-Century Intellectual: Jean de Meun and the "Roman de la Rose"* [Newcastel upon Tyne, U.K.: University of Durham, 1961] 11). Reason's social doctrine is egalitarian only to the extent that each of the social orders had to justify its existence by performing productive labor. She does not advocate an abolition of the social hierarchy, however.

71. 18577–88. On Jean's respect for the working classes, see Cohn 20–22.

72. "Travail," *Dictionnaire de l'ancien français;* "travail," *Dictionnaire de l'ancienne langue française et de tous ses dialectes du IXe au XVe siècles*, defined as "gêne, tourment, effort penible" (difficulty, torment, laborious effort), as well as "effort soutenu" (sustained effort).

amusements (18833). Nature does not target the *otium* of the clerical classes the way Andreas Capellanus did in *De amore*. She does, however, mention in passing that clerics must also work well, and she obviously includes clerical work among those works that are productive (18681–84).

While, again, the polyphonic nature of Jean's text makes it impossible to identify Nature's position here with that of Jean himself, we should note that Nature's work ideology complements and develops that which we have already seen in the discourses of Friend and Genius. These two voices affirm that the obligation to work is the universal condition of a fallen world. Nature's discourse underscores the idea that the work obligation extends beyond members of the third estate to those of the first and second estates, neither of whom have any rights to unproductive *otium otiosum*.

The discourse of Reason on labor, however, shows that there is a limit to the apparent universal support of hard work in *RII*. That limit is reached when Reason considers "travaill d'aquerre," labor directed toward the accumulation of wealth, which was one of the distinguishing marks of the bourgeoisie according to medieval satirists.[73] Jean de Meun was no protocapitalist. In her discussion of different kinds of love, Reason argues that one should strive for sufficiency but not wealth, and she bitterly condemns those "foolish" people—merchants, physicians, aristocrats, even clergymen—who, directing their love toward money, spend their time simply trying to amass wealth beyond what they need to live.[74] Reason suggests that three great misfortunes befall those who seek wealth (5097–99, 5166–74). First, they have to work hard to acquire wealth (5067). Second, they fear losing their wealth, and thus spend their lives in anxiety. *RII* might indeed represent an "embourgeoisement de l'eros" as Payen claims, but Reason is clear-sighted enough to realize that "nul marchaant ne vit a ese" (no merchant lives at ease; 5042). The same can be said for lawyers and physicians (5061–62). Third, those who amass great wealth eventually die, and thus grieve to give it up. These same misgivings about the acquisition of great wealth via the "travaill d'aquerre" are repeated by Nature during her confession (18797–814). Reason and Nature's distrust of the accumulation of riches and their support of work only to the extent that it is used to acquire the necessities of life fit well with the ideological developments attending the growth of the money economy in the thirteenth century.

---

73. Alter 72–73. 74. See comments in Payen 201.

This review of Jean's treatment of labor helps establish some key points about *RII*. First, unlike Guillaume de Lorris, who celebrates the aristocratic claim to idleness and makes it a sine qua non of *fin amors*, Jean de Meun distrusts leisure when it represents *otium otiosum* rather than an opportunity for *otium negotiosum*. He is a strong supporter of productive labor. While none of his characters can be taken as representing his position completely, it is surely significant that all of his *praeceptores* take complementary positions on the obligation to work. For Jean, the obligation to work was a fact of life in a fallen world, and he strongly respects the dignity of those who work with their hands. While he generally recognizes the traditional division of labor according to the three estates model, he does not take the model as giving any license for either clerical or aristocratic *otium otiosum*. On the contrary, he probably believed that the friars' claim to be free of the obligation to perform manual labor was invalid. Although he recognized the legitimacy of intellectual labor (18682), unlike the friars, he does not emphasize the need for labor specialization. Indeed, when he treats labor, he continuously focuses on the obligation to work with one's hands. Finally, despite his strong defense of the obligation to work, Jean was no capitalist and strongly distrusted the accumulation of wealth. We shall see all of these general positions on labor coloring the discourse of love's labor occurring in other sections of *RII*.

VI

Jean's discourse of love's labor, to which we now turn, is not univocal in *RII*. Sarah Kay calls *RII* a compilation or montage of "different subject positions all held in play" (47). Jean's poem can also be seen as an encyclopedic *ars amatoria*, and in its completeness it treats the Ovidian labor of courtship within the discourses of the characters Friend and the Old Woman.[75] Like Guillaume, Jean uses the character Friend as the lover's

75. On Jean de Meun's debt to Ovid, see Leslie Cahoon, "Raping the Rose: Jean de Meun's Reading of Ovid's *Amores*," *Classical and Modern Literature* 6 (1986): 261–85; and Pelen, *Latin Poetic Irony*. Allen argues that Jean borrowed heavily from both the *Ars* and the *Remedia*. Citing Ernest Langlois (*Origines et sources du Roman de la Rose* [Paris: Ernest Thorin, 1891] 119–27), Allen claims that Jean borrowed 2,000 lines from Ovid, largely from the *Ars amatoria*. Nevertheless, Allen claims that Jean suffered from anxiety of influence and rebelled against much of his Ovidian material (79–84). If one goes beyond the discourse of Friend, this is certainly the case with respect to Ovid's discourse of love's labor.

On *RII* as an *ars amatoria*, see Cohn 18 and Payen 195–96. Payen writes that *RII* "participe à une offensive de démythification fondée sur le réalisme cynique des nouveaux arts d'aimer" (participates in a demythologizing offensive based upon the cynical realism of the new arts of love; 195).

praeceptor for the parts corresponding to Books 1 and 2 of the *Ars amatoria*. For the section corresponding to Book 3, Jean creates a new *praeceptor*, the Old Woman.[76]

After the Dreamer rejects the advice of Reason, he seeks out Friend to help him win the rose. The teaching credentials of Friend, like those of the *praeceptores* in the *Ars amatoria* and in the *De amore*, come from experience (7960–66). Friend tells the Dreamer to serve Love, employing labor vocabulary similar to that of *RI* and the *De amore*.[77] However, while in the *De amore* service was meant to demonstrate the worth of the inner person, Friend's approach to love's labor effects a return to Ovidian playfulness and cynicism.[78] Friend is much more interested in teaching the Dreamer how to pursue love effectively than in teaching him how to reveal his inner person. He begins with the second labor of the *Ars amatoria*, winning the lady.[79] Like Ovid's *praeceptor*, he counsels his pupil to employ deceit and strategy in his efforts. For example, the Dreamer is *to pretend* to serve the character Foul Mouth, but this service is only a strategy finally to defeat him (7316–22). It is no sin, says Friend, to trick the trickster (7323–24). From here on, Friend dishes out a steady stream of Ovidian ploys to win over the lady's servants and guardians: flatter them, give them gifts, weep, send anonymous letters. For Friend, the labor of courtship is truly an art, the labor of a skilled craftsman. He emphasizes the skill required to accomplish love's work by comparing courtship and seduction to the guiding of a ship (7519–28). Just as skill and perseverance are required to steer a ship through a storm, so too the lover must steer his own ship carefully and never give up.

Once the rose's guardians are won over, the Dreamer must direct his efforts toward the lady herself. The first step in winning a lady, says Friend, is to ask for her love. Let no man wait for the woman to make the first move (7619–28). He then advises the most direct form of labor of all: if the lady does not respond positively to the Dreamer's approach, then,

---

76. Allen finds Friend to be "the most like the Ovidian *praeceptor amoris*" of all the characters in *RII* (86). He finds the Old Woman to be "the transvestite *praeceptor amoris* of *Ars Amatoria* 3" (89). In fact, the two characters are "the two faces of the Ovidian teacher" (88).

77. 7269–71. His formal instructions in the art of seduction begin on line 7277: "Or vos dirai que vos ferez" (now I will tell you what to do).

78. On Friend's moral relativism and its relation to Ovid, see Allen 86–87.

79. Ovid describes the three labors of love as follows: "Principio, quod amare uelis, reperire labora, / qui noua nunc primum miles in arma uenis; / proximus huic labor est placitam exorare puellam; / tertius, ut longo tempore duret amor" (First, for you, as a soldier, who come fresh into new arms, are the labors of finding someone to love; the next labor is to win the attractive girl; the third is to make love long endure; *Ars amatoria* 1.35–38).

like Ovid's *praeceptor*, the Dreamer may "cut the rose by force."[80] Once this extreme and immoral position is stated, however, Friend seems to retreat from it by suggesting other Ovidian strategies for winning the lady. The Dreamer, for example, should learn how to play games and study how to lose at the games to please the lady.[81] Many of these, one notes, are the same idle pastimes suggested in *RI*, but Jean, unlike Guillaume, does not call attention to their socially unproductive nature.

Up to this point, all of Friend's teaching involved Ovid's second labor, winning the woman. At line 8227, however, Friend begins his teaching regarding Ovid's third labor, keeping the lady one has won.[82] He says,

> Mes quant l'en a la chose aquise,
> si recovient il *grant mestrise*
> au bien garder et sagement,
> qui joïr en veut longuement;
> car la vertu n'est mie mendre
> de bien garder et de deffendre
> les choses, quant eus sunt aquises,
> que d'eus aquerre en quelque guises.
>
> (8227–34; emphasis added)

[But when one has acquired something, he must exercise *great mastery* in keeping it well and wisely if he wants to enjoy it for long, for to keep and protect things after they are acquired is no less a virtue than to acquire them in various ways.]

Keeping one's lover also is subject to the rules of art. Friend begins instruction in the "grant mestrise" with another important Ovidian labor: cultivation of the mind. The lover must not trust his looks alone, but rather must cultivate his manners and his mind to keep himself interesting.[83] Friend further counsels that the lady be given lots of freedom, and when lovers quarrel, to use sex—called here the "geu d'amors" (9731)—as a device for reconciliation. He follows this with advice on how to take care of her if she becomes ill, and, finally, he concludes his teaching of love's labors by treating what he considers the most powerful strategy to keep women: flattery (9905–28).

---

80. 7664. Cf. Ovid, *Ars amatoria* 1.699ff.

81. 7737–46. This advice is given to women rather than to men in the *Ars* (3.367–70).

82. Ovid, *Ars amatoria* 2.12–15.

83. 8284–85. Just learning pretty little songs will not be enough to keep her either (8307–16). Jean's Friend has less trust in writing poetry as a labor of love than did Ovid.

Friend, like Ovid's praeceptor in the Ars amatoria, Books 1 and 2, is not explicitly preoccupied with labor productivity per se. However, unlike Ovid's praeceptor, he does not make a special point of underscoring how hard it is to work at love's labor. For example, no comparisons of court-ship with the rigors of army life are found in the discourse of Friend. At the same time, however, he is driven, if not to produce material artifacts, at least to succeed in his projects, and to that end he will employ any strategy to bring the labor of courtship to a successful conclusion.

Another praeceptor is the Old Woman, a former prostitute. Her per-spective is just as cynical as but also substantially different from that of Friend. With her advice we pass to a section of RII that corresponds roughly to Book 3 of the Ars amatoria, love advice for women. Unlike Ovid, however, Jean creates a new praeceptor for his section. In addition, the new praeceptor addresses her lesson to a male character, Fair Welcom-ing, a personification of the part of the female psyche willing to welcome the amorous advances of the male lover.[84]

The Old Woman invites Fair Welcoming to learn her art and the "geus d'Amors" (game of love; 12973, 12976), for art, she says at one point, is a great aid to nature (13570). At the end of the instruction, Fair Welcoming thanks the Old Woman for instruction in her art, but he feigns both igno-rance of the art and lack of interest in learning it. He says it is "trop es-trange matire" (14583). The reader suspects, however, that he knows it all too well and that his reluctance to express interest in the art is in fact a sign of his mastery of it. Like Friend and Ovid himself, the Old Woman's qualifications to be a lecturer in love come from experience.[85] Unlike Ovid's praeceptor of Book 3, however, the Old Woman passes on her "en-seignemenz" by conferring on Fair Welcoming license to be a praeceptor in his own right (13469–86).

Both Book 3 of the Ars amatoria and the instructions of the Old Woman are worldly texts, but there is a bitter edge to the Old Woman's instruction that is not found in Ovid. Unlike those of Ovid's praeceptor, her games of love are not ultimately playful. This is so for two reasons: first, because love's labor for the Old Woman is wage labor, and, second,

84. 12351–14777. Kay notes that subjectivity in RII is essentially a male prerogative. The rose, therefore, can become a subject only if it is replaced by a masculine entity, that is, Fair Welcoming.

85. She says, "Bele iere, et jenne et nice et fole, / n'onc ne fui d'Amors a escole / ou l'en leüst la theorique, / mes je sai tout par la practique. / Experimez m'en ont fet sage, / que j'ai hantez tout mon aage" (I was young and beautiful, foolish and wild, and had never been to a school of love where they read in the theory, but I know everything by practice. Experiments, which I have fol-lowed my whole life, have made me wise in love; 12771–76).

because she wants to use Fair Welcoming to exact revenge upon all males (12850–54). The Old Woman hates idleness, and Fair Welcoming will not be idle, she argues, when he works with his beauty to earn money and/or gifts (12915–18). Indeed, in her own gloss on the courtly code outlined by Guillaume's Love, she argues that Fair Welcoming should know the commandments of love but not love itself (12981–84), and that it is the man's duty to be generous, not the woman's (13007). Like a good bourgeois merchant, she argues that Fair Welcoming should never *give* his heart to any single man, but *sell* it to the highest bidder (13008–12).

What is the reason that love should be sold? The reason is that women need to stock up wealth for old age (14411–26). The end toward which all life moves is *viellece*, the cold and barren years that the *bon tens* of Diversion's garden are meant to hide. In accordance with this insight, she argues that wise women never forget that their beauty lasts but for a moment, and thus they prepare for old age. One is reminded here of Alan of Lille's sermon on *acedia*, discussed above, in particular the *exemplum* of the ants, which are held up as models of good industry. Crafty women, like the ants, work hard to prepare for the winter of old age. Here, again, the Old Woman teaches from experience, for she, like the proverbial grasshopper, spent her youth in careless pleasures and has not stocked up anything for her own winter (14427–40).

With this in mind, the Old Woman teaches strategies for "investing" one's beauty, youth, and charm, all of which, she argues, can be made to yield rich dividends for later in life. Her art, then, consists of the strategies necessary to turn love into cash or gifts. One of her teachings, for example, is to delay gratification because delay raises the price of love.[86] This is a strategy that Fair Welcoming will employ later in the romance to good effect.

As we have seen, the theme of labor enhancing value occurs regularly in the *De amore*. In the teachings of the *Rose*, however, it is *price* rather than labor per se that enhances value, perhaps reflecting the thirteenth-century increase in the use of money.[87] Indeed, the Old Woman's discourse breaks new ground by adding prostitution to the list of activities

86. See, for example, the Old Woman's axiom that "demeure les amanz atise" (delay excites lovers; 13631).

87. It comes as a shock to note, for example, that the attitude of the Old Woman is almost identical with that of Guillaume's Love, who says to the Dreamer: "Biaus amis, par l'ame mon pere, / nus n'a bien s'il ne le compere; / s'en aime l'en mieuz la chaté / quant l'en l'a plus chier acheté; / et plus en gré sont receü / li bien ou l'en a mal eü." (Fair friend, [I swear on the soul of my father] no one has anything good unless he pays for it. *Men love a possession more when they have bought it at a higher price,*

associated with love's labor. To be sure, Ovid taught women how to milk
their lovers for gifts just as he taught men how to avoid being generous to
the point of bankruptcy. Overall, however, the focus of the *Ars amatoria* is
more on love's labor as a form of play rather than on using love's labor
for economic gain. In contrast, the Old Woman measures the productivity of love's labor strictly by the amount of wealth the young woman can
win:

> Mes s'el veult mon conseill avoir,
> ne tande a riens fors qu'a l'avoir.
> Fole est qui son ami ne plume
> jusqu'a la darreniere plume;
> car qui mieuz plumer le savra,
> c'iert cele qui meilleur l'avra
> et qui plus iert chiere tenue,
> quant plus chier se sera vendue.
>
> (13665–72)

[But if she wants my advice, she should think only of what she can get. She is a
fool who does not pluck her lover down to the last feather, for the better she can
pluck the more she will have, and she will be more highly valued when she sells
herself more dearly.]

Such productivity is important because, as we have seen, the Old Woman
has a keen sense of the transitory nature of what Fair Welcoming has to
sell. Because she knows from experience that Old Age is not allowed
within the Garden of Love, she notes that Fair Welcoming should not
wait too long to begin using his looks for gain. To this end, she employs
the carpe diem theme for economic gain rather than simply for pleasure.[88]

The primary figure used by the Old Woman to describe love's labor is
hunting, and she often refers to trapping men in her "nets" (e.g., 12798,
13045). The bitter nature of this hunt is revealed in the simile the Old
Woman uses to describe it:

---

and the good things for which one has suffered are received with greater thanks; 2583–88; emphasis
added). Compare this to the opinions of the Old Woman in 13665–72.

88. 13445–68. When he suggests to women that they should "seize the day," Ovid does not mention economic gain (*Aa* 3.61–64).

> Torjorz doit fame metre cure
> Qu'el puist la louve resembler
> quant el vet les berbiz enbler;
> car, qu'el ne puist du tout faillir,
> por une en vet .M. assaillir,
> qu'el ne set las quele el prendra
> devant que prise la tendra.
> Ausinc doit fame par tout tendre
> ses raiz por touz les homes prendre.
>
> (13552–60)

[A woman must always take care to imitate the she-wolf when she wants to steal ewes, for, in order not to fail completely, the wolf must attack a thousand to capture one; she doesn't know which she will take before she has taken it. So a woman ought to spread her nets everywhere to catch all men.]

Ovid employed hunting as one of the love's labors in the *Ars amatoria*. For example, he writes that catching women is like catching birds. This imagery, however, does not dominate. In fact, when he refers to women as "she-wolves," he is merely reporting what he hears from worried men, an opinion to which the *praeceptor* himself does not subscribe.[89]

In the discourse of the Old Woman, the labor of women becomes active and aggressive rather than passive. The imagery suggests that self-cultivation is not simply passive but that these activities are those of an active predator. To this extent, one could argue that Jean de Meun here fashions a discourse of love's labor that is female-oriented rather than male-oriented. The references to prostitution, however, make this discourse rather sordid, and one is tempted to respond that the discourse of the Old Woman is not truly female-oriented but, in fact, represents traditional antifeminist male anxiety regarding female sexuality.

Among the Ovidian labors to which the Old Woman refers is to dress well, but, she concludes, it is unnecessary for her to teach this labor, for Fair Welcoming already knows well how to do it (13059–62). Self-cultivation, especially dressing well, is apparently a "mestier," a trade, that Fair Welcoming has already perfected.[90] Nevertheless, after a brief digression on how all men are sensualists, the Old Woman reviews some specific Ovidian strategies: a woman should use clothes and cosmetics to empha-

---

89. Ovid, *Ars amatoria* 1.270, 3.8. Other passages with the hunting motif occur in 1.45ff., 2.2, and 3.669–70.

90. 13059–62. Cf. Ovid, *Ars amatoria* 3.169ff.

size her best parts (13253–304). She should keep her body clean and her breath fresh (13305–20). She should laugh and cry with decorum (13321–54). She should mind her table manners (13355–444, 13499–551). All are taken directly from Book 3 of the *Ars amatoria*.[91] In addition, the woman, as well as men, should play roles. For example, she should pretend to be fearful whenever they have an assignation (13765–804, 14173–250).

Finally, the Old Woman, like Ovid, turns to techniques in the "labor" of lovemaking. She says,[92]

> Et quant se seront mis an *l'euvre*,
> chascuns d'aus si sagement *euvre*,
> et si a point, que il conviegne
> que li deliz ensamble viegne
> de l'une et de l'autre partie
> ainz que *l'euvre* soit departie,
> et s'antredoivent entr'atendre
> por ansamble a leur bonne tendre.
>
> (14263–70, emphasis added)

[And when they set about their *labor* each of them should *work* so carefully and so exactly that the pleasure must come together for the one person and the other before they leave off *the task;* and between them, they should wait for each other so that they can direct their desires toward their good.]

The purpose of an art is to teach how one might "sagement euvre," wisely work, to reach one's goal. In this section of the Old Woman's art, unlike in the rest, the goal is not monetary gain but pleasure. As in Ovid, creating mutual pleasure in lovemaking is also work. The Old French noun *euvre* meant work or labor or the result of those activities. In agriculture, it meant the amount of work one could complete in a day.[93] The verb *ovrer* had a similar range of meanings: to work, to act, to serve someone.[94] The point is that the Old Woman, like Ovid's *praeceptor*, represents even the act of making love as an act of labor. However, when she emphasizes that sex ought to be productive, unlike Alan of Lille, she is thinking of producing pleasure, not babies. With respect to the dis-

---

91. Cf. Ovid, *Ars amatoria* 3.101ff., 193ff., 281ff., 747–68.

92. Cf. Ovid, *Ars amatoria* 3.769–808.

93. "Oeuvre, uevre" (1, 3, 4), *Dictionnaire de l'ancien français;* "uevre," *Dictionnaire de l'ancienne langue française et de tous ses dialectes du IXe au XVe siècles,* defined as "oeuvre, application du travail, de l'industrie . . . resultat du travail" (work, application of work or of industry . . . result of work).

94. "Ovrer," *Dictionnaire de l'ancien français.*

course of love's labor in *RII*, this representation of copulation is a crucial connection between the Ovidian labors taught by Friend and the Old Woman and the reproductive labors taught in the discourses of Reason, Nature, and Genius, to which we now turn.

Although Reason argues against being involved in *fin amors*, she is not against erotic love. However, like Nature and Genius, Reason insists that erotic love, to be healthy, must be a form of productive work. Like Andreas, Reason employs the discourse of passion first to define love as a "maladie" caused by the sight of and obsessive thinking about the loved one.[95] Unlike Andreas, however, Reason qualifies her definition to exclude sexual desire leading to procreation (4355–58). Copulation performed with procreation in mind is distinguished from *fin amors* by its potential productivity. Like Alan of Lille, then, Reason believes that lovers are workers, to whom are entrusted the absolutely serious work of reproduction:

> Nature veust que li filz saillent
> pour recontinuer *ceste euvre*,
> si que par l'un l'autre requeuvre.
> Pour ce i mist Nature delit,
> pour ce veust que l'en si delit
> que *cist ovrier* ne s'en foïssent
> et que *ceste euvre* ne haïssent.
>
> (4382–88; emphasis added)

[Nature wills . . . that children rise up to continue *the work* of generation, and that one's life may be regained by means of another. For this purpose Nature has implanted delight in man because she wants the *workman* to take pleasure in his *task* in order that he might neither flee from it nor hate it.]

Copulation is "ceste euvre," this work, and a person who engages in it is "cist ovrier." Since the Old French noun *ouvrier* signified someone who performed manual labor to earn his bread, in this model sexual pleasure is the wages necessary to attract good workers.[96] This theme is repeated in 4527–32 with the added condemnation of those (like the Old Woman)

---

95. 4347–58. This definition is clearly derived from that found in the *De amore*. Compare it with "Amor est passio quaedam innata procedens ex visione et immoderata cogitatione formae alterius sexus" (Love is an inborn suffering which results from the sight of, and uncontrolled thinking about, the beauty of the other sex; Andreas Capellanus, *De amore: Andreas Capellanus on Love*, ed. and trans. P. G. Walsh [London: Duckworth, 1982] 32–33).

96. "Ouvrier," *Dictionnaire de l'ancienne langue française et de tous ses dialectes du IXe au XVe siècles*, defined as "celui que travaille des mains pour gaigner un salaire" (he who works with his hands to

who use sex to gain money. Employing a condemnation based on class prejudice, Nature argues that those who seek the wages without producing are like "serfs and wretches" (4397). Among these wretches is the Dreamer himself (4573–74). The misguided aristocrats who only play at sex lose their youth and their time (4585–94).

Reason further develops her idea of love as productive labor in a later passage. This love, which she characterizes as "natural," is far from being a "maladie," but, rather, is a kind of *officium*, or duty. The discourse of passion is completely left behind in Reason's description of natural love:

> C'est naturiex enclinemenz
> de volair garder son semblable
> par entencion convenable,
> soit part voie d'engendreüre,
> ou par cure de norreture.
>
> (5740–44)

[It is a natural inclination to wish to preserve one's likeness by a suitable intention, either by engendering or by caring for nourishment.]

Later the sexual organs are styled as *estrumenz*, tools, by which men, like skilled craftsmen, can labor effectively (6931). Borrowed directly from the *De planctu*, this figure fits in neatly with Jean's general views of labor outlined above. Reason believes that reproductive copulation is neither to be praised nor blamed because it is simply a kind of work made necessary in a fallen world. Furthermore, this work is not a game in disguise. It is a serious labor that must be productive in order for humankind to survive. By participating in it—and *all* people should—individuals contribute materially to the common good. It is with the speeches of Nature and Genius that the full impact, both ideologically and artistically, of the discourse of love's labor from the *De planctu* is felt in *RII*. As with Reason, both characters turn the discourse of love's labor away from the work of courtship or seduction toward that of reproductive labor. Nature, for example, first appears not as a transcendent goddess dressed in fine robes, but as a blacksmith at her forge (15863–68). This description is repeated just a few lines later, where the seriousness of Nature's work is underscored: her work is productive and necessary because it defeats the efforts of death (15975–87).

---

gain a salary). *Ouvrier* also had the more general meaning of "he who acts" ("ovrier" [1], *Dictionnaire de l'ancien français*).

Later, in her confession to Genius, Nature describes herself as constable, vicar, and even chambermaid of God's creation (16751–52). As in the *De planctu*, Nature is found weeping, but in *RII* she weeps *not* because of homosexual unions but because Love and his forces are about to assault a maiden castle for the wrong reasons. Love and the Dreamer assault the castle for mere pleasure, not for reproduction, and this, according to the distinction made by Reason, is merely sport, not productive labor. Jean thus constructs love's labor in a way that seems, at first, thoroughly consistent with natural law ethics. In a passage heavily indebted to the *De planctu*, Nature states that humankind is the end of all her labor: "c'est la fins de tout mon labeur" (18998). Nevertheless, humankind alone disregards her work rules (19161–66). From here follows a short list of unproductive sexual practices. Like Nature in *De planctu*, Jean's Nature condemns sodomy (19204), and it is in keeping with her overall labor ideology that Nature characterizes the sodomite as "pareceus" (lazy) because his labor does not materially contribute to the common good. The message that Nature sends to Venus and Love is *not* that they are wrong to assault the castle, but that the assault must be carried out in the proper way, according to the rules in her book, which call for stalwarts to multiply their lines. This is the duty of all those who are gifted with the tools of Nature ("mes oustilz"; 19304). All who refuse those rules are to be excommunicated (19348–59).

Genius takes the basic labor discourse from Reason and Nature and again enlarges upon it. In even greater detail, he describes reproductive sex in the language of love's labor. Reproductive sex is likened not only to the work of blacksmiths and scribes but also to that of farmers. This is seen in the very beginning of Genius's address to the troops of Love. He blesses all those who work loyally, "qui leaument i travaille" (19507), and promises them paradise as a reward for their labors. To those who engage in unproductive sex, he offers excommunication and even castration. The richness of the imagery in this passage calls for a long quotation:

> Mar leur ait Nature doné,
> au faus don j'ai ci sarmoné,
> greffes, tables, marteaus, anclumes,
> selonc ses lais et ses coustumes,
> et sos a pointes bien aguës
> a l'usage de ses charrues,

et jaschieres, non pas perreuses,
mes planteïves et herbeuses,
qui d'arer et de trefoïr
ont mestier, qui an veust joïr,
quant il n'an veulent labourer
por lui servir et honourer,
ainz veulent Nature destruire
quant ses anclumes veulent fuire,
et ses tables et ses jaschieres,
qu'el fist precieuses et chieres
por les choses continuer,
que Mort ne les peüst tuer.

(19513–30)

[It was an evil hour when Nature, in accordance with her laws and customs, gave to those false ones of whom I have been speaking their styluses and tablets, hammers and anvils, the plowshares with good sharp points for the use of their plows, and the fallow fields, not stony but rich and verdurous, that need to be plowed and dug deep if one wants to enjoy them; it is an evil hour when they do not want to labor at serving and honoring Nature, but wish rather to destroy her by preferring to flee from her anvils, her tablets and fallow fields, which she made so precious and so dear in order to continue things so that Death might not kill them.]

Here the sex act is described using the verb *labourer*, an Old French verb carrying many of the same denotations and connotations of its Latin counterpart.[97] Not fearing a mixed metaphor, Genius describes the sexual organs as *greffes* and *tables* (styluses and tablets), *marteaus* and *anclumes* (hammers and anvils), and *sos a pointes bien agues* (plowshares with good sharp points; 19515, 19517). What is notable in *RII* is that Genius condemns not only those who use their tools unproductively but also those celibates who refuse to use them at all: those who flee the anvils, the tablets, and the fertile fields (19521–30). It is shameful, he argues, not to engage in this work because tools that are unused ("in oiseuse tenues") become rusty and useless. Fields that are not plowed remain fallow (19531–52). In addition, if all men ceased such work for sixty years, the

---

97. *Laborer* could mean simply "to work" or specifically "to work the earth." It could mean "to make something" or simply "to extend efforts to some end." It also carried the negative denotations of Latin *laborare*: to suffer ("Laborer," *Dictionnaire de l'ancienne langue française et de tous ses dialectes du IXe au XVe siècles;* "laborer" [1–4], *Dictionnaire de l'ancien français*).

human race would die out (19553–68). Genius therefore insists that the work of procreation is for *all* men and then goes on to list particular examples of slackers: homosexuals, those who engage in oral sex, and even the celibates (19569–19632). After excommunicating such people and even wishing them to be buried alive, Genius turns his attention to the loyal barons and encourages them to begin their work: Don't be lazy with respect to the works of Nature and put your tools to work (19657–70).

While the imagery employed in these passages comes from the *De planctu*, it is likely that the vehement insistence that the labor of procreation belongs to *all* people comes from Guillaume's *De periculis*. While Guillaume emphasized that manual labor was imposed as an obligation on each individual, the mendicants countered that the obligation to manual labor was imposed on mankind as a whole but not on individuals. Jean takes Guillaume's position on manual labor and merely transposes it into a different key, one that Bonaventure, who wrote his *De paupertate* years before Jean composed *RII*, had anticipated. As noted earlier, he wrote that the obligation to procreate, like the obligation to work with one's hands, is given to the species, not to individuals, and he consistently upheld the legitimacy of a division of labor. In this matter, as well as on the matter of manual labor for friars, *RII* is clearly imbued with the work ideology of *De periculis*.

Hence, what starts as an orthodox presentation of sexuality that is in line with natural law ethics becomes, in Jean's hands, heterodox. Although Thomas Aquinas defends sexuality leading to reproduction, he along with his Church also holds that virginity is nobler and more virtuous than marriage.[98] Jean's presentation suggests the opposite, that celibacy is somehow inferior to reproductive sexual relations because celibacy is not productive. Thus, a conservative strand of the discourse of love's labor, the strand fostering social control of sexuality in *De planctu*, takes a subversive although not Ovidian twist in *RII*. Jean, accepting the labor ideology of the *De periculis*, follows the premises of natural law ethics to an unorthodox conclusion: the common good of all mankind is best served when *everyone* performs the labor of reproduction.

As noted earlier, Genius in *RII* delights in comparing reproductive labor not only to labor in the shops but also to the labor of the fields. For

---

98. *Summa theologiae*, ed. Thomas Gilby, 60 vols. (New York: Blackfriars Press, 1963) 2a.2ae.152.4–5.

example, mixing up of the *officia* of the various estates, Genius encourages the aristocrats, to "plow the fields": "Arez, por Dieu, baron, arez, / et voz lignages reparez" (19671–72). In fact, he develops this image in lavish detail: the barons are to tuck up their shirts, raise the guideboards of their plows, and push their plowshares stiffly into the straight furrows. They are to stir up the horses fiercely, and never quit working, even when they are completely exhausted (19671–705).

Not content with only the agricultural metaphor, Genius continues his exhortation with the other two metaphors developed at length in the *De planctu:*

> Ne vos lessiez pas desconfire,
> greffes avez, pansez d'escrire.
> N'aiez pas les braz anmouflez:
> martelez, forgiez et souflez;
> aidiez Cloto et Lachesis,
> si que, se des fils cope .VI.
> Atropos, qui tant est vilaine,
> qu'il an resaille une dozaine.
>
> (19763–70)

[Don't let yourselves be overcome. You have styluses; think about writing. Don't leave your arms in muffs; hammer away, use forge and bellows; help Cloto and Lachesis so that if Atropos, who is so villainous, cuts six threads, a dozen more may spring from them.]

That the approach of Genius and Nature is meant as a critique of Guillaume's approach in *RI* becomes clear in Genius's explicit contrast of a lovely, fertile park with Guillaume's square garden (20213–596). One corresponds to the truth, while the other is a mere fable. The most important difference between the two parks, however, is one of productivity. The labor described in the square garden is sterile. It produces nothing for the common good, whereas the labor performed in the fertile park is productive. Genius concludes by admonishing his audience to "Pensez de Nature honorer, / servez la par bien laborer" (Think how to do honor to Nature; serve her by working well; 20608–9).

This is exactly what the Dreamer finally does. The climax of *RII* is a raucous description of the Dreamer's copulation with the rose, described using the discourse of love's labor. The Dreamer describes his own sexual tools in several ways, one of which is as two hammers (".II. martelez"). He then recognizes Nature's role in making him a good workman:

Mout me fist grant honeur Nature
quant m'arma des ceste armeüre
et m'an ansaigna si l'usage
que m'an fist bon ouvrier et sage.
(21347–50; emphasis added)

[Nature did me a great honor when she equipped me with this armor and so
taught me its use that *she made me a good and wise workman.*]

And, indeed, coition is here described as a work of labor, the Dreamer
going so far as to compare his labors with that of Hercules, a mythological figure whose defining characteristic was hard work.[99] Although the
poem ends before revealing the outcome of this action, its productive nature is at least suggested by the Dreamer's noting the scattering of his
seed over the rose. There is an implicit contrast, I believe, between this
passage and the passage in *RI* in which the frustrated Dreamer compares
himself to a peasant scattering seed in vain.[100] At least one critic, Kelly,
thinks that the rose becomes pregnant.[101]

The productive nature of the act is suggested in another way as well—
through Jean's story of Pygmalion, whose labors for love parallel in many
ways those of the Dreamer (20787–21184). This story is identified by
many critics as central to the message of *RII*, and another aspect of its
significance is revealed when it is read as part of Jean's discourse of love's
labor.[102] Pygmalion, whose central characteristic is that he is a craftsman,
a sculptor, "uns antaillierres" (20787), begins with an "unnatural" love. It
is unnatural because, in turning away from real women and serving an
ivory statue, it can never be productive. Pygmalion himself realizes that
his love does not come from Nature (20829–33). Pygmalion specifically
compares his love with that of Narcissus, whose fountain is central to the
experience of the sterile courtly lovers of *RI* (20846–49).

Although he is a craftsman, Pygmalion's art cannot duplicate Nature's
labor, and he fears that all his labors are in vain (20891–92). While human
art, as Jean explained earlier, attempts to copy Nature's work, it never

99. 21589–606. On the ideological meaning of Hercules, see Birgit van den Hoven, *Work in Ancient and Medieval Thought*, Dutch Monographs on Ancient History and Archaelogy (Amsterdam: J.
C. Gieben, 1996) 31–38.

100. *Rose* 3932–44, 21689–700.

101. Kelly 132.

102. Gunn writes "the theme of both the *exempla* [i.e., Pygmalion and Venus and Adonis] is the
same as that of the poem as a whole, love's progress and love's art" (151). See Allen (100–103) for a
recent summary of scholarship on the Pygmalion story in *RII*.

equals the work of Nature. No matter how cleverly she copies Nature, Art can never bring her products to life (15987–16034). The labors of Pygmalion's courtship are those performed by lovers following the art of *fin amors* outlined in *RI*. He buys clothes, gems, and flowers for the statue (20901–83). He sings to it, plays a dazzling array of instruments, and makes his clocks chime to announce his love (20991–21028). Finally, after asking the statue to be his wife, he even takes the statue to bed (20984–90, 21029–34).

It is only when Pygmalion renounces chastity, however, and implicitly agrees to productive sexual union that Venus takes pity on him and changes the statue into a living woman (21053–90). At last Pygmalion has a lover whose "anvil" can be productive when struck by his "hammer." At last he has a fertile field to plow. The result is a child: "Tant ont joué qu'ele est anceinte / de Paphus, don dit Renomee / que l'ille an fu Paphos nomee" (They played so well that she became pregnant with Paphus, whose fame gave the island of Paphos its name; 21154–56). Despite the polyphony of voices in *RII*, this myth captures the dominant (although not the sole) work ideology in the love's labor discourse of *RII*. It is a repudiation of that found in *RI* and, to some extent, that found in the *De amore* and even in the *Ars amatoria*. The work of love is more than just a courtly pastime. Love's workers do not rejoice in idleness but in what they can produce for the common good. Although this labor ideology does not come near to exhausting the possible meanings of *RII*, let alone of the *Rose* as a whole, it runs with remarkable consistency through the heart of *RII* and, as Alan M. F. Gunn has suggested, is certainly among the major motifs of the poem.

As noted earlier, in the *Rose*'s discourse of love's labor, love is quintessentially "repos travaillant," an oxymoron that captures the paradoxical nature of aristocratic love practices. One of the relationships between *RI* to *RII* is that of a dialog over the nature of love's labor. Guillaume de Lorris, perhaps an envious outsider from the bourgeoisie, writes of love's labor as a form of courtly effort but, in the character of Idleness, highlights the "repos" of "repos travaillant." For Guillaume, the courtly games of love do not have to be socially productive. They are essentially the fruits of *otium otiosum*. In contrast, Jean de Meun, perhaps a cleric with bourgeois roots, emphasizes the "travaillant" of this oxymoron. Indeed, except for sections of the discourse of Friend, the "repos" of love is almost banished completely from *RII*, where love is not only "travaillant," but "travaillant *an touz termes*," a phrase that can be translated "working *at all times,*" or *"in all places,"* or *"in all manners."*[103] *RII* is, on one level, an encyclopedia of all manners of love's labors. Its central message includes not only an exhortation to its readers that one must work hard at this skilled labor, but also that the work must be productive and must benefit the entire human community. It is a message constructed with words, figures, and ideologies taken not only from his literary predecessors, Ovid and Alan of Lille, but also from the powerful labor dispute that Jean de Meun no doubt witnessed not long before he composed *RII*.

---

103. *Rose* 4296. "'Termes,'" *Dictionnaire de l'ancienne langue française et de tous ses dialectes du IXe au XVe siècles*, defined as "territoire," "terme," "fin d'une période de temps," and "manière d'agir."

CHAPTER 6

The Vice of *Acedia* and the *Gentil Occupacioun* in Gower's *Confessio Amantis*

And it is a marvel he outdwells his hour,
For lovers ever run before the clock.
—*Shakespeare's Graziano*

Sloth in nobility, courtiers, schollers, or any men is the
chiefest cause that brings them in contempt.
—*Thomas Nashe*

I

Like all of the works studied so far, John Gower's *Confessio Amantis* treats the subject of love.[1] Unlike most of the others so far, however, the *Confessio* is not an art of love. It is a story collection framed by the confession of a frustrated lover. Far from an *ars amatoria*, in fact, the *Confessio* is a *remedia amoris*.[2] By the end of the work, the narrator, Amans, whom we eventually discover to be an old man, learns to accept the limits of his age and is cured of his illness, the hopeless love of a young woman. The discourse of love as passion, then, plays a significant and continuous role in the *Confessio*.

The *Confessio*'s frame narrative is built around a dialog between Amans and his confessor, Genius, a character from the *Romance of the rose* and the *De planctu naturae*.[3] Through this confession, Amans is led to ana-

1. This chapter is a substantially revised and enlarged version of my article "John Gower's *Confessio Amantis*, Ideology, and the 'Labor' of 'Love's Labor,'" *Re-visioning Gower: New Essays*, ed. R. F. Yeager (Asheville, N.C.: Pegasus Press, 1998) 147–58.

2. "Remedia Amoris" is, in fact, the title of Theresa Tinkle's chapter on the *Confessio* in *Medieval Venuses and Cupids: Sexuality, Hermeneutics, and English Poetry* (Stanford, Calif.: Stanford University Press, 1996).

3. For a summary of the scholarship on Genius, see Peter Nicholson, introduction, *An Annotated Index to the Commentary on Gower's "Confessio Amantis"* (Binghamton, N.Y.: Medieval and Renaissance

lyze the quality of his love and his behavior toward the young woman. The stories in the collection serve as *exempla* to illustrate various points Genius wishes to make about love. The structure of the collection is built around the tradition of the Seven Deadly Sins. In each of the books, the confessor analyzes one of the sins as it relates to love. While the sin of lust is excluded, the sin of *acedia*, or sloth, is not. Thus, in Book 4, Genius and Amans grapple with the question of what it means to be slothful in love, and whether Amans is guilty of this sin.[4] If sloth is a sin, then purposeful activity, work, must be a virtue "in amoris causa" (in the condition of love). Hence, the discourse of love as labor overshadows the discourse of passion in Book 4. In a crucial passage, for example, Genius defines love as an occupation fit for all gentle hearts:

Texts and Studies, 1989) 11–13. On the conception of Genius and his relationship to reason and to Venus in the *Confessio*, see especially George Economou, "The Character of Genius in Alan de Lille, Jean de Meun, and John Gower," *Chaucer Review* 4 (1970): 203–10. Economou argues that Gower modeled his character on the Genius in Alan of Lille's *De planctu* rather than on the character in Jean de Meun's *Rose*. For a summary of the scholarship on Amans, see Nicholson 15–17.

1. Several notable treatments of Book 4 of the *Confessio* serve as the background to this study. Russell Peck (*Kingship and Common Profit in Gower's "Confessio Amantis"* [Carbondale: Southern Illinois University Press, 1978] 79–98) treats the discrepancy between the unproductive nature of Amans's "labor" and his view that these are constructive activities. Peck sees Genius's role as trying to teach Amans "the proper industry of the third estate" (93). Rozalyn Levin ("The Passive Poet: Amans as Narrator in Book 4 of the *Confessio Amantis*," *Proceedings of the Illinois Medieval Association* [DeKalb, Ill., 1986] 3.114–29) argues that Book 4 reveals Gower's understanding of the courtly concept of "gentilesse." Linda Marie Zaerr ("The Dynamics of Sloth: Fin amour and Divine Mercy in John Gower's *Confessio Amantis*" [Diss. Univ. of Washington, 1987]) analyzes Gower's adaptation in Book 4 of Christian teachings regarding *acedia*, particularly the relationship of the *exempla* and the frame narrative. She finds that the book reveals fatal inconsistencies and flaws in the concept of *fin amors*. R. F. Yeager (*John Gower's Poetic: The Search for a New Arion* [Cambridge, U.K.: Brewer, 1990]) points out Gower's debt in Book 4 to Dame Nature's discussion of labor in the *Roman de la rose* and sees the book's discussion of labor as a counterexample to the slothful behavior of lovers (34, 161). He asserts that Gower's treatment of work is structured not according to the three estates model, but according to the division of believers into those in the active life or those in the contemplative life. The discussion serves as a foreshadowing and justification of Venus's eventual order in Book 8 for Amans to turn to the intellectual life (169).

Kurt Olsson's treatments of Book 4 are found in "Aspects of *Gentilesse* in John Gower's *Confessio Amantis*, Books III–V" (*John Gower: Recent Readings*, ed. R. F. Yeager [Kalamazoo, Mich.: Medieval Institute, 1989] 225–76) and chapter 10 of his book *John Gower and the Structures of Conversion: A Reading of the "Confessio Amantis"* ([Cambridge, U.K.: Brewer, 1992] 119–30). Within his treatment of the *Confessio* as an authored but multivoiced *compilatio*, Olsson argues that the discussion of love's labor and idleness is a form of "recreation," a genteel pasttime akin to the *demande d'amour*, designed to lead Amans to his eventual recognition of good and "honeste" love in Book 8 (*Structures of Conversion* 124–25, 226). The discussion is played out against the ambiguity of the sense of *otium*, with meanings ranging from "idleness" and "laziness" through "leisure" and "the fruits of leisure" (120). These studies all richly contribute to our understanding of Gower's use of his literary past, but none focuses specifically on the interplay of various traditional and contemporary ideologies of labor in Books 4 and 8.

> Among the gentil nacion
> Love is an occupacion,
> Which forto kepe hise lustes save
> Scholde every gentil herte have.[5]

[Among aristocrats, love is an occupation, in which every aristocratic heart should engage in order to keep its pleasures safe.]

Employing an even stronger term in a different passage, Genius suggests that love's labor is "mannes werk" that the timid of heart lack the courage to undertake (4.316–18). The slothful in love, claims Genius, have little chance of success. For Gower, however, what specifically is the work of love? In Book 4 of the *Confessio*, as in the *Ars amatoria* and the *De amore*, love's labor is primarily the labor of courtship although Genius will mention the labor of reproduction briefly. The frame narrative of the *Confessio* offers not an art of how to carry out this "occupacion" but rather a moral analysis of it based on Gower's adaptation of the traditional Christian vices and virtues. If not an *ars erotica*, it may be best classified as an early contribution to what Michel Foucault calls *scientia sexualis*, or perhaps more correctly the *scientia amoris*, for it attempts to examine the truth about matters of love and sexuality.[6]

In Book 8, when Amans is cured of his love malady, Gower returns to the discourse of love's labor to explain why Amans is not a fit lover. The conception of love's labor, however, is fundamentally altered in Book 8. Ostensibly influenced by either the *De planctu* or Jean de Meun's *Rose*, Gower now depicts love's labor as primarily the work of copulation and reproduction. Because Amans is revealed to be too old to perform this labor, Venus grants him a cure from his malady as well as the chance to take a retirement from love's labors, to enjoy, as it were, the fruits of monastic *otium*.

In analyzing the discourse of love's labor in the *Confessio*, one encounters interpretive difficulties similar to those that one encountered in the

---

5. John Gower, *Confessio Amantis: The English Works of John Gower*, ed. G. C. Macaulay, 2 vols., Early English Text Society 81–82 (1900; London: Oxford University Press, 1979) 4.1451–54 (1.340). All quotations of the *Confessio*'s English verses will be taken from this edition and cited in the text by book and line numbers. Modern English translations are my own. Quotations of the Latin introductory verses or glosses will be taken from this edition and cited in the text by volume and page numbers.

This passage, however, is qualified by the Latin marginal gloss, which reads: "Non quia sic se habet veritas, set opinio Amantum" (This is not true, but the opinion of lovers).

6. *A History of Sexuality*, trans. Robert Hurley, vol. 1 (New York: Vintage Books, 1978) 68.

Roman de la rose. Like the *Rose*, the *Confessio* is an immensely complex work of literature. One finds, for example, a mixture of themes from social policy to personal morality. On the level of morality, two different systems, the code of *fin amors* and that of Christianity, are ostensibly mixed together. In addition, although at various times the voices of Genius, Venus, and even Amans sound authoritative, none of these voices is consistently so. Finally, the *Confessio* comes with Latin introductory verses and marginal glosses that have a prima facie authority because of their language and their position. These glosses often give a more strictly moralistic interpretation than does the English text. While it is probable that Gower himself wrote the glosses, his authorship has not been proven beyond a doubt.[7] Hence, far from a monology, the *Confessio* contains a polyphony of voices, languages, and ideologies.

The somewhat strange mixture of amatory and moral discourses in the *Confessio* has been a concern throughout the recent history of Gower criticism. Some scholars have made attempts to reconcile the divergent discourses into one unified message, usually a Christian moral message.[8] Others believe that the *Confessio* is a failed work of literature because the discourses cannot finally be reconciled.[9] Still other scholars recognize that no reconciliation is possible but do not conclude that Gower has therefore failed. Theresa Tinkle, for example, writes:

By incorporating amatory as well as pastoral discourses, Gower accentuates the heterogeneity apparent in late medieval discussions of sexuality. He does not present us with a single hegemonic (ecclesiastical) discourse but rather invites contemplation of the relationships among the sundry and sometimes contradictory discourses that formulate medieval sexualities.[10]

7. On Gower's Latin verses and marginal notations, see R. F. Yeager, "English, Latin, and the Text as 'Other': The Page as Sign in the Work of John Gower," *Text* 3 (1987): 251–67. Yeager finds a polyphony of voices in the *Confessio* but identifies the Latin verses and glosses as the "authoritative" voice. Tinkle, however, does not agree that the Latin verses are meant as the authoritative interpretation of the English ones (182).

8. For a summary of scholarship, see Nicholson 3–10. See, for example, Alaistar Minnis, "'Moral Gower' and Medieval Literary Theory," *Gower's "Confessio Amantis": Responses and Reassessments* (Woodbridge, Suffolk, U.K.: Brewer, 1983) 50–78, and "John Gower: *Sapiens* in Ethics and Politics," *Medium Aevum* 49 (1980): 207–29.

For a critique of moralized readings that ignore Gower's humor and his debt to the French tradition of *fin amors*, see William Calin, "John Gower's Continuity in the Tradition of French *Fin' Amour*," *Mediaevalia* 16 (1990): 91–112.

9. Hugh White, "Division and Failure in Gower's *Confessio Amantis*," *Neophilologus* 72 (1988): 615.

10. Tinkle 179. On Gower's subversive discrepancies and contradictions, see also James Simpson, "Ironic Incongruence in the Prologue and Book I of Gower's *Confessio Amantis*," *Neophilologus* 72 (1988): 617–32.

Kurt Olsson, who treats the *Confessio* as an example of the medieval genre of *compilatio*, believes that, in terms of style, the entire collection speaks with one voice to the extent that Gower effaces the individual voices of his sources. At the same time, however, he argues that Gower creates his own discordant polyphony of voices, much like that found in the *Canterbury Tales*.[11] Unlike Tinkle, however, Olsson believes that readers are meant to work through the text's discords to achieve Gower's fundamentally moral message.

With respect to the discourse of love's labor, my understanding of the *Confessio*'s polyphony of voices and ideologies is consistent in part with both Tinkle's and Olsson's views. Specifically, with respect to labor, the *Confessio* is an ideological crossroads, containing many different voices with many different ideological colorings.[12] In the end, however, Gower's favored labor ideology is one that presents work as a necessary but positive human activity, one whose value derives not merely because it is an antidote to idleness but primarily because of its material contributions to the common profit. The same ideology emerges as Gower's last word in his treatment of love's labor.

II

Work ideology is not readily apparent from the collection's major structuring principle, the moral analysis based on the Seven Deadly Sins. Book 4 is structured using a standard treatment of the vice of *acedia* found in popular works of morality and confession manuals.[13] The traditional labor ideology implied in the treatment of *acedia* valued labor primarily as an antidote to idleness and not for what it produced for the community. However, while this ideology is found in the *Confessio*, it is not the dominant ideology of the work.

Acedia represented a much more complex constellation of moral failings than those denoted by the modern English "sloth."[14] Siegfried Wen-

11. Olsson 10–15.

12. I take the term "ideological crossroads" from the French "carrefour idéologique" of Jean-Charles Payen, "*Le Roman de la rose* et la notion de carrefour idéologique," *Romanistische Zeitschrift für Literaturgeschichte* 1 (1977): 193.

13. On Gower's debt to the tradition of medieval penitential literature, see John McNally, "The Penitential and Courtly Traditions in Gower's *Confessio Amantis*," *Studies in Medieval Culture*, ed. John R. Somerfeldt (Kalamazoo, Mich.: Medieval Institute, 1964) 74–94; Gerald Kinneavy, "Gower's *Confessio Amantis* and the Penitentials," *Chaucer Review* 19 (1984): 144–63; and Mary Flowers Braswell, *The Medieval Sinner* (Rutherford, N.J.: Fairleigh Dickinson University Press, 1983) 81–87.

14. See Morton Bloomfield, *The Seven Deadly Sins* (East Lansing: Michigan State College Press, 1952) 157–202. John Bowers (*The Crisis of Will in "Piers Plowman"* [Washington, D.C.: The Catholic

zel has treated the subject thoroughly, and the following short summary of its history is heavily indebted to his research.[15] Greek in origin, *acedia* means literally "lack of care."[16] The discussion of the vice begins with the fourth-century Egyptian desert fathers. Evagrius Ponticus identified *acedia* with the "noonday demon" of Psalm 90, who tempts monks to leave their way of life. He used it to refer to the depression and listlessness caused by the monotony of life in the desert.[17] According to Evagrius, its chief remedy was patience. Later, John Cassien offered the classic definition of the vice as "taedium cordis," weariness of the heart. Further, not only did he establish for the first time the branches of the vice—idleness, somnolence, rudeness, restlessness, wandering about, instability of mind, chattering, and inquisitiveness—but he also added two new remedies: courage and manual labor.[18]

By the late Middle Ages, two major traditions concerning *acedia* clearly existed: one was scholarly, the other popular.[19] On the one hand, *acedia* was thought to be a sin of the spirit. In the words of Hugh of St. Victor it is: "ex confusione mentis nata tristitia, sive taedium et amaritido animi immoderata" (a sadness born of confusion of the mind, or weariness and immoderate bitterness of the soul).[20] On the other hand, *acedia* was also thought to be a sin of the flesh, idleness. While Geoffrey Chaucer's Parson speaks primarily of spiritual *acedia* in his sermon, calling it at one point "the angwissh of troubled herte" (the anxiety of a troubled heart), his Second Nun opens her tale with a treatment of fleshly *acedia*, which

---

University of America Press, 1986] 62) gives three reasons why modern readers either do not recognize *acedia* in medieval literature when they see it or do not sympathize with the writer's concerns when he treats the vice: (1) the subject was hidden under specialized terminology; (2) the symptoms were so well known that, rather than mentioning the vice by name, medieval writers often mentioned only the symptoms; and (3) the concept of "sloth" has narrowed so much over time that today it means little more than a tendency to procrastinate.

Some of this summary has already appeared in my article "Love, Labor, and Sloth in Chaucer's *Troilus and Criseyde,*" *Chaucer Review* 26 (1992): 350–68.

15. See Siegfried Wenzel, *The Sin of Sloth: Acedia in Medieval Thought and Literature* (Chapel Hill: University of North Carolina Press, 1967) 174–81. See also Wenzel's "Acedia, 700–1200," *Traditio* 22 (1966): 72–102; and Reinhard Kuhn, *The Demon of Noontide: Ennui in Western Literature* (Princeton, N.J.: Princeton University Press, 1976).

16. Wenzel, *Sin of Sloth* 6.

17. For a recent treatment of *acedia* as a form of depression, see Kathleen Norris, *The Cloister Walk* (New York: Riverhead Books, 1996) 130–34.

18. John Cassien, *Institutions cénobitiques*, ed. Jean-Claude Guy (Paris: Editions du Cerf, 1965) 5.1 (191). See also Wenzel, *Sin of Sloth* 5–22.

19. Wenzel, *Sin of Sloth* 174.

20. Hugh of St. Victor, *Summa de sacramentis fidei, Patrologiae cursus completus, Sive bibliotheca universalis*, ed. J.-P. Migne, 221 vols. (Paris, 1844–1864) 2.13.1 (176.526).

she calls "the ministre and the norice unto vices" (the minister and nurse-maid of the vices).[21] If the remedy for fleshly *acedia* was "bysynesse," the major remedy for spiritual *acedia* was *fortitudo*, or courage, that, as the Parson says, "may endure by long suffraunce the travailles that been covenable" (may endure by patience the labors that are appropriate; 10.730).

Even in the popular moral tradition of *acedia*, however, the emphasis was on *spiritual* laziness or *spiritual* lack of industry, not on their secular applications.[22] In the *Book of Vices and Virtues*, an English translation of Frère Lorens's thirteenth-century *Somme le Roi*, for example, the treatment of sloth focuses almost exclusively on spiritual torpor and laziness. In the brief treatment of "heuynesse," or somnolence, for example, the author defines the branch as "whan a man is so heuy þat he loueþ not but to lyn and reste & slepe" (when a man is so heavy that he loves nothing but lying down for rest and sleep), but he immediately adds, "oþerwhile þei beþ a-waked wel y-now as to werkes of þe world, but to þe werkes of God þei beþ a-sleped" (at other times they are perfectly awake for the works of this world, but are asleep for the works of God).[23] Hence, an industrious but religiously tepid worker could be guilty of *acedia*.

Nevertheless, as *acedia* came to be identified more and more closely with plain idleness, the failure to perform secular work also came to be included. Accordingly, the value of labor arose primarily from its quality as an antidote to idleness, not necessarily from what it could produce for the community. Just as Benedict instructed his monks to perform manual labor primarily as a way of avoiding idleness, the fifteenth-century author of *Jacob's Well*, quoting St. Jerome, writes: "Alwey do sum good werk, þat þe feend may fynde þe occupyed; for he may noȝt lyȝtly be takyn of þe devyll þat alwey hauntyth good occupacyoun" (Always do some good work so that the fiend might find you occupied, for he who is always occupied in a good way may not easily be taken by the devil).[24] Indeed, when treating *acedia*, Frère Lorens compares the activity of the

---

21. *The Riverside Chaucer*, ed. Larry D. Benson, 3rd ed. (Boston: Houghton Mifflin, 1987) 10.677, 8.1. All quotations from Chaucer will be taken from this edition. The modern English translations are my own.

22. Wenzel, *Sin of Sloth* 88, 90, 96.

23. *The Book of Vices and Virtues*, ed. W. Nelson Francis, Early English Text Society, OS, 217 (London: Oxford University Press, 1942) 27. *Acedia* is similarly a lack of spiritual work in John Myrc, *Instructions for Parish Priests*, ed. Edward Peacock, 2nd rev. ed., Early English Text Society, OS, 31 (1902; Rochester, N.Y.: Boydell & Brewer, 1996) 33–34.

24. *Jacob's Well*, ed. Arthur Brandeis, Early English Text Society, OS, 115 (1900; Millwood, N.Y.: Kraus, 1988) 1.105.

virtuous Christian to the struggles of knights and specifically contrasts it to the acquisitive and productive labor of city dwellers.[25] St. Thomas Aquinas argued that idleness is sinful for all Christians, but any activity, not just productive manual labor, that can defeat idleness is a licit way to combat it.[26]

III

Both John Gower and Geoffrey Chaucer were citizens of late-fourteenth-century England. The late fourteenth century, in the midst of what one historian has called "The Age of Anxiety," was an important time in the history of labor.[27] The depopulation resulting from the Black Plague, for example, had an unsettling effect on the value, and thus the stability, of manual labor, both rural and urban. In England this led in 1349 to such artificial means of keeping down wages as Edward III's royal ordinance, and in 1351 to Parliament's Statute of Laborers. Written in French, the statute begins by castigating the idle and those workers who sought to take advantage of the labor shortage to demand "outrageous" wages.[28] The statute ordered a rollback to wage levels common in 1346–1347 and forced workers to swear an oath of obedience to the terms of the Statute. Failure to abide by the terms of the oath was the mechanism by which the statute's terms could be enforced. The statute was generally vigorously enforced in England and was somewhat successful in counteracting the effects of the marketplace.[29] Bronislaw Geremek argues that such statutes attempted to ground all vice in the sin of sloth, but they went beyond a simple moral condemnation. The unwillingness to work was seen as a social danger, a crime.[30]

25. *Book of Vices and Virtues* 161–62.

26. *Quaestiones Quodlibetales*, ed. Raymund Spiazzi, 8th ed. (Rome: Marietti, 1949) 149–50.

27. William Bouwsma, "Anxiety and the Formation of Early Modern Culture," *After the Reformation: Essays in Honor of J. H. Hexter*, ed. Barbara C. Malament (Philadelphia: University of Pennsylvania Press, 1980) 215–46. See also Steven A. Epstein, "Labor and Guilds in Crisis: The Fourteenth Century," *Wage Labor and Guilds in Medieval Europe* (Chapel Hill: University of North Carolina Press, 1991) 207–56. And, finally, see the comments of Wenzel, *Sin of Sloth* 92.

For a skeptical assessment of the magnitude of fourteenth-century changes in labor ideology, see R. B. Dobson, introduction, *The Peasants' Revolt of 1381* (New York: St. Martin's Press, 1970) 12.

28. The original French text of the statute can be found in Bertha Putnam, *The Enforcement of the Statute of Labourers during the First Decade after the Black Death, 1349–1359*, Studies in History, Economics, and Public Law 32 (1908; New York: AMS, 1970) 12*–17*. An English translation is found in Dobson 63–68.

29. On the Statute of Laborers, see Putman 1–6; Epstein 232–39; and Robert C. Palmer, *English Law in the Age of the Black Death, 1348–1381* (Chapel Hill: University of North Carolina Press, 1993).

30. Bronislaw Geremek, "Le refus du travail dans la société urbaine du bas moyen âge," *Le travail*

Social unrest was common in many of the Western European countries during the late Middle Ages, and the unrest brought labor issues to the forefront. The causes of the English Peasants' Revolt of 1381 are numerous and may have varied from region to region, but an unhappiness with the consequences of the Statute of Laborers was at least an indirect influence.[31] In addition, rebels arose not only from among the peasants but also from among various urban classes, particularly artisans, and even from among the gentry.[32] Gower himself lamented the revolt and criticized its participants in his Latin work, the *Vox Clamantis*. In the *Vox*, Gower criticizes the failings of all the various estates, but among his criticisms of the third estate is the abandonment of agricultural work.[33]

Labor issues arose in the writings of religious reformers. Like Guillaume de Saint-Amour, John Wycliffe and the Lollards rejected the idea of religious mendicancy and criticized the idleness of monks, friars, and "clerks possessioners." They argued that all religious should perform manual labor.[34] The argument for work in *An Apology for Lollard Doctrines*, for example, is fairly traditional, quoting, as it does, the Bible, St. Augustine's *De opere monachorum*, and St. Benedict's *Rule*. The author ends, however, with an encomium to the productivity of labor: "gloriouse is þe frut of good labors; for þe Psalme seiþ, For þu schalt ete þe labor of þi handis, þu art blessid, and wel schal be to þe" (the fruit of good labors

---

au moyen âge: Une approche interdisciplinaire, ed. Jacqueline Hamesse and Collette Muraille-Samaran (Louvain-la-Neuve: Institut d'études médiévales de l'Université Catholique de Louvain, 1990) 387–92.

31. Rodney Hilton, *Bond Men Made Free: Medieval Peasant Movements and the English Rising of 1381* (London: Temple Smith, 1973) 151–56, 230.

32. On the revolt of 1381, see Dobson 1–31; Hilton 137–236; Christopher Dyer, "The Social and Economic Background to the Rural Revolt of 1381," *The English Rising of 1381*, ed. R. H. Hilton and T. H. Aston (Cambridge, U.K.: Cambridge University Press, 1984) 9–42; A. F. Butcher, "English Urban Society and the Revolt of 1381," *The English Rising of 1381* 84–111; and Epstein 248–56.

33. "*Vox Clamantis*": *The Latin Works: The Complete Works of John Gower*, ed. G. C. Macaulay, vol. 4 (Oxford, U.K.: Clarendon Press, 1901) 1.3 (28–30).

34. On the idleness of the friars, see Wycliffe's translation and commentary on the *Rule* of St. Francis (*The English Works of Wyclif*, ed. F. D. Matthew, 2nd ed. [1902 Millwood, N.Y.: Kraus, 1978] 50–51) and a passage on "Mendicancy" (*Selections from English Wycliffite Writings*, ed. Anne Hudson [Cambridge, U.K.: Cambridge University Press, 1978] 95). Another attack on the friars is contained in "Tractatus de Pseudo-Freris" (*English Works* 294–324). On the obligation to work and the idleness of "clerks possessioners," see "Of Clerks Possessioners" (*English Works* 136).

On Wycliffe's hatred of the friars, see Herbert Workman, *John Wyclif: A Study of the English Medieval Church* (1926; Hamden, Conn.: Archon Books, 1966) 2.97–108. Although Wycliff praised the virtue of labor, the necessity for clergy to work arose primarily from his theory of the disendowment of the clergy (Anne Hudson, *The Premature Reformation: Wycliffite Texts and Lollard History* [Oxford, U.K.: Clarendon Press, 1988] 340–41).

is glorious, for the Psalm says: because you will eat the labor of your hands, you are blessed and you will be well).[35]

Finally, changes in the methods of timekeeping affected ideas of work and work productivity. The advent of the mechanical clock, which rapidly became installed in city squares during the late fourteenth century, changed old work rhythms and inaugurated new conceptions of urban "work time."[36] "The unusual anxiety of the period after 1300," writes William Bouwsma, "is . . . implicit in its novel concern with the passage of time, which found general expression in the familiar new historical consciousness of the Renaissance and was manifested more particularly in efforts to mark the flow of time with chronometers and to control its use by profitably filling the hours.[37]

This new urgency about time contrasts starkly with attitudes toward time in the earlier Middle Ages. Marc Bloch, for example, writes that early medieval man had a vast indifference to time.[38] To support this claim, he relates an anecdote from the *Chronicle of Hainault* in 1188 C.E. showing the confusion about the exact time. The chronicle relates that a duel was supposed to begin at the hour of nones. While one party put in an appearance at the ninth hour, dawn, his adversary did not show up. The judges became confused as to whether, in fact, the hour of nones had passed and which monastic bells to use as the standard for the time became a subject of debate.[39] This vast indifference to time was to change dramatically over the course of the fourteenth century.

Historians agree that the invention of the mechanical clock occurred in the middle of the thirteenth century. It was the invention of the verge escapement with foliot that allowed its creation.[40] The exact date of its invention and the name of the inventor are unknown, for medieval writ-

35. See, for example, the sections "þat religious men are bounde to bodily warks" and "þat it is not leful to religious to beg" in *An Apology for Lollard Doctrines, Attributed to John Wicliffe*, ed. James Henthorn Todd (1842; New York: AMS, 1968) 105–13.

36. See Jacques LeGoff, "Merchant's Time and Church's Time in the Middle Ages," and "Labor Time in the 'Crisis' of the Fourteenth Century: From Medieval Time to Modern Time," *Time, Work, and Culture in the Middle Ages*, trans. Arthur Goldhammer (Chicago: University of Chicago Press, 1980) 29–52.

37. Bouwsma 218–19. Gerhard Dohrn-van Rossum writes: "Scholars of European history discovered that the fundamental change in time consciousness occurred with the transition from an agrarian to an industrial society that began in the Middle Ages" (*History of the Hour: Clocks and Modern Temporal Orders*, trans. Thomas Dunlap [Chicago: University of Chicago Press, 1996] 2).

38. Marc Bloch, *Feudal Society*, trans. L. A. Manyon (Chicago: University of Chicago Press, 1961) 73.

39. Giselbert of Mons, *Chronicle of Hainault;* quoted in Bloch 74.

40. Carlo M. Cippola, *Clocks and Culture, 1300–1700* (London: Collins, 1967) 39.

ers generally used the Latin word *horologium* for all kinds of timekeeping devices, including sundials, water clocks, fire clocks, and mechanical clocks.[41] It is not until the fourteenth century that one finds indisputable references to mechanical clocks. Two of these early references are to clocks in England: Roger Stoke's clock for Norwich Cathedral (1321–1325) and Richard of Wallingford's clock for St. Albans (1330–1364).[42]

Although it is not necessarily true that public clocks preceded private clocks, by the end of the fourteenth century, public clocks were standard in most European towns. Moreover, until the mid-fifteenth century, most clocks were public rather than private. Gerhard Dohrn van Rossum argues that the year 1370 marks the beginning of a significantly new period. Between 1370 and 1380, just preceding the composition of the *Confessio*, Dohrn van Rossum finds records of seventy-six new public clocks in Western Europe. By 1400, all large cities in Western Europe had a public clock.[43]

Why were these clocks first installed in towns? Jacques LeGoff argues that the merchant class was behind clocks. For the merchant, writes LeGoff, time was a commodity to be sold, and the clock helped him sell or buy more efficiently. In fact, LeGoff sees the clock as the merchants' instrument of social, economic, and political domination.[44] Dohrn van Rossum, however, has challenged LeGoff's argument. He argues that, if anything, the merchants initially *opposed* the expenses associated with the purchase of the mechanical timepieces. The public clock was most often introduced by princes, who were interested in adding a new element of prestige to their towns.[45] Regardless of the role of the merchants, most historians agree that civic pride was a motivating factor in having the clocks installed. Landes even speaks of the "totemic role" of the new clocks.[46]

41. David S. Landes, *Revolution in Time: Clocks and the Making of the Modern World* (Cambridge, Mass: Belknap Press of Harvard University Press, 1983) 53. See also Gerhard Dohrn van Rossum, "Les 'orlogeurs' artistes et experts (XIVᵉ–XVᵉ siècles)," *Prosopographie et genèse de l'état moderne*, ed. Françoise Autrand (Paris: Centre National des Lettres, 1986) 233.

42. Landes 53.

43. Dohrn van Rossum, "Les 'orlogeurs' artistes" 235. Starting in the middle of the fourteenth century, chamber clocks begin to show up in inventories and accounts (Landes 80).

44. LeGoff, "Merchant's Time" 34–35.

45. Dohrn-van Rossum, *History of the Hour* 138–71.

46. Cippola also regards civic pride as the prime motivation for the installation of the public clock (42). Landes says that mechanical clocks were the technological marvel of their age and cites Froissart's poem on clocks to prove it (57, 81–82). The remark on the "totemic role" of clocks appears on page 79.

What were the effects of the installation of public clocks? First of all, the marking of the hours by the monastery and, later, by the public clock meant that time in medieval Europe was public and communal, not individual.[47] Second, the mechanical clock forced the transition from thinking of time in larger units—such as the day or the season—toward smaller units. Third, the concept of the hour, the length of which initially varied according to the season of the year, changed to denote twenty-four equal parts of the day.

As clocks began to be common in public squares, the daily rhythms of urban workers began to change.[48] For example, in 1306 the city of Sarum passed a law regulating marketplace activity. The law read, in part, that "before the clock of the Cathedral had struck one, no person was to purchase or cause to be purchased flesh, fish or other victuals."[49] An even better reference to the effect of the clock on city life comes from an early-fifteenth-century didactic work called *Dives and Pauper*, an extended dialog aimed at an audience of newly literate, worldly, but also pious laymen. The audience is represented by the character Dives. The character Pauper, who probably represents a well-educated preaching friar, is his mentor. In one relevant section of the work, Pauper speaks of time and how the heavenly bodies are natural timekeepers.[50] He calls the heavenly bodies natural "horloges" and insists that, although they are set in the heavens for men to use to govern their behavior, they do not determine that behavior. At this point, however, Pauper makes a critical distinction between city folk and rural folk: city folk use clocks, not heavenly bodies, to regulate their lives. He says: "þe relygious rewlyn hem be þe lamppe and be þe horlege, and in cyteis and tounnys meen rewlyn hem be þe clokke" (The persons in religious orders rule themselves by means of the lamp and the clock, and in cities and towns men rule themselves by the clock; 120). For monks and city folk, then, instead of a time linked solely to heavenly events or to the irregular ecclesiastical hours, a more certain, regular time arose. The clock began to govern the lives of men. LeGoff writes: "Time was no longer associated with cataclysms or festivals but

47. Landes 69.
48. LeGoff, "Labor Time" 44; and Landes 77.
49. Cited in Landes 77; and in C. F. C. Beeson, *English Church Clocks, 1280–1850* (London: Antiquarian Horological Society, 1971) 16.
50. *Dives and Pauper*, ed. Priscilla Heath Barnum, Early English Text Society 275 (London: Oxford University Press, 1976) 1.1.120. The quotation from this text is taken from this edition and cited in the text by page number. The modern English translation is my own.

rather with daily life, a sort of chronological net in which urban life was caught."[51]

The "chronological net" made possible by the public clock was a source of some anxiety to urban dwellers but had not yet affected the rural population.[52] Landes agrees that the late-medieval urban sense of time was different from the agrarian sense of time. Urban life was still governed by bells, but the tempo of these time signals increased. He writes:

As commerce developed and industry expanded, the complexity of life and work required an ever larger array of time signals. These were given, as in the monasteries, by bells: the urban commune in this sense was the heir and imitator of the religious community. Bells sounded for the start of work, meal breaks, end of work, closing of gates, start of market, close of market, assembly, emergencies, council meetings, end of drink service, time for street cleaning, curfew, and so on through an extraordinary variety of special peals in individual towns and cities.[53]

What is particularly significant is that the change in the measurement of time led also to a change in attitudes toward labor. LeGoff, for example, argues that earlier agrarian attitudes toward work were tied to seasonal agrarian rhythms and not concerned so much with productivity.[54] With the advent of the clock, however, work time, and thus productivity, could be more accurately measured. This led to bitter disputes between management and labor over the length of the working day.[55] The new methods of time measurement were a two-edged sword for workers: employers now had a more accurately measured period of time to fill, but employees now had more accurate boundaries marking off the limits of their work obligations. Landes believes that the invention of the clock made things better rather than worse for the workers. At least they knew that the length of the working hours would stay more or less constant.[56]

Finally, this change in concepts of work time led to changes in the ethics of work. The theme of using one's time profitably became more dramatic and insistent in moral and ethical instruction.[57] This, in turn,

---

51. LeGoff, "Labor Time" 48.

52. According to Bousma, "In cities time was experienced differently from in the country; change became a function not merely of the eternal rhythms of nature but of the unpredictable human will, and with the future always dependent on the actions of other men it became increasingly uncertain" (227–28).

53. Landes 72.   54. LeGoff, "Labor" 44.

55. LeGoff, "Labor" 45–49.   56. Landes 74–75.

57. Landes 74–75.

led to the notable preoccupation of the Italian humanists (and of late-fourteenth and fifteenth-century English and French poets) with the profitable use of time. This attitude can be found, for example, in the *Canterbury Tales*. In the Man of Law's Prologue, after the Host determines the exact hour, he exhorts the pilgrims to waste no more time and continues:

> Lordynges, the tyme wasteth nyght and day,
> And steleth from us, what pryvely slepynge,
> And what thurgh necligence in oure wakynge,
> As dooth the streem that turneth nevere agayn,
> Descendynge from the montaigne into playn.
> Wel kan Senec and many a philosophre
> Biwaillen tyme moore than gold in cofre;
> For "Los of catel may recovered be,
> But los of tyme shendeth us," quod he.
> It wol nat come agayn, withouten drede,
> Namoore than wole Malkynes maydenhede,
> Whan she hath lost it in hir wantownesse.
> Lat us nat mowlen thus in ydelnesse.
>
> (2.20–32)

[Gentlemen, time wastes away night and day, and steals away from us, either sleeping privately or being negligent when awake. It flows away as does a stream descending down from a mountain to the plain and never returning again. Seneca and many other philosophers may indeed lament the loss of time more than the loss of gold in chests. As Seneca says, "Lost possessions may be recovered, but lost time ruins us." Without a doubt, time will not come again, any more than will Malkin's virginity, when she has lost it by being wanton. Let us not grow moldy in idleness.]

Although the Host cites an ancient authority for his views, he is really exhibiting here a typically late-medieval concern. Not satisfied with simply lamenting the passage of time, he insists that his fellow pilgrims use their time productively.

Landes also notes that the waves of plague made late-medieval people more aware of time's passing and of the need to save time. Moreover, this awareness can be seen in members of all social classes. The preaching clergy, for example, did their part to highlight this. "The clergy—those old keepers of the clocks, ringers of bells, masters of the calculus of purgatory and redemption," Landes writes, "waxed eloquent on this point, since it was precisely here that their own regimen intersected with, translated into, a spiritual discipline for the layman."[58] For example, Thomas à Kempis, who authored one of the most popular late-medieval books of private devotion, *The Imitation of Christ*, writes:

But how sad that you do not spend this time well while you have strength to gather the merit which will allow you to live forever! The time will come when you will wish for one day or one hour for changing your ways, and I do not know whether you will get it.[59]

Petrarch quoted Emperor Charles IV as saying that time "is so precious, nay so inestimable a possession, that it is the one thing that the learned agree can justify avarice."[60] Another example comes from the Dominican Domenico Calva of Pisa, who died in 1342. Using the vocabulary of the merchant, Calva gave over two chapters of his *Disciplina degli Spirituali* to the "waste of time" and to the duty to save and make the most of one's time.[61]

If one ought to employ time well for the saving of one's soul, the merchant classes saw its value for making money. Leon Battista Alberti, for example, wrote:

In the morning when I get up, the first thing I do is think as though to myself: what am I going to do today? So many things: I count them, think about them, and to each I assign its time. . . . I'd rather lose sleep than time, in the sense of the proper time for doing what has to be done. [The important thing is] to watch the time, and assign things by time, to devote oneself to business and never lose an hour of time. . . . He who knows how not to waste time can do just about anything; and he who knows how to make use of time, he will be lord of whatever he wants.[62]

Alberti's remarks suggest that such an ethic was alive and well, at least in Italy.

Labor and productivity issues, then, played an important role in late-fourteenth-century England and were essential parts of the writing context for both Chaucer and Gower. While evidence on typical fourteenth-century labor ideologies is not consistent, historians such as Margo Todd, Paul Münch, and LeGoff have argued that certain aspects of what Max

58. Landes 90.

59. Thomas à Kempis, *The Imitation of Christ*, trans. William C. Creasy (Macon, Ga.: Mercer University Press, 1989) 27.

60. *Petrarch: A Humanist among Princes*, trans. David Thompson (New York: Harper & Row, 1971) X.1 (101).

61. Domenico Calva, *Disciplina degli Spirituali*; quoted in LeGoff's "Labor Time" 50–51.

62. Leon Battista Alberti, *I Libri della famiglia*; quoted in Landes 91–92.

Weber identified as the Protestant work ethic are to be found in the writings of the early humanists.[63] Christopher Dyer has also recently conducted a study of work attitudes in late-fourteenth-century Europe and has found that, indeed, evidence exists of a new work ethic or ethics at that time. Dyer found that different groups had different attitudes toward work. Intellectuals, he found, were more likely to stress the dignity of work rather than its roots in sin. Employers advocated fixed working hours, labor discipline, and regular contracts. The government, Dyer finds, was interested in regulating not only work but also unsuitable uses of leisure time. Even peasants and lower-level wage earners of the time began to be aware of a rudimentary work ethic.[64] To be specific, in this context a "new" work ethic means a general belief in the dignity of work (as opposed to seeing the work obligation as merely an effect of man's fall), an intense concern for labor productivity, and the belief that time is a commodity to be spent wisely.[65] Not included, however, are the conviction of labor as a "calling" and a commitment to the acquisition of riches as a sign of election.[66] Nevertheless, since concerns with work productivity arose in the writings of Alan of Lille and Jean de Meun, it may be just as valid to see fourteenth-century developments as intensifications of twelfth-century changes in medieval work ideologies rather than as radically new positions.[67]

63. Max Weber, *The Protestant Ethic and the Spirit of Capitalism*, trans. Talcott Parons (1930; New York: Charles Scribner's Sons, 1956); Margo Todd, "Work, Wealth and Welfare," *Christian Humanism and the Puritan Social Order* (Cambridge, U.K.: Cambridge University Press, 1987) 118–75; Paul Münch, "The Thesis before Weber: An Archaeology," *Weber's "Protestant Ethic": Origins, Evidence, Contexts*, ed. Hartmut Lehmann and Guenther Roth, Publications of the German Historical Institute (Cambridge, U.K.: Cambridge University Press, 1993) 51–71; and LeGoff, "Labor Time" 48–52.

G. R. Owst finds foreshadowings of the Protestant work ethic in fourteenth-century sermons (*Literature and Pulpit in Medieval England*, 2nd ed. [New York: Barnes & Noble, 1961] 557). Yeager calls Gower a fourteenth-century humanist (*John Gower's Poetic* 13–14).

64. Christopher Dyer, "Work Ethics in the Fourteenth Century," *The Problem of Labour in Fourteenth-Century England*, ed. James Bothwell et al. (York, U.K.: York Medieval Press, 2000) 21–41.

65. Weber 157–59, 178–79.

66. Weber 62–63, 79ff., 162–63.

Although Gower praises work, he is no protocapitalist. In the *Mirour*, he cautions that the person who works to acquire wealth risks falling into the sin of covetousness (14485–90). Quotations from the *Mirour* will be taken from *The French Works: The Complete Works of John Gower*, ed. G. C. Macaulay, vol. 1 [Oxford, U.K.: Clarendon Press, 1899], and cited in the text by line numbers. English translations will be taken from *Mirour de l'Omme*, trans. William Burton Wilson [East Lansing, Mich.: Colleagues Press, 1992]).

67. George Ovitt, Jr., for example, believes the crucial shift in attitudes toward labor occurred in the twelfth century (*The Restoration of Perfection* [New Brunswick, N.J.: Rutgers University Press, 1987] 137).

Late-medieval attitudes toward work can be perceived in the preaching of the age. G. R. Owst, for example, finds in preaching a concern for the health of medieval society and a corresponding insistence that all classes contribute by doing their appropriate work. He quotes, for example, the *Summa predicantium* of the Dominican John Bromyard, compiled during the fourteenth century in England:

God has ordained three classes of men, namely, labourers such as husbandmen and craftsmen to support the whole body of the Church after the manner of feet, knights to defend it in the fashion of hands, clergy to rule and lead it after the manner of eyes. And all the aforesaid who maintain their status are of the family of God. The Devil, however, finds a certain class, namely, the slothful, who belong to no Order. They neither labour with the rustics, nor travel about with the merchants, nor fight with the knights, nor pray and chant with the clergy.[68]

Owst also finds much of the old attitude toward work: that it is punishment for Adam's sin and a good remedy for idleness. Nevertheless, he finds a new interest in the positive benefits of work. One preacher notes:

But natheles, thou3 werkes doon in dedli synne profiteth no3t to encrecyng of blisse, 3eet thei profiten to thre thynges: oon is that the worldli goodes of suche men schul encrece the more . . . And therfore it is good evere to wirche wel.[69]

[But nonetheless, although works done in deadly sin are not capable of increasing bliss, yet they are good for three things: one is that the worldly good of such men shall increase the more . . . And, therefore, it is good always to work well.]

---

68. Owst 554. Very similar to this are the remarks of Gower's contemporary, Bishop Thomas Brinton: "Nam cum homo naturaliter nascitur ad laborem, exercitus Christianorum qui principaliter stat in tribus gradibus, scilicet prelatorum, religiosorum, et laboratorum, sub spe regni Dei debet continue occupari vel in operibus actiue vite . . . vel in operibus vite contemplatiue, . . . vel in operibus seruitutis humane, qualia sunt fodere, orare, serere, metere, et propriis manibus laborare in tantum quod miseri ociosi, qui in nullo gradu istorum trium sunt vtiliter occupati et per consequens infructuosi priuant se per diuinam iusticiam regno Dei" (For as man is naturally born to labor, the army of Christians, which principally exists in three states, namely, prelates, religious, and laborers, in the hope of the reign of God, must be occupied continuously either in the works of the active life . . . or in the works of the contemplative life, . . . or in the works of human service, which are to dig, to pray, to sow, to reap, and they must work with their own hands inasmuch as those miserable idle ones, who are not occupied in any level of these three states and who are not bearing any fruit consequently also deprive themselves through divine justice of the kingdom of God; *The Sermons of Thomas Brinton, Bishop of Rochester [1373–1389]*, ed. Mary Aquinas Devlin [London: Royal Historical Society] Sermon 20 [1.83]).

69. Ms. Add. 41321, fols. 106–11; quoted in Owst 555–56.

Although the spiritual benefits of work had long been recognized, the mention of productivity, the increase of worldly goods, suggests the positive and secular value of labor.

One especially important sermon, delivered in 1357, was Richard FitzRalph's "Defensio curatorum," delivered before the pope and the college of cardinals.[70] David Aers writes that the sermon "shows at least some signs of what looks like a new work ethic in which the production of material goods and material work seems glorified as an end in itself."[71] The basic topic of the sermon is an attack on the Franciscans, and thus the sermon seems to be indebted to Guillaume de Saint-Amour. Two of FitzRalph's basic prongs of attack are against the Franciscan ideal of poverty and the Franciscan practice of begging.

While he admits that Jesus himself was poor, FitzRalph denies that Jesus loved poverty. Poverty equals "wrecchednesse," and no man loves "wrecchednesse." Since poverty cannot be loved in itself "pouert schuld nouȝt be loued & y-holde of God, noþer of man, noþer of þe deuel of helle" (poverty should not be loved nor held to be of God, nor man, nor the devil of hell). On the contrary, "riches is good hauyng & worþi to be loued of God" (riches are good to have and worthy to be loved by God) because God is the "richest of alle" (80). This attack goes to the very heart of the Franciscan ideal. Indeed, St. Francis began with an idealization of poverty, and every other detail of his life followed from that ideal.

If poverty is bad and riches are good, how does one obtain riches? Certainly not by begging. FitzRalph saves an extensive attack against the idea of healthy persons begging for the end of his powerful sermon. Jesus himself, he claims, never begged and never taught his disciples to beg. On the contrary, he taught them to "ete & drynke of þe mede of her trauail" (eat and drink from the reward of their work; 86). He also quotes the Apostle Paul on Paul's own habit of hard manual work: "we ete noon ydel brede þat we hadde of eny man, but we trauailede bisiliche & wrouȝt day & nyȝt" (We do not eat the bread of idleness given by any man, but we worked busily and labored both day and night; 88). He also quotes the dictum of the apostle: "Who þat wole nouȝt trauaile schal

70. "Defensio Curatorum," trans. John Trevisa, *Dialogus inter Militem et Clericum*, ed. Aaron Jenkins Perry, Early English Text Society, OS, 167 (London: Oxford University Press, 1925) 39–93. Quotations will be taken from this edition and cited in the text by page number.

71. David Aers, "*Piers Plowman*: Poverty, Work, and Community," *Community, Gender, and Individual Identity: English Writing 1360–1430* (New York: Routledge, 1988) 25.

nouȝt ete" (Whoever will not work shall not eat; 88). In addition, he also points to the argument for work given by St. Augustine in his book on the labor of monks (89).

One obtains the good of riches, then, by working. But what is the origin of work? Here FitzRalph completely ignores the standard negative etiology of work as a result of original sin. Instead, he writes that God put man in Paradise to work:

> & in þe first ordynaunce of man God ordeyned hym so þat anoon as man was made, God put hym in Paradys for he schuld worche & kepe Paradys; so hit is writen in þe bygynnyng of Hooly Writ.

[And in the first decree concerning man, God ordained that as soon as man was made, He put him in Paradise to work and keep it. So it is written in beginning of Sacred Scripture.]

He then takes the next logical step in his argument:

> Hit semeþ me þat þere God tauȝt þat bodilich werk, possessioun and plente of riches & vnmebles, & warde & keping þerof for mannes vse, schuld be sett tofore beggerie; for god sett man in Paradys for he schuld worche. (71)

[It seems to me that there God taught that bodily work, possession, and plenty of riches and properties and guardianship thereof for man's use should be set before beggary. For God set man in Paradise to work.]

Thus, engaging in productive work, work that renders riches and real estate and control of property, is the *prelapsarian* condition of mankind. Riches are not yet a sign of election, but they are part of the divine plan for man. One could not ask for a more positive evaluation of the nature of productive labor.

If each class had an essential role to play in the health of society, then the work of each class, including the peasant worker, had an inherent importance.[72] During the late Middle Ages, the peasant worker came to be idealized in some forms of preaching.[73] Adam was seen as his ancestor, and the plowman was sometimes put forward as the image of Christ. William Langland's *Piers Plowman* is certainly the best example of this, but Owst argues that Langland's glorification of the working classes was

---

72. Owst 557–62.

73. For a recent review of the image of the plowman in late-fourteenth-century England, see Christopher Dyer, "Piers Plowman and Plowmen: A Historical Perspective," *Yearbook of Langland Studies* 8 (1994): 155–76. Dyer argues that it was the independent plowman, who owned his own tools and property, who was idealized in *Piers Plowman* and not the hired workers, who are identified with the lazy and indolent in that poem.

no innovation. It was, argues Owst, merely a repetition of widespread current pulpit doctrine.[74]

While some preachers glorified the laboring classes, some late-medieval authorities were preoccupied with their idleness. One remembers most clearly Langland's condemnations of "wastours" in Passus 6 of *Piers Plowman*. His solution is to invoke a personified Hunger to move the poor toward work.[75] Geremek notes that the lack of employment, either forced or voluntary, appeared centrally in the social debates of the late Middle Ages. The laziness of workers was often mentioned in the public and civic documents of the late Middle Ages. Moreover, refusing to work was thought to represent a revolt against the established order.[76]

The productive nature of work came to be highlighted in some of the moral literature of the late Middle Ages. The author of *Jacob's Well*, for example, defines idleness not only as inactivity but also "warkys of no profy3t" (works of no profit) or activities that are not "frutefull."[77] Similarly, Bishop Thomas Brinton wrote:

Sicut proprium est aui volare et pisci natare, sic proprium est condicioni humane a mane vite vsque ad vesperam laborare *et vtiliter operari*. . . . Et hoc est contra *ociosos et inutiliter occupatos*, qui secundum omnem statum hominis saluti sue anime aduersantur.[78]

[Just as it is natural for a bird to fly and a fish to swim, so it is also appropriate for the human condition to toil and to work usefully from the morning of life until evening. . . . And this goes against *the slothful and those uselessly occupied*, who, in accordance with any assessment of humankind, act contrary to the health of their souls.]

What is noteworthy is that Brinton stresses that *productive* work, not just keeping busy, is part of the nature of man. He specifically includes those engaged in useless activities with the idle. Another example of this attitude comes from John Gower himself. His most straightforward treatment of the vice of "Accidie" is found in his Anglo-Norman French poem, the *Mirour de l'Omme*, written between 1376 and 1379, roughly ten years before the composition of the *Confessio*.[79] Gower here identifies the

---

74. Owst 568–69.

75. William Langland, *Piers Plowman: The B Version*, ed. George Kane and E. Talbot Donaldson (London: Athlone Press, 1975) 6.171–331.

76. Geremek 381.

77. *Jacob's Well* 1.105.

78. Brinton, Sermon 59 (2.269; emphasis added).

79. The first version of the *Confessio* was completed sometime about 1390. Key revisions were in-

branches of *accidie* as *sompnolence* (somnolence), *peresce* (laziness), *lachesce* (slackness), *oedivesce* (idleness), and *negligens* (negligence) (5125–6180). Noticeably lacking are the more spiritual categories of *tristitia* and despair. As in many treatises on the virtues and vices, the *Mirour* also identifies antidotes to the vices. With respect to *accidie*, the antidote is the virtue *prouesce* (prowess), which Gower divides into *vigile* (vigilance), *magnanimité* (magnanimity), *constance* (steadfastness), *sollicitude* (industry), and *science* (knowledge) (14101–15180).

In the section on laziness, for example, Gower writes that the lazy

> . . . n'ose commencer
> Sur soy d'enprendre ascun office,
> Ou de labour ou de service,
> Du quoy se porroit proufiter.
>
> (5487–90)

[dares not commence to take on herself any office—either of work or of service—from which she could profit.]

It is not simply that the lazy are inactive—they do not contribute to the common good. Similar sentiments occur in the section on idleness, which is incomplete.[80] The idleness section reveals the extension of the meaning of *acedia* beyond spiritual labors to labor in general, for Gower writes that idleness performs neither spiritual nor physical labors. The "mestier" of the idle is to play games, that is, to engage in unproductive activities (5773–84). The idle man is compared to the grasshopper, who plays all summer but has nothing to eat during the winter (5821–44).

In the *Mirour*, the antidote to idleness is industry. In his treatment of industry, Gower makes a reference to St. Paul's dictum that people who do not work should not eat. He also notes the Genesis story of the fall and the command to eat from the "sweat of the brow" (14425–33). Almost immediately, however, he emphasizes the productive value of labor. He notes, for example, that one labors because "corps et alme en ont proufit" (both body and soul have profit from it; 14436). Industry, he writes,

---

corporated during the early years of the 1390s, the end of the fourteenth century (Macaulay, introduction, *English Works* xxi–xxvi). See also John H. Fisher, *John Gower: Moral Philosopher and Friend of Chaucer* (New York: New York University Press, 1964) 116–27.

On the date of the *Mirour*, see Wilson, introduction, *Mirour de l'Omme* xv.

80. A part of this section is missing in the unique manuscript, Cambridge University Additional 3035 (R. F. Yeager, foreword, *Mirour de l'Omme*, trans. Wilson vii).

Toutdis labourt, toutdis estrive,
Et quiert le bien dont l'alme vive,
Et dont le corps en sa destresce
Ait sa viande sustentive.

(14407–10)

[Always . . . labors, always . . . strives and seeks the good from which the soul lives and from which the body in its need should have its nourishing food.]

The emphasis in this section is not on labor as punishment nor as an antidote to idleness but rather on the positive value of labor for fulfilling human needs, both physical and spiritual. Pamphilus, he notes, admonishes that God and labor bring us all good things. In addition, no good thing comes without labor (14449–60). Labor, associated with the active life, is judged less worthy than the contemplative life but is still valuable for what it produces for the common good (14569–80). For Gower, then, work is characterized just as much by its productivity as by its ability to keep one from falling into sin.

Unlike Jean de Meun, Gower does not praise manual labor at the expense of clerical labor. He distinguishes between the manual labor of the farmer and clerical labor but finds that both are productive and serve the community (14467–72). Gower makes no mention of knightly labor here, but earlier, under the section on laziness, he contrasts the lazy person to those workers who cultivate the fields or who conquer by arms (5377–88). Also, within the *Mirour*'s satire on the estates, Gower mentions that each estate has its own form of labor and specifies the labor of the knights specifically:

Chascun estat, le quel qu'il soit,
Est ordiné par son endroit
De faire au siecle auscun labour;
Dont pour garder le commun droit
Ly chivalers combatre doit,
Car ce partient a son honour.

(23617–22)

[Each estate, whichever it be, is ordained by its character to perform some task in the world. So the knight should fight to guard the rights of the people, for this pertains to his honor.]

The duties of the priest and knight, like that of the peasant, are forms of necessary "labour." Unlike Guillaume de Lorris's *Rose*, there is no celebration of aristocratic *otium* in the *Mirour*.

Gower's social position (among the professional classes that had significant contact with the social worlds of franklins and merchants as well as the more refined world of the aristocracy) would not only have allowed him to be aware of these labor concerns but also would have given him access to the ideologically charged languages of several key groups.[81] The labor ideologies of these languages, I will argue, are present in the discourse of love's labor in the *Confessio Amantis*. Like the *Roman de la rose*, then, with respect to attitudes toward labor, the *Confessio* is a "carrefour idéologique," an ideological crossroads in which traditional ways of thinking about work in the literature of *acedia* come into sustained literary engagement with the evolving labor ideologies of the late fourteenth century.

IV

The first place in which readers perceive this engagement of ideologies is in Gower's labor lexicon in the *Confessio*. It is striking that he employs at least six different words to describe love's labor: *travail, servise, labour, werk, bysynesse, bisischipe*, and *occupacioun*.[82] The word *bysynesse*, however, was by far Gower's favorite word for love's labor. While he uses the others inconsistently, he employs *bysynesse* ten times. A review of the denotations and, to the extent the dictionaries allow, the connotations of these words helps us see the range of meanings Gower had to choose from as he constructed his review of love's labor.

Middle English *werk*, the word with the longest history in English, descended from Anglo-Saxon *weorc* and had a range of meanings, with apparently neutral to negative connotations, including those covered by the Latin *labor*, that is, hard, strenuous labor, trouble, and affliction.[83] Several new synonyms for *werk* were borrowed in the thirteenth century but gained wide currency only over the course of the fourteenth century. While the *Middle English Dictionary* has only one or two thirteenth-centu-

---

81. On Gower's social position, see John Fisher, "Life Records," *John Gower* 37–70. In particular, Fisher writes: "The different bodies of material show Gower moving in the same two worlds as Chaucer, the upper middle class society of the franklin, merchant, and lawyer, and the aristocratic society of a trusted retainer in a noble household" (41). For further information on Chaucer's and Gower's social position, see Paul Strohm, *Social Chaucer* (Cambridge, Mass.: Harvard University Press, 1989) 1–46.

82. For examples of Gower's use of "travail" referring to love's labor, see 4.1105 and 1604. For "servise," see 4.341 and 1130. For "labour," see 4.2023. For "werk," see 4.301 and 317. For "bysynesse," see 4.298, 513, 725, 1155, 1261, 1747, 1751, 1757, 2289, and 3492. For "besischipe," see 4.119. For "occupacioun," see 4.1257 and 1452.

83. "Work" (4, 4b, 6a), *Oxford English Dictionary (OED)*, 1989 ed.

ry citations of *travail*, it gives a significantly larger number of citations from the fourteenth and fifteenth centuries. Even more strongly than *werk*, *travail* seems to have carried the negative denotations and connotations of Latin *labor*.[84] *Servise* entered the English language from French at the beginning of the thirteenth century but, like *travail*, is not widely attested until the fourteenth century. From the very beginning, it carried the sense of generalized effort or assistance to another. However, it often carried the suggestion of some kind of legal obligation to a master, such as that owed by a servant, feudal tenant, or knight.[85] It is noteworthy that Gower was almost certainly among the first English poets to use Middle English *servise* to refer to love's labor.[86] Borrowed from Latin or French, Middle English *labour* first appeared at the beginning of the fourteenth century but, again, is not often found in Middle English texts until the end of the century. Like *travail*, *labour* carried with it some of the same denotations and negative connotations as its Latin cognate. By the end of the fourteenth century, however, it could also refer specifically to *mental* labor.[87]

While Anglo-Saxon *bisig*, from which *bysynesse* and *bisischipe* were derived, had a long history in English by Gower's day, its range of meanings expanded in the thirteenth and fourteenth centuries.[88] One instance of Anglo-Saxon *bisignisse* meaning "anxiety" or "solicitude" can be found.[89] However, the word seems not to have been in wide circulation until the end of the fourteenth century, when it developed a range of meanings from "industry" and "diligence" to the familiar "task appointed or undertaken; a person's official duty [or] function."[90] *Bysynesse* could still refer to

---

84. "Travail" (1a, 2b, 3a–d), *Middle English Dictionary (MED)*, 1956 ed.

85. "Servise" (7), *MED*, defined as "assistance, help; a helpful act, requested favor," is cited as early as 1230 C.E. However, definitions 1, 2, 3, and 4, all quite current in the fourteenth century, suggest some kind of legal obligation of the server to the one served. Definition 6, appearing only at the end of the fourteenth century, is "slavery, servitude, bondage."

86. "Servise" (5), *MED*; *Confessio* 8.2012 is first on the list of citations here.

87. "Labour," *MED*. Definitions 1(a–c) all refer to difficult manual work, in particular, agricultural work. Definition 1(d), however, refers to "mental work," and, here again, a quotation from the *Confessio* (4.2396) is the first citation. Meanings given under definitions 4(a–c) all refer to generalized troubles and difficulties, mental anguish, and even disease. These latter meanings all developed around the end of the fourteenth century.

88. "Busy" (1.a), *OED*, defined as "occupied with constant attention," is not found until 1225. Definition 4(a), "constantly or habitually occupied," is not found until about the same time.

89. "Business" (5), *OED*.

90. "Business" (1, 2, 8, 1.a), *OED*. See also "bisinesse" (1, 2), *MED*. The entries in the *MED*, even more than those in the *OED*, suggest that *bysynesse* carried far fewer negative connotations than did *werk, labour, servise,* or *travail*.

troubles and anxieties, but unlike the Latin *labor*, it seems to have carried less of the negative connection to *physical* labor. Middle English *bisischipe* meant simply "effort" or "exertion."[91]

Something similar can be said of *occupacioun*. The *Middle English Dictionary's* first citation for this word is dated 1325, but the first citation in which it meant an "activity," an "exercise," a "craft," a "trade," a "profession," or a "business"—denotations that are relevant to this discussion— is dated 1387, precisely when Gower was working on the *Confessio*.

Two important points arise from this brief philological survey. First, the thirteenth and fourteenth centuries were times of growth in the part of the English lexicon relating to work. Even more significant, however, than the growth in the *number* of relevant labor words is what seems to have been a significant *semantic* growth in this area. Even long-established words like *werk* developed new meanings toward the end of the fourteenth century.[92] As a rule, the newly developed meanings did not bear such negative connotations as "strenuous toil," "trouble," and "affliction." Evidence from the history of the English lexicon, then, supports the claim of some historians that the fourteenth century was a critical time in the history of English labor ideology. The expansion of lexicon and meanings in the labor vocabulary is at least circumstantial evidence suggesting both an interest in work issues and an ideological movement toward a humanist work ethic.

Second, John Gower was a participant in the cultural discussion of work. His positive assessment of the nature of work in the *Mirour* has already been noted. Concerns about the lack of productivity also arise in the *Vox Clamantis*. In the *Confessio*, Genius's discussion of labor, and, in particular mental labor, for example, indicates that Gower continued to think about work ideologies in general.[93] Gower also stretched the tradi-

---

91. "Bisichipe," *MED*.

92. The plural form *works*, for example, first came to refer to "moral actions considered in relation to justification" at the end of the fourteenth century ("Work" [I.1.b.], *OED*).

93. 4.2363–700. The Latin gloss says that the poet "ponit exemplum de diligencia predecessorum, qui ad tocius humani generis doctrinam et auxilium suis continuis laboribus et studiis, gracia mediante diuina, artes et sciencias primitus inuenerunt" (gives examples of the diligence of [his] predecessors, who, by means of continual work and study, originally discovered the arts and sciences for the teaching and aid of the entire human race). The Latin verse introducing this section explicitly defends the value of mental labor over that of physical labor: "Set qui doctrine causa fert mente labores, / Preualet et merita perpetuata parat" (But he who toils in mind for wisdom's sake / Prevails, for he lays up perpetual meed). The translation of the latter is taken from Sian Echard and Claire Fanger, *The Latin Verses in the "Confessio Amantis": An Annotated Translation* (East Lansing, Mich.: Colleagues Press, 1991) 53.

tional English lexicon for love's labor. Although the Old French *servise* had long been used to denote love's labor, Gower was among the first to employ it in English. Beyond the traditional *labour* and *travail*, for example, he used newly coined words like *occupacioun*. In addition, the Latin *negotium*, the closest Latin equivalent to *bysynesse*, was one word that was never used for love's labor in the works of Ovid, Andreas Capellanus, or Alan of Lille. It is impossible to say exactly why this was, but a possible reason is that it was too closely associated with the activities of merchants. Gower, however, perhaps because of his social position between the aristocracy and the merchant class, did not have the same misgivings about labor words associated with the business world. For him, love's labor could indeed be *bysynesse* or *occupacioun* as well as the more aristocratic *servise*. This suggests that the *Confessio* goes even beyond Jean's *Rose* toward the "embourgeoisement de l'eros."[94] Finally, the connotations of *bysynesse* and *occupacioun*, both of which were overwhelmingly either neutral or positive, stand out in contrast to the connotations of traditional medieval labor words such as Latin *labor*, which connect work with suffering and backbreaking physical toil.[95]

Moving from lexicon to the level of argument, one first notes that Book 4's major structuring principle is taken from the traditional branches of the vice of *acedia*. Genius begins his treatment of sloth in love with the subcategory of *lachesce*, procrastination. He continues with treatments of pusillanimity, forgetfulness, negligence, idleness, somnolence, and despair. Particularly revealing of the schema's traditional foundation is the inclusion of pusillanimity and despair, medieval branches of the vice no longer associated with modern English "sloth."

By *lachesce*, Gower signifies the tendency to procrastinate and waste time (4.4–13). Thus, Gower begins Book 4 with a consideration of "work time" *in amoris causa*, but his treatment shows only slight influence of the arrival of the mechanical clock and hours of unchanging duration. It is surprising that neither the word "horloge" nor the word "clock" appears in the *Confessio*. Nevertheless, the word "hour" appears often (e.g., 4.241, 277, 642, 969). Indeed, since in Book 7 Gower speaks of the "four and twenty houres *evene*"—that is, twenty-four *equal* hours—which the sun takes to complete his circle, it is clear that he is speaking of hours as measured by a mechanical clock rather than the traditional unequal hours (7.860; emphasis added).[96]

---

94. Payen 195, 197.
95. "Occupacioun" (2, 3 [a, b, c]), *MED*.
96. Before the fourteenth century, medieval men and women did not divide the day and night

Although the mechanical clock makes no appearance in the *Confessio*, one finds in Book 4 a fairly persistent concern with the waste of time. For example, in the section on *lachesce*, Amans at first confesses to "letting time slide" (4.41) and not pursuing his courtship as promptly as he might, yet later he reverses his judgment and says "And natheles of mi lachesse / Ther hath be no defalte I gesse / Of time lost" (And, nonetheless, from my lachesse, there has been no failure with respect to the loss of time, I guess; 4.281–83). He insists that he keeps his appointments (4.277). Simply keeping appointments, however, does not produce results: "I seche that I mai noght finde, / I haste and evere I am behinde" (I seek what I may not find; I haste but ever am behind; 4.289–90), a sentiment that reminds one of Chaucer's witty remark about the Man of Law: "Nowher so bisy a man as he ther nas, / And yet he semed bisier than he was" (Nowhere was there a man so busy as he, and yet he seemed busier than he was; 1.321–22). This is the first time the question of labor productivity arises in Book 4. Genius, however, does not seem to hear Amans's point, for, reflecting a traditional attitude toward labor implied in the schema of the Seven Deadly Sins, he responds that Amans should simply keep up his *bysynesse* in order to avoid *lachesce*. "For Slowthe," he says, "is mihti to confounde / The spied of every mannes werk" (For Sloth is powerfully able to destroy the success of every man's work; 4.300–301). For much of Book 4, Genius sticks to this ideology.

In addition, Genius presents the story of Dido and Aeneas as an *exemplum* of *lachesce*. Aeneas, he states, tarries in his return to Dido: "His time lette, and that was rowthe" ([He] delayed his time and that was a pity; 4.120). In the section on idleness, Genius again reminds Amans that "Men mai recovere lost of good, / Bot so wys man yit nevere stod, / Which mai recovere time lore" (Men may recover lost goods, but no man is so wise that he can recover lost time; 4.1485–87). He illustrates this proverbial wisdom with the story of Jephthah's daughter, who, because of her father's rash oath, was condemned in the flower of her youth to be a human sacrifice. Her state of virginity is lamented as "lost time" (4.1573). Genius says the same about those suffering from *tristesse*, or depression, who cannot bring themselves to complete necessary tasks during the day and then fall into even deeper despondency when they consider how much time they have lost (4.3393).

---

into twenty-four equal units. The canonical hours were originally the so-called *temporal* or unequal hours. The day and night were each divided respectively into twelve equal parts, but the length of these parts varied with the seasons and were equal only at the equinoxes. On the hours, see Landes 403n.

In Book 4's section on *pusillamite*, cowardice, labor issues arise in surprising ways. First, Genius defines *pusillamite* as the opposite not of courage in battle but of willingness to undertake work. The pusillanimous soul is "He that hath litel of corage / And dar no mannes werk beginne" (He who has little spirit and dares not begin a man's work; 4.316–17). For (male) lovers, the "mannes werk" is to pursue courtship aggressively, and Genius illustrates this with the tale of Pygmalion. Whereas, in the *Roman de la rose*, the Pygmalion story illustrated the conversion from sterile *fin amors* to fruitful reproductive love, in the *Confessio* Gower uses it to illustrate that work overcomes the resistance of nature. For when Pygamalion "hath his word travailed" (caused his word to work; 4.428), his statue comes to life. "Be this ensample thou miht finde," concludes Genius, "That word mai worche above kinde" (By this example you might find that a word may work beyond natural limits).[97] The same thesis is presented, but much less effectively, by the following tale, the tale of Iphis, a young woman who, after impersonating a prince and marrying another woman, is changed into a man. Unlike Pygmalion, Iphis does not *work* to change her sex. Genius, however, blithely overlooks this detail to draw the same conclusion. Love looks favorably on those with "besy herte":[98]

> Wherof, my Sone, in this matiere
> Thou miht ensample taken hiere,
> That with thi grete besinesse
> Thou miht atteigne the richesse
> Of love, if that ther be no Slowthe.
>
> (4.511–15)

[Whereof, my son, from this matter you might take an example here. With your great business you might attain the riches of love, if you are not slothful.]

---

97. *Confessio* 4.437–38. Carole Koepke Brown analyzes the changes Gower made to Ovid's version in the *Metamorphoses* and concludes that Gower's point in the tale of Pygmalion is to illustrate Pygmalion's inability to speak because of sloth ("The Tale of Pygmalion," *John Gower's Literary Transformations in the "Confessio Amantis": Original Articles and Translations*, ed. Peter G. Beidler [Washington, D.C.: University Press of America, 1982] 29–32). While this is literally true, Brown misses the larger significance of the tale with respect to Gower's labor ideology.

98. *Confessio* 4.509. This is clearly a tale on which Genius forces a moral that is simply not illustrated. While it is true that Genius concludes that the tale illustrates the worth of a "besy herte" as an antidote to sloth (see Nicolette Stasko, "The Tale of Iphis," *Literary Transformations* 33–36), the tale does not actually illustrate the point because Iphis does not do any work.

For Genius, as for Virgil in the *Georgics*, labor conquers all, even unnatural love. Moreover, it is interesting to note that Genius's statement is an ironic double voicing of Ovid's dictum from the *Remedia amoris:* "qui finem quaeris amoris, / (cedit amor rebus) res age, tutus eris" (you who seek an end to love, love yields to business: be busy, you will be safe).[99] Genius repeats the same counsel in the next section, on forgetfulness. When Amans confesses that fear leads him to forget what he would say to his mistress, Genius counsels him simply to keep busy: "Forthi pull up a besi herte, / Mi Sone, and let nothing asterte / Of love fro thi besinesse" (Therefore, call up a busy heart, my son, and let nothing hinder your business in love; 4.723–25).

Under the section on idleness, however, Amans again raises concerns about productivity. When Genius introduces the subject of idleness, he employs a traditional image—the cat who would eat fish without wetting his paws—to suggest that idle men cannot be successful in their endeavors.[100] Since the reason for this confession was Amans's despair over his lack of success in love, Genius asks whether he is guilty of idleness. Amans, however, vehemently denies that he is idle. On the contrary, he claims to be continually busy with love's labor. When pressed to define his labor, Amans describes how he passes his days trying to meet every desire of his lady:

> What thing sche bit me don, I do,
> And wher sche bidt me gon, I go,
> And whanne hir list to clepe, I come.
> Thus hath sche fulliche overcome
> Min ydelnesse til I sterve.
>
> (4.1161–65)

[I do whatever she asks me to do. I go wherever she asks me to go. And when it pleases her to call, I come. Thus, she has fully overcome my idleness until I die.]

One has the slightly comic picture here of a man, tormented by an obsessive need to please his lady, running himself to death performing inconsequential acts under the pretense that they are absolutely crucial to her well-being: "I serve, I bowe, I loke, I loute," he proclaims, "Min yhe folweth hire aboute" (I serve, I bow, I look, I bow again. My eye follows her

---

99. *"Amores," "Medicamina Faciei Femineae," "Ars Amatoria," "Remedia Amoris,"* ed. J. E. Kenney (Oxford, U.K.: Clarendon Press, 1961) *Ra* 143–44.

100. 4.1105–11. On common medieval images of sloth, see Wenzel, *Sin of Sloth* 105ff.

around; 4.1169–70). Among his particular works of love, Amans cites playing with the lady's dog or birds and chatting with her maids. He recites Ovidian songs of love and helps lift his lady onto her horse if she wants to go out riding.[101] If all else fails, he simply waits in attendance and invents what he calls "tariinges," another relatively new term in Gower's English, which carried the negative connotations of the modern English "loitering."[102] Like Ovid's *praeceptor amoris* and his successors, Amans packages activities that are essentially the fruits of *otium otiosum* as purposeful work. But whereas Ovid's treatment is subversive of the social norm, that is, supporting as legitimate work the idle activities of his *praeceptor*, Gower's treatment subverts his protagonist.

While Genius at first agrees with Amans that his "tariinges" are legitimate examples of love's labor, he soon attempts to define "love's labor" more closely and introduces a distinction based on gender: the proper labor of women, unlike the "idle" Rosiphelee, is simply to allow themselves to love and be loved, while the proper *travail* for men is knightly combat.[103] Here again one sees the essential male orientation of the discourse of love's labor with the man being assigned the active role.

As in the *De amore*, knightly deeds of arms are undertaken to prove the man's inner character. They are undertaken, says Genius, "for worschipe" and that the lady might hear of his "prouesce."[104] At this point the usually docile Amans begins vigorously to disagree with his confessor. Rejecting the tradition found in the *De amore*, he denies that engaging in battle is truly love's labor on grounds that are both moral and pragmatic.[105] Christ, he argues, forbids us to kill other men, even if they are not Christians (4.1659–63). Amans's real objection, however, is grounded

101. Other of Amans's activities are described under the section on somnolence: caroling and dancing, playing at dice, reading the *Troilus*, and procrastinating when it is time to leave his lady (*Confessio* 4.2771–831).

102. "Tarrying" (1), *OED*, first attested in the period 1340–1370.

103. 4.1620–44. Genius uses the word "travail" three times in the space of about twenty-five lines to refer to this kind of love's labor (4.1623, 1628, and 1645). See also Genius's insistent comments at 4.1804–10 and 4.2029–39, where he cites the example of Lancelot's labors for Guinevere.

Genius, however, does suggest that knights, like ladies, should also allow themselves to be loved (4.1456–62).

104. Genius describes exactly how the process works for successful knights in *Confessio* 4.1632–41.

105. In the *Vox Clamantis*, Gower had condemned the very activity that Genius now advocates as the true labor of love. In Book 5, chapter 4, Gower writes that lustful love extinguishes all knightly virtue. Book 5, chapter 5, is a condemnation of all those who undertake "armorum labores" in order to impress women (*Vox Clamantis* 207–9).

in concerns about productivity, for he continues, "What scholde I winne over the Se, / If I mi ladi loste at hom?" (What should I win overseas if I lost my lady at home?; 4.1664–65). What good is work if it does not produce the intended results?[106] Indeed, Amans's labor has not yet produced results for him:

> For everemore I finde it so,
> The more besinesse I leie,
> The more that I knele and preie
> With goode wordes and with softe,
> The more I am refused ofte.
>
> (4.1746–51)

[For I always find that the busier I am, the more that I kneel and pray with good, soft words, the more often I am refused.]

Amans indeed "hath his word travailed," yet, unlike Pygmalion, his work can not overcome nature. Here Gowers shifts the discussion significantly and anticipates in an unexpected way the final resolution of Book 8.

Genius tries to calm his fears by stating that the knightly labors of battle are sufficient to accomplish Amans's ends (4.2014–19). Working knights are sure to be successful in their love because, says Genius, "every labour axeth why / Of som reward" (every labor asks to be rewarded; 4.2023–24). He cites the examples of Lancelot and other romance heroes, who won their loves through great deeds in battle (4.2034–39). Against this argument, Amans can do no more than change the subject, so he asks Genius to define "gentilesce" (4.2200–203).

To be sure, Amans's labor ideology here is inconsistent. Although earlier he argued that he was not guilty of idleness because he kept himself busy, he now admits that just keeping busy, just countering the vice of sloth, is not enough. One's work must produce results. In a key passage, he reasons:

> Bot thogh my besinesse laste,
> Al is bot ydel ate laste,
> For whan theffect is ydelnesse,
> I not what thing is besinesse.[107]

---

106. Later, Amans repeats this idea, 4.1720–23.

107. *Confessio* 4.1757–60. Note also Amans's remark: "Bot certes if I mihte spede / With eny maner besinesse / Of worldes travail, thanne I gesse, / There scholde me non ydelschipe / Departen

[But although my business lasts, in the end all my works are idle, for when the effect is the same as idleness, I do not know what business is.]

In the traditional schema of the Seven Deadly Sins, the antidote to idleness is simply to be busy, but Amans's position here is close to that found in *Jacob's Well*, that is, *bysynesse* without productivity is just another example of *ydelnesse*. Moreover, he now concludes that, despite his activities, he is an idle man. It is important to note, however, that he does not judge himself idle on the basis of Christian morality, but rather on the basis of a labor ideology that equates labor with *productive* activity.

In other books, Genius is aware of this ethic of productivity. In Book 5, for example, after explaining that virtue lies in the "golden mean" between two extremes (5.7641–45), Genius treats sexual promiscuity under prodigality in love. In describing the promiscuous lover, Genius twice explains that he wastes his time by giving his love to too many women (5.7765, 7774). Although Amans denies that he is guilty of such a waste of time, he notes that, despite his fidelity, his love has not met with success. Genius's reply is couched in terms of productivity and the waste of time:

> Mi Sone, that I mai wel lieve:
> And natheles me semeth so,
> For oght that thou hast yit misdo
> Of time which thou hast despended,
> It mai with grace ben amended.
>
> (5.7810–14)

[My son, that I may well believe. And, nonetheless, it seems to me that for anything that you have yet done badly, with respect to the time that you have dissipated, with grace it may be amended.]

In other words, Genius asserts that positive results can transform wasted time into productive work time.

An even more striking example occurs in Book 3. Here Genius treats the proverbial wisdom that "haste makes waste" and counsels Amans to work wisely and not just to keep busy. "Men sen alday that rape reweth" (One sees all the time that men repent haste), he notes, and then continues with a host of similar proverbs (3.1625–38). The point is that Amans should not force love by acting too hastily, and the story of Pyramus and

---

fro hir ladischipe" (But, certainly, if I might succeed in any manner of the world's work, then, I guess, no idleness should keep me from her ladyship; 4.1726–30).

Thisbe is cited as a tragic *exemplum* of hasty labor producing tragic results. Instead of counseling *bysynesse*, Genius here suggests that Amans
slow down his labor: "Yit sit it wel that thou eschuie / That thou the
Court noght overhaste, / For so miht thou thi time waste" (Yet it is well
that you avoid being too hasty at the Court of Love, for otherwise you
might waste your time; 5.1674–76). This is yet another striking example
of how Genius raises concerns of work productivity.

Returning to Book 4, one finds a similar concern with productivity
arises in the section dealing with the subcategory of negligence. Amans
is aware of the Ovidian tradition that love is an art to be learned, and in
the section on negligence he acquits himself of that vice by noting that
he has done his best to learn the art of love. He says:

> I am so trewly amerous,
> That I am evere curious
> Of hem that conne best enforme
> To knowe and witen al the forme,
> That falleth unto loves craft.
>   (4.921–25)

[I am so truly amorous that I am always inquisitive with respect to those who
can best relate how to know all the rules of love's craft.]

Judging from the "labors" he names in the section on idleness, Amans is
learning from an art in the original Ovidian tradition. The problem is
that the arts of love cannot teach him a foolproof method:

> Yit so fer cowthe I nevere finde
> Man that be resoun ne be kinde
> Me cowthe teche such an art,
> That he ne failede of a part.
>   (4.931–34)

[Yet I have not yet been able to find anyone who could teach such an art, either
by reason or by nature, and who did not, at least in part, fail.]

He has practiced all of love's craft, yet he is nowhere nearer to enjoying
the fruits of his labor (4.935–39). Indeed, he jauntily assures Genius that if
there were a successful strategy to employ, he would have learned it long
ago (4.940–43). Perhaps his wits are not strong enough to comprehend
the subtleties of love's craft, yet he assures Genius that he cannot be fault-
ed for not trying his best (4.945–55). His protest is somewhat insincere,

however, for, as we have seen, he refuses Genius's advice concerning the knightly labor of combat, which is the one labor he rejects out of hand.

Regarding love, the work ethics of Alan of Lille and Jean de Meun were ethics of productivity as well. When speaking of productivity, however, they focused on the sexual act and its reproductive function, not courtship. The major difference between Amans's position and theirs, then, is that Amans applies this same ethic of productivity to the labor of courtship. Amans calls his labor "idle" not because it has not produced new offspring, but rather because it has not yet caused his lady to fall in love with him. In addition, whereas natural law ethics insists that sex is meant to serve the common needs of the human community, Amans's ethic here simply ignores the needs of the community and focuses narrowly on his own needs.

Genius, however, does not limit the idea of success in love's labor to success in courtship. In a short passage that seems underdeveloped but that gives a foreshadowing of his position in Book 8, Genius alludes to the reproductive model of love's labor. In this passage, he affirms that the best love is aimed at marriage, "Whereof the love is al honeste."[108] To support this argument, Genius makes several assertions. First, he asserts that he who will "in his degre / Travaile so as it belongeth" (work in accordance with his status) will receive both "worshipe" and "ese" (4.2292–95). The implied question is, Which is the proper work for someone in Amans's "degre"? In a second statement he asserts that although men may recover lost goods, they can never recover lost time (4.1485–87; see also 4.1572–73). Genius concludes that idle people are those "Which unto thing that love demeth / Forslowthen that thei scholden do" (who neglect by sloth those things they should do, those things love thinks good; 4.2318–19). The context of this passage, however, has changed the meaning of love's labors from courtship activities to reproduction.

At this point, Genius's words are aimed more pointedly at women rather than men. However, he does not specifically cite the carpe diem motif because women's beauty is fleeting. Rather, he worries that the woman who tarries will lose her chance at bearing children (4.1493–97). As we noted above, he then tells the *exemplum* of Jephthah's daughter,

---

108. *Confessio* 4.1476–79, 1484. On "honeste love," that is, married, reproductive love, as Gower's ideal in the *Confessio*, see J. A. W. Bennett, "Gower's 'Honeste Love,'" *Gower's "Confessio Amantis": A Critical Anthology*, ed. Peter Nicholson (1966; Cambridge, U.K.: D. S. Brewer, 1991) 49–61. Zaerr speaks of "honeste love" as Gower's moral response to *fin amors*. She characterizes it as flexible, forgiving, and selfless (14–18).

who, because of her father's rash oath, is forced to die before she was able to marry. When she learns of her sentence, Jephthah's daughter begs a forty-day reprieve from her sentence. She asks for the delay in order to mourn her lost youth, but the loss that she feels most keenly is not the loss of the joys of courtship or even of the sexual act. What she mourns is the fact that she will never be able to bear children, "So that the poeple is noght encressed" (so that the people are not increased; 4.1571). Clearly, this story has direct relevance to Amans, but the reader will not realize just how relevant it is until Book 8, when it is revealed that Amans is too old to copulate and reproduce. Here, then, Genius in an understated way employs the discourse of love's labor from the *De planctu* and from Jean de Meun's portion of the *Rose* to offer a subtle correction to Amans's view of productivity. Productive love, "honeste love," is love that produces not only a successful courtship but also material benefits for the entire community.

It is significant that, later in Book 4, Genius leads a discussion on the great workers of history, emphasizing in each case the productive contributions made by their work (4.2396–671). Before he begins this encomium, however, Genius briefly treats labor in general (4.2363–95). This treatment is much shorter than that found in Jean de Meun's *Rose*. Besides its brevity, however, two notable qualities exist in Genius's treatment of labor that distinguish it from the treatment of labor in Jean's *Rose*. First, Genius does not mention that human labor is the result of man's fallen nature. While he does quote Solomon—"As the briddes to the flihte / Ben made, so the man is bore / To labour" (As birds are made to fly, so man is born to labor; 4.2342–44)—he does not present labor as a loathsome burden. On the contrary, when he chooses to praise the ancients, he cites not only their long lives, their great wits, and their mighty strength, but also their "hertes ful of besinesse" (hearts full of business; 4.2355). Nor does Genius mention a Saturnian Golden Age, a time when the earth yielded its fruits without work. In fact, he simply states that before men sowed corn and labored to cultivate it, there was simply none to eat (4.2374–77). Thus, Genius consistently stresses both the positive nature of work and its role in producing necessities for the common good. This is a position on work that is consistent with Gower's treatment of labor in *Mirour de l'Omme*. People engage in productive labor for common profit.[109]

---

109. The importance of the theme of "common profit" has been thoroughly explored by Peck in

Second, from the very start, Genius stresses the dignity of intellectual labor. By "intellectual labor" he means not only scholarship but also the discovery of practical arts by which life is made better. The Latin introductory verse sets the tone:

> Expedit in manibus labor, vt de cotidianis
>   Actibus ac vita viuere possit homo.
> Set qui doctrine causa fert mente labores,
>   Preualet et merita perpetuata parat.

> [Manual labor's useful, so a man
> can live in daily life by daily deeds;
> But he who toils in mind for wisdom's sake
> Prevails, for he lays up perpetual meed.][110]

Although he does not denigrate the dignity of manual labor, Genius insists that those who provide intellectual labor are not idle. In fact, they work just as hard as manual laborers do:

> Thus was non ydel of the tuo,
> That on the plogh hath undertake
> With labour which the hond hath take,
> That other tok to studie and muse,
> As he which wolde noght refuse
> The labour of hise wittes alle.
>   (4.2382–87)

[Thus, neither was idle—not the man who undertook with labor to plow, nor the other who chose study and musing, as a man who would not refuse to work his wits.]

Both kinds of labor are valuable because both make contributions to the common good. If Gower's contemporary John Wycliffe tended to follow Guillaume de Saint-Amour's highlighting of the importance of manual labor, Gower tends to take the position of Guillaume's opponents, Bon-

---

Kingship and Common Profit. Unlike some of his contemporaries, Gower was no social leveler. On the contrary, his assessment was that the age's troubles arose not from a corrupt social structure but rather from corrupt individual moral choices. Indeed, the *Vox Clamantis* presents an anatomy of such corrupt choices made by members of each estate.

Peck argues that Gower's idea of common profit was "the mutual enhancement, each by each, of all parts of the community for the general welfare of the community taken as a whole" (xxi). For a list of passages in which the term is used, see Fisher 178–79.

110. Macaulay, *English Works* 1.365.

aventure and Thomas Aquinas, who pointed out the equal value of all kinds of productive labor.

With this remarkably positive characterization of labor, Genius then sets the stage for his praise of all those intellectual workers who contributed knowledge or skills to the human fund of learning. Thus, for example, Cham is praised for inventing Hebrew letters, while Cadmus is praised for inventing the Greek alphabet (4.2396–402). Heredot is praised for discovering rhyme, meter, and cadence, while Prometheus is credited with inventing sculpture (4.2413–15, 2422). Jadahel is credited with the invention of the net, the fish hook, and hunting (4.2427–30), while Minerva is credited with the invention of weaving (4.2435–36). Saturn, not Jupiter, is credited with the invention not only of farming but also of coining money (4.2439–50).

At the end of this section, Genius comes to the discovery of Latin (by Carmente) and to the long list of Latin writers who made positive contributions (4.2633–71). At the end of this list, Ovid is mentioned. It is significant, however, that it is Ovid's *Remedia amoris*, not the *Ars amatoria*, that is cited (4.2668–71). At the mention of the *Remedia*, Genius quickly suggests that "if that thou fiele, / That love wringe thee to sore, / Behold Ovide and take his lore" (If you feel that love wrings you too grievously, behold Ovid and take his lore; 4.2672–74). Amans quickly replies that, if any of Ovid's books will help him succeed in love, he will read them. He will not, however, read any books that would help him withdraw from love (4.2675–86). Amans is not yet ready to retire from his labors.

Book 4 of the *Confessio*, then, contains a dialog among various ideologically colored voices. The voice of the traditional medieval ideology of work based on the schema of the Seven Deadly Sins is present. Aristocratic voices which speak, on the one hand, of "tariinges" (the fruit of aristocratic *otium*) being the true work of love and, on the other, of knightly combat as love's proper work can also be found. Finally, the voice of a humanist work ethic in process, arising in part from Gower's literary sources and in part from his cultural context, also exists in Book 4. This ethic insists that legitimate work, including intellectual labor, is a positive aspect of the human condition, but that work must be judged on its ability to produce concrete results. It is impossible, however, to align these voices neatly with the two major characters. Although Amans's position on love's labor through a large part of Book 4 is influenced by an ethic of productivity and careful use of time, he not only endorses his "tariinges" as legitimate work, but he also uses *travail*, a word bearing pe-

jorative connotations, as well as the more positive *bysynesse* to refer to
love's labor. At the same time, although in many ways Genius's presentation of love's labor clearly reflects the traditional ethic of work's value
arising from its opposition to *acedia*, he not only calls love by the newly
borrowed *occupacioun* but also warns Amans repeatedly against the wasting of time. In short, Gower's ideology of labor in Book 4 is neither simply traditional nor avant-garde, neither completely aristocratic nor bourgeois. It is an ideology in process, mirroring to some extent ideological
shifts in Gower's language and his society. Book 4 is, then, a "site of action" in which various late-medieval labor ideologies undergo a "sustained literary engagement."

V

    The conclusion of the *Confessio Amantis* adds another layer of com-
plexity. At this point, Amans has finished his confession to Genius, but his
spiritual condition, his passion in love, seems no closer to being healed.[111]
After relating the story of Apollonius of Tyre, Genius changes his position on love's labor. He now uses the word *servise* to refer to it, and by using that word brings to the foreground the social context of love's work,
in particular, the obligations owed by love's servant to the one served.
Venus is served by love's labor, but exactly what kind of labor does she
expect? While Genius notes that the rewards of love come from *servise*
(8.2009–12), he says that *servise* must be carried out according to reason,
and reason says that love's labor should be directed to procreation. As a
result, Genius argues that *for Amans* romantic love is unreasonable *servise*,
and he counsels Amans to turn his love to a different master, Jesus Christ
(8.2085–90). The courtship that Amans has conducted to date has proved
fruitless, and, picking up on Amans's earlier concern with productivity,
Genius adds, "if thou travaile, / Wher thou no profit hast ne pris, / Thou
art toward thiself unwis" (If you work where you have no profit nor
prize, you are to yourself unwise; 8.2092–94). However, Amans at this
point is not ready to give up love's labor, and he issues a direct appeal to
Venus to reward his service: "For Service in thi Court withouten hyre /
To me, which evere yit have kept thin heste, / Mai nevere be to loves
lawe honeste" (In my opinion, who have ever kept your commands, service in your court without reward can never be seemly with respect to
love's law; 8.2291–93). In the Gospel of St. Luke, Jesus says that the labor-

---

111. On the direct link between Books 4 and 8, see Olsson 129.

er deserves his wages (Luke 10.15). In the *De amore*, one of the characters notes that "A bonae videtur rationis ordine deviare, si non benefacta suis actoribus debita commoda ferant" (For it seems a departure from the order of right reason if fine deeds do not win the appropriate rewards for those who perform them).[112] In the same spirit, Amans claims to have performed the labor. He now is simply asking for his wages.

But has he really? Venus and Genius definitively modify here the definition of productive labor: it now becomes reproduction. Thus, while Amans has complained about his lack of productivity in the labor of courtship, Venus and Genius raise an even more profound question about his lack of productivity. Can he produce children? The answer to this question is withheld from the reader until the point when Venus returns to heal Amans of his malady. It is at this point that the link between Amans and the author John Gower is forcefully established (8.2321), and the reader finds out that Amans/Gower is simply too old to enter into a productive relationship with the woman he loves.

At this point of the narrative, the significant influence of the love's labor discourse of the *De planctu*, Jean de Meun's *Rose*, and natural law ethics becomes apparent. While Alan of Lille condemned homosexuals for engaging in fruitless copulation and Jean de Meun widened this condemnation to include heterosexual sodomy and even celibacy, Gower adds yet another category of unproductive lovers: the aged. The Latin introductory verse makes this point clear:

> Qui cupit id quod habere nequit, sua tempora perdit,
> > Est vbi non posse, velle salute caret.
> Non estatis opus gelidis hirsuta capillis,
> > Cum calor abcessit, equiperabit hiems.
>
> >   (2.450)

> [He wastes his time who wants what he can't have;
> Where might is missing, wanting wants a cure.
> When warmth departs, then frosty bristled Winter
> Will not be up to Summer's exercise.]

Hearkening back to Genius's concerns in Book 5, yet another of Gower's voices raises the issue of the waste of time in idle, unproductive activities. Venus's words are even more blunt as she addresses Amans "in scorn":

---

112. Andreas Capellanus, *De amore: Andreas Capellanus on Love*, ed. and trans. P. G. Walsh (London: Duckworth, 1982) 58–59.

For loves lust and lockes hore
In chambre acorden neveremore,
And thogh thou feigne a yong corage,
It scheweth wel be the visage
That olde grisel is no fole.

(8.2403–7)

[For love's pleasure and grey locks never accord in the bedroom. Although you feign a young spirit, your face reveals clearly that "Old Grisel" is no foal.]

Although "feigning" was an essential strategy in the Ovidian courtship, Venus here declares that in the work of reproduction, sexual potency must match outward show (8.2408–11). As for Amans, she notes that his labor to date has been an "ydel peine" because "thou art noght sufficant / To holde love his covenant" (you are not sufficient to uphold love's covenant; 8.2419–20).

In dismissing Amans, Venus employs a figure from the world of rural labor when she affirms that Amans cannot "plow his field" (8.2421–27). Jean de Meun had used the image of "plowing" to great effect in the ending of his portion of the *Rose*. Gower also employs a figure from commerce, however, to make the same point: "What bargain scholde a man assaie, / Whan that him lacketh forto paie?" (How can a man try to bargain when he lacks means of payment?; 8.2431–32). As with his use of *occupacioun* and *bysynesse*, Gower again demonstrates his conviction that work from the world of commerce is an apt figure for love's labor.

Venus's solution is given in terms of a retreat from unproductive labor, that is, idleness, to productive leisure, *otium negotiosum*. She commands Gower to make "a beau retret" (8.2416) from the labor of courtship, thus contradicting Genius's earlier assertion that love was an "occupacioun" for *every* "gentil herte." After Cupid removes his arrow, Venus annoints his wound with a cold ointment (8.2794–2819). She gives him a rosary with the words "por reposer" (for resting) engraved on it (8.2904–7). In essence, she allows Amans / Gower the privilege of monastic *otium*. This *otium negotiosum* is licit because with it Gower can at last become socially productive. Venus reminds Gower pointedly of his books (8.2924–27), and he himself understands that the rosary was meant to suggest that he now must spend his time in prayer (8.2958–61).

In the last chapter, I noted Jean-Charles Payen's characterization of Jean de Meun as the poet of productivity.[113] Much the same can be said of

113. Payen 197.

John Gower, which, given the overt structure of Book 4, is at first surprising. In the traditional labor ideology inherent in the moral schema of the Seven Deadly Sins, in particular the popular moral tradition of *acedia*, sloth opened the soul up to the devil, and thus activity of any sort was the recommended remedy. Traditionally this schema did not concern itself overtly with productivity. However, a consistent labor motif in the *Confessio*, one that is linked to Gower's cultural and ideological contexts, pushes the traditional thinking about sloth a step further toward a humanist work ethic. Through the dynamics of the dialog among Amans, Genius, and Venus, Gower emphasizes that keeping busy is not enough; one's labor must produce something for the common good.

To conclude, Gower's treatment of love's labor in the *Confessio* condemns the wasteful idleness of loving "par amour" every bit as strongly as Reason's discourse in *Le Roman de la rose* did, but the *Confessio* is not simply traditional in its treatment of love's labor. Gower's masterpiece does not speak with a single ideological voice, but the ideological "taste" of its condemnation of *acedia* is rooted not only in the traditional rhetoric of "love's labor" but also in the developing labor ideologies of his own time and culture.

CHAPTER 7

Love's *Bysynesse* in Chaucer's Amatory Fiction

The lyf so short, the craft so long to lerne,
Th'assay so hard, so sharp the conquerynge, . . .
Al this mene I by Love.

[The life so short, the craft so long to learn; the attempt
so hard, so sharp the conquering; In all this, I refer to love.]

    —*Chaucer*

For youre love I swete ther I go.

[For your love, I sweat wherever I go.]

    —*Chaucer's Absalom*

I

Chaucer's love poetry, like that of Ovid, takes its particular coloring from the discourse of love's labor, and his labor discourse double-voices not only that of Ovid, Alan of Lille, and the authors of the *Roman de la rose* but also that of his own contemporary society. Of course, the discourse of love's labor is placed into dialog with the discourse of passion in many of Chaucer's works. The love sicknesses of Palamon, Arcite, Troilus, and even Absalom come immediately to mind. However, these are more than counterbalanced by the labor discourses of Pandarus, Diomede, Daun John, Nicolas, Januarius, and the Wife of Bath. As we shall see, Chaucer was a man imbued with a respect for *bysynesse*, a word that carried little of the negative connotations of the Latin *labor* or the French *travail*, in all aspects of life, including love. Since the word's Latin equivalent, *negotium*, played no role at all in the discourse of love's labor in Ovid, Andreas Capellanus, or Alan of Lille, it is noteworthy that *bysynesse* here plays so large a role. It is a sign, I believe, of the significant "embourgeoisement de l'eros" in Chaucer's adaptations of the aristocratic traditions of love poetry.[1] For example, despite the key role played by Idleness in Guillaume de Lorris's *Roman de la rose*, Chaucer, himself a busy civil servant who had to steal time for his art from the night, found idleness terribly suspect.[2] In this chapter's first epigraph, the narrator of the *Parlement of Foules*, like Ovid himself, presents love as a craft to be learned. Chaucer's successful lovers are more often than not those who learn this art well and apply it diligently. Since love is "sharp" in "conquerynge," lovers like the Miller's "hende Nicholas" earn their love by their wits, by their dogged perseverance, and by the "sweat of their brows." The failed lovers are often the ones who allow passion or *otium otiosum* to overwhelm their better judgment.

Since the general labor situation and labor attitudes of fourteenth-century England were discussed in the previous chapter, a review of these matters is not necessary here. Chaucer has not left us a treatise on his own personal labor ideology. As with the other works treated in this book, one is dealing with ideologies double-voiced in works of creative literature. One can never be absolutely certain, then, how closely the discourse of a particular Chaucerian character reflects the author's own work ideology. The various texts must be read with care and with tact. Nevertheless, taking into consideration what we know of Chaucer's so-

1. John Scattergood briefly notes the theme of love's labor in Chaucer's writings ("The 'Bisynesse' of Love in Chaucer's Dawn-Songs," *Essays in Criticism* 37 [1987]: 110–20). Scattergood does not tie Chaucer's use of this imagery to the literary tradition or the discourse of love's labor. In addition, he argues that Chaucer uses love's labor imagery only with respect to the "work of the night," that is, sex (118). The discourse of love's labor is much more pervasive in Chaucer and is used to construct courtship as well as sex.

2. In the *House of Fame* (*HF*), Chaucer's narrator, who shares many personal characteristics with his creator, spends his evenings alone writing and reading in his study until his head aches (*The Riverside Chaucer*, ed. Larry D. Benson, 3rd ed. [Boston: Houghton Mifflin, 1987], lines 629–40. All quotations from Chaucer's work will be taken from this edition and cited in the text. Modern English translations are my own). After a full day of regular work, the eagle says: "For when thy labour doon all ys, / And hast mad alle thy rekenynges, / In stede of reste and newe thynges / Thou goost hom to thy hous anoon, / And, also domb as any stoon, / Thou sittest at another book / Tyl fully daswed ys thy look" (For when your labor is all done and you have paid all your bills, instead of rest and new things, you go home immediately to your house, and still as a stone, you sit at another book until you are thoroughly dazed; *HF* 652–58).

On Chaucer as an "urban" poet with little patience for idleness, see Craig E. Berelot, "'My Wit is Sharp: I Love No Taryinge': Urban Poetry in the *Parlement of Foules*," *Studies in Philology* 93 (1996): 365–89. On Chaucer's use of the bourgeois realistic style in conjunction with high, aristocratic styles, see Charles Muscatine, *Chaucer and the French Tradition* (Berkeley and Los Angeles: University of California Press, 1957). Lee Patterson highlights what he sees as an "ideology of commerce" in Chaucer's writings, especially in the Shipman's Tale and the Merchant's Tale. He is not convinced, however, that this ideology should necessarily be identified only with the urban bourgeoisie (*Chaucer and the Subject of History* [Madison: University of Wisconsin Press, 1991] 322–66).

cial backgrounds and his biography, one can harvest from Chaucer's entire corpus a general feeling of his attitudes toward labor and idleness.
On the whole, they reveal a profound respect for and even an obsession
with productive effort at every level of society.

Chaucer's biography has been written and rewritten many times. His
roots were bourgeois. He came from a family of successful wine merchants, with apparent close contacts with the ruling aristocracy. These
contacts allowed Chaucer himself to rise above his family's social class—
to be raised in a royal household, to acquire close contacts with the royal
family, and to become an important civil servant and even a member of
Parliament.[3] He had a large and varied network of social contacts, particularly in the middle and upper levels, a network of contacts reflected,
perhaps, in the social composition of his Canterbury pilgrims. He also
had a good ear for different social languages, which he took in as a detached observer.

To begin a review of his writings touching labor, one must note an exception that confirms the rule, Chaucer's short poem "The Former Age,"
in which he praises the simplicity of life in the Golden Age, when "Yit nas
the ground nat wounded with the plough" (the ground was not wounded yet with the plow) and the mill was not yet invented (6, 9). Nor had
men first begun "hir swety bysinesse" (their sweaty business) of mining
the earth for gold and jewels (28). Andrew Galloway analyzes the poem
as Chaucer's last negotiation with applied knowledge "as an ideology."[4]
He argues that Chaucer understood that the obligation to subdue the
earth through the rational application of technology was a result of
man's fall, but that Chaucer's attitude toward this phenomenon was both
"anxious" and "fascinated" (537–38). That is, Chaucer regretted postlap-
sarian man's obligation to work but took pride in man's ability to subdue
nature through the mechanical arts.

This may well be, but the poem does contain all the traditional pejorative associations of work with sin and sweaty manual labor. It directly ties
labor to luxuriousness and covetousness (31–32). Unlike their "lambish"
forbears, modern people, says Chaucer's persona, are "forpampred with

---

3. For the most recent of Chaucer's biographies, see Derek Pearsall, *The Life of Geoffrey Chaucer: A
Critical Biography* (Cambridge, Mass.: Basil Blackwell, 1992). On Chaucer's social position, as a civil
servant straddling the borders of the merchant class and the aristocracy, see also Paul Strohm, *Social
Chaucer* (Cambridge, Mass.: Harvard University Press, 1989) 10–21.

4. Andrew Galloway, "Chaucer's *Former Age* and the Fourteenth-Century Anthropology of Craft:
The Social Logic of a Premodernist Lyric," *ELH* 63 (1996): 538.

outrage" (overindulged with excess; 5) and afflicted with "pryde," "en-vye," and "avaryce" (53). The poem, based on classical treatments of the Golden Age such as that found in Ovid's *Metamorphoses*, betrays a nostal-gia for primitive living, not only when there was no work but also when men's lives and tastes were simpler. In this, its labor discourse is not char-acteristic of what one normally finds in Chaucer.

More characteristic not only of Chaucer but also of a notable strain of medieval labor ideology is Chaucer's treatment of labor in the Parson's Tale, a traditional confession manual composed from various Latin sources.[5] Here, in the section on *acedia* (10.676–737), the Parson praises labor and condemns all manner of sloth, including "sloggy slombrynge" (sluggish sleeping). The Parson's treatment of this vice falls well within the general tradition of *acedia* and includes the sins of despair and *tristi-cia*. Given that a significant portion of this section deals with fleshly *ace-dia*, that is, idleness, it is curious that the traditional remedy for *spiritual acedia, fortitudo,* is highlighted but not the remedy for *fleshly acedia,* labor.[6] At one point the Parson calls idleness the "yate of alle harmes" (gate of all harms), a bilge containing "alle wikked and vileyns thoghtes" (all wicked and villainous thoughts; 10.713–14). At this point the Parson af-firms that "Certes, the hevene is yeven to hem that wol labouren, and nat to ydel folk" (Certainly, heaven is given to laborers and not to idle folk; 10.715). Thus, labor plays a small role in the Parson's discourse as a reme-dy for one branch of *acedia*. It belongs to other Chaucerian texts, howev-er, to highlight the dignity of labor an integral part of ordinary life.

The pernicious character of idleness, for example, is a special concern of Chaucer's Second Nun. Rather than beginning her tale with an invoca-tion of heavenly aid, the Second Nun chooses to begin with a condemna-tion of idleness. Idleness she identifies as the "ministre and the norice unto vices" (the minister and governess of vices), and she even knows that Idleness was the porter of the love garden in the *Roman de la rose* (8.1, 3). Issues of productivity are not brought to the fore, but they can be found. For one thing, the Second Nun recognizes that from idleness "ther nevere comth no good n'encrees" (there never comes any good or in-

---

5. On the genre of the Parson's Tale, see Helen Cooper, *The Oxford Guide to Chaucer's "Canterbury Tales"* (Oxford, U.K.: Oxford University Press, 1987) 400–402. See also Siegfried Wenzel, "Notes on the Parson's Tale," *Chaucer Review* 16 (1982): 248–51.

6. 10.727–37. On the late-medieval distinction between spiritual and fleshly *acedia*, see Siegfried Wenzel, *The Sin of Sloth: Acedia in Medieval Thought and Literature* (Chapel Hill: University of North Carolina Press, 1967) 173–74.

crease; 8.18). Idleness also brings forward the question of fairness, for, like William Langland, the Second Nun notices that the idle person consumes the "swynke" (work) of other persons.[7] Therefore, to avoid this condition, the Second Nun recommends its opposite, "leveful bisynesse" (lawful business; 8.5), a term echoed later in the passage (8.24). What is interesting about this prologue is that it grounds the motivation for the Second Nun's impressive poetic and didactic composition, the life of St. Cecilia, in neither heavenly nor personal inspiration, nor in her sense of vocation, nor even in her duty to instruct—foundations that one might have expected—but rather in her fear of idleness. Here is a nun who gives the rhetorical place of honor to labor ideology, not theology. In this, I believe, she shows herself a particularly Chaucerian nun, valuing *bysynesse* above contemplation, Martha over Mary.

While issues of productivity are hardly mentioned in the Parson's Tale and are not developed in the Second Nun's Prologue, they are highlighted in the treatment of labor found in the Tale of Melibee. When Melibee considers revenge against his enemies, he notes that he is richer and thus more powerful than his enemies (7.1546–48). This comment leads his wife, Dame Prudence, into a consideration of how riches can be gained and used. In this section, labor is strongly linked to production and reward, and not, as in the Parson's Tale, presented simply as an antidote to idleness. This is a text to warm the hearts of the bourgeoisie. Its approach to worldly wealth spurns the traditional Christian rejection of wealth and glorification of worldly poverty. On the contrary, poverty is condemned as a source of many evils: "And right so as by richesses ther comen manye goodes, right so by poverte come ther manye harmes and yveles" (And just as through riches come many goods, so too many harms and evils come through poverty; 7.1563). Poverty, says the clever Dame Prudence, puts one at the mercy of one's enemies (7.1565–66).

Riches, the antidote to poverty, however, are good only to the extent that they are properly gained and used. Dame Prudence has no sympathy for the idle rich, for, like Max Weber's Protestants, she links wealth strongly with diligent labor. "And, sire," she says, "ye shul geten richesses by youre wit and by youre travaille unto youre profit" (And, sir, you shall acquire riches by your wits and by your profitable works; 7.1580). Here

---

7. 8.21. See *Piers Plowman: The B Version*, ed. George Kane and E. Talbot Donaldson (London: Athlone Press, 1975) 6.133 (356). All subsequent quotations from *Piers Plowman* will be taken from this edition and cited in the text by *passus* and line numbers. The modern English translations are my own.

the labor of one's mind, one's "wit," is put on an equal footing with manual labor, for both can be the source of worldly prosperity. Indeed, idleness is condemned in this passage, but the reason for its condemnation is significantly broadened from those found in the Parson's Tale or the Second Nun's Prologue. Of course, Dame Prudence notes that idleness can lead to sin (7.1588). However, sin is not the focus of her lesson here. On the contrary, the primary danger of idleness is lack of productivity, which leads inevitably to poverty and destitution. One is reminded of Piers Plowman's appeal to Hunger to cure the laziness of idlers (6.171–98). Dame Prudence says:

And the same Salomon seith that "he that travailleth and bisieth hym to tilien his land shal eten breed, / but he that is ydel and casteth hym to no bisynesse ne occupacioun shal falle into poverte and dye for hunger." / And he that is ydel and slow kan nevere fynde covenable tyme for to doon his profit. (7.1589–91)

[And the same Solomon says: "he who labors and busies himself with the tilling of land shall eat bread, but he who is idle and does not apply himself to business or an occupation shall fall into poverty and die from hunger." And he that is idle and sluggish can never find an appropriate time to do what is profitable.]

Lack of production, in this key passage, is the main reason to flee idleness. An idle person can never find the time to increase his wealth. This is clearly a foreshadowing of the ideology that Weber identified as the Protestant work ethic, where work is a blessed vocation and is tied to the accumulation of worldly property.[8] Rather than emphasize labor's being rooted in original sin, this ethic presents it as a worthy and dignified part of daily life that is directly tied to one's worldly well-being.

The Tale of Melibee is a close translation of Renaud de Louens's work of moral instruction, Le livre de Melibée et de Dame Prudence, which was written around 1336.[9] Again, it is difficult to be sure how closely the work ideology in the translation, taken in isolation, reflects Chaucer's own beliefs. Yet I hope to demonstrate that in the context of the entire Chaucerian corpus, this passage can be safely taken as representative. At the very least, Renaud's labor ideology is put into dialog here with other labor discourses in the rest of the Chaucerian canon. One noteworthy indication of Chaucer's ideological stance is the labor vocabulary he employs. The French "travail," which, as we saw in the previous chapter, carried much

8. Max Weber, The Protestant Work Ethic and the Spirit of Capitalism, trans. Talcott Parsons (1930; New York: Charles Scribner's Sons, 1956) 62–63.
9. Benson 923. On the genre of the Melibee, see Cooper 313–14.

of the pejorative connotation of "suffering" and "hard manual labor," is in this passage made more complex and positive by the addition of the English *bysynesse* and the newly coined *occupacioun*.[10] Both of these words carried more positive connotations, and thus are further indications of Chaucer's progressive work ideology.

Another indirect indication of Chaucer's labor ideology is found in the characterizations of the *Canterbury Tales*. As a general rule, those characters accorded the most profound respect are those that work well, while idlers are held up to scorn. On the one hand, the Plowman is praised as a "trewe swynkere" (true worker).[11] Moreover, his brother, the Parson, who, we are told, "This noble ensample to his sheep . . . yaf, / That first he wroghte, and afterward he taughte" (gave this noble example to his sheep: first he did the right thing and afterward he taught about it; 1.496–97), teaches that "Usage of labour is a greet thyng" (the habit of work is a great thing; 10.689). On the other hand, Chaucer's Monk, described by the Pilgrim with not too subtle Chaucerian irony, is presented as someone who finds not only manual labor but also clerical labor beneath his dignity. The Pilgrim reports his attitude as follows:

> What sholde he studie and make hymselven wood,
> Upon a book in cloystre alwey to poure,
> Or swynken with his handes, and laboure,
> As Austyn bit? How shal the world be served?
> Lat Austyn have his swynk to hym reserved!
>
> (1.184–88)

[Why should he study and drive himself crazy, always poring over a book in a cloister, or work with his hands and labor as St. Augustine commands? How shall the world be served? Let Augustine keep his work to himself!]

The word "swynken" was not used by Gower, but it is used occasionally by Chaucer. It inevitably suggests unpleasant manual labor and the sweat of one's brow, even, as we shall see below, when it is used in the discourse of love's labor.[12] In this passage the meaning is made clear by

10. See my discussion of Gower's labor words in the previous chapter, pp. 189–91.

11. 1.531. On the Plowman and conflicting medieval attitudes toward labor, see Daniel F. Pigg, "With Hym Ther Was a Plowman, Was His Brother," *Chaucer's Pilgrims: A Historical Guide to the Pilgrims in the "Canterbury Tales,"* ed. Laura C. Lambdin and Robert T. Lambdin (Westport, Conn.: Praeger, 1996) 263–70.

12. The verb *swynken,* a word that is first found around the middle of the twelfth century, carried all the pejorative connotations and denotations of the Latin *labor.* It meant primarily "to engage in physical labor, work hard, toil" ("Swinken" [1 (a)], *Middle English Dictionary* [MED], 1956 ed.). It also

the qualification "with his handes" and by the parallel English word "laboure." Although the Pilgrim may be taken in by the Monk's authority, most readers see that Chaucer is here satirizing those monks who have wandered from the traditional incorporation of some kind of productive labor in the daily monastic routine.[13] The reference here is certainly to Augustine's treatise on monastic labor in which he defends manual labor and attacks those who argued that true Christians avoid labor and live like the birds of the air.[14]

An even worse scoundrel is the Pardoner. Like the Monk, he has little respect for manual labor. "I wol nat do no labour with myne handes" (I will do no labor with my hands; 6.444), he boasts. He is not an idle character, however. In fact, since he presents his preaching as a form of "bisynesse" (6.399), he and Harry Bailey are the only pilgrims who engage in their own proper labor during the course of the pilgrimage to Canterbury. Even the Pilgrim realizes, however, that although preaching keeps the Pardoner from idleness, this labor is flawed because it is not socially productive. The Pardoner himself admits that it is a "gaude" (trick; 6.389) to convince the "lewed peple" that they should give him money in exchange for false and worthless relics. "For myn entente," he says, "is nat but for to wynne, / And nothyng for correccioun of synne" (For my intent is only to win money and not to correct sin; 6.403–4). Moreover, the Pardoner, a busy entrepreneur who, like Dame Prudence in the Tale of Melibee, finds poverty hateful and links wealth to *bysynesse*, nevertheless breaks Prudence's first rule in the accumulation of wealth: do no harm. Indeed, she proclaims, "that nature deffendeth and forbedeth by right that no man make hymself riche unto the harm of another persone" (that nature rightfully forbids and prohibits that a man make himself rich with the effect of harming another person; 7.1583). The Pardoner does not care at all that he is the spiritual equivalent of a snake-oil salesman and that his customers are putting their spiritual health at risk by buying his goods. "I rekke nevere, whan that they been beryed," he admits, "Though that hir soules goon a-blakeberyed!" (When they are buried, I never care even if their souls go blackberry picking!; 6.405–6). Within a Christian context, then, the potential for doing harm is great. In

referred specifically to work as a punishment for sin (1 [e]) and to the suffering of pain and physical discomfort (4 [a]). From at least 1330, it was also used to refer to sexual toil, that is, copulation (2 [e]).

13. And, in general, from most aspects of the monastic rule. See John P. Hermann, "A Monk Ther Was, A Fair for the Maistrie," Lambdin and Lambdin 75–76.

14. St. Augustine, *De opere monachorum*, *Oeuvres completes de Saint Augustin*, ed. Péronne et al. (Paris: Louis Vivès, 1870) 22.84–129. See, especially, 101–2, 107, 110–15.

other contexts, the energy of Chaucer's Pardoner might be admirable, but clearly Chaucer presents him as a case of unproductive and hence perverted *bysynesse*. One is reminded of Alan of Lille's character Iocus, who perverts the true work of love into mere play. So too with respect to spiritual labor, does the Pardoner. Guillaume de Saint-Amour would have found him very much like the stereotypical friar in the *De periculis*, a shifty usurper of the work of others.

The Sergeant of Law presents yet another example of an at least partially flawed worker. The Pilgrim recognizes that the Sergeant of Law keeps himself occupied, yet he concentrates only on the effects of his work, the money he makes. The close ties between work and reward are nowhere more evident than in the description of this character. Indeed, we are told that "For his science and for his heigh renoun, / Of fees and robes hadde he many oon" (For his learning and his high renown, he had many a fee and robe; 1.316–17). Nevertheless, the Pilgrim suspects that his companion's reported activity is somewhat inflated: "Nowher so bisy a man as he ther nas," reports the Pilgrim, "And yet he semed bisier than he was" (Nowhere was there a busier man, and yet he seemed busier than he really was; 1.321–22). For the Sergeant at Law, "bysynesse" clearly carries none of the pejorative connotations of the old ideas of work. If it did, he would have no reason to pretend to be busier than he was. This self-presentation is an indication of a progressive labor ideology that values labor both in its own right and for what it can produce. With that aspect of the Sergeant at Law, one can be reasonably certain, Chaucer had no quarrel. What Chaucer mildly satirizes, however, is the hypocrisy of someone who pretends to work harder than he really does. He is the bourgeois equivalent of Jean de Meun's hypocrite Pope-Holiness, a character who pretends to be holier than he really is. Nevertheless, the condemnation of the Sergeant of Law's industry is nowhere near as brutal as that accorded the Pardoner. Chaucer is amused, not outraged, because the Sergeant of Law's activity at least causes no harm.

Another character concerned with productivity, at least within the context of the storytelling game, is Chaucer's Host, Harry Bailly. Introduced as a good-natured innkeeper of Southwerk, the Host takes his duties as the tour guide seriously. He provides the initial dinner and lodging, arranges the rules of the game, and, except for his embarrassing contretemps with the Pardoner, keeps order during the pilgrimage masterfully. One of the Host's special concerns is the proper use of time. We saw in the previous chapter that the initial diffusion of the mechanical clock on public squares during the late fourteenth century brought to the foreground concerns with the proper use of time and that this was a characteristic concern of the early humanists.[15] Although he makes only a passing reference to the clock, Harry Bailly shares the humanists' time anxiety.[16] In the introduction to the Man of Law's Tale, he carefully notes the position of the Sun, makes his calculations, and concludes that it is "ten of the clokke" (2.14). At that point, he decides that the pilgrims are not making the progress he would expect in their game. Rather than simply calling on the next teller, however, he offers a little sermon on the proper use of time, quoted at length in the previous chapter (2.18–24). After a quick citation from Seneca, the Host concludes that while one may recover lost property, one cannot recover lost time.[17] Therefore, time must be put to productive use; it must not be spent in idleness. In this case, the most productive use of time is simply to speed up the story-telling game. This passage, then, highlights another aspect of Chaucer's work ethic, his humanist concern with the efficient use of one's time.

In sum, a broad range of approaches to labor exists in Chaucer's writings, suggesting that, as in Gower, several different work ideologies are in dialog. Nevertheless, in almost all the passages cited above, the idea of work is held in high regard, whether due to its nature as an antidote to idleness or its ability to produce wealth for the worker.[18] These same atti-

15. On the time concerns of the humanists, see Gerhard Dohrn-van Rossum, *History of the Hour: Clocks and Modern Temporal Orders*, trans. Thomas Dunlap (Chicago: University of Chicago Press, 1996) 252.

16. Peter Travis's comment on the Host is worth quoting in this regard: "Throughout the pilgrimage Harry suffers from a very modern obsession with the passage of time, an obsession that is an instantiation of the mercantile mentality characterized by Le Goff. Harry is thus very much a man of the hour, epitomizing the burgeoning bourgeois fascination with the process of gaining and losing the measurable *minutiae* of time" ("Chaucer's Chronographiae, the Confounded Reader, and Fourteenth-Century Measurements of Time," *Disputatio* 2 [1997]: 11).

17. Dohrn van-Rossum notes that Seneca's essay "On the Brevity of Life" became notably influential among the humanists. Under Seneca's influence, he argues, "Petrarch introduced notions about the 'incalculable value of time' into literature" (4).

18. Elsewhere I have treated Chaucer's adaptations of the character Idleness from the *Roman de la rose* ("Interpreting Guillaume de Lorris' Oiseuse: Geoffrey Chaucer as Witness," *South Central Review* 10.1 [1993]: 22–37). In that article, I argued that: "It is one thing to argue that many of the various denotations of 'oiseuse' find support in the Chaucer canon; it is quite another, however, to suggest that Chaucer's overall attitude toward idleness was noncommittal. On the contrary, taken as a whole I find that his *oeuvre* conveys an attitude of disapproval or, at least, distrust. In fact, one sees this distrust not only in the comments of those favorites of the Exegetes, the Parson and the Second Nun, but also in the treatment of his aristocratic knights—the 'verray, parfit gentil knight' of the *Canterbury Tales*, the Black Knight, and Troilus. . . . Nowhere in Chaucer's works can one find support for the courtly argument that Oiseuse is a virtue to be celebrated or a secular parallel to religious contemplation. On the whole, Chaucer's attitude toward Oiseuse [is that] . . . idleness emasculates lovers. Chaucer seems to believe that one should always be busy about something, whether the

tudes can be seen in Chaucer's construction of the discourse of love's labor.

II

A good place to begin the treatment of Chaucer's discourse of love's labor is with his poem *The Parlement of Foules*, from which the first epigraph of this chapter is taken. At the beginning of the poem, Chaucer uses a rhetorical flourish, the *ars longa vita brevis* topos, to announce one of the central themes of the poem: love's labor.[19] As in Ovid's *Ars amatoria*, love is a craft to be learned. What is notable here is that this is one of the examples of "craft" that Chaucer uses in a positive or neutral way to denote either a technique or a skill. In fact, throughout much of the Chaucerian canon, the word "craft" carries pejorative connotations. It is used, for example, to refer to the tricks of the Shipman and of the Pardoner (1.401, 692). The Friar uses the word to refer to the tricks of the devil, which are more subtle than those of a "jogelour" (3.1468). The Merchant has Januarius refer to the craft of deceitful old widows (4.1424), and he later uses it to refer to Damian's smarmy flattery: "For craft is al, whoso that do it kan" (For craft is everything for people who know how; 4.2016). The word is used most often in the Canon Yeoman's Tale, where it is employed fourteen times to refer to the dishonest alchemical tricks of the Canon. For the Canon's Yeoman, alchemy is an "elvysshe," "cursed," "false," and "soory" craft.[20]

---

labor is physical, spiritual, or amatory. Like his Parson, he affirms that heaven, the heaven of the Christian religion or the secular paradise of Courtly Lovers, is the reward of laborers and not of idle folk" (32–33).

19. The central theme of the poem, whether it concerns primarily love or politics, has been the subject of much controversy. For a helpful summary of the arguments in favor of the theme of politics, see Russell Peck, "Love, Politics, and Plot in the *Parlement of Foules*," *Chaucer Review* 24 (1990): 290–305. Two important articles that elaborate the political themes in the poem are Paul A. Olson, "The *Parlement of Foules*: Aristotle's *Politics* and the Foundations of Human Society," *Studies in the Age of Chaucer* 2 (1980): 53–69; and Bruce Kent Cowgill, "The *Parlement of Foules* and the Body Politic," *Journal of English and Germanic Philology* 74 (1975): 315–35. For an argument that the poem concerns love and not politics, see A. C. Spearing, "Al This Mene I Be Love," *Studies in the Age of Chaucer. Proceedings* 2 (1986): 169–77. On (various kinds of) love as the primary theme, see also comments by J. A. W. Bennett, *"The Parlement of Foules": An Interpretation* (Oxford, U.K.: Clarendon Press, 1957) 23, 29; A. J. Minnis, *Oxford Guides to Chaucer: The Shorter Poems* (Oxford, U.K.: Clarendon Press, 1995) 299, 315; and Helen Cooney, "The *Parlement of Foules*: A Theodicy of Love," *Chaucer Review* 32 (1998): 373–74. My reading of the poem supports the latter group, especially that of Minnis, although the poem, seen through the lens of the love's labor theme, is more coherent and unified than Minnis thinks.

20. Canon's Yeoman's Tale, 8.619, 621, 751, 785, 830, 838, 866, 882, 952, 1247, 1320, 1349, 1369, 1395.

What is apparently a direct and positive reference to Ovid's art of love, then, becomes suspicious in the context of Chaucer's normal associations with "craft." It is probable, then, that "craft" here bears both positive and negative connotations, connotations that become apparent only as the poem progresses. Indeed, love's labor, from the very start of this poem, is an ambiguous concept, and, as we shall see below, the double nature of love's work is among its central concerns. The dialog about the nature of that work, then, begins in the first line of the poem.

A few lines farther into the poem, the Dreamer/Narrator admits that he himself is not a lover, but rather a student of love:

> For al be that I knowe nat Love in dede,
> Ne wot how that he quiteth folk here hyre,
> Yit happeth me ful ofte in bokes reede
> Of his myrakles and his crewel yre.
>
> (8–11)

[For although I do not know love in deed, nor how he pays lovers' wages, yet it happens that I often read in books of his miracles and his cruel ire.]

He extends the work metaphor logically: if love is a craft, then the god of love must pay wages for its practice. It is the Dreamer's task to discover what these wages are. On the face of it, this is a surprising statement, for the narrator has done his research. He has read many books on love. How can someone who has done all that book research not know what the wages of love are?

Several possible answers suggest themselves. First, the verb *witen* may be taken in the sense of "to have experience of."[21] Since the narrator has never practiced love, he has never received or experienced the wages of love. Moreover, it would be logical to equate the wages of love with sexual pleasure. The narrator has book knowledge of love's wages, but he has not yet experienced them.

In the context of the entire poem, however, another, less obvious, but perhaps more fitting interpretation presents itself. In this reading, the wages of love are children, for the discourse of love's labor in *The Parlement of Foules* is highly influenced not only by that in Jean de Meun's *Roman de la rose* but also by Alan of Lille's *De planctu naturae*.[22] It is a dis-

---

21. "Wit" (2 [b]), *Oxford English Dictionary (OED)*, 1989 ed.

22. Chaucer cites the *De planctu* in the poem (316), and the influence of the *De planctu* on the *Parlement of Foules* is a critical commonplace. See, for example, Bennett 12–14, 139; and Minnis 265, 271–76.

course in which love is constructed as *productive* labor, in which the sexual organs are presented as tools, and in which any nonproductive sexual practices are presented as perverse. Indeed, Alan's Dame Nature plays a pivotal role in the *Parlement of Foules*, and the *De planctu* is even cited specifically as a source of information on the goddess (316). It is not surprising, then, to find Alan's labor ideology woven into the fabric of Chaucer's poem as well. In this reading, the Dreamer does not know love's wages in two different senses. First, not having practiced the craft of love, he has engendered no children. Second, it is also possible that he does not even recognize that offspring *are* the proper wages of love. He is looking for love's wages in all the wrong places, and this confusion is driven home in the parliament scene and in his exploration of the dream garden.

The contrast between productive love and sterile love is first presented as the Dreamer enters through the gate of the dream garden, a garden with two presiding deities, Venus and Nature. On one side, the garden is presented as verdant and healthful, a "welle of grace" (129). On the other, the garden is described as a wasteland in which the trees bear no fruit. The ponds are dry. Daunger (Resistance) and Disdayn, we are told, are the garden's proper guides (134–40). Read from the perspective of the *De planctu*, this double inscription, which is meant for "Loves servaunts" only (159), becomes a reference to the contrast between reproductive and unproductive love, between the work of Cupid and the work of Iocus. This contrast is further highlighted in the descriptions of the two goddesses. Venus, her hair tressed by lifeless golden wires, accompanied by Riches, draped seductively on a bed of gold in a dark and private corner, and surrounded by the images of dead and unhappy lovers, is clearly an unattractive figure (260–94). Nature, on the other hand, presiding nobly in a sweet and green place over a joyous route of happy birds, is just as clearly a sympathetic authority figure.[23] Her beauty, we are told, surpasses every creature as much as the light of the sun surpasses every star (299–301).

The contrast between Venus and Nature is elaborated in the parliament scene proper. Here the noble birds, who are more inclined to serve Venus than Nature, are contrasted with the commoners, eager servants of Nature.[24] Both groups are brought before Nature to accomplish love's

23. 295–308. For Bennett, Nature represents "ageless fecundity, the endless multiform going on of life" (121–22).

24. For the birds as representatives of various social classes, see Bennett 140; David Aers, "The

"werk," specifically, in this context, the choosing of mates (666). The high rhetoric of the birds of prey features the discourse of love's service prominently.[25] The eagles occupy the discourse world of Andreas Capellanus's *De amore* or Chaucer's own Knight's Tale, in which the discourse of love's service is also foregrounded.[26] Their conception of love's labor, which includes only rhetoric and knightly combat, descends directly from Andreas. Implicitly rejecting Nature's discourse, the royal tersel refuses to call the formel eagle his "fere" (mate) and insists on calling her his "soverayn lady" (416). The labor he chooses is not the labor of reproduction but of knightly service (440). Indeed, both of the first two suitors attempt to convey the depth of their love for the formel eagle by boasting of their service. The second argues that he has served the formel eagle longer than the first (453). The third tercel eagle admits that he has not served the formel as long as the other two, but his service, nonetheless, could be of higher quality if given the chance: "A man may serven bet and more to pay," he argues, "In half a yer, although it were no moore, / Than som man doth that hath served ful yoore" (A man may serve better and more satisfactorily in half a year, no more, than others do who have served a long time; 474–76). Immediately, however, he expresses an exaggerated humility topos by claiming "I seye not this by me, for I ne can / Don no servyse that may my lady plese" (I'm not referring to myself, for I cannot perform service pleasing to my lady; 477–78). In the context of the entire poem, this exaggerated rhetoric is at the heart of love's "craft" in the pejorative sense. One suspects that none of the eagles, particularly the last, really means what he says, or, if he does, he is deceiving himself, yet these exaggerated claims all form a part of the aristocratic rhetoric of love.

The discourse of love's labor in the *Parlement* is, of course, well mixed with the discourse of passion. The first and third eagles highlight their sufferings, and thus make claims on the lady's *pité* as well as her sense of fairness for services rendered (424–27, 435–38, 470–73). All three suffer

---

Parliament of Fowls: Authority, the Knower, and the Known," *Chaucer Review* 16 (1981): 10–14; and Clement Hawes, "'More Stars, God Knows, than a Pair': Social Class and the Common Good in Chaucer's *Parliament of Fowls*," *Publications of the Arkansas Philological Association* 15 (1989): 12.

25. See lines 419, 440, 453, 474, and 476.

26. Upon seeing Emily, both Palamon and Arcite, striken by love sickness, are moved "to serve" her faithfully (1.1143). When confronted with the battling cousins, Theseus speaks movingly of the "service" of love to Palamon and Arcite and admits that he himself was a "servant" (1.1803, 1814). Love's "servants" are depicted in Venus's temple (1.1923), where Palamon pledges himself to be a "servant" of Venus (1.2235). And at the end of the tale, Arcite, Theseus, and the Knight/Narrator all agree that Palamon has "served" and will continue to "serve" Emily very well indeed (1.2795, 3078, 3086, 3104).

grievously for love, yet it is the courtly discourse of love's service that predominates. All three, in fact, are prepared to engage in the labor of knightly combat to win the wages of love (540).

The sterility of this highly rhetorical and codified form of love is brought into focus not only by the formel's inability to choose from among her suitors but also by the businesslike attitudes of the lower birds.[27] They understand Nature's command to choose a mate as a job to be done. Like Chaucer's Host and unlike the terselets, who devote the entire day to profitless rhetoric, the lower birds realize that time lost cannot be recovered. The goose, for example, exclaims "My wit is sharp; I love no taryinge" (My wit is sharp; I don't like delay; 565). Nor can they understand unproductive work. "Wel bourded," says the Duck, "That men shulde loven alwey causeles! / Who can a resoun fynde or wit in that?" (You're joking . . . to claim that men should love without cause. Who can find reason or wit in that?; 589–91). Although the noble birds find this kind of talk vulgar and although Chaucer's double voicing of the bourgeois work ideology is at times comic ("Lo, here a parfit resoun of a goos!" [Lo, hear the perfect reason of a goose!; 568]), nevertheless this work ideology certainly forms the spine of Chaucer's discourse. After all, the happy ending of the poem resides not in the frustrated and sterile nondecision of the formel eagle, but in the joy of the lower birds in a job well done. Their "werk," unlike that of the birds of prey, "al brought was to an ende" (was all brought to an end; 666).

This reading of the parliament scene nicely ties the second half of the poem with the first, where Scipio the Elder instructs Scipio the Younger always to work for the common profit.[28] The Elder says,

27. Bertolet has nicely analyzed the rhetoric of the two classes of birds, especially with respect to their attitudes toward time. "The upper fowls model their addresses on the courtly love lyric, which . . . encodes aristocratic leisure, *otium*—surplus time, a form of wealth—by refusing to economize time." On the other side, the rhetoric of the lower-class birds is an "urban" rhetoric, one emphasizing profitable industry and the understanding that time is a commodity that should not be wasted (366–70).

28. The question of the poem's unity, of how its parts fit together, is an enduring critical problem. The problem arises because the parts, especially the opening dream and the parliament scene, do not seem to be related. While there have been consistent efforts to demonstrate that the poem is unified (see, e.g., R. M. Lumiansky, "Chaucer's *Parlement of Foules:* A Philosophical Interpretation," *Review of English Studies* 24 [1948]: 81–89; Bennett 6, 23; Cowgill 315; and Cooney 339–76), many recent critics have insisted that there is no formal unity in the poem (Robert M. Jordan, "The Question of Unity and the *Parlement of Foules," English Studies in Canada* 3 [1977]: 373–85; Spearing 175–76; and Minnis 312, 317). While I would not argue that the poem has an organic unity, I do believe that reading the poem through the lens of love's labor helps make its parts cohere more strongly.

And loke ay besyly thow werche and wysse
To commune profit, and thow shalt not mysse
To comen swiftly to that place deere
That ful of blysse is and of soules cleere.

(74–77)

[Always look that you busily work and direct yourself toward the common profit, and you shall not fail to come swiftly to that dear place full of bliss and bright
souls.]

While the aristocratic rhetoric and the exaggerated feelings of the birds
of prey might be fashionable on certain levels of society, the poem suggests that they do not serve the common good. Particularly in a society
that suffered significant depopulation caused by extended wars and dev-
astating waves of the plague, one of the most fundamental ways to serve
the common good would be to engender more children. This, within
Alan of Lille's discourse of love's labor, is to use Nature's tools to fashion
new "coins" for the realm.[29] While the common birds have not at this
point actually coined new money, they have metaphorically set up shop
and are ready to continue to the next step of their legitimate craft.

But what of love's wages, which play so prominent a role in the opening of the poem? If the work has been accomplished, why do we not hear
of wages being paid? At the end of the poem, Chaucer mentions neither
sexual pleasure nor offspring. Of course, the birds of prey, from Nature's
perspective, have performed no productive labor, and thus deserve no reward. And what of the lower species? We actually do hear of reproduction in the earlier part of the poem when the narrator, pausing to describe the birds in the garden, says "Some besyede hem here bryddes
forth to brynge" (Some busied themselves here to bring forth birds; 192).
The reason that we do not hear of their offspring at the end of the poem
is that it is too early in the process. Reproduction, however, is implied in
that the birds have chosen their mates, and thus have fulfilled the first
necessary conditions for reproduction. Yet they have, in a sense, begun to
reap their wages: the ability to rest within the healthful aspects of the
garden. At the beginning of the poem, Scipio the Elder promises the
Younger a "place deere / That ful of blysse is and of soules cleere" (76–
77) as a reward to everyone who works for the common good. Nature's

29. Bertolet argues that the lower fowl see procreation as their contribution to "common profit"
(379–80).

summery garden, in which the lower orders of birds dance and play with "blisse and joye" is indeed such a place (669).

Another reason that offspring are not mentioned may be the estate of the narrator. After seeing the sterility of the noble birds and the happiness of the lower orders, one might suppose that the Dreamer would have awakened from his dream with the conviction that he needed to follow Nature's counsels and seek out his own mate. That is not the case. Instead, the Dreamer reverts to his earlier habits and seeks to discover love's wages through further reading: "I wok, and othere bokes tok me to, / To reede upon, and yit I rede alwey" (I woke and devoted myself to reading other books, and still I continue to read; 695–96). This, however, is the proper labor for a *cleric* of love, who, like the narrator of *Troilus and Criseyde*, serves the servants of Love (*Troilus* 1.15). Earlier in the poem, he identifies reading as his labor (93). Somewhat later in the poem, Scipio the Elder reveals that the dream itself is the Dreamer's appropriate reward. "Sumdel of thy labour wolde I quyte" (I would reward a part of your labor), he says (112). The dream is not the reward appropriate for a servant of love—that wage the Dreamer can never have—but it is a reward appropriate for a cleric. What's more, in correctly admonishing the lovers who will read his poem, the Dreamer has performed his *officium*, has contributed to the common profit in a way appropriate to his estate, and thus has earned his wages. Nevertheless, since he himself still does not and cannot "know," that is, experience, the wages of love "in dede," he leaves it to the lovers in his audience to fill in the details.

Thus, Chaucer's discourse of love's labor in the *Parlement of Foules* is a light and imaginative double voicing of the labor discourse from the *De planctu* and, ultimately, from natural law ethics. One can detect a certain bourgeois humor in the tone of the poem, but on the whole the ideological import is clear and straightforward. However, while the *Parlement*'s work ideology is close to that found in the *De planctu*, in other of Chaucer's writings a new twist is added to a work ideology that foregrounds productivity. While Alan of Lille, Jean de Meun, and even John Gower tend to link productivity in love's labor to reproduction, Chaucer in other works of his amatory fiction, but especially in the *Troilus*, explores the problem of productivity *in courtship*. In some ways, this is a return to Ovidian love discourse, but in others it seems to reflect a growing fourteenth-century concern with productivity and the proper use of one's time.

III

Before turning to the *Troilus*, however, we should in passing note Chaucer's consistent use of labor diction in various parts of the *Canterbury Tales* to describe the sexual act. For example, in the Shipman's Tale, the lusty friar Daun John first approaches the Merchant's wife with the words: "I trowe, certes, that oure goode man / Hath yow laboured sith the nyght bigan / That yow were nede to resten hastily" (I believe, certainly, that our good man has put you to work since the night began so that now you quickly need some rest).[30] Here the term *labouren* is employed as a joke to emphasize the wife's need for rest the morning after hard sexual activities. The underlying sarcasm in this passage, however, suggests just the opposite, that the Merchant is no such workman. In pointing this out, the friar silently suggests that he himself would be better.

This passage is directly tied to the Host's own obsession with the sexual potency of the clergy and their legal inability to perform the labor of reproduction. In this he seems a clear ally of Jean de Meun. He says to the Monk, for example:

> I pray to God, yeve hym confusioun
> That first thee broghte unto religioun!
> Thou woldest han been a tredefowel aright.
> Haddestow as greet a leeve as thou hast myght
> To parfourne al thy lust in engendrure,
> Thou haddest bigeten ful many a creature.
>
> (7.1943–48)

[I pray to God to confuse the person who first led you into the monastic life! You certainly would have been a breeding fowl. If you had permission matching your sexual potency, you would have begotten many, many creatures.]

Here the focus is not on pleasure but on potency, a motif that is confirmed by the Host's comparison of the potency of monks to that of laymen:

> God yeve me sorwe, but, and I were a pope,
> Nat oonly thou, but every myghty man,
> Though he were shorn ful hye upon his pan,

---

30. 7.107–9. Many of these examples are noted in Scattergood 115–18.

Sholde have a wyf; for al the world is lorn!
Religioun hath take up al the corn
Of tredyng, and we borel men been shrympes.

(7.1950–55)

[God give me sorrow, but if I were the pope, not only you but every potent man,
whether he were tonsured or not, should have a wife, because (as things now
stand) all the world is lost! Religious orders have taken up the best men for copu-
lating, and we laymen are shrimps.]

Here the Host offers a locker-room compliment to the monk and a complementary self-denigration: yours, he says, is much bigger than mine.
This is obviously not the kind of compliment that the Monk wants to
hear in public. What is noteworthy, however, is that the compliment
refers specifically to productivity in love's labor. According to Harry, the
religious orders have taken up all the mightiest of workers for the labor
of reproduction.

   Alan of Lille's labor discourse, however, is put to other uses by
Chaucer. Whereas Alan's discourse conveys a serious concern with un-
derpopulation and the precarious position of the human species vis-à-vis
nature, Chaucer's double voicing is ironic and sarcastic. The Host is not
really suggesting that the Monk take a wife. He wants the Monk and his
ilk to keep their vows. The implicit criticism of the sexual profligacy of
monks and friars is made obvious later in the passage, when the Host
pointedly explains that the Monk's potency is the reason why so many
wives seek out religious men for the wages of love's labor, "for ye mowe
bettre paye / Of Venus paiementz than mowe we" (for you can better offer Venus's payments than we can; 7.1960–61). However, are these payments in sexual pleasure or in children? Chaucer probably has it both
ways. His Host playfully satirizes the Monk's sexual promiscuity, but he
also makes a serious point about productivity because the emphasis in
the passage is on reproduction. This becomes especially clear when Harry Bailley adds "God woot, no lussheburghes payen ye!" (God knows you
don't pay with inferior coins!; 7.1962). Here the evocation of inferior
coins imported from Luxembourg may well carry an indirect reference
to Venus as "mistress of the mint" in the *De planctu*. Indeed, F. N. Robin-
son notes that, although a lively debate on the merits of clerical celibacy
occurred in the late fourteenth century, the Host's arguments regarding
sexual productivity in the engendering of children were seldom heard.[31]

31. See Benson 929.

This, then, is Chaucer's appropriation of the discourse of Jean de Meun's Genius, who, as we have seen, goes even farther than Alan of Lille in condemning those healthy celebates who refuse Nature's work. The underlying seriousness of this double voicing becomes apparent in the Host's double-edged apology: "But be nat wrooth, my lord, though that I pleye, / Ful ofte in game a sooth I have herd seye!" (But don't be angry, my lord, even though I play. Many times I have heard a truth told in jest; 7.1963–64).

The Host's preoccupation with clerical reproductive labor is again reflected in an almost identical satirical compliment to the Nun's Priest: "But by my trouthe, if thou were seculer, / Thou woldest ben a tredefoul aright" (But by my truth, if you were a layman, you would have certainly been a breeding fowl; 7.3450–51). However, the Host takes the opposite approach with the Pardoner, whose description has raised so many questions about his sexuality or lack thereof. The Host denigrates the Pardoner by highlighting his apparent lack of sexual potency with the rough proposition:

> I wolde I hadde thy coillons in myn hond
> In stide of relikes or of seintuarie.
> Lat kutte hem of, I wol thee helpe hem carie;
> They shul be shryned in an hogges toord.
>
> (6.952–55)

[I wish I had your testicles in my hand instead of relics or a sacred object. Let's cut them off. I will help you carry them. They shall be enshrined in a hog's turd.]

Earlier, the Pardoner had exclaimed when he begins his false preaching, "it is joye to se my bisynesse" (6.399), but here the Host implies that, despite the Pardoner's outward show, he does not have the "tools" to perform the most essential work of Nature.

Besides the verb *laboren*, Chaucer uses the verb *swynken* to emphasize the raw physicality and somewhat comic nature of sexual work. When the Reeve, for example, describes Aleyn's weariness in the morning, he explains it by noting his activities with Malyne: "he had swonken al the longe nyght" (he had toiled all the long night; 1.4235). In addition, the Wife of Bath, who prides herself on being a good "werkman" (3.44e), expects no less from her husbands: "As help me God, I laughe when I thynke / How pitously a-nyght I made hem swynke!" (So help me God, I laugh when I think how piteously I made them toil at night; 3.201–2). There is no glorious poetry in this sexual labor. These acts involve no sacrament in the religion of love, nor are they in any way tied to the work of reproducing the species, for there is no indication that the Wife of Bath ever had any children. Instead, the labor discourse simply highlights the brutish effort involved in these liaisons. Whereas the Miller's Nicholas and Alisoun rejoice in the "bisynesse of myrthe and of solas" (the business of mirth and comfort; 1.3654), for Alisoun's husbands sex is "swynke" and, like the luckless Absalom, quoted in the second epigraph, they must sweat for simple sexual release.

The best, most detailed use of labor diction to highlight the comic physicality of sex in the *Canterbury Tales* is found in the Merchant's Tale. After the Merchant lingers over the unpleasant description of Januarius's rough and scratchy beard, he has Januarius prepare his bride for what he suspects she will find unpleasant work. "Allas! I moot trespace / To yow, my spouse, and yow greetly offende" (Alas! I must trespass on you, my spouse, and greatly offend you), he laments (4.1828–29). Yet he justifies his activities by invoking a tongue-in-cheek work ethic:

> Ther nys no werkman, whatsoevere he be,
> That may bothe werke wel and hastily;
> This wol be doon at leyser parfitly.
>
> (4.1832–34)

[There is no workman, whosoever he be, who may work both well and hastily. This work will be done leisurely and perfectly.]

Januarius, of course, is a knight, and thus should, like Chaucer's Theseus or the *Parlement*'s Royal Tersel, be employing the discourse of "service" and not "labor." It is unlikely that he (or, for that matter, the Merchant) has had personal experience as a manual laborer. As a result, this labor discourse, the praise of the craftsman's work ethic, has a very different effect than that found in the *De planctu*. Rather than dignifying the status of the craftsman, it comically degrades the speaker. After noting that the state of marriage protects them from all sin, "laboureth he til that the day gan dawe" (he labors until the dawn; 4.1842). Had there been any indication that this laboring would produce children, such discourse could easily be linked in a positive way with the labor discourse in the *De planctu* or in the *Roman de la rose*. There is none, however. Instead, Chaucer again signals his satiric intent by focusing on the disjunction between Januarius's youthful "ragerye" (wantonness) and the distasteful appearance of the sagging skin of his neck. Chaucer also notes that "fresshe May" was not particularly satisfied by the quality of Januarius's work: "She preyseth nat his pleyyng worth a bene" (She does not find his sexual play worth a bean; 4.1854).

As suggested in this passage, Chaucer in the Merchant's Tale creates an Ovidian conflation of sex as both work and play. Januarius sees his activity as play when he notes that such activity is not sinful for married couples (4.1835–36). For May, one suspects that "play" is used in the more pejorative sense of Alan of Lille: unproductive work. Thus, a lingering mixture of bitter irony and real insight is created when the Merchant notes that May kept to her bed on the fourth day while Januarius roamed about, "For every labour somtyme moot han reste" (For one must take a rest sometime from every labor; 4.1862).

IV

One is prepared for labor discourse used for comic purposes in certain of the *Canterbury Tales*. The complex double voicing of labor discourse comes unexpectedly, however, in Chaucer's complex "tragedie," *Troilus and Criseyde*.[32] Such is the case, however, and the double voicing contributes to the work's mixed style. Nevertheless, stylistic concerns are not the whole story. Labor discourse is, surprisingly, at the very heart of this work. Chaucer, for example, uses the word *slouthe* (sloth) more often in *Troilus* than he does in his confession manual, the Parson's Tale. Moreover, his palette of labor diction in the *Troilus* is at least as broad as anything found in Book 4 of the *Confessio Amantis*. Like Gower, Chaucer does not use the noun *swynk* or the verb *swynken* to refer to love's labor in the *Troilus*, although he does use it one time to refer to the work of writing poetry (5.272). However, for love's labor Chaucer does employ such words as *labour; bysynesse; travail; werk* and various forms of *werken; service* and various forms of *serven* continuously throughout this masterpiece.[33] In addition to these, Pandarus once likens himself to an *instru-*

32. The criticism on the poem is voluminous. The best review of the poem and its criticism is found in Barry Windeatt, *Oxford Guides to Chaucer: "Troilus and Criseyde"* (Oxford, U.K.: Clarendon Press, 1992).

No one generic description fits the *Troilus* exactly. *Troilus* is sui generis, a creative mixture of many different kinds of genres, and this generic indeterminacy is part of the reason why the thematic ambiguity runs so high in it. For a thorough and insightful treatment of the genre of *Troilus*, see Windeatt 138–79.

33. For Chaucer's use of *labour* in the *Troilus*, see 1.199, 955, 972, 1042; 2.1204; 3.1075; and 5.94. For his use of *bysynesse*, see 2.1316; 3.165, 244, 363, 1610; and 4.1488. For *werk* and forms of *werken*, see 1.265, 959, 1066, 1071; 2.960, 1401; 3.471, 697, 702, 735, 943; 4.166, 852; and 5.1823. For *service* and forms of *serven*, see 1.332, 370, 458, 816, 1058; 2.234, 273, 839, 996, 1150; 3.174, 390; 4.400, 713, 1265, 1290; and 5.279, 442, 1306. For his use of *servant*, see 1.15, 48, 328, 371, 912; 3.983, 1487; and 5.173, 1345. For his use of *travail*, see 1.21, 372, 475; 2.3, 1437; 3.522; and 5.184, 1852.

ment to help Troilus with his affair, and he calls the love affair an *emprise* on several occasions.[34] Concerns about productivity are recurrent. However, unlike the *De planctu* or the *Roman de la rose*, the *Troilus* never links productivity with reproduction. Instead, Chaucer's labor discourse here touches continuously on the productivity of lovers in courtship.

The *Troilus* is a rich and complex poem that resists single foundational readings. While most scholars agree that the poem is about "love" in a general sense, disagreements have continually arisen over the quality of the love in question. David Benson has nicely summarized three of the various options.[35] First, C. S. Lewis and others saw the poem as focusing on "courtly love," with Troilus being the ideal courtly lover. For Lewis, the greatest literary influence, after, of course, the *Filostrato*, is the *Roman de la rose*. He concluded that "the writing of *Troilus* betokens no apostasy from the religion of Cupid and Venus. Chaucer's greatest poem is the consummation, not the abandonment, of his labours as a poet of courtly love. It is a wholly medieval poem."[36] Later, however, D. W. Robertson and the Exegetes denied that the poem reflected "courtly love" at all. Instead, they argued that the poem focused on sinful "passionate love" set against the background of the *Consolation of Philosophy*. In this Augustinian reading, Troilus is first and foremost a sinner, a man who misdirects his love toward a frail, earthly goal rather than toward the highest good. Pandarus, rather than being a true incarnation of *Ami*, is a "priest of Satan."[37] A third kind of love, according to Benson, is that love described by Elizabeth Salter. For Salter, the focus of *Troilus* is love "not simply as a gay, sensual episode, nor as an ennobling example of 'amour courtois', nor indeed as proof of the 'worldes brotelnesse,' but as an embodiment of 'the holiness of the heart's affections.'" Salter argued that the *Troilus* is not a totally consistent poem, especially when one comes to the ending, but that Book 3 carries the central message of the poem and that is a courageous and blunt celebration of earthly love.[38]

To these three kinds of love could be added two more. One is love as a disease. Starting from the pioneering work of John Livingston Lowes in

---

34. For Pandarus as "instrument," see 1.631. Pandarus uses the word "emprise" to refer to the love affair in 2.73 and 2.1391. Troilus, also, calls the affair an "emprise" in 3.416.

35. C. David Benson, *Chaucer's "Troilus and Criseyde"* (London: Unwin Hyman, 1990) 120–21.

36. C. S. Lewis, *The Allegory of Love* (Oxford, U.K.: Oxford University Press, 1936) 176.

37. D. W. Robertson, Jr., *A Preface to Chaucer: Studies in Medieval Perspectives* (Princeton, N.J.: Princeton University Press, 1962) 472, 479.

38. Elizabeth Salter, "*Troilus and Criseyde*: A Reconsideration," *Patterns of Love and Courtesy: Essays in Memory of C. S. Lewis*, ed. John Lawlor (London: Edward Arnold, 1966) 88–90.

1913, we have been made aware that a certain kind of love, *amor hereos*, was presented as a bona fide disease in medieval medical manuals.[39] Because the symptoms of the disease match almost exactly those that Chaucer ascribes to Troilus, various scholars have argued that Troilus is a victim of *amor hereos*. This reading finds, contrary to the Exegetes, that Troilus is sick physically, not morally. Mary Wack adds that "[n]o ethical valuation is attached to the causal mechanisms in any of the texts—the patient is not held 'guilty' or 'responsible' for his illness."[40] In this reading, Pandarus acts as the physician who, eventually, brings Troilus to Criseyde's bed because intercourse with the desired person was given as the best medical cure for the disease. This is a variation on passionate love. It is passionate love because the lover is acted upon; he or she suffers rather than acts.

Then, finally, there is love as labor.[41] In this reading, Troilus and Diomede are interpreted primarily as workers in love's fields, and Pandarus is a teacher of love's labor, a *praeceptor amoris*. Indeed, because he even takes on Troilus's work when Troilus refuses to do it or does it halfheartedly, Pandarus can also be interpreted as a worker in his own right. Speaking of Pandarus as *praeceptor amoris*, however, leads to a consideration of Chaucer's debt to Ovid, for Ovid wrote the first manual of love's labor, and he influenced Chaucer greatly in the *Troilus*. Indeed, Chaucer's affinity to Ovid is a scholarly commonplace.[42] What is important to stress here, however, is that Ovid brought a playful attitude to the discourse of love's labor, and love's work for the *praeceptor* was, at its most basic, a game. That is, Ovid used language reflecting the ideology of labor of his own time to construct the discourse of love's labor, but he did so playful-

39. "The Loveres Maladye of Hereos," *Modern Philology* 11 (1913–14): 491–546.

40. Mary Wack, "Lovesickness in *Troilus*," *Pacific Coast Philology* 19 (1984): 56. See also Giles Y. Gamble, "Troilus Philocaptus: A Case Study in *Amor Hereos*," *Studia Neophilologica* 60 (1988): 175–78; and Carol Falvo Heffernan, *The Melancholy Muse: Chaucer, Shakespeare, and Early Medicine* (Pittsburgh, Pa.: Duquesne University Press, 1995) 67–89.

41. For an earlier treatment of love's labor in *Troilus*, see Gregory M. Sadlek, "Love, Labor, and Sloth in Chaucer's *Troilus and Criseyde*," *Chaucer Review* 26 (1992): 350–68. Some of what follows is taken directly from that article.

42. On Chaucer and Ovid, see Richard Lanham, *The Motives of Eloquence: Literary Rhetoric in the Renaissance* (New Haven, Conn.: Yale University Press, 1976) 65–66, and John M. Fyler, *Chaucer and Ovid* (New Haven, Conn.: Yale University Press, 1979) 1–2. On Ovid and the *Troilus* in particular, see Winthrop Wetherbee, *Chaucer and the Poets: An Essay on "Troilus and Criseyde"* (Ithaca, N.Y.: Cornell University Press, 1984) 92–93. The most recent contribution to our understanding of *Troilus* as a kind of *Ars amatoria* and also *Remedia amoris* is found in Michael Calabrese, *Chaucer's Ovidian Arts of Love* (Gainesville: University Press of Florida, 1994). Calabrese calls Pandarus an "*ars amatoria* incarnate" (39).

ly. Much of this same playful and "rhetorical" spirit will be seen in the discourse of love's labor in the *Troilus*, especially in the first three books. Here Chaucer will construct the "game" of love as a form of "work," an "emprise," an occasion for "bysynesse."[43] The work ideology embedded in these words and images, however, is different from the work ideology in Ovid. It is a new protohumanist kind of work ideology that values work as a good in itself and also for what it can produce, not a Roman ideology or an early medieval ideology valuing labor simply as a remedy for idleness. Nevertheless, although Chaucer's work ideology is different from Ovid's, what he does with this work ideology is similar to what Ovid did. He double-voices the labor discourse for his own artistic purposes, and those artistic purposes are often for the sake of humor but sometimes, especially in Book 5, for the sake of pathos.

This reading will focus on the discourse of love's labor in the *Troilus*, but strong cases can and have been made for all of the above kinds of love. As Windeatt writes, the *Troilus* is a sort of *"summa* of approaches to love."[44] At least since the time of Charles Muscatine, various scholars have been warning readers not to reduce *Troilus* to a single, coherent style or a single, coherent theme, particularly with regard to love. Arguing that the *Troilus* was constructed in the interplay of aristocratic and bourgeois styles, Muscatine, for example, writes:

The *tertium quid* created by the interplay of these styles and these philosophical traditions is best called a genre unto itself, for the result is a qualitative difference from romance or novel that requires a different kind of attention from the reader. It needs . . . "multiconsciousness," the simultaneous awareness of different and opposite planes of reality.[45]

Donald Rowe argues that the poem is built on the principle of contraries united and that its most basic characteristic is not ambiguity but paradox.[46] Benson adds that "[t]he range of interpretations advocated by these . . . powerful readings can help us to understand that the love between Chaucer's Troilus and Criseyde is never simple and always in question. No single approach can explain it, and thus none is comprehen-

43. A. J. Minnis has opined that "[i]ndeed, *Troilus* is to some extent a mirror for lovers, a work designed to demonstrate to its immediate audience the rules of the game of love" (*Chaucer and Pagan Antiquity* [Cambridge, U.K.: D. S. Brewer, 1982] 90).

44. Windeatt 214.

45. Muscatine 132–33.

46. Donald W. Rowe, *O Love, O Charite!: Contraries Harmonized in Chaucer's "Troilus"* (Carbondale: Southern Illinois University Press, 1976) 5.

sive."[47] Discussing the unity of the *Troilus*, Windeatt agrees. The fullness of the poem, he opines, prevents it from being seen satisfactorily from one single, unifying perspective. On the contrary, Windeatt argued that *Troilus*

progressively educates its reader into accepting that there can be no single fixed point of view in this world. . . . By reaching out toward certain polarities within its vision, *Troilus* promotes a kind of multiconsciousness in which any interpretation of the text must necessarily be offset by its opposite or contain its contrary within itself.[48]

Finally, Rosemarie P. McGerr demonstrates convincingly that the poem resists closure on all levels.[49] Indeed, the *Troilus* has a definite "novelesque" quality to it in that is open-ended, favoring what Bakhtin called centrifugal rather than centripetal linguistic forces.[50] Thus, the discourse of love's labor is just one of the many love discourses running through the poem.[51] It forms an especially important thematic and lexical thread through Books 1 to 3, and then, again, with Diomede's wooing of Criseyde, in Book 5. There is little of the discourse of love's labor in Book 4, in which Chaucer's attention is focused not on how love may be acquired, but how the two lovers deal with a setback of fortune.

In addition, the discourse of love's labor can best be seen by focusing on the poem's three principal male characters and not much on Criseyde. Again, the discourse of love's labor remains male-oriented. Although Criseyde is a vibrant character in her own right, she does not normally voice the discourse of love's labor.[52] Or, perhaps, it is better to say that she engages in a different kind of labor from the men, the cultivation of the self. In this, Chaucer remains faithful to Ovidian lore, for in the *Ars amatoria* the proper labor for women was passive self-cultivation.

Troilus and Criseyde constructs Criseyde as the object of male loves

47. Benson 122.

48. Windeatt 299.

49. Rosemarie P. McGerr, *Chaucer's Open Books: Resistance to Closure in Medieval Discourse* (Gainesville: University Press of Florida, 1998) 96–118.

50. See Gregory M. Sadlek, "Bakhtin, the Novel, and Chaucer's *Troilus and Criseyde*," *Chaucer Yearbook: A Journal of Late Medieval Studies* 3 (1996): 87–101.

51. "The poem may be Chaucer's most extended attempt not only to celebrate the variousness of human discourse, but also to realize the humanist sense that the study of speech is a kind of sociology, a way of understanding human behavior and human interaction" (Michaela Paasche Grudin, *Chaucer and the Politics of Discourse* [Columbia: University of South Carolina Press, 1996] 55).

52. On the character of Criseyde, see Windeatt 280–87 and Rowe 79–84. For Criseyde in her role as "widow," see Margaret Hallissy, *Clean Maids, True Wives, Steadfast Widows: Chaucer's Women and Medieval Codes of Conduct* (Westport, Conn.: Greenwood Press, 1993) 145–55.

and, from this perspective, she is more acted upon that acting. Gretchen Mieszkowski has argued that Criseyde is a remarkably passive character. "She initiates nothing of any consequence, drifts into decisions rather than making them, and is rarely shown accepting any responsibility. . . . She has no personal substance and no projects of her own; she never chooses and acts or sets goals and tries to reach these goals."[53] In this, she agrees with Donald Rowe, who, when comparing Troilus and Criseyde, notes that "Troilus tends to consider the world what he wishes it to be; he subordinates it to his own vision and his own feelings. . . . Criseyde, on the contrary, conforms her private world, her own inner life, to the demands and expectations of the public world."[54] Whether this is a personal flaw or one inherent to the socially constructed role of medieval women is a debatable question. Roberta Milliken, for one, believes that "[t]he woman's role . . . is a rather impotent one, one that is distinguished by forced inactivity."[55] Criseyde does not, on the whole, engage in love as active labor.

Troilus is a problem worker in love's fields as well, but his inactivity is always explicitly or implicitly compared with the aggressive activity of Pandarus or Diomede. Criseyde's inactivity stands apart. She is not expected to perform the same kinds of labors as those performed by the male characters. While she is not as passive as Mieszkowski paints her—for example, she covertly helps Pandarus to bring the affair to fruition and she is particularly willful in Book 4—she does not produce the discourse of love's labor. It is in the discourses of Troilus, Pandarus, and Diomede that the key terms and images are to be found.

Chaucer used the branches of the vice of both spiritual and fleshly *acedia* as major characteristics of Troilus in his role as courtly lover (but not public warrior).[56] As with all of Chaucer's major characters, disagree-

---

53. Gretchen Mieszkowski, "Chaucer's Much Loved Criseyde," *Chaucer Review* 26 (1991): 109.

On Criseyde's powerlessness, Arlyn Diamond argues that Criseyde, although the idealized beloved of Troilus, is in fact simply a pawn of the male patriarchy ("*Troilus and Criseyde*: The Politics of Love," *Chaucer in the Eighties*, ed. Julian N. Wasserman and Robert J. Blanch [Syracuse, N.Y.: Syracuse University Press, 1986] 93–104).

54. Rowe 49–50.

55. Roberta Milliken, "Neither 'Clere Laude' nor 'Sklaundre': Chaucer's Translation of Criseyde," *Women's Studies* 24 (1995): 197.

56. Sadlek, "Love, Labor, and Sloth" 351, 355.

Piero Boitani treats the vice of *acedia* in conjunction with lover's melancholy in his article "O quike deth: Love, Melancholy, and the Divided Self," *The Tragic and the Sublime in Medieval Literature* (Cambridge, U.K.: Cambridge University Press, 1989) 56–74. In this article Boitani explores the paradoxes of passionate love, especially its "dark pleasures," as forms of melancholy and hence spiritual

ments over how to interpret Troilus exist. Many scholars have advanced strong arguments for Troilus as a noble character, the true hero of the poem. He is certainly the poem's only nonpragmatic idealist and always speaks in the "high style."[57] All these arguments can be persuasive to a degree, yet from the perspective of love's labor, Troilus is pitifully inadequate. C. S. Lewis writes that "Troilus, throughout the poem, suffers more than he acts."[58] Muscatine adds: "It is difficult to think of a single hero of French romance who is quite so prostrated by love, so removed from the actual business of courtship, who depends so completely on an intermediary."[59] Winthrop Wetherbee writes: "The most striking feature of Troilus' role is his passivity. . . . The tendency of Troilus' emotions to turn in upon themselves rather than to cause him to actively pursue love is perhaps the most consistent feature of his behavior."[60] Most courtly lovers suffer from fear and melancholia, but Troilus suffers from these and from passivity to an extreme degree. Largely because of this passivity, June Hall Martin argues that Troilus is a parody of a courtly lover.[61] In other places, Troilus's passivity has led scholars to question his masculinity and to call him a "feminised hero."[62] Others see him as manly enough but just very, very young.[63]

Unless one believes that a bad case of *amor hereos* absolves Troilus of any moral responsibility, he certainly is a victim of spiritual *acedia*—as manifested in his melancholia, *tristesse*, and despair. Troilus's *tristesse* occupies a major portion of both early and late books of the *Troilus*. In fact,

acedia. The article focuses on the lover of the Petrarchan sonnet, but it also briefly touches on Troilus. It does not cover the various branches of *acedia*, nor does it treat Troilus's fleshly *acedia*.

On the distinction between the public and the private Troili, see Windeatt 277; and William H. Brown, "A Separate Peace: Chaucer and the Troilus of Tradition," *Journal of English and Germanic Philology* 83 (1984): 492–508.

57. On Troilus as hero, see Alfred David, "The Hero of the *Troilus*," *Speculum* 37 (1962): 566–81. For insightful overviews of Troilus's character, see Rowe 74–78 and Windeatt 275–78. On Troilus's "high style" of discourse, see Muscatine 133–37; Rowe 39–41; and Grudin 64–68.

58. Lewis 194.

59. Muscatine 137.

60. Winthrop Wetherbee, *Chaucer and the Poets* (Ithaca, N.Y.: Cornell University Press, 1984) 65–67.

61. June Hall Martin, *Love's Fools: Aucassin, Troilus, Calisto and the Parody of the Courtly Lover* (London: Tamesis, 1972) 37.

62. Jill Mann, *Geoffrey Chaucer*, Feminist Readings (New York: Harvester Wheatsheaf, 1991) 166–69. For a more recent argument about Troilus's lack of "masculine" qualities, see Maud Burnett McInerney, "'Is this a mannes herte?': Unmanning Troilus through Ovidian Allusion," *Masculinities in Chaucer: Approaches to Maleness in the "Canterbury Tales" and "Troilus and Criseyde,"* ed. Peter Beidler (Cambridge, U.K.: D. S. Brewer, 1998) 221–35.

63. Derek Brewer, "Troilus' 'Gentil' Manhood," *Masculinities* 237–52.

the narrator opens the poem by identifying Troilus's "double sorwe" as a major theme of the poem (1.1). It is not just that Troilus is sad; it is the severity and duration of the sadness coupled with Troilus's passivity that makes it a symptom of spiritual *acedia*. In addition, Chaucer uses the term "malencholie" four times in Book 5 to describe Troilus's condition.[64] Troilus's spiritual *acedia*, however, is not central to my argument here although it suggests that Chaucer had a coherent constellation of qualities (i.e., those of both spiritual and fleshly *acedia*) in mind when he created his protagonist. What is directly relevant to my argument, however, is that Troilus *the lover* also tends to suffer from fleshly *acedia* in the service of love: passivity, idleness, and somnolence.[65] If Chaucer's writings suggest that he favored a strong work ethic, it is clear that Troilus the lover does not share it. While he does sometime engage in love's labor, he is not a self-confident worker. He works at love when it is easy, but he is just as easily defeated by doubts, fears, and bad fortune. If it were not for Pandarus, Troilus's love affair would never have gotten off the ground. From this perspective, Troilus's lack of a work ethic contrasts sharply with the work ethics of both Pandarus and Diomede.

First of all, the *Troilus* begins with Chaucer's protagonist openly admitting his distaste for love's labor. Unlike Boccaccio's Troiolo, Chaucer's Troilus has not experienced love's labor, and he is proud of his innocence. While swaggering through the temple, he boasts:

> I have herd told, pardieux, of youre lyvynge,
> Ye loveres, and youre lewed observaunces,

---

64. 5.360, 5.622, 5.1216, and 5.1646.

65. Besides manifesting itself in idleness and passivity, fleshly *acedia* is also manifested in somnolence. When Troilus suffers the blows of bad fortune or his own negligence, he characteristically takes to his bed, where he slumbers "as in a litargie" (1.730). This may be a normal symptom of depression, yet Troilus goes to bed even when he is happy. Chaucer's description of his behavior after the first night with Criseyde is enlightening. He writes that Troilus "Retorned to his real paleys soone, / He softe into his bed gan for *to slynke*, / To slepe longe, *as he was wont to doone*" (Soon returned to his royal palace. He began *to slink* quietly into his bed to sleep a long time *as he was used to doing;* 3.1534–36; emphasis added). Chaucer emphasizes Troilus's somnolence here by using the verb "to slink," which hardly seems an appropriate movement for an exultant lover, and by adding the phrase "as he was wont to doone," which suggests that "sloggy slombrynge" was one of Troilus's habits. Neither of these characterizations is in Boccaccio's text. Boccaccio writes: "Tornato Troilo nel real palagio, / Tacitamente ne n' entrò nel letto, / Per dormir se potesse alquanto ad agio" (After Troilus had returned to the royal palace, he went thence silently to bed to sleep a little, if he could, for ease; *The Filostrato of Giovanni Boccaccio*, ed. and trans. Nathaniel Griffin and Arthur Myrick [Philadelphia: University of Pennsylvania Press, 1929] 3.53. Subsequent quotations from the *Filostrato* and English translations will be taken from this edition and cited in the text by part and line numbers.)

And which a labour folk han in wynnynge
Of love, and in the kepying which doutaunces.
. . . .
O veray fooles, nyce and blynde be ye!

(1.197–200, 202)

[You lovers, I have heard told, by God, of your manners of living and your ignorant customs and what labor is required to win love and what uncertainties in
keeping it. . . . O true fools! You are foolish and blind.]

While Troiolo is experienced in love and glad to be out of it at this point
in *Il Filostrato*, Troilus has only heard talk of what it is like to be a lover.
Rumor has it that lovers are ignorant fools and frustrated workers, and
Troilus accepts the common wisdom completely. Poetic justice is served,
however, when he is smitten with love for the beautiful Crisyede.

From the perspective of the discourse of love's labor, it is noteworthy
that the narrator, in a passage that has no parallel in *Il Filostrato*, almost
immediately compares Troilus to a *work* horse, "proude Bayard."[66] Although Bayard for a time believes he is free from the law of horses, a lash
of the whip reminds him quickly that he is but a horse and must join his
fellows in the labor of pulling the wagon. So too with Troilus. The sight
of Criseyde is his "lash of the whip," his call to labor. This is a surprisingly nonaristocratic image of love, constructed from the discourse of love's
labor and emphasizing the significant effort necessary for a successful
love affair. The effect of this discourse at this point is comic. It deflates
the high, aristocratic pretensions of Troilus and puts him on the same
level as all his followers.

Indeed, the reference to labor is an appropriate transition to the next
scene, where, humbled and contrite, Troilus retreats from the temple. His
mind runs immediately to the labor and sorrow in the process of love. He
imagines that "travaille nor grame / Ne myghte for so goodly oon be
lorn" (neither work nor suffering for such a goodly person might be lost;
1.373–74). In fact, at this point, Troilus makes a conscious decision to
learn and apply "loves craft" but to "werken pryvely" (1.379–80). Thoroughly imbued with aristocratic ideology, he conceives love's labor as
"service" and begins his service, like the birds of prey in the *Parlement of
Foules*, with aristocratic but ultimately unproductive rhetoric on love, a

---

66. 1.218–25. In determining Chaucer's debt to Boccaccio throughout this chapter, I have benefited greatly from Barry Windeatt's parallel-column edition of *Troilus* and *Il Filostrato* (*"Troilus and
Criseyde": A New Edition of "The Book of Troilus"* [New York: Longman, 1984]).

Petrarchian song (1.400–420). He next adds a prayer by which Cupid becomes his feudal lord, and he becomes Cupid and Criseyde's "man."[67] In this prayer, as well, he fashions his labor as service (1.422–34). Finally, in an apostrophe to the absent Criseyde, "to whom serve[th] [he] and laboure[th]" (for whom he serves and labors; 1.458), he links service and labor but formally asks *not* for wages but for pity. When Troilus speaks of love's labor, he usually employs the aristocratic discourse of love's service, but this practice does not absolutely distinguish his discourse from that of Pandarus or Diomede. All three employ that word as well as others for love's labor, as does the narrator. When Criseyde, for example, first sees Troilus and is emotionally moved, the narrator steps in to defend her against the charge of loving at first sight. At this point the narrator proclaims that Troilus won her love "by good servyse . . . and in no sodeyn wyse" (by good service . . . and not in a sudden manner; 2.678–79).

The real distinction comes in their work ethics. Troilus, like Theseus in the Knight's Tale (1.1802–3), is skeptical about the fairness of the god of love in the distribution of rewards for his service, and this may be the reason Troilus is less inclined to put forth effort on his own behalf. His first reaction to finding himself smitten by love is to doubt whether it will all be worth the effort. In an apostrophe to lovers that is original with Chaucer, Troilus cries:

> . . . Lord, so ye lyve al in lest,
> Ye loveres! For the konnyngeste of yow,
> That serveth most ententiflich and best,
> Hym tit as often harm therof as prow.
> Youre hire is quyt ayeyn, ye, God woot how!
> Nought wel for wel, but scorn for good servyse.
>
> (1.330–35)

[Lord, you all live in delight, you lovers! For the most skillful among you, who serves most diligently and best, experiences harm as much as profit. You are repaid again, God knows how! Not well for well, but scorn for good service.]

Beginning with biting sarcasm, Troilus brings up the question of how love's laborers are paid for their efforts. He has heard that they are paid in scorn for "good servyse." What reasonable worker, then, would put

---

67. For a thorough treatment of feudal imagery in the poem, see Sanford B. Meech, "Subjugation and Feudal Relationship," *Design in Chaucer's "Troilus"* (Syracuse, N.Y.: Syracuse University Press, 1959) 271–89. See also Windeatt 228–31.

forth effort without the promise of an appropriate reward? Thus, although he decides to take up love's craft a few verses later, it is generally a half-hearted attempt. He proposes to learn "what to arten hire to love" (how to persuade her to love; 1.388), and the labors he learns are the typical aristocratic labors reflected in Andreas Capellanus's *De amore*: rhetoric and deeds of arms. He quickly composes a song to love and doubles his efforts at the "travaille / In armes" to build up his reputation so that Criseyde will fall in love with him (1.475–76). When these labors prove unproductive (1.491–97), however, he just as quickly succumbs to overwhelming anxiety, depression, and passivity. Moreover, he worries that the aristocratic labor that he has done for the winning of Criseyde will be wasted. In Book 3, for example, when he fears that Criseyde will be angry over his feigned jealousy, he decides that all his previous labor has been in vain: "al that labour he hath don byforn, / He wende it lost" (he thought lost all that labor he did before).[68]

This is not to say that Troilus never accomplishes love's work. Both before and after the first tryst he does manage to serve. Early in Book 3, for example, after the first meeting with Criseyde, he actually becomes a model in love's service. He is even able to anticipate Criseyde's every desire (3.463–67). So well does he attend to "his werk," says the narrator, that Criseyde thanks God twenty thousand times for him (3.471–74). The narrator adds, "So koude he hym governe in swich servyse, / That al the world ne myght it bet devyse" (He could so well govern himself in such service that no one could contrive to do it better; 3.475–76). He seems to have learned his lesson, for on the night of the first tryst, in his prayer to Love, he notes that the god does come to the aid of those "That serven best and most alwey labouren" (Who serve best and most continuously labor; 3.1265). Troilus's service continues after the night of the first tryst, and, indeed, he not only becomes the perfect lover but also comes to believe that everyone who is not in love's service is lost (3.1793–94). The author concludes the happy third book by stating that he has "fully" sung "Th'effect and joie of Troilus servise" (3.1815).

It is significant, however, that even in Book 3, Troilus does not conceive Love as paying wages due. Rather, he sees Love as aiding workers out of his own generosity, "of bownte" (1.1264). This is the theology of unmerited grace, not the work ideology of wages paid for honest labor. Given Troilus's earlier skepticism about love, Troilus's approach here has

68. 3.1072, 1075–76. There is no parallel passage in *Il Filostrato*.

some merit. The approach, however, marks a fundamental difference in his construction of love from that of Diomede and Pandarus. For Troilus, love remains first and foremost a religion; for Pandarus and Diomede, it is a job or "an emprise."[69]

After the conclusion of the second of Ovid's labors, winning a lover, the third labor, keeping a lover begins. Pandarus, for one, realizes that keeping the beloved is just as difficult as gaining a lover. As he tells Troilus:

> Thow art at ese, and hold the wel therinne;
> For also seur as reed is every fir,
> As gret a craft is kepe wel as wynne
>
> (3.1632–34)

[You are at ease, and hold yourself well therein; for as sure as fire is red, it takes as much skill to keep love as to win it.]

Troilus must work as subtly as ever to keep Criseyde. Comparing Troilus to a horse, Pandarus counsels "Bridle alwey wel thi speche and thi desir" (Bridle always your speech and desire well; 3.1635). Troilus must exercise masterful control over his emotions in order to accomplish the third labor of love. While times are good, Troilus manages adequately. It is at the first sign of trouble in Book 4, however, that things again start to go wrong. Troilus's self-confidence is easily shattered, and he once again loses faith in the promise of his own labor: "I, combre-world," he complains, "that may of nothyng serve" (I, an encumbrance on the world, who serves for nothing; 4.279). Indeed, he later worries (prophetically) that the "bisynesse" of some suave Greek will make Trojan efforts look boorish in comparison (4.1485–91). Until Pandarus again intervenes, he is reduced to inactive despair. He becomes, as one critic put it, "a composite of the scorned women in the *Heroides*, waiting endlessly for the return of his lover, recalling past promises, writing letters, and wishing for death."[70] Once roused by Pandarus, however, he does manage a few weak efforts and proposals. Most notably, he suggests to Criseyde that they flee Troy (4.1506–26). He is quickly overruled by Criseyde, however, and thus spends most of Book 5 in passive melancholy, waiting for Criseyde to set things right. "Who koude telle aright or ful discryve,"

---

69. On love as religion, and especially on Troilus's use of the "theology of grace," see Windeatt 231–34. See also Wetherbee 59.

70. Calabrese 48.

comments the Narrator, "His wo, his pleynt, his langour, and his pyne?" (Who could truly tell or fully describe his woe, his complaint, his suffering, and his pain?; 5.267–68). During the ten-day wait, he can do no more than visit her house (5.512–60), compose laments (5.638–44), and linger, daydreaming, on the city ramparts (5.666–79). Here, again, the focus is on the private Troilus, not the public warrior, who continues to perform his knightly duties and who is "in no degree secounde / In durrying don that longeth to a knyght" (in no degree second in the daring-do pertaining to knighthood; 5.836–37). Pandarus tries to take the lover's mind off Criseyde by suggesting a visit to Sarpedon, but the strategy does not work (5.430–501). When the ten-day period has passed and Crisyede has still not returned, at Pandarus's suggestion Troilus—as in Book 2—rouses himself enough to write Criseyde a letter (5.1317–1421). When that does not bring Criseyde back to him, he dreams of taking even more drastic action, of disguising himself as a pilgrim and sneaking into the Greek camp (5.1576–82). These plans, however, remain only dreams. He does nothing more than write another letter (5.1583–86). At this point the narrator somewhat weakly and ironically remarks "he lefte it nought for slouthe" (he did not overlook it due to sloth; 5.1584).

The discovery of undeniable proof of Crisyede's infidelity rouses Troilus to redouble his work on the battlefield, but this decidedly is not love's labor. It is action rooted in despair, not in the hope of winning Criseyde back. Rather than capturing a lover's just wages for love's service, Troilus seeks his own death in battle. When Troilus charges off to seek Diomede in battle, a reader's first impression may be that Troilus has finally conquered his *acedia* and that his private and public personae have finally met. This is only an illusion, however, because at this point Troilus is motivated by the last, most terrible manifestation of *acedia*, despair, "that comth," says the Parson, "somtyme of to muche outrageous sorwe, and somtyme of to muche drede" (which comes sometime from too much outrageous sorrow and sometime from too much dread; 10.693). Only just barely saved from despair and suicide in Book 4, Troilus, who discovers Criseyde's broach on Diomede's cloak, now seeks both to kill and to be killed; he says:

> And certeynly, withouten moore speche,
> From hennesforth, as ferforth as I may,
> Myn owen deth in armes wol I seche;
> I recche nat how soone be the day!
>
> (5.1716–19)

[And, certainly, without more speech, from henceforth, to the extent that I can, I will seek my own death in arms. I care not how soon the day comes.]

Wetherbee says of Troilus's motivation at this point: "The necessary condition for Troilus' final display of courage is not madness or hatred, but despair, and the only motive for his 'wrath' is the desire to achieve his own death."[71] However, unlike Troilus, Troiolo at the corresponding point in Boccaccio's story is motivated by anger and a desire for vengeance. Although he recognizes that he might die in pursuit of his vengeance, his chief intent is not to kill himself but to kill Diomede:

> Mandimi Iddio Diomede davanti
> La prima volta ch'esco alla battaglia!
> Questo disio tra li miei guai cotanti,
> Sì ch' io provar gli faccia come taglia
> La spada mia, e lui morir con pianti
> Nel campo faccia, e poi non me ne caglia
> Che mi s'uccida, sol ch' e' muoia, e lui
> Misero trovi nelli regni bui.
>
> (8.21)

[May the gods send Diomede in my way the first time that I go forth in battle. This do I desire among my great woes, that I may let him know by experience how my sword cutteth and put him to death with groans on the field of battle. And then I care not if I die provided only that he die and that I find him wretched in the realm of darkness.]

While Troiolo's anger is directed outwardly and pushes him into desperate action, Troilus's anger is primarily inwardly directed. With respect to his spiritual *acedia*, then, the Troilus of Book 5 differs little from the Troilus of the earlier books.

Troilus's lack of love's labor as well as his *acedia* are brought into relief by the productive work done by his go-between, Pandarus, and his rival, Diomede. Both of these conceive courtship primarily as a labor to be accomplished, and both have a strong work ethic. Upon discovering Troilus's despair, Pandarus, good friend, vice figure, physician, and stand-in for Lady Philosophy or for the male patriarchy,[72] is perfectly willing to assume Troilus's work. As Lewis remarks, "Pandarus . . . is, above all, the

---

71. Wetherbee 222.

72. On the character of Pandarus, see Wetherbee 45; Windeatt 289–92; Diamond 97; Rowe 85–91; and Muscatine 138–46. See also Larry Bronson, "Chaucer's Pandarus: 'Jolly Good Fellow' or 'Reverend Vice'?," *Ball State University Forum* 24 (1983): 34–41; and Martin Camargo, "The Consola-

practical man, the man who 'gets things done.'"[73] Indeed, he does so with boundless energy. He exclaims to Criseyde: "O verray God, so have I ronne! / Lo, nece myn, se ye nought how I swete?" (O true God, I have run so hard that, lo, niece, don't you see how I sweat?; 2.1464–65). Although he likens himself to an "instrument," a whetstone, Pandarus is not simply a passive tool, sharpening Troilus's work habits.[74] On the contrary, he is an active, creative workman himself. In the *Ars amatoria*, Ovid had written of three different labors of love: finding a lover, winning a lover, and keeping a lover. With respect to Troilus and Criseyde's love affair, Pandarus assumes complete responsibility for the direction of the second.

References to labor are a distinctive characteristic of Pandarus's discourse. In Book 1, for example, taking a line directly from Boccaccio, Chaucer has Pandarus say: "Yef me this labour and this bisynesse, / And of my spede be thyn al that swetnesse" (Give me this labor and this business, and be yours the sweetness of my success).[75] He uses the same discourse when he asks Criseyde to respond to Troilus's first letter. In a line not found in the *Filostrato*, Pandarus begs: "Yif me the labour it to sowe and plite" (Give me the labor of folding and sewing the letter; 2.1203). Chaucer adds many more such comments to Boccaccio's story line. For example, when Pandarus learns from Troilus that his favorite brother is Deiphebus, he merrily goes off to arrange the first meeting of the lovers with the words "Now lat m'alone, and werken as I may" (Now let me alone to work as I may; 2.1401). Again, in Book 4, Pandarus, in an attempt to calm his despairing friend, begs: "and shortly, brother deere, / Be glad, and lat me werke in this matere" (and shortly, dear brother, be glad and let me work on this matter; 4.650–51). Pandarus not only knows the ins and outs of the game of love—he "wel koude ech a deel / Th'olde daunce" (knew fully the "old dance"; 3.694–95)—but he is willing to work at it on Troilus's behalf.

Key passages in Book 1 bring important aspects of Pandarus's single-

---

tion of Pandarus," *Chaucer Review* 25 (1991): 214–28. For Pandarus as the Ovidian *praeceptor amoris*, see Calabrese 37.

73. Lewis 190.

74. 1.631. "Instrument," *MED*, defined as "a device operated by hand, a tool, an implement, a utensil" (1a). According to the *MED*, although instances of *instrument* meaning "musical instrument" can be found as early as 1300, the word was used in the sense of "tool" beginning only in Chaucer's lifetime.

75. 1.1042–43. In the *Filostrato*, Pandaro says to Troiolo: "Questa fatica tutta sarà mia, / E'l dolce fine tuo voglio che sia" (This labor will all be mine and the sweet result I wish to be thine; 2.32).

minded work ideology to the fore. Whereas in the *Filostrato* Pandaro
merely bears messages between the two lovers, in Chaucer's *Troilus* he
takes complete charge of the affair down to the smallest details. First,
however, he must try to force (or woo) Troilus into some minimal cooperation.[76] To this end he argues:

> Thow mayst allone wepe and crye and knele—
> But love a womman that she woot it nought,
> And she wol quyte it that thow shalt nat fele;
> Unknowe, unkist, and lost that is unsought.
>
> (1.806–9)

[You may weep and cry and kneel here all alone, but love a woman when she
does not know it, and she will requite it in ways you won't feel. Unknown, un-
kissed, and lost is she who is unsought.]

Sick though he may be, Troilus must understand that success in love demands work. There are no wages paid to those who do not work, Pandarus says. If you want to enjoy the wages of love's labor, you must make
an effort to serve the lady. Indeed, the service itself is part of the wages of
love. As Pandarus suggests, a lover should always be ready "To serve and
love his deere hertes queene, / And thynke it is a guerdon hire to serve, /
A thousand fold moore than he kan deserve" (to serve and love his dear
heart's queen, and to think that service alone is a thousand times more
reward than he deserves; 2.817–19).

However, just working, just keeping busy at love's labor is not enough
for Gower's Amans, and it is not sufficient for Pandarus. For Pandarus,
love's labor must be *productive* labor. Although his work is not successful
with respect to his own love interests (1.621–23), his efforts at directing
Troilus and Criseyde's love affair are masterfully productive precisely because he believes that real work must be so. Early in Book 1, in a riot of
proverbial wisdom not found in the *Filostrato*, he explains to Troilus that,
to be productive, work must be planned and executed carefully:

76. As Robert Hanning writes: "Chaucer's poem reorients Pandarus's efforts toward convincing
Troilus to stop pining and get to work (or, more precisely, let Pandarus get to work) winning the object of his desire. That is, much more than Pandaro, Pandarus must devote his persuasive powers to
'wooing' Troilus before he can woo Criseyde. The goal of this wooing is to transform Troilus' lyric
posture of static, hopeless longing into a narrative form of active quest for the object of desire"
("Come in Out of the Code: Interpreting the Discourse of Desire in Boccaccio's *Filostrato* and
Chaucer's *Troilus and Criseyde*," *Chaucer's "Troilus and Criseyde": "Subgit to alle Poesie": Essays in Criticism*, ed. R. A. Shoaf [Binghamton, N.Y.: Medieval and Renaissance Texts and Studies, 1992] 131).
Hanning's argument supports my basic line of reasoning, except that I argue that Pandarus has very
little luck in changing Troilus's "lyric posture of static, hopeless longing."

> Now loke that atempre be thi bridel,
> And for the beste ay suffre to the tyde,
> Or elles al oure labour is on ydel:
> He hasteth wel that wisely kan abyde.
> Be diligent and trewe, and ay wel hide;
> Be lusty, fre; persevere in thy servyse,
> And al is wel, if thow werke in this wyse.
>
> (1.953–59)

[Now see to it that your bridle is restrained, and suffer the passing of time for the best, or else all our labor is in vain. He hastens well who wisely can abide. Be diligent and true, and always conceal your love. Be vigorous and generous. Persevere in your service, and all will be well if you work in this way.]

Here inactivity, "not swimming against the tide," is *not* a mark of idleness or sloth but a part of Pandarus's work strategy, part of love's service. The passage is riddled with labor diction, and it becomes clear that Pandarus's labor ideology has nothing to do with the traditional medieval and monastic ideology of work as simply a remedy for idleness. If it were, he wouldn't counsel Troilus to moderate his bridle at this point. Real work, for Pandarus, must produce concrete results. Here he expresses the same concerns as those of Gower's Amans, who, in a passage quoted in the previous chapter, complained that he could not distinguish his own work from idleness because it produced no results.[77] Unlike Amans, however, Pandarus is full of good hope. Until now, Troilus had engaged only in unproductive "bysynesse," and the failure of these tactics has pushed him into despair. Pandarus thus conceives the first goal of his mission as awakening his friend from unproductive lethargy (1.729–30). He decides that his second goal is to move Troilus away from unproductive work strategies toward productive ones. Productive work strategies, he is convinced, should bring success. He comments that, unless Troilus's depression or his own "over-haste" undermines his work, he expects to bring his labor to a productive conclusion (1.970–72). Ideologically his discourse reflects a kind of humanist work ethic in which "bysynesse" plays a dignified role in life and in which time must be carefully expended for maximum results.

This ideology is again reflected in the notable passage at the end of Book 1—a passage with no parallel in the *Filostrato*—in which Pandarus

77. John Gower, *The English Works of John Gower*, ed. G. C. Macaulay, 2 vols., Early English Text Society 81–82 (1900; London: Oxford University Press, 1979) 4.1757–60.

conceives the conducting of a love affair as analogous to the building of a
house. The narrator reports his thought in the following passage, adapted from Geoffrey of Vinsauf's *Ars Poetica:*

> For everi wight that hath an hous to founde
> Ne renneth naught the werk for to bygynne
> With rakel hond, but he wol bide a stounde,
> And sende his hertes line out fro withinne
> Aldirfirst his purpos for to wynne.
> Al this Pandare in his herte thoughte,
> And caste his werk ful wisely or he wroughte.[78]

[For no person who wishes to build a house rushes off with hasty hand to begin
the work. No. He will wait a while and, first, send out an imaginary line from
within, so that he can succeed in his purpose. All this Pandarus thought in his
heart and planned his work very wisely before he acted.]

Here Chaucer double-voices Geoffrey's advice on the careful structuring
of poetry to reflect Pandarus's concerns with hasty or sloppy work. In
the *Ars amatoria* and the *De amore*, the labor of creating love poetry and
the labor of courtship are often compared, equated, or conflated. Here,
Chaucer follows his mentors. Since courtship must be carefully planned
in order to be productive, Pandarus "caste[th] his werk ful wisely or he
wroughte," and the results of his careful planning are seen in the successful tryst of Book 3.

Yet another key labor passage, again original to Chaucer, occurs at the
end of Book 2, when, after successfully managing the first exchange of
letters, Pandarus begins to consider the next step: bringing the two lovers
together for the first time. Here again Pandarus must work to shore up
Troilus's spirits, which are quite apt to flag at the least hindrance. Realiz-
ing this, Pandarus takes the offensive and wonders whether, perhaps,
Troilus is thinking that Criseyde will never be won over (2.1360–79). On

---

78. 1.1065–71. Geoffrey of Vinsauf wrote: "Si quis habet fundare domum, non currit ad actum, /
Impetuosa manus: intrinseca linea cordis / Praemetitur opus, seriemque sub ordine certo / Interior
praescribit homo, totamque figurat / Ante manus cordis quam corporis; et status ejus / Est prius
archetypus quam sensilis" (If a man has a house to build, his hand does not rush, hasty, into the very
doing: the work is first measured out with his heart's inward plumb line, and the inner man marks
out a series of steps beforehand, according to a definite plan; his heart's hand shapes the whole before his body's hand does so, and his building is a plan before it is an actuality). For the original text,
see Edmond Faral, ed., *Les arts poétiques du XIIͤ et du XIIIͤ siècle* (Paris: Honoré Champion, 1962) 198.
The English translation is taken from James J. Murphy, ed., *Three Medieval Rhetorical Arts* (Berkeley
and Los Angeles: University of California Press, 1971) 34.

the contrary, he counters, Criseyde is like an oak tree, which is difficult to chop down but which eventually falls quickly. He says,

> Thenk here-ayeins: whan that the stordy ook,
> On which men hakketh ofte, for the nones,
> Receyved hath the happy fallyng strook,
> The greet sweigh doth it come al at ones,
> As don thise rokkes or thise milnestones.
>
> (2.1380–84)

[Think, on the contrary, that when the sturdy oak, on which men have often hacked, finally receives the happy, falling blow, the great falling momentum comes all at once, as it does for rocks and millstones.]

The wooing of Criseyde does take work, but it is work that will be rewarded swiftly once it takes effect. "Men shal rejoissen of a gret empryse / Acheved well" (Men shall rejoice in a well achieved, great enterprise), he exclaims. The wooing of Criseyde is an *empryse*, a difficult task or undertaking, sometimes a chivalric enterprise or deed.[79] This was another new labor word in Chaucer's day. The earliest citation in the *Middle English Dictionary* dates only from 1330, but most of the others are later, in the 1390s and even 1400s. The word did not carry any of the traditionally negative connotations of *labour* or *swynk* and thus is more evidence suggesting the positive evaluation of labor of both Pandarus and his creator.

Pandarus, of course, is not all talk, for he works harder than anyone else to bring the two lovers together. He concocts the brilliant (if also dishonest) ruse by which the two lovers meet at the house of Deiphebus. After that successful meeting, he redoubles his efforts to bring the two lovers together for the first tryst. The narrator, commenting on how hard and how carefully Pandarus worked to bring about his plans, notes:

> For he with gret deliberacioun
> Hadde every thyng that herto myght availle
> Forncast and put in execucion,
> And neither left for cost ne for travaille.
>
> (3.519–22)

[For he, with great deliberation, planned ahead of time and executed everything that might be helpful, and skimped on neither cost nor labor.]

---

79. 2.1391–92. "Emprise" (1–4), *MED*. Pandarus also thinks of his work for Troilus and Criseyde as an "emprise" in 2.73.

In this passage Chaucer employs some brand-new words to fully describe Pandarus's exceptional commitment to love's labor. It recalls the earlier passage in which Pandarus likens the building of the affair to the building of a house. Here he continues to plan ahead *(forncasten)* "with gret deliberacioun." It is significant that the *Middle English Dictionary* lists only passages from Chaucer's works to illustrate the meaning of *forncasten*. Certainly it was a new word in Chaucer's day, and it may well have been one of the poet's own contributions to the language. At the very least it underscores Chaucer's (and Pandarus's) concerns that labor not only combat idleness but also be productive. To be productive, labor must be carefully planned.

Moreover, it must be carefully executed. According to the *Middle English Dictionary*, the word *execucioun* was a new word in Chaucer's day as well. This passage from the *Troilus*, in fact, antedates the earliest attestation in the *Middle English Dictionary*. The word may well have started out as a purely legal term, for the first meaning of the word was "the carrying out, putting into effect, or enforcing (of the provisions of a statue, law, will, etc.) or a penalty." Almost immediately, the word's meaning broadened to include (as in this passage) "the performance (of an act), the carrying out or realization (of a request, plan, or plot)." To "put in execucioun" meant to "carry out or perform (a request, someone's will)."[80] While it is now clear that Chaucer could not have studied at the Inns of Court, he is clearly drawing on his experience with lawyers to paint this image of a man who carries out Troilus's will as if it were a court order. Pandarus spares neither cost nor effort *(travaille)* to effect the union of the two lovers.

Pandarus's labor ideology is also reflected in his concern for sloth in the labor of love. Unlike Alan of Lille's Nature, Pandarus focuses exclusively on the "bysynesse" of courtship, not the labor of reproduction, but like Dame Nature, Pandarus is concerned with sloth not because it makes room for the devil's work, but because sloth (and idleness in particular) hinders productivity. Six times he uses the Middle English *slouthe* in attempts to goad Troilus and Criseyde into some kind of minimal productive activity. For example, when he returns to Troilus after he has presented the young knight's request to Criseyde, he warns Troilus:

---

80. "Execucioun" (1–3), *MED*.

> Sire, my nece wol do wel by the,
> And love the best, by God and by my trouthe,
> But lak of pursuyt make it in thi slouthe.
>
> (2.957–59)

[Sir, by God and on my word of honor, my niece will do well by you and love you best unless your sloth hinders your pursuit of her.]

Here "slouthe" is directly contrasted to active, productive work, "pursuyt." Indeed, Pandarus refers to the love affair as "*thi* werk" in the very next line. Because at this point Troilus seems minimally ready to respond, Pandarus suggests that he write a love letter to Criseyde and adds: "Now help thiself, and leve it nought for slouthe!" (Now help yourself and don't quit out of sloth!; 2.1008). Later, in the house of Deiphebus, before Criseyde is led into Troilus's sick room, Pandarus, for the third time in less than six hundred lines, urges Troilus not to let sloth hinder the progress of the affair (2.1499–1502). None of these references to sloth are found in the *Filostrato*.

Although Criseyde does not take part in the active labor of love, Pandarus still urges her to cooperate with his plans by warning her against sloth. When he first encounters Criseyde in Book 2, for example, he tantalizes her with talk of some vague good fortune on her horizon, but he also warns her:

> For to every wight som goodly aventure
> Som tyme is shape, if he it kan receyven;
> But if he wol take of it no cure,
> Whan that it commeth, but wilfully it weyven,
> Lo, neyther cas ne fortune hym deceyven,
> But ryght his verray slouthe and wrecchednesse;
> And swich a wight is for to blame, I gesse.
>
> (2.281–87)

[A lucky chance is ordained for every person during some time of his or her life if the person can receive it. But if, when it comes, the person pays no attention and willfully forgoes it, lo, neither fate nor fortune deceives him. He is, indeed, deceived by his own true sloth and wretchedness. And such a person is to blame, I guess.]

Good fortune, argues Pandarus, must be actively seized, not simply accepted passively. If the slothful fail to benefit from the opportunities presented by good fortune, it is their own fault, not that of either fortune or chance. Pandarus repeats this exact warning in Book 3 at the point in which Criseyde is unable to decide whether to receive Troilus in Pandarus's bedroom or not.[81] In this regard, the most ideologically pregnant comment of Pandarus occurs just a few lines earlier, when Criseyde suggests that Pandarus carry her ring to Troilus as a token of her good will. At this suggestion, Pandarus roughly replies that this is an inadequate response to a dangerous situation and that Criseyde must work quickly and wisely: "O tyme ilost, wel maistow corsen slouthe!" (O lost time. You may well curse sloth!; 3.896). In this statement, the medieval concern with sloth is quite neatly married with something akin to humanist anxieties over the proper management of time. Obviously, since Criseyde needs only to allow Troilus in the room, Pandarus is being manipulative and not really sincere in this appeal for active labor. Nevertheless, the duplicitous double voicing of contemporary labor discourse here is undeniable.

Pandarus's anxieties over the proper management of time come out even more strongly when he is trying to bolster the lovers' courage before they meet each other at the house of Deiphebus. In a passage noted just above, Pandarus exclaims to Troilus:

> . . . Now is tyme, if that thow konne,
> To bere the wel tomorwe, and al is wonne.
> Now spek, now prey, now pitously compleyne;
> Lat nought for nyce shame, or drede, or slouthe!
>
> (2.1497–1500)

[Now is the time, if you know how, to carry yourself well tomorrow, and all is won. Now speak, now pray, now piteously complain. Don't forget anything because of foolish shame or dread or sloth.]

Warning specifically against sloth, Pandarus argues that Troilus must act now, or the opportunity will be lost forever. On the next day, he uses a similar argument to convince Criseyde to cooperate. This is the opportunity, he argues, for her to speak in private with Troilus. "While folk is blent," he argues, "the tyme is wonne" (While folk are deceived, the time is won; 2.1743). Time spent in delay, "taried tyde," however, is time lost, he insists (2.1739). "Las, tyme ylost!" he concludes in good humanist fashion.

These warnings about sloth in love and mismanagement of time are manipulative, but they are also serious and straightforward to the extent

81. 3.935. Earlier, Pandarus suggested that sloth might be the reason for Criseyde's hesitancy in reading Troilus's letter (2.1136).

that Pandarus is determined to produce results in his direction of the love affair. At the same time, however, Pandarus's dialog reveals Chaucer in his most Ovidian double voicing of the language of love's labor. Pandarus wants results, but he also wants fun. In this, and in his facility with words and with strategy, he is very much like Ovid's *praeceptor amoris*. When Troilus first reveals his love, Pandarus exclaims: "Here bygynneth game" (Here begins the game; 1.868), which is the mirror image of the ending of the *Ars amatoria*, "lvsus finem habet." This is a game, as Richard F. Green, has argued, that Troilus, in contrast, never quite understands.[82] Pandarus's intense plotting in Book 2 and the early parts of Book 3 is carried out with energy, high spirits, and a good dose of complex theater. The climax of the game occurs in the comic antics of Troilus just before the affair is consummated. Here, Pandarus must do almost everything for the lovers, including taking off some of Troilus's clothes and throwing him into Criseyde's bed. Criseyde too seems to take much of her interaction with Pandarus as a form of game, and when Troilus finally awakes in bed and complains about her lack of discretion, she replies: "Is this a mannes game?" (Is this a man's game?; 3.1126). She characterizes their interactions as a "game" again just a few lines later (3.1494).

Another industrious worker in love's fields is Diomede although he, unlike Pandarus, works only for himself. Most critics see Diomede as an unsavory, self-centered character, and that evaluation is not unjust.[83] However, from the perspective of love's labor, he is as diligent and as clever a worker as Pandarus. In the words of Michael Calabrese, he is a "textbook Ovidian lover."[84] Indeed, his first words in the *Troilus*, adapted from Book 4, stanza 10 of *Il Filostrato*, underscore this. When he is sent to pick up his beautiful prisoner, he says to himself: "Al my labour shal nat ben on ydel, / If that I may, for somwhat shal I seye" (All my labor shall not be in vain if I can help it, for I will say something; 5.94–95). While the "bysynesse" of the passive Troilus is performed by his friend Pandarus, Diomede needs no such help. He can do his own work. It is noteworthy

82. Richard F. Green, "Troilus and the Game of Love," *Chaucer Review* 13 (1979): 201–20. On the *Troilus* as presenting life as a "game" and the rhetorical view of life, see Lanham 65–66.

83. Larry Bronson, for example, writes that Diomede is a composite of Troilus and Pandarus, but that he is self-centered and ultimately responsible for the destruction of all the major characters in the poem ("The Sodeyn Diomede: Chaucer's Composite Portrait," *Ball State University Forum* 25 [1985]: 14–19). Green believes that Diomede lacks "basic integrity" (211). Grudin speaks of Diomede's "patent duplicity" (78). Alexandra Hennessey Olsen, however, defends Diomede, but on the grounds that Diomede was just as "aristocratic" as Troilus ("In Defense of Diomede: 'Moral Gower' and *Troilus and Criseyde*," *In Geardagum* 8 [1987]: 1–12).

84. Calabrese 70.

that while Chaucer makes Troilus more passive than Troiolo, he recon-
figures Diomede to be even more self-confident and aggressive than his
counterpart in *Il Filostrato*. Boccaccio's Diomede, who at this point comments "Vana fatica credo sia la mia" (I think this labor of mine an idle
one; 6.10), fears his labor will be vain. In contrast, Chaucer's Diomede
begins with the conviction that his labor will *not* be in vain.

Shrewd, fearless, and practical as a lover, Diomede is ideologically akin
to Pandarus and the opposite of Troilus. He too employs the discourse of
love's labor and, like Pandarus, plans his amorous strategy carefully. Indeed, the narrator notes that Diomede "koude his good," that is, knew
what was to his own advantage (5.106). After closely observing Troilus
and Criseyde and deciding to pursue the latter, he reasons (in a passage
for which no parallel exists in *Il Filostrato*):

> . . . Certeynlich I am aboute nought,
> If that I speke of love or make it tough;
> For douteles, if she have in hire thought
> Hym that I gesse, he may nat ben ybrought
> So soon awey; but I shal fynde a meene
> That she naught wite as yet shal what I mene.
>
> (5.100–105)

[Certainly I am wasting my time if I speak of love or become too bold, for
doubtless, if she has on her mind him that I guess, he may not be chased from
her thoughts so soon. But I shall find a way so that she will not yet discover my
intent.]

Like Pandarus, Diomede believes that labor is used to produce results,
not just to keep from idleness. Thus, he analyzes Criseyde's situation to
discover the most productive route to his goal. On the way back to the
Greek camp, he speaks first not of love but of friendship, brotherhood,
and the nobility of the Greeks (5.106–40). He does, however, rather
quickly bring up the possiblity of being Criseyde's "servant" in love
(5.173). Although Criseyde does not respond very warmly to his first approaches, she does thank him "Of al his travaile and his goode cheere"
(for all his labor and his good cheer) and accepts his friendship.[85] Thus,
while Troilus in Book 1 wastes time worrying that love is nothing but "labor" and "suffering," Diomede, who successfully wins Criseyde away
from him, cheerfully accepts the labor necessary for love.[86]

---

85. 5.183. In the parallel passage of *Il Filostrato*, Griseida rebuffs Diomede but notices his "ardir,"
his daring (6.26).

86. Although Alain Renoir ("Criseyde's Two Half Lovers," *Orbis Litterarum* 16 [1961]: 239–55) ex-

After describing in detail the profitless passivity of Troilus, the narrator returns to the work of the industrious Diomede and his expertise in the craft of love. Indeed, the narrator states that Diomede "koude more than the crede / In swich a craft" (knew more than the basic essentials of such a craft), a description not found in *Il Filostrato* (5.89–90). His successful winning of Criseyde in a relatively short time proves it,[87] and his active planning of his own courtship is reminiscent of Pandarus's. While the narrator suggests that Pandarus thought of the construction of a love affair to be similar to the construction of a house, the narrator here suggests that Diomede compared it to fishing. He, like Ovid's *praeceptor amoris*, is prepared to use every trick in the book to accomplish his task. In another passage for which there is no parallel in *Il Filostrato*, the narrator comments:

> This Diomede, of whom yow telle I gan,
> Goth now withinne hymself ay arguynge,
> With al the sleghte and al that evere he kan,
> How he may best, with shortest taryinge,
> Into his net Criseydes herte brynge.
> To this entent he koude nevere fyne;
> To fisshen hire he leyde out hook and line.
>
> (5.771–77)

[This Diomede, about whom I began to tell you, goes about now arguing with himself about how he may best, with the shortest delay, bring Criseyde's heart into his net with all his ingenuity and all he knows how to do. This project never left his mind: to fish for her he laid out hook and line.]

Crafty Diomede is, like Harry Bailey, time-conscious; he must accomplish his task with the "shortest tarynge." He is also driven: he can never stop thinking about how to successfully accomplish his work. Indeed, later, in the set portrait of Book 5, he is described as "in his nedes prest

---

plores the differences between Troilus and Diomede in terms of the former's passivity and the latter's aggressive activity, he does not use the discourse of love's labor as his starting point; rather, he analyzes their differences in Jungian terms. He claims that Criseyde, whose fear suggests that she has a stronger *anima* than *animus*, is drawn to Diomede almost against her will because his *animus* is clearly dominant. On the other hand, Troilus's passivity suggests that he, like Criseyde, is dominated by his *anima*. Thus, Criseyde, in choosing Diomede, finds a psychic complement that she did not have in Troilus.

87. To save face for Criseyde, the narrator protests that no one knows how long it took for Diomede to win Criseyde (5.1086–90). However, earlier he had remarked that "er fully monthes two . . . she wol take a purpose for t'abide" (Before two months pass, . . . she will decide to stay; 5.766, 770), and the relative narrative brevity (less than half a book) of Diomede's campaign for Criseyde suggests speed.

and corageous" (eager and courageous with respect to his needs; 5.800).

Imagery in this passage also supports the contrast between the two knight/lovers. The fishing discourse may be a double voicing of the tradition in which slothful people are likened to cats who refuse to fish because they do not want to get their paws wet. In the *Confessio Amantis*, for example, Genius uses this image to describe the idle lover:

> For he ne wol no travail take
> To ryde for his ladi sake,
> Bot liveth al upon his wisshes;
> And as a cat wolde ete fisshes
> Withoute wetinge of his cles,
> So wolde he do, bot natheles
> He faileth ofte of that he wolde.
>
> (4.1105–11)

[For he will make no effort to ride out for his lady's sake, but he lives upon his wishes, and just as the cat who would eat fish without wetting his claws, so would he do. Nevertheless, he fails often to accomplish his goal.]

Chaucer himself uses the image in the *House of Fame* when the Goddess of Fame describes the idlers who want good fame without doing anything to merit it. "Ye be lyke the sweynte cat," she says, "That wolde have fissh; but wostow what? / He wolde nothing wete his clowes" (You are like the lazy cat who wants to eat fish, but you know what? He would not wet his claws; 1783–85). This description of Diomede's work planning, then, obliquely suggests that Diomede is no such "cat," and, by implication, that Troilus is.[88]

Diomede presses forward with his labor even in the face of self-doubt (5.782). Although he is not sure his strategy will be successful, he says "But for t'asay … naught n'agreveth, / For he that naught n'asaieth naught n'acheveth" (It doesn't hurt to try; nothing ventured, nothing gained; 5.783–84). He repeats a similar thought just a few lines later and thinks that whoever might win a "flower" like Criseyde "He myghte seyn he were a conquerour" (He might say that he was a conqueror; 5.792, 794). Both the content and the proverbial nature of this extended passage are reminiscent of Pandarus's style.[89] Moreover, the narrator underscores

---

88. Wenzel (105) says that this was the most widespread simile of its kind.

89. On Pandarus's proverbial speech, see R. M. Lumiansky, "The Function of Proverbial Monitory Elements in Chaucer's *Troilus and Criseyde*," *Tulane Studies in English* 2 (1950): 5–48; and Windeatt 320, 352–53.

his cleverness and perseverance by describing in detail his final assault on "the rose," Criseyde (5.855–945). While the discourse of Troilus is centered on his own feelings and his own sufferings, the discourse of Diomede at this point is wholly centered on Criseyde's feelings. He notes her sorrow and her loneliness (5.871–82). Without ever naming Troilus, he shrewdly manipulates her fears and her own inherent sense of practicality as a remedy for her love of Troilus (5.883–917). Troy is lost, he, in essence, says. Go with a winner. Indeed, Diomede, like Troilus, employs the discourse of love's service, but he rejects the aristocratic ideology inherent in that discourse.[90] He, like Troilus, identifies himself as her "man" (5.939). One gets the impression (although it can not be unquestionably demonstrated in the text) that even his use of a gesture of aristocratic humility is simply a ruthless ploy (5.925–31).

All this work does not immediately gain Criseyde's heart for Diomede, but it does move her heart in the right direction. While she weakly defends the nobility of the Trojans and explains that things are much too complicated for her to consider taking on a lover at this point, she admits that, after the Greeks have won the town, then, perhaps, she would consider accepting his proposal (5.956–94). The work strategy also wins him permission to return to see her at will (5.995–97). Moreover, it wins Criseyde's surprising declaration that "If that I sholde of any Grek han routhe, / It sholde be youreselven, by my trouthe!" (If I should have pity on any Greek, upon my word, it would be you; 5.1000–1001).

This encouragement is all that a good worker needs. Thus, Diomede, instead of taking his wages and leaving, continues his work. He presses on and asks for her "mercy," a code word for her love (5.1011). For this extra effort, he wins her glove, and, unbeknownst to him, her firm decision not to return to Troy (5.1013, 1029). Little more remains to be accomplished on the next day. When Diomede returns, additional wages come quickly: a horse, a broach, her sleeve, and "Men seyn—I not—that she yaf hym hire herte" (It is said—not by me—that she gave him her heart; 5.1050).

From a moralistic perspective, Troilus is an idealist and Diomede an opportunistic cad, but from the perspective of the discourse of love's labor, the former is a slacker and the latter a determined, practical worker. It would be just as easy to see Diomede as an embodiment of the principles of Ovid's *Ars amatoria* as it would be to see Troilus's second letter in

---

90. See, for example, 5.921, 923, 941.

the collection of Ovid's *Heroides*. Because it takes so long to unite Troilus and Criseyde as lovers, the images and particularly the labor diction are much more developed in the case of Pandarus (who is the actual worker in the first half of the poem) than in the case of Diomede, who is not only a smart worker but a quick worker. Getting Troilus and Criseyde together was a great "emprise," but, comparatively speaking, Diomede makes short work of Criseyde.

Chaucer did not believe, however, in good Weberian fashion, that success in work was a necessary sign that one was going to heaven. At least no specific connection exists between Troilus's lack of work ethic in love and his final place in the heavens. We do not know where Troilus's spirit finally ends up (5.1826–27), but since he is lifted into the heavens rather than put under the earth, his final dwelling place must be a good one. Chaucer apparently thought that bourgeois labor ideology was appropriate, after all, only to those who are both in the world and "of the world." It does not apply to those in the afterlife. Thus, Chaucer's ending (or endings), in which he deifies Troilus in the pagan heavens, presents another aspect of Chaucer's polyphony of meaning. As the author of *Everyman* insisted, worldly goods cannot accompany human beings to the other world.[91] Worldly goods are the "guerdoun for travaille / Of Jove, Appollo, of Mars, of swich rascaille" (reward for the work of Jove, Apollo, Mars, and other such rabble), wages that serve only "thise wrecched worldes appetites" (5.1851–53). Criseyde is still the wages for labor, but now the labor serves only the "wretched" appetites of this world. So it is that, after death, the otherworldly Troilus can laugh not only at those who weep for his death but also at love's toil—at "oure werk that foloweth so / The blynde lust" (our work by which we pursue blind lust; 5.1823–24). From the perspective of the other world, all earthly labors are, perhaps, blind and unproductive, all loves "feynede" (5.1848). From the moral perspective of Christianity, only the wages of Christ are truly worthwhile (5.1835–48). Indeed, the discourse of medieval Christianity's coming into dialog with the discourse of love's labor also creates a part of the polyphony of meaning in the *Troilus*.

Nevertheless, the religious discourse of the ending does not cancel out insistent and pronounced discourse of love's labor that went before it. Troilus, Diomede, and Pandarus are workers in love's fields, and each is

---

91. *The Summoning of Everyman*, ed. Geoffrey Cooper and Christopher Wortham (Nedlands: University of Western Australia Press, 1980) 29–31.

rewarded on this earth according to his labor. I have already stated that Criseyde is not as passive as Mieszkowski has painted her, and certainly viewed from several of the poem's competing interpretive perspectives, Criseyde is a fully alive and well-developed character. From the perspective of the discourse of the "laboring" male characters, however, she represents the wages of love's labor. Diomede enjoys the wages of love's labor on his own merits, while Troilus enjoys the wages of love's labor *primarily* due to the labor of his go-between. Perhaps that is why Criseyde shares some of the characteristics of Langland's Lady Mede, who is agreeable to anyone who courts her vigorously. Lady Mede is a beautiful woman who rewards all her faithful servants with rich gifts. Her most notable traits are generosity and fickleness—her willingness to take up with all who work for her. Lady Church contrasts her with Truth, who is identified as the best of all treasures (1.207). Mede is the daughter of Fals, "þat haþ a fikel tonge" (who has a fickle tongue; 2.25). Her popularity is rooted in the gifts she gives to others (2.20–24, passim). Read with Lady Mede in mind, the narrator's description of Criseyde in Book 5 is striking. He writes that Criseyde was:

> . . . goodly of hire speche in general,
> Charitable, estatlich, lusty, fre;
> Ne nevere mo ne lakked hire pite;
> Tendre-herted, slydynge of corage.
> (5.822–25)

[In general gracious in her speech, she was charitable, dignified, lively, generous, tender-hearted, changeable of mood, nor did she lack pity.]

These are all of the qualities that could be attributed to Lady Mede. What's more, after betraying Troilus, Criseyde becomes aware that she too will bear the stigma of unfaithfulness, but she decides to make the best of it (5.1054–68). She will, she tells herself, at least be true to Diomede. Langland's knight Conscience, aware of Mede's fickle nature, refuses to marry her, even though he is commanded by the king to do so (3.110–41). Troilus, totally prostrated by "passionate love" or *amor hereos*, is not so cold-blooded.

The comparison of Criseyde to Lady Mede does not hold if one takes Lady Mede, as John Yunck does, to be a personification of human venality.[92] To be sure, Yunck notes that Langland understood Mede to be a

---

92. John A. Yunck, *The Lineage of Lady Meed: The Development of Mediaeval Venality Satire* (South Bend, Ind.: University of Notre Dame Press, 1963) 5–6.

complex character, who could, under the proper conditions, for example, as wages for honest labor, make a positive contribution to society.[93] On the whole, however, Yunck believes that the sensitive and insecure Langland, a Church cleric, presents her as essentially evil, dressing her up as the Whore of Babylon (2.7–19) and having her brutally rejected by the good knight Conscience. Chaucer, on the other hand, the descendant of successful merchants, the dedicated but worldly civil servant, the tariff collector, but most importantly the nascent Renaissance humanist, was much easier on his own version of Lady Mede than Langland was. His narrator's deep sympathies for Criseyde, however "slyding of corage," have often been noted. Moreover, from the perspective of love's labor, Chaucer's sympathies lay at least as much with Pandarus and Diomede as with Troilus. *Troilus and Criseyde* can, at one level, be read as an *exemplum* of the principle that the productive worker enjoys the wages of love. Specifically, Chaucer saw hidden in Boccaccio's story the principle that love rewards those "That serven best and most alwey labouren" (3.1265). He exploited this potential in his own version. While he admired Troilus's idealism, his bourgeois heart sided with the geese rather than with the falcons. In this sense, then, it would be perhaps more fitting to identify Criseyde with "mercede" of the C-text, who, argues Yunck, unambiguously stands for the just wages of labor.[94]

Whether or not one is convinced that Criseyde is like Lady Mede, the significance of this analysis is that, as Bakhtin would have predicted, the language by which Chaucer constructed his famous love poem is not pure, but dialogically "contaminated" with discourses from other aspects of human life, in this case, labor. Furthermore, the majority of the passages cited here were not found in the *Filostrato* but were Chaucer's own additions. Indeed, the discourse of love's labor in *Troilus and Criseyde* dovetails very nicely with evidence from other of Chaucer's works about Chaucer's work ethic. He was a man who, in general, believed in the dignity of work and distrusted aristocratic idleness. However, work for him was more than just an antidote for idleness; it was the means to produce something of value. He also believed that hard diligent work should be given its just reward, but, apparently, a reward only on this earth. An analysis of the discourse of love's labor, and, indeed, of productive labor in general, therefore, takes us closer to the beating heart of Chaucer's most polished and complex portrayal of the human phenomenon of love.

93. Yunck 10.
94. Yunck 293.

Conclusion

> Your brother and my sister no sooner met but they looked; no sooner
> looked but they loved; no sooner loved but they sighed; no sooner
> sighed but they asked one another the reason; no sooner knew the rea-
> son but they sought the remedy; and in these degrees have they made
> a pair of stairs to marriage, which they will climb incontinent, or else
> be incontinent before marriage.
>
> —*Shakespeare's Rosalind*

> Work is love made visible.
>
> —*Kahlil Gibran*

Rosiland's description in Shakespeare's *As You Like It* of the
progress in the relationship between Oliver and Celia encapsu-
lates in many ways an ideal paradigm in the discourse of love's
labor.[1] While the lovers fall in love at first sight, they are not
prostrated by overwhelming emotion. On the contrary, love
sets them to work in a reasonable and purposeful manner. The
dart of love enters through a glance; the glance leads to sighs,
but the sighs immediately lead to a search for both reasons and
remedies. Shakespeare's remedy, however, is not a rejection of
love in the tradition of Ovid's *Remedia amoris* or Gower's *Confessio Amantis*. On the contrary, the remedy includes analysis and determined effort:
the building of a set of stairs, a series of discrete but ascending steps leading to the fulfillment of their love, which is the marriage that occurs at
the end of the play. Contrary to the assertion of Denis de Rougemont,
happy love does have a history. Shakespeare's comedies present a part of
that history, and the ancient and medieval literary tradition that has been
the focus of this study presents another. In the earlier tradition, however,
marriage is not presented as the top of love's stairway; that end comes
later, further along in the "embourgeoisement de l'eros." The end in the

---

1. *As You Like It: Comedies: The Norton Shakespeare*, ed. Stephen Greenblatt et al. (New York: W. W.
Norton, 1997) 5.2.29–35 (643).

ancient and medieval tradition is either successful courtship or reproduction or both.

Indeed, a notable tradition of constructing love as a form of labor begins with Ovid and continues through the Middle Ages. The tradition is saturated with the labor ideologies of the times and cultures of the various authors who contributed to it. More correct, however, two literary traditions of love's labor were created. One starts with Ovid, a literary figure who had an impressive and continuous influence on medieval writers. In the *Ars amatoria*, Ovid writes an *ars erotica*, a manual of love's labor. He begins a tradition in which constructing such labor is "rhetorical," playful, and centered on the labor of courtship. In contrast, the second tradition is centered on the labor of procreation, and it tends to be, at least in its beginnings, philosophical, conservative, and serious. The first begins with Ovid and continues through the *De amore*, Guillaume de Lorris's *Roman de la rose (RI)*, and the *Troilus*. The second begins with the *De planctu naturae* and then is put into dialog with the first in Jean de Meun's *Roman de la rose (RII)*, the *Confessio Amantis*, and the *Parlement of Foules*. In the first, the object is to "work" at courtship, which is ultimately a game, and the anticipated results include finding a lover, winning a lover, and keeping a lover, the three major labors of the *Ars amatoria*. In this tradition, the labor discourse is double-voiced and, in the earlier texts, often subversive not only of the mainstream labor ideologies but also of orthodox moralities. In the second, the object is to labor to produce children. Here the writers picture the genitals as tools. The work is serious, and it plays a key role in the communal effort to build human population. Those who refuse to perform this work, because they are homosexuals, celibates, or just too old, are either condemned or corrected. The labor discourse in the second tradition supports or even goes beyond the prevailing labor ideologies in that it always considers labor a positive value and judges labor by means of what it can produce. Although progressive in its labor ideology, it is conservative in its morality, usually supporting traditional natural law sexual ethics. Marriage, however, plays no overt role even in this second tradition.

This dual tradition is starkly highlighted in a comparison of the first two medieval works discussed in this book: the *De amore*, representing the first tradition, and the *De planctu*, representing the second. In the first, Andreas writes a treatise that looks very much like a medieval combination of the *Ars amatoria* and the *Remedia amoris*. In this treatise, although love is defined as a passion, it is constructed as a call to labor, to performing aristocratic services. The treatise explains how to carry out these services, which are, above all, knightly activities and polite conversation. In eight dialogs between potential lovers of various ranks, the *De amore* even models this service of love. The dialogs are "rhetorical" and focused on the labor of courtship.

Although the *De amore* falls within the first tradition, the love's labor discourse found therein is in many key ways different from that found in the *Ars amatoria*. What has Andreas really done to Ovid, the original *filostrato* (love-striken one)?[2] He has, of course, medievalized him. Andreas's labor lexicon has evolved, for example, with positive labor words like *obsequium, ministerium,* and *servitium* being used to designate the specifically aristocratic character of love's labor. Moreover, a strong class consciousness exists in the *De amore* that is not evident in the *Ars amatoria*. Love's labor in the *De amore* is strictly and self-consciously a labor of the aristocracy. The *De amore* is also concerned with love's labor as external evidence revealing the worth of the inner person, whereas Ovid, on the contrary, presents love's labor as a form of playacting, which does not by definition reveal the inner man. Finally, the *De amore* fashions love as a sort of economic transaction, with the lady's response to wooing being cast as "wages" due for honest labor.

The *De planctu* was written at just about the same time as the *De amore*. Here, however, the discourse of love's labor becomes serious and morally conservative. Indeed, Alan's discourse has none of the subversive, Ovidian levity found in the *De amore*. The discourse is serious and nonironic when it insists that sex must be (re)productive labor. The sexual organs are described as tools and the woman's body as a workshop. Idleness and *otium* corrupt Venus's work if mankind is not thoughtful. When this corruption occurs, sexual activity is best symbolized by Iocus, sport, and not Cupid, who stands for productive sexual labor. Love's labor, for Alan, is not agricultural labor but rather the labor of scribes and artisans, people who work with their hands but in cities, not in the fields. Although morally conservative with respect to the uses of sex, Alan's discourse is also ideologically progressive in that it consistently reflects changes in the ideology of labor and laborers evolving in the twelfth century. While the typical Christian (and monastic) ideology of labor portrayed work as an antidote to idleness, Alan's discourse praises mechani-

2. I am, of course, playing here with the title and content of C. S. Lewis's seminal article on the *Troilus:* "What Chaucer Really Did to Il Filostrato," *Essays and Studies by Members of the English Association* 17 (1932): 56–75.

cal labor as a dignified activity and identifies work productivity as a serious issue for the first time. In this way, Alan's discourse anticipates what
will become a new bourgeois work ethic.

Turning to the *Roman de la rose* and Gower's *Confessio Amantis*, we see
both traditions of love's labor as well as various contemporary labor issues being brought into dialog. They are intense "sites of action" in
which various labor ideologies meet and comment upon each other. In
RI, Guillaume de Lorris continues exclusively the Ovidian strain of the
discourse of love's labor. Here love's labor is courtship, but unlike Ovid,
Guillaume celebrates, in the character of Idleness, the aristocratic leisure
necessary to engage in the service of courtship. In *RI* work is clearly in
quotation marks. In *RII*, however, the two strains are placed into dialog
by various allegorical *praeceptores* created by Jean de Meun for just that
purpose. Friend and the Old Woman are Ovidian teachers, who discuss
the work of courtship for both the lover and his beloved. The emphasis is
on strategy and game; they counsel the lover to do what is necessary to
win—either in terms of sex or money. Coming into dialog with this
Ovidian strain is the discourse of love's labor as a means of procreation.
Discourse favoring natural law ethics is put into the mouths of Nature
and Genius, who want the courtship to succeed just as much as Friend
does but only on the condition that procreation occurs, only on the condition that Nature's tools are used to fashion new human beings. From
the perspective of Christian morality, however, Jean de Meun is heterodox rather than conservative because he pushes natural law ethics beyond orthodox limits. Taking an amusing position that certainly did not
amuse orthodox clerics, he condemns celibates, who refuse love's labor,
as well as homosexuals, who perform it unproductively. In the raucous
conclusion of *RII*, the serious labor discourse of the *De planctu* becomes
playful, energetic, and, in the end, almost violent. Christine de Pisan was
probably right to be concerned about it.

Moving from *RII* to the *Confessio Amantis* is like moving from the climax of an epic adventure into the small and quiet confines of a confes-
sional. Michel Foucault argues that confession is the archetypal form of
discourse from which is constructed our modern *scientia sexualis*.[3] To the
extent that Amans believes he is interrogating Genius for "the truth"
about love and sex, this fourteenth-century dialog is a contribution to *scientia sexualis* in its infancy. Unlike Ovid or Andreas, Gower does not offer

---

3. *The History of Sexuality*, trans. Robert Hurley, vol. 1 (New York: Vintage Books, 1990) 58–65.

an *ars erotica* but rather a "philosophical" discourse that is sometimes playful and sometimes serious and morally conservative, that is, supporting natural law ethics. Nevertheless, in Amans's confession various labor discourses are brought fully into dialog with each other. In Book 4 of the *Confessio*, Gower brings the Ovidian strain of love's labor, especially as it was developed in the *De amore*, into a pseudomoralistic focus. Here the work of love is the various activities of courtship as well as the service of battle and conquest for the sake of the beloved. Inactivity in love's labor is fashioned as lover's *acedia*, and the lover is slothful if he does not keep himself actively engaged in all kinds of love's labor. The lover, however, questions the value of military service. He brings up new concerns about productivity in love's labor because his own efforts have produced no concrete results. What is significant here is that the concern for productivity arises *outside* of the second tradition of love's labor, the tradition that focuses on procreation. Instead, Amans is thinking about productivity *in courtship*. Here the effect of new fourteenth-century work ethics—especially those that emphasize the dignity of labor and concerns with productive uses of time—arises in Gower's discourse of love's labor. In Book 8, however, Gower makes a move similar to that of Jean de Meun in *RII*. He abruptly turns from consideration of the labor of courtship and places the whole question of Amans's productivity in the context of the command of Genius and Nature to multiply the race. Placed in this context, Amans's argument that he has been "busy" about love's labor is shown to be self-deluding. Yes, one can be busy about courtship, but if one will not (or cannot) use Nature's tools productively to increase the species, then the labors of courtship are no better than idleness. Prayer and a retreat from love are the only remedies.

Chaucer, like Gower, is concerned with (re)production in the *Parlement of Foules*. Chaucer's poem concerns love, but it also concerns service for the common good. In the parliament scene of the poem, Chaucer juxtaposes the first and second discourses of love's labor. The birds of prey represent the first discourse. Here the labor of courtship is the aristocratic service of rhetorically elaborate debates and knightly combat. The female is valued not so much as a prospective mother but rather as a courtly lady, not a "fere" but a "soverayn lady." The three birds of prey in the *Parlement* are all active workers in the tradition of Andreas Capellanus. Their rhetoric is polished to a high degree. However, in this poem, Chaucer presents the three aristocratic birds as somewhat silly, and their discourse as sterile. The reason for this is that Chaucer, like

Gower, merges the first tradition of love's labor with the second. In addition, unlike Alan of Lille, Chaucer constructs the discourse playfully. The followers of Nature in the *Parlement* are the lower-class birds, and they alone are concerned with completing the work of procreation. They completely ignore the aristocratic works of elaborate speech and military service and proceed without ceremony to choosing their mates. Chaucer, however, manages to get even more comedy out of the discourse of the lower-class birds than he does out of the discourse of the upper-class birds of prey. As in *RII*, discourse in the second tradition of love's labor becomes playful and full of high energy. Chaucer's poem ends on a comic note, with order restored and the work of reproduction set to continue reliably.

The two bookends of this study are Ovid and Chaucer. Linking Ovid and Chaucer is a commonplace of literary criticism, for Chaucer's poetry is heavily indebted to Ovid's with respect to its themes, tropes, and spirit. Both Ovid and Chaucer are "rhetorical" poets. Both delight in a mixture of earnestness and game. While Ovid writes against the background of a labor ideology that condemned *otium otiosum*, he really advocates courtship activities that from a civic perspective could be classified under idleness. In the *Troilus*, Chaucer does something similar. He approves the labor of such good workers as Pandarus and Diomede, and he disapproves of the sloth in love of his protagonist Troilus. Nevertheless, if one considers the *Troilus* from a civic perspective, the work that Troilus ignores and that Diomede does so well is not work at all but leisure activity. From the strict Roman perspective, courtship activities are the fruits of *otsium otiosum*. Neither the work of procreation nor marriage is ever mentioned in the *Troilus*. From the perspective of public virtue, Troilus *is* a good worker, for he attends to the *officium* of his class, which is the defense of his city. He is second only to Hector in the "durryng don that longeth to a knyght" (the daring-do appropriate to knighthood).[4] Pandarus is indeed right that the work of love is but a game. Thus, in many ways, Chaucer employs the same strategy that Ovid did, appealing to an ethic that encourages "work" while really defending *otium otiosum*.

However, apart from the fact that the *Ars amatoria* is a mock didactic work and the *Troilus* a verse narrative, subtle differences in the labor discourse separate the two works. These are differences that normally

---

4. Geoffrey Chaucer, *Troilus and Criseyde*, in *The Riverside Chaucer*, ed. Larry D. Benson, 3rd ed. (Boston: Houghton Mifflin, 1987) 5.837 (571).

would not be perceived without a Bakhtinian appreciation of the ideological coloring of language. On the one hand, Ovid was reacting to the ethic(s) surrounding the concept of *otium* in classical Rome. He was also building on a social structure in which certain kinds of work were considered beneath the dignity of free men. Romans believed that a free man's agriculture, the fruit of *otium negotiosum*, was one of the highest callings, but that the work of artisans, slaves, and even merchants was illiberal. Ovid avoided the terms *servitium*, which linked work to the activities of slaves, and *negotium*, which linked work to the activities of merchants.

Chaucer, on the other hand, lived in a society in which a new work ethic was beginning to emerge. It was a work ethic that perceived labor as a positive quality, detached from the traditional etiology of work as a result of sin. It was an ethic that valued labor *productivity*, rather than simply valuing labor as an antidote to idleness. It was also an ethic that valued the work of merchants and the accumulation of wealth. Because Chaucer was writing in English rather than Latin, his lexicon cannot be compared directly with that of Ovid. However, Chaucer painted love's labor using a much fuller palette of words than Ovid had. He used labor words that were just coming into use, reflecting new attitudes toward labor and not necessarily linking work to pain, suffering, and drudgery. Beyond such traditional terms as *labour, werk, swynk, service,* and *travail,* Chaucer was able to use such new, positive terms as *bysynesse* and *emprise* for the work of love. While Ovid's relationship to the prevailing work ideology of his time is defensive and subversive, Chaucer's attitude reflects a wholehearted acceptance of the emerging labor ideology of his own time. While in the *Troilus* Chaucer operates completely within the first tradition of love's labor, he still sets up *productive* labor as his ideal. Thus, the discourse of love's labor in Chaucer reflects an "embourgeoisement de l'eros," a discourse in which the bourgeois values of labor and productivity are foregrounded although within the context of love. Writing hundreds of years later, Shakespeare superbly captures Chaucer's can-do spirit in Romeo's affirmation, as he explains to Juliet how he came to be in her garden: "With love's light wings did I o'erperch these walls, / For stony limits cannot hold love out, / And what love can do, that dares love attempt."[5] For the emphasis of the labor discourse in the *Troilus* focuses consistently on love as a project to be conquered with ingenuity and grit. Love in the discourses and actions of Pandarus and Diomede is

---

5. *Romeo and Juliet: Tragedies: The Norton Shakespeare* 2.2.107–10 (170).

active, rather than passive; courageous, rather than prostrated; happy, rather than tragic. What those two laborers can do, they dare attempt. This is strikingly not true of Troilus, who tragically suffers more than he acts. Troilus is all about feeling and little about action.

Indeed, the discourse of love's labor embodies in many ways the exact opposite of those qualities admired in Troilus. The discourse stresses action above emotion, and this is probably the reason that it has not been given the recognition it deserves. After all, the primary definition of "love" in the *Oxford English Dictionary* speaks of warm, affectionate *feelings* which, in response to attractive qualities or sympathy, manifest themselves in delight in the beloved's presence and solicitude for his or her welfare.[6] Nevertheless, little analysis of feeling per se occurs in the discourse of love's labor; the discourse is focused much more either on the behaviors associated with the feelings of love or on the results of those behaviors. It highlights what ought to be done rather than what is felt. For that reason, Troilus, unlike Romeo, could never be a hero in the discourse world of love's labor. To appreciate Troilus, one must shift registers and enter the discourse world of love as passion.

Kahlil Gibran's remark that "Work is love made visible" is an appropriate place to end this study.[7] Gibran, of course, is commenting about physical labor rather than love's labor. His essay is a genuine encomium to the joys of productive labor, and he has little patience for idleness. "To be idle," he writes, "is to become a stranger to the seasons, and to step out of life's procession."[8] Rather than being the result of a curse, labor for Gibran is a way of loving life and learning life's secrets. In that sense, then, work becomes love made visible. Gibran's insight, however, is also true in a narrower sense with respect to love's labor. While the discourse of passion is focused inwardly on feelings, the discourse of love's labor looks outward to the actions that make love visible to anyone with eyes to see. With respect to lovers, the discourse proclaims: By their fruits, you shall know them. Whether engaged in amorous dialog, active courtship, or sex and reproduction, love's laborers are thoroughly involved in the procession of life and, in that sense, happy and fulfilled. Happy love does, then, have a history. In literature, love's workers make love visible, while at the same time their creators make visible their own evolving ideologies of work and creative effort.

6. "Love" (1.a), *Oxford English Dictionary*, 1989 ed.
7. Kahill Gibran, "On Work," *The Prophet* (1923; New York: Knopf, 1971) 28.
8. Gibran 25.

Bibliography

Primary Texts

Abelard, Peter, and Heloise. *The Letters of Abelard and Heloise.* Trans. Betty Radice. New York: Penguin Books, 1974.

Adalbéron de Laon. *Poème au roi Robert.* Ed. and trans. Claude Carozzi. Les Classiques de l'histoire de France au moyen âge. Paris: Les Belles Lettres, 1979.

Alan of Lille. *De Planctu Naturae.* Ed. Nikolaus M. Häring. *Studi Medievali,* 3rd sers., 19.2 (1978): 797–879.

———. *Plaint of Nature.* Trans. James J. Sheridan. Toronto: Pontifical Institute, 1980.

———. *Summa de arte praedicatoria.* In *Patrologiae cursus completus, sive bibliotheca universalis. Series Latina.* Ed. J.-P. Migne. 221 vols. Paris, 1844–1864. 210.110–98.

Andreas Capellanus. *Andreas Capellanus on Love.* Ed. and trans. P. G. Walsh. London: Duckworth, 1982.

Augustine of Hippo. *The City of God against the Pagans.* Ed. and trans. William M. Green. Loeb Classical Library. Cambridge, Mass.: Harvard University Press, 1972.

———. *De Genesi ad litteram: Libri duodecim.* In *Oeuvres complètes de Saint Augustin.* Ed. Péronne et al. 33 vols. Paris: Librairie de Louis Vivès, 1870. 7.39–381.

———. *De Genesi contra Manichaeos.* In *Oeuvres complètes de Saint Augustin.* Ed. Péronne et al. 33 vols. Paris: Librairie de Louis Vivès, 1870. 3.423–91.

———. *De opere monachorum.* In *Oeuvres complètes de Saint Augustin.* Ed. Péronne et al. 33 vols. Paris: Librairie de Louis Vivès, 1870. 22.84–129.

———. *Enarrationes in psalmos.* In *Oeuvres complètes de Saint Augustin.* Ed. Péronne et al. 33 vols. Paris: Librairie de Louis Vivès, 1870. 11.609–15.562.

Benedict of Nursia. *Benedicti regula.* Ed. Rudolph Hanslik. Corpus Scriptorum Ecclesiasticorum Latinorum 75. Vienna: Hoelder-Pichler-Tempsky, 1960.

———. *The Rule of St. Benedict.* Trans. Cardinal Gasquet. New York: Cooper Square, 1966.

Biblia sacra iuxta vulgatam clementinam: Nova editio. Ed. Albert Colunga and Laurence Turrado. 7th ed. Madrid: Biblioteca de Auctores Christianos, 1985.

Boccaccio, Giovanni. *"The Filostrato" of Giovanni Boccaccio.* Ed. and trans. Nathaniel Griffin and Arthur Myrick. Philadelphia: University of Pennsylvania Press, 1929.

Bonaventure, Saint. *"De paupertate Christi: Contra Magistrum Guilelmum." Opera Omnia.* Ed. A. C. Peltier. 15 vols. Paris: Ludovicus Vives, 1868. 14.364–409.

The Book of Vices and Virtues. Ed. W. Nelson Francis. Early English Text Society, OS, 217. London: Oxford University Press, 1942.

Brinton, Thomas. *The Sermons of Thomas Brinton, Bishop of Rochester (1373–1389).* Ed. Mary Aquinas Devlin. 2 vols. London: Royal Historical Society, 1954.

Cassien, John. *Institutions cénobitiques*. Ed. Jean-Claude Guy. Paris: Les éditions du Cerf, 1965.

Cato, Marcus Porcius. *De agri cultura: Marcus Porcius Cato "On Agriculture" and Marcus Terentius Varro "On Agriculture."* Trans. William Hooper and Harrison Ash. Rev. ed. Loeb Classical Library. Cambridge, Mass.: Harvard University Press, 1935. 1–157.

Chaucer, Geoffrey. *The Riverside Chaucer*. Ed. Larry D. Benson. 3rd ed. Boston: Houghton Mifflin, 1987.

———. *Troilus and Criseyde: A New Edition of "The Book of Troilus."* Ed. Barry Windeatt. New York: Longman, 1984.

Chrétien de Troyes. *Erec and Enide*. Ed. and trans. Carleton W. Carroll. Garland Library of Medieval Literature 25. New York: Garland, 1987.

Cicero, Marcus Tullius. *De officiis*. Trans. Walter Miller. Loeb Classical Library. Cambridge, Mass.: Harvard University Press, 1913.

———. *Tusculan Disputations*. Ed. and trans. J. E. King. Loeb Classical Library. Cambridge, Mass.: Harvard University Press, 1927.

Dives and Pauper. Ed. Priscilla Heath Barnum. Early English Text Society 275. London: Oxford University Press, 1976.

Faral, Edmond, ed. "Les responsiones de Guillaume de Saint-Amour." *Archives d'histoire et littéraire du moyen âge* 18 (1950–1951): 337–94.

FitzRalph, Richard. "Defensio curatorum." In *Dialogus inter Militem et Clericum*. Trans. John Trevisa. Ed. Aaron Jenkins Perry. Early English Text Society, OS, 167. London: Oxford University Press, 1925. 39–93.

Francis of Assisi. *Écrits*. Ed. Kajetan Esser et al. Sources Chrétiennes. Paris: Les éditions du Cerf, 1981.

Geoffrey of Vinsauf. *Ars poetica: Les arts poétiques du XIIe et du XIIIe siècle*. Ed. Edmond Faral. Paris: Honoré Champion, 1962.

Gibran, Kahlil. *The Prophet*. New York: Knopf, 1971.

Gower, John. *The Complete Works of John Gower*. Ed. G. C. Macaulay. 4 vols. Oxford, U.K.: Clarendon Press, 1901.

———. *The English Works of John Gower*. Ed. G. C. Macaulay. 2 vols. Early English Text Society, ES, 1. Oxford, U.K.: Oxford University Press, 1900.

———. *The Latin Verses in the "Confessio Amantis": An Annotated Translation*. Trans. Sian Echard and Claire Fanger. East Lansing, Mich.: Colleagues Press, 1991.

———. *Mirour de l'omme*. Trans. William Burton Wilson. East Lansing, Mich.: Colleagues Press, 1992.

Guillaume de Lorris and Jean de Meun. *Le Roman de la rose*. Ed. Félix Lecoy. 3 vols. Paris: Librarie Honoré Champion, 1983.

———. *The Romance of the Rose*. Trans. Charles Dahlberg. Hanover, N.H.: University Press of New England, 1983.

Guillaume de Saint-Amour. "De periculis ecclesiae." In *Fasciculum rerum expetendarum et fugiendarum*. Ed. Edward Brown. 1690. Tucson, Ariz.: Audax Press, 1967. 2.18–41.

Horace (Quintus Horatius Flaccus). *Odes and Epodes*. Ed. and trans. C. E. Bennett. Rev. ed. Loeb Classical Library. Cambridge, Mass.: Harvard University Press, 1927.

Hugh of St. Victor. *Didascalicon: A Medieval Guide to the Arts*. Trans. Jerome Taylor. New York: Columbia University Press, 1961.

———. *Hugonis de Sancto Victore Didascalicon de studio legendi: A Critical Text*. Ed. Charles

Henry Buttimer. Studies in Medieval and Renaissance Latin 10. Washington, D.C.: The Catholic University of America Press, 1939.

———. *Summa de sacramentis fidei*. In *Patrologiae cursus completus, sive bibliotheca universalis. Series Latina*. Ed. J.-P. Migne. 221 vols. Paris, 1844–1864. 176.173–618.

Idung. *Dialogus duorum monachorum*. Ed. R. B. C. Huygens. *Studi Medievali*, 3d sers., 13.1 (1972): 375–470.

Jacob's Well. Ed. Arthur Brandeis. Early English Text Society, OS, 115. 1900. Millwood, N.Y.: Kraus, 1988.

Jerome, Saint. *Lettres*. Ed. and trans. Jérome Labourt. Vol. 1. Paris: Les Belles Lettres, 1949.

Langland, William. *Piers Plowman: The B Version*. Ed. George Kane and E. Talbot Donaldson. London: Athlone Press, 1975.

Libellus de diversis ordinibus et professionibus qui sunt in aecclesia. Ed. and trans. Giles Constable and B. Smith. Oxford, U.K.: Oxford University Press, 1972.

Murphy, James J., ed. *Three Medieval Rhetorical Arts*. Berkeley and Los Angeles: University of California Press, 1971.

Myrc, John. *Instructions for Parish Priests*. Ed. Edward Peacock. 2nd rev. ed. Early English Text Society, OS, 31. 1902. Rochester, N.Y.: Boydell & Brewer, 1996.

Ovid (Publius Ovidius Naso). *P. Ovidi Nasonis: "Amores," "Medicamina Faciei Femineae," "Ars Amatoria," "Remedia Amoris."* Ed. E. J. Kenney. Oxford, U.K.: Clarendon Press, 1961.

———. *Metamorphoses: Ovid*. Ed. and trans. Frank Justus Miller and G. P. Gould. 3rd ed. Loeb Classical Library. Cambridge, Mass.: Harvard University Press, 1984.

Petrarca, Francesco. *Petrarch: A Humanist among Princes*. Trans. David Thompson. New York: Harper & Row, 1971.

Plato. "Phaedrus." In *Plato: "Euthyphro," "Apology," "Crito," "Phaedo," "Phaedrus."* Ed. and trans. Harold North Fowler. Loeb Classical Library. Cambridge, Mass.: Harvard University Press, 1914. 405–579.

Selections from English Wycliffite Writings. Ed. Anne Hudson. Cambridge, U.K.: Cambridge University Press, 1978.

Shakespeare, William. *The Norton Shakespeare*. Ed. Stephen Greenblatt et al. 4 vols. New York: Norton, 1997.

Sophocles. *Antigone: Sophocles*. Ed. and trans. F. Storr. Loeb Classical Library. Cambridge, Mass.: Harvard University Press, 1981. 1.309–419.

The Summoning of Everyman. Ed. Geoffrey Cooper and Christopher Wortham. Nedlands: University of Western Australia Press, 1980.

Terence (Publius Terentius Afer). *The Brothers: Terence*. Ed. and trans. John Sargeaunt. Loeb Classical Library. Cambridge, Mass.: Harvard University Press, 1965. 2.213–323.

Thomas à Kempis. *The Imitation of Christ*. Trans. William C. Creasy. Macon, Ga.: Mercer University Press, 1989.

Thomas Aquinas. *Quaestiones quodlibetales*. Ed. Raymundi Spiazzi. 8th ed. Rome: Marietti, 1949.

———. *Summa contra gentiles*. Trans. Vernon J. Bourke et al. 5 vols. South Bend, Ind.: University of Notre Dame Press, 1975.

———. *Summa theologiae*. Ed. Thomas Gilby. 60 vols. New York: Blackfriars Press, 1963.

Virgil (Publius Vergilius Maro). *Virgil*. Ed. and trans. H. Rushton Fairclough. Rev. ed. 2 vols. Loeb Classical Library. Cambridge, Mass.: Harvard University Press, 1986.

———. *Virgil, Georgics: Volume 1, Books I–II*. Ed. Richard F. Thomas. Cambridge, U.K.: Cambridge University Press, 1988.

Wyclif, John. *An Apology for Lollard Doctrines, Attributed to John Wicliffe*. Ed. James Henthron Todd. 1842. New York: AMS Press, 1968.

———. *The English Works of Wyclif*. Ed. F. D. Matthew. 2nd ed. 1902. Millwood, N.Y.: Kraus, 1978.

Secondary Texts

Ackerman, Diane. *A Natural History of Love*. New York: Random House, 1994.

Aers, David. "The *Parliament of Fowls*: Authority, the Knower and the Known." *Chaucer Review* 16 (1981): 1–17.

———. "*Piers Plowman*: Poverty, Work, and Community." *Community, Gender, and Individual Identity: English Writing 1360–1430*. New York: Routledge, 1988. 20–72.

Alexander, Jonathan. "*Labeur* and *Paresse*: Ideological Representations of Medieval Peasant Labor." *Art Bulletin* 72 (1990): 436–52.

Allen, A. W. "Elegy and the Classical Attitude toward Love: Propertius 1,1." *Yale Classical Studies* 11 (1950): 255–77.

Allen, Peter. *The Art of Love: Amatory Fiction from Ovid to the "Romance of the Rose."* Philadelphia: University of Pennsylvania Press, 1992.

Alter, Jean V. *Les origines de la satire anti-bourgeoise en France: Moyen âge–XVIᵉ siècle*. Geneva: Droz, 1966.

Alvar, Carlos. "Oiseuse, Vénus, Luxure: Trois dames et un miroir." *Romania* 106 (1985): 108–17.

André, J. M. *L'otium dans la vie morale et intellectuelle romaine des origines à l'époque augustéenne*. Paris: Presses Universitaires de France, 1966.

Applebaum, Herbert. *The Concept of Work: Ancient, Medieval, and Modern*. Albany: SUNY Press, 1992.

Arden, Heather. "*The Roman de la Rose*": An Annotated Bibliography. New York: Garland, 1993.

Badel, Pierre-Yves. "*Le Roman de la rose*" au XIVᵉ siècle: Étude de la réception de l'oeuvre. Geneva: Droz, 1980.

Bakhtin, M. M. "Discourse in the Novel." *The Dialogic Imagination*. Ed. Michael Holquist. Trans. Caryl Emerson and Michael Holquist. Austin: University of Texas Press, 1981. 259–422.

———. "From the Prehistory of Novelistic Discourse." Bakhtin, *The Dialogic Imagination* 41–83.

———. *Problems of Dostoevsky's Poetics*. Trans. Caryl Emerson. Minneapolis: University of Minnesota Press, 1984.

Balsdon, J. P. V. D. *Life and Leisure in Ancient Rome*. New York: McGraw-Hill, 1969.

Batany, Jean. *Approches du "Roman de la rose."* Bordas Études 363. Paris: Bordas, 1973.

———. "Miniature, allégorie, idéologie: 'Oiseuse' et la mystique monacale récupérée par la 'classe de loisir.'" *Études sur "Le Roman de la rose" de Guillaume de Lorris*. Ed. Jean Dufornet. Paris: Honoré Champion, 1984. 7–36.

Beeson, C. F. C. *English Church Clocks, 1280–1850*. London: Antiquarian Horological Society, 1971.

Beidler, Peter G., ed. *John Gower's Literary Transformations in the "Confessio Amantis": Original Articles and Translations.* Washington, D.C.: University Press of America, 1982.

———, ed. *Masculinities in Chaucer: Approaches to Maleness in "The Canterbury Tales" and "Troilus and Crisdeyde."* Chaucer Studies 25. Cambridge, U.K.: D. S. Brewer, 1998.

Bennett, J. A. W. "Gower's 'Honeste Love.'" *Gower's "Confessio Amantis": A Critical Anthology.* Ed. Peter Nicholson. Cambridge, U.K.: D. S. Brewer, 1991. 49–61.

———. *"The Parlement of Foules": An Interpretation.* Oxford, U.K.: Clarendon Press, 1957.

Benson, C. David. *Chaucer's "Troilus and Criseyde."* London: Unwin Hyman, 1990.

Benton, John F. "The Court of Champagne as a Literary Center." *Speculum* 36 (1961): 551–91.

Benveniste, Emile. *Le vocabulaire des institutions indo-européenes.* Paris: Éditions de Minuit, 1969.

Berelot, Craig E. "'My Wit is Sharp: I Love No Taryinge': Urban Poetry in the *Parlement of Foules.*" *Studies in Philology* 93 (1996): 365–89.

Bergmann, Martin S. *The Anatomy of Loving: The Story of Man's Quest to Know What Love Is.* New York: Columbia University Press, 1987.

Berger, Peter, and Thomas Luckmann. *The Social Construction of Reality.* New York: Doubleday, 1966.

Binns, J. W., ed. *Ovid.* London: Routledge, 1973.

Bloch, Marc. *Feudal Society.* Trans. L. A. Manyon. 2 vols. Chicago: University of Chicago Press, 1961.

Bloomfield, Morton. *The Seven Deadly Sins.* East Lansing: Michigan State College, 1952.

Boase, Roger. *The Origin and Meaning of Courtly Love.* Totowa, N.J.: Rowman & Littlefield, 1977.

Boissonnade, P. *Life and Work in Medieval Europe.* Trans. Eileen Power. 1927. Evanston, Ill.: Harper & Row, 1964.

Boitani, Piero. "*O Quike Deth:* Love, Melancholy, and the Divided Self." *The Tragic and the Sublime in Medieval Literature.* Ed. Piero Boitani. Cambridge, U.K.: Cambridge University Press, 1989. 56–74.

Bouwsma, William. "Anxiety and the Formation of Early Modern Culture." *After the Reformation: Essays in Honor of J. H. Hexter.* Ed. Barbara C. Malament. Philadelphia: University of Pennsylvania Press, 1980. 215–46.

Bowden, Betsy. "The Art of Courtly Copulation." *Medievalia et Humanistica* 9 (1979): 67–85.

Bowers, John. *The Crisis of Will in "Piers Plowman."* Washington, D.C.: The Catholic University of America Press, 1986.

Braswell, Mary Flowers. *The Medieval Sinner: Characterization and Confession in the Literature of the English Middle Ages.* Rutherford, N.J.: Fairleigh Dickinson University Press, 1983.

Brewer, Derek. "Troilus' 'Gentil' Manhood." Beidler, *Masculinities* 237–52.

Bronson, Larry. "Chaucer's Pandarus: 'Jolly Good Fellow' or 'Reverend Vice'?" *Ball State University Forum* 24 (1983): 34–41.

———. "The 'Sodeyn Diomede': Chaucer's Composite Portrait." *Ball State University Forum* 25 (1985): 14–19.

Brooke, Rosalind. *The Coming of the Friars.* Oxford, U.K.: Allen & Unwin, 1975.

Brown, Carole Koepke. "The Tale of Pygmalion." Beidler, *John Gower* 29–32.

Brown, William H., Jr. "A Separate Peace: Chaucer and the Troilus of Tradition." *Journal of English and Germanic Philology* 83 (1984): 492–508.

Brownlee, Kevin. "The Problem of Faux Semblant: Language, History, and Truth in the *Roman de la Rose.*" *The New Medievalism.* Ed. Marina S. Brownlee, Kevin Brownlee, and Stephen G. Nichols. Baltimore: Johns Hopkins University Press, 1991. 253–71.

Butcher, A. F. "English Urban Society and the Revolt of 1381." Hilton and Aston 84–111.

Cahoon, Leslie. "Raping the Rose: Jean de Meun's Reading of Ovid's *Amores.*" *Classical and Modern Literature* 6 (1986): 261–85.

Calabrese, Michael A. *Chaucer's Ovidian Arts of Love.* Gainesville: University Press of Florida, 1994.

Calin, William. "John Gower's Continuity in the Tradition of French *Fin'Amor.*" *Mediaevalia* 16 (1993): 91–111.

Camargo, Martin. "The Consolation of Pandarus." *Chaucer Review* 25 (1991): 214–28.

Cerquiglini, Jacqueline. "Actendez, actendez." *Le nombre du temps: En hommage à Paul Zumthor.* Paris: Honoré Campion, 1988. 39–47.

Chenu, Marie Dominique. *Nature, Man, and Society in the Twelfth Century: Essays on New Theological Perspectives in the Latin West.* Ed. and trans. Jerome Taylor and Lester K. Little. Chicago: University of Chicago Press, 1968.

Cherchi, Paolo. *Andreas and the Ambiguity of Courtly Love.* Toronto: University of Toronto Press, 1994.

Cherniss, Michael. "The Literary Comedy of Andreas Capellanus." *Modern Philology* 72 (1975): 223–37.

Cipolla, Carlo M. *Clocks and Culture, 1300–1700.* London: Collins, 1967.

Cohn, Norman. *The World-View of a Thirteenth-Century Intellectual: Jean de Meun and the "Roman de la Rose."* Newcastel upon Tyne, U.K.: University of Durham, 1961.

Cooney, Helen. "The *Parlement of Foules:* A Theodicy of Love." *Chaucer Review* 32 (1998): 339–76.

Cooper, Helen. "Chaucer and Ovid: A Question of Authority." Martindale 71–81.

———. *The Oxford Guide to Chaucer's "Canterbury Tales."* Oxford, U.K.: Oxford University Press, 1987.

Copley, F. O. "*Servitium amoris* in the Roman Elegists." *Transactions of the American Philological Association* 78 (1947): 285–300.

Cowgill, Bruce Kent. "The *Parlement of Foules* and the Body Politic." *Journal of English and Germanic Philology* 74 (1975): 315–35.

Curtius, Ernst Robert. *European Literature and the Latin Middle Ages.* Trans. Willard R. Trask. New York: Harper & Row, 1953.

David, Alfred. "The Hero of the *Troilus.*" *Speculum* 37 (1962): 566–81.

de Lage, G. Raynaud. *Alain de Lille, poète du XIIᵉ siècle.* Montreal: Institute d'Études Médiévales, 1951.

Delehaye, Philippe. "Quelques aspects de la doctrine thomiste et néothomiste du travail." Hamesse and Muraille-Samaran 157–75.

Demats, Paul. "D'Amoenitas à Deduit: André le Chapelain et Guillaume de Lorris." *Mélanges de langue et de litterature du moyen âge et de la Renaissance, offerts à Jean Frappier.* Geneva: Droz, 1970. 217–33.

Denomy, Alexander. *The Heresy of Courtly Love.* New York: Declan X. McMullen, 1947.

de Rougemont, Denis. *Love in the Western World*. Trans. Montgomery Belgion. New York: Schocken Books, 1983.

Diamond, Arlyn. "*Troilus and Criseyde:* The Politics of Love." *Chaucer in the Eighties*. Ed. Julian N. Wasserman and Robert J. Blanch. Syracuse, N.Y.: Syracuse University Press, 1986. 93–102.

Dobson, R. B. *The Peasants' Revolt of 1381*. New York: St. Martin's Press, 1970.

Dodds, E. R. *The Greeks and the Irrational*. Berkeley and Los Angeles: University of California Press, 1966.

Dohrn van Rossum, Gerhard. *The History of the Hour: Clocks and Modern Temporal Orders*. Trans. Thomas Dunlap. Chicago: University of Chicago Press, 1996.

———. "Les 'orlogeurs' artistes et experts (XIVe–XVe siècles)." *Prosopographie et genèse de l'état moderne*. Ed. Françoise Autrand. Paris: Centre National des Lettres, 1986. 231–47.

Dragonetti, Roger. *Le mirage des sources: L'art du faux dans le roman médiéval*. Paris: Seuil, 1987.

Duby, Georges. *The Three Orders: Feudal Society Imagined*. Trans. Arthur Goldhammer. Chicago: University of Chicago Press, 1980.

Dufeil, M.-M. *Guillaume de Saint-Amour et la polémique universitaire parisienne, 1250–1259*. Paris: Picard, 1972.

Dyer, Christopher. "*Piers Plowman* and Plowmen: A Historical Perspective." *Yearbook of Langland Studies* 8 (1994): 155–76.

———. "The Social and Economic Background to the Rural Revolt of 1381." Hilton and Aston 9–42.

———. "Work Ethics in the Fourteenth Century." *The Problem of Labour in Fourteenth-Century England*. Ed. James Bothwell et al. York, U.K.: York Medieval Press, 2000. 21–41.

Economou, George. "The Character of Genius in Alan de Lille, Jean de Meun, and John Gower." *Chaucer Review* 4 (1970): 203–10.

Edwards, Catharine. *The Politics of Immorality in Ancient Rome*. Cambridge, U.K.: Cambridge University Press, 1993.

Edwards, Robert R., and Stephen Spector. *The Olde Daunce: Love, Friendship, Sex, and Marriage in the Medieval World*. Albany: SUNY Press, 1991.

Epstein, Steven. *Wage Labor and Guilds in Medieval Europe*. Chapel Hill: University of North Carolina Press, 1991.

Finley, Moses. *The Ancient Economy*. 2nd ed. London: Hogarth Press, 1985.

Fisher, John. *John Gower: Moral Philosopher and Friend of Chaucer*. New York: New York University Press, 1964.

Fleming, John V. "Further Reflections on Oiseuse's Mirror." *Zeitschrift für Romanische Philologie* 100 (1984): 26–40.

———. *Reason and the Lover*. Princeton, N.J.: Princeton University Press, 1984.

Foucault, Michel. *The History of Sexuality*. Trans. Robert Hurley. Vol. 1. New York: Vintage Books, 1990.

Frank, R. I. "Catullus 51: *Otium* versus *Virtus*." *Transactions of the American Philological Association* 99 (1968): 233–36.

Frantzen, Allen J. "The Work of Work: Servitude, Slavery, and Labor in Medieval England." Frantzen and Moffat 1–15.

Frantzen, Allen J., and Douglas Moffat, eds. *The Work of Work: Servitude, Slavery, and Labor in Medieval England*. Glasgow, U.K.: Cruithne Press, 1994.

Fyler, John M. *Chaucer and Ovid*. New Haven, Conn.: Yale University Press, 1979.

Galloway, Andrew. "Chaucer's *Former Age* and the Fourteenth-Century Anthropology of Craft: The Social Logic of a Premodernist Lyric." *ELH* 63 (1996): 535–53.

Gamble, Giles Y. "Troilus Philocaptus: A Case Study in *Amor Heroes*." *Studia Neophilologica* 60 (1988): 175–78.

Gaylin, Willard, and Ethel Person, eds. *Passionate Attachments: Thinking about Love*. New York: Free Press, 1988.

Geoghegan, Arthur. *The Attitude towards Labor in Early Christianity and Ancient Culture*. Washington, D.C.: The Catholic University of America Press, 1945.

Geremek, Bronislaw. "Le refus du travail dans la société urbaine du bas moyen âge." Hamesse and Muraille-Samaran 379–94.

Green, Peter. Introduction. *Ovid: The Erotic Poems*. New York: Penguin Books, 1982. 15–81.

Green, Richard. "Alan of Lille's 'De Planctu Naturae.'" *Speculum* 31 (1956): 649–74.

———. "Troilus and the Game of Love." *Chaucer Review* 13 (1979): 201–20.

Greenblatt, Stephen, and Giles Gunn. Introduction. *Redrawing the Boundaries: The Transformation of English and American Literary Studies*. New York: MLA, 1992. 1–11.

Grudin, Michaela Paasche. *Chaucer and the Politics of Discourse*. Columbia: University of South Carolina Press, 1996.

Gunn, Alan M. F. *The Mirror of Love: A Reinterpretation of "The Romance of the Rose."* Lubbock: Texas Tech Press, 1952.

Hallissy, Margaret. *Clean Maids, True Wives, Steadfast Widows: Chaucer's Women and Medieval Codes of Conduct*. Westport, Conn.: Greenwood Press, 1993.

Hamesse, Jacqueline. "Le travail chez les auteurs philosophiques du 12ᵉ et du 13ᵉ siècle." Hamesse and Muraille-Samaran 115–27.

Hamesse, Jacqueline, and Collette Muraille-Samaran, eds. *Le travail au moyen âge: Une approche interdisciplinaire*. Louvain-la-Neuve: Institut d'études médiévales de l'Université Catholique de Louvain, 1990.

Hanning, Robert W. "Come Out of the Code: Interpreting the Discourse of Desire in Boccaccio's *Filostrato* and Chaucer's *Troilus and Criseyde*." *Chaucer's "Troilus and Criseyde": "Subgit to alle Poesie": Essays in Criticism*. Ed. R. A. Shoaf. Binghamton, N.Y.: Medieval and Renaissance Texts and Studies, 1992. 120–37.

Harbert, Bruce. "Lessons from the Great Clerk: Ovid and John Gower." Martindale 83–97.

Harley, Marta Powell. "Narcissus, Hermaphroditus, and Attis: Ovidian Lovers at the Fontaine d'Amors in Guillaume de Lorris's *Roman de la rose*." *PMLA* 101 (1986): 324–37.

Hatton, Thomas. "Nature as Poet: Alanus de Insulis' *The Complaint of Nature* and the Medieval Concept of Artistic Creation." *Language and Style* 2 (1969): 85–91.

Hawes, Clement. "'More Stars, God knows, than a Pair': Social Class and the Common Good in Chaucer's *Parliament of Fowls*." *Publications of the Arkansas Philological Association* 15 (1989): 12–25.

Heffernan, Carol Falvo. *The Melancholy Muse: Chaucer, Shakespeare, and Early Medicine*. Pittsburgh, Pa.: Duquesne University Press, 1995.

Herescu, N. I., ed. *Ovidiana: Recherches sur Ovide*. Paris: Les Belles Lettres, 1958.

Hermann, John P. "A Monk Ther Was, A Fair for the Maistrie." Lambdin and Lambdin 69–79.

Hexter, Ralph J. *Ovid and Medieval Schooling: Studies in Medieval School Commentaries on Ovid's "Ars Amatori," "Epistulae ex Ponto," and "Epistulae Heroidum."* Munich: Bei der Arbeo-Gesellschaft, 1986.

Hicks, Eric, ed. *Le débat sur le Roman de la Rose.* Paris: Honoré Champion, 1977.

Hilton, Rodney. *Bond Men Made Free: Medieval Peasant Movements and the English Rising of 1381.* London: Temple Smith, 1973.

Hilton, Rodney, and T. H. Aston, eds. *The English Rising of 1381.* Cambridge, U.K.: Cambridge University Press, 1984.

Hinnebusch, William. *The History of the Dominican Order.* Staten Island, N.Y.: Alba House, 1966.

Hoffman, Richard L. *Ovid and "The Canterbury Tales."* Philadelphia: University of Pennsylvania Press, 1966.

Hollis, A. S. "The *Ars Amatoria* and *Remedia Amoris.*" Binns 84–115.

Hudson, Anne. *The Premature Reformation: Wycliffite Texts and Lollard History.* Oxford, U.K.: Clarendon Press, 1988.

Hult, David F. *Self-Fulfilling Prophecies: Readership and Authority in the First "Roman de la Rose."* Cambridge, U.K.: Cambridge University Press, 1986.

Hunt, Morton M. *The Natural History of Love.* New York: Knopf, 1959.

Huot, Sylvia. *"The Romance of the Rose" and Its Medieval Readers.* New York: Cambridge University Press, 1993.

Jaeger, C. Stephen. *Ennobling Love: In Search of a Lost Sensibility.* Philadelphia: University of Pennsylvania Press, 1999.

Jordan, Robert M. "The Question of Unity and the *Parlement of Foules.*" *English Studies in Canada* 3 (1977): 373–85.

Joyce, Patrick. "The Historical Meanings of Work: An Introduction." *The Historical Meanings of Work.* Ed. Patrick Joyce. Cambridge, U.K.: Cambridge University Press, 1987. 1–30.

Kavanagh, James H. "Ideology." *Critical Terms for Literary Study.* Ed. Frank Lentricchia and Thomas McLaughlin. 2nd ed. Chicago: University of Chicago Press, 1995. 306–20.

Karnein, Alfred. *"Amor est Passio:* A Definition of Courtly Love?" *Court and Poet.* Ed. Glyn S. Burgess. Liverpool, U.K.: Cairns, 1981. 215–21.

———. "La réception du *De amore* d'André le Chapelain au XIIIᵉ siècle." *Romania* 102 (1981): 324–51.

Kastan, David Scott. "Shakespeare and the 'Element he Lived in.'" *A Companion to Shakespeare.* Ed. David Scott Kastan. Oxford, U.K.: Blackwell, 1999. 3–6.

Kay, Sarah. *The Romance of the Rose.* London: Grant & Cutler, 1995.

Kelly, Douglas. *Internal Difference and Meanings in the "Roman de la rose."* Madison: University of Wisconsin Press, 1995.

Kenney, E. J. "Nequitiae poeta." Herescu 201–9.

Kinneavy, Gerald. "Gower's *Confessio Amantis* and the Penitentials." *Chaucer Review* 19 (1984): 144–63.

Köhler, E. "Lea, Matelda und Oiseuse." *Zeitschrift für Romanische Philologie* 78 (1962): 464–69.

Kolb, H. "Oiseuse, die Dame mit dem Spiegel." *Germanisch-Romanische Monatsschrift* 15 (1965): 139–49.

Kuhn, Reinhard. *The Demon of Noontide: Ennui in Western Literature.* Princeton, N.J.: Princeton University Press, 1976.

Lambdin, Laura C., and Robert T. Lambdin, eds. *Chaucer's Pilgrims: An Historical Guide to the Pilgrims in "The Canterbury Tales."* Westport, Conn.: Praeger, 1996.

Landes, David S. *Revolution in Time: Clocks and the Making of the Modern World.* Cambridge, Mass.: Belknap Press of Harvard University Press, 1983.

Lanham, Richard. *The Motives of Eloquence: Literary Rhetoric in the Renaissance.* New Haven, Conn.: Yale University Press, 1976.

Leach, E. W. "Georgic Imagery in the *Ars Amatoria.*" *Transactions of the American Philological Association* 95 (1964): 142–54.

Leclercq, Jean. *Otia monastica: Études sur le vocabulaire de la contemplation au moyen âge.* Rome: Herder, 1963.

LeGoff, Jacques. "Le travail dans les systèmes de valeur de l'Occident médiéval." Hamesse and Muraille-Samaran 7–21.

———. *Time, Work, and Culture in the Middle Ages.* Trans. Arthur Goldhammer. Chicago: University of Chicago Press, 1980.

Leicester, H. Marshall. "Ovid Enclosed: The God of Love as *Magister Amoris* in the *Romance of the Rose* of Guillaume de Lorris." *Res Publica Litterarum* 2 (1984): 107–29.

Levin, Rozalyn. "The Passive Poet: Amans as Narrator in Book 4 of the *Confessio Amantis.*" *Proceedings of the Illinois Medieval Association* 3 (1986): 114–30.

Lewis, C. S. *The Allegory of Love.* 1936. Oxford, U.K.: Oxford University Press, 1979.

———. "What Chaucer Really Did to *Il Filostrato.*" *Essays and Studies by Members of the English Association* 17 (1932): 56–75.

Little, Lester. "Pride Goes before Avarice: Social Change and the Vices in Latin Christendom." *American Historical Review* 76 (1971): 16–49.

———. *Religious Poverty and the Profit Economy in Medieval Europe.* Ithaca, N.Y.: Cornell University Press, 1978.

Lowes, John L. "The Loveres Maladye of Hereos." *Modern Philology* 11 (1913–1914): 491–546.

Lumiansky, R. M. "Chaucer's *Parlement of Foules*: A Philosophical Interpretation." *Review of English Studies* 24 (1948): 81–89.

———. "The Function of Proverbial Monitory Elements in Chaucer's *Troilus and Criseyde.*" *Tulane Studies in English* 2 (1950): 5–48.

Lyne, R. O. A. M. "Servitium amoris." *Classical Quarterly* n.s. 29 (1979): 117–27.

Mann, Jill. *Geoffrey Chaucer: Feminist Readings.* Atlantic Heights, N.J.: Humanities Press International, 1991.

Martin, June Hall. *Love's Fools: Aucassin, Troilus, Calisto and the Parody of the Courtly Lover.* London: Tamesis, 1972.

Martindale, Charles, ed. *Ovid Renewed: Ovidian Influences on Literature and Art from the Middle Ages to the Twentieth Century.* Cambridge, U.K.: Cambridge University Press, 1988.

McGerr, Rosemarie P. *Chaucer's Open Books: Resistance to Closure in Medieval Discourse.* Gainesville: University Press of Florida, 1998.

McInerney, Maud Burnett. "'Is This a Mannes Herte?': Unmanning Troilus through Ovidian Allusion." Beidler, *Masculinities* 221–35.

McNally, John J. "The Penitential and Courtly Traditions in Gower's *Confessio Amantis*." *Studies in Medieval Culture*. Ed. John R. Somerfeldt. Kalamazoo: Medieval Institute, 1964. 74–94.

Meech, Sanford. *Design in Chaucer's "Troilus*." Syracuse, N.Y.: Syracuse University Press, 1959.

Michel, Alain. "Rhétorique, poétique et nature chez Alain de Lille." Roussel and Suard 113–24.

Middleton, Anne. "Medieval Studies." Greenblatt and Gunn 12–40.

Mieszkowski, Gretchen. "Chaucer's Much Loved Criseyde." *Chaucer Review* 26 (1991): 109–32.

Miles, Gary B. *Virgil's "Georgics": A New Interpretation*. Berkeley and Los Angeles: University of California Press, 1980.

Milliken, Roberta. "Neither 'Clere Laude' nor 'Sklaundre': Chaucer's Translation of Criseyde." *Women's Studies* 24 (1995): 191–204.

Minnis, Alastair. *Chaucer and Pagan Authority*. Totowa, N.J.: Brewer, 1982.

———. "John Gower: *Sapiens* in Ethics and Politics." *Medium Aevum* 49 (1980): 207–29.

———. "'Moral Gower' and Medieval Literary Theory." *Gower's "Confessio Amantis": Responses and Reassessments*. Woodbridge, Suffolk, U.K.: D. S. Brewer, 1983. 50–78.

———. *Oxford Guides to Chaucer: The Shorter Poems*. Oxford, U.K.: Clarendon Press, 1995.

Moi, Toril. "Desire in Language: Andreas Capellanus and the Controversy of Courtly Love." *Medieval Literature: Criticism, Ideology, and History*. Ed. David Aers. New York: St. Martin's Press, 1986. 11–31.

Monson, Don. "Andreas Capellanus and the Problem of Irony." *Speculum* 63.3 (1988): 539–72.

———. "*Auctoritas* and Intertextuality in Andreas Capellanus' *De Amore*." *Poetics of Love in the Middle Ages: Texts and Contexts*. Ed. Moshe Lazar and Norris J. Lacy. Fairfax, Va.: George Mason University Press, 1989. 69–79.

Moorman, John. *A History of the Franciscan Order: From Its Origins to the Year 1517*. Oxford, U.K.: Clarendon Press, 1968.

Münch, Paul. "The Thesis before Weber: An Archaeology." *Weber's "Protestant Ethic": Origins, Evidence, Contexts*. Ed. Hartmut Lehmann and Guenther Roth. Publications of the German Historical Institute. Cambridge, U.K.: Cambridge University Press, 1993. 51–71.

Murgatroyd, P. "*Servitium amoris* and the Roman Elegists." *Latomus* 40 (1981): 87–100.

Muscatine, Charles. *Chaucer and the French Tradition*. Berkeley and Los Angeles: University of California Press, 1969.

Myerowitz, Molly. *Ovid's Games of Love*. Detroit: Wayne State University Press, 1985.

Nerlich, Michael. *The Ideology of Adventure*. Trans. Ruth Crowley. Minneapolis: University of Minnesota Press, 1987.

Newman, F. X., ed. *The Meaning of Courtly Love*. Albany: SUNY Press, 1968.

Nicholson, Peter. *An Annotated Index to the Commentary on Gower's "Confessio Amantis*." Medieval and Renaissance Texts and Studies 62. Binghamton, N.Y.: Center for Medieval and Early Renaissance Studies, 1989.

Norris, Kathleen. *The Cloister Walk*. New York: Riverhead Books, 1996.

Oexle, Otto Gerhard. "Le travail au XIᵉ siècle: Réalités et mentalités." Hamesse and Muraille-Samaran 49–60.

Olsen, Alexandra H. "In Defense of Diomede: 'Moral Gower' and *Troilus and Criseyde.*" *In Geardagum* 8 (1987): 1–12.

Olson, Paul A. "The *Parlement of Foules:* Aristotle's *Politics* and the Foundations of Human Society." *Studies in the Age of Chaucer* 2 (1980): 53–69.

Olsson, Kurt O. "Aspects of *Gentilesse* in John Gower's *Confessio Amantis,* Books III–V." Yeager, *Recent Readings,* 225–76.

———. *John Gower and the Structures of Conversion: A Reading of the "Confessio Amantis."* Cambridge, U.K.: D. S. Brewer, 1992.

Ott, Karl A. "Pauvreté et richesse chez Guillaume de Lorris." *Romanistische Zeitschrift für Literaturgeschichte* 2 (1978): 224–39.

Ovitt, George, Jr. "The Cultural Context of Western Technology: Early Christian Attitudes toward Manual Labor." Frantzen and Moffat 71–94.

———. *The Restoration of Perfection: Labor and Technology in Medieval Culture.* New Brunswick, N.J.: Rutgers University Press, 1987.

Owst, G. R. *Literature and Pulpit in Medieval England.* 2nd ed. New York: Barnes and Noble, 1961.

Palmer, Robert C. *English Law in the Age of the Black Death, 1348–1381.* Chapel Hill: University of North Carolina Press, 1993.

Patterson, Lee. *Chaucer and the Subject of History.* Madison: University of Wisconsin Press, 1991.

———. *Negotiating the Past: The Historical Understanding of Medieval Literature.* Madison: University of Wisconsin Press, 1987.

Paxson, James J., and Cynthia Gravlee, eds. *Desiring Discourse: The Literature of Love, Ovid through Chaucer.* Selinsgrove, Pa.: Susquehanna University Press, 1998.

Payen, Jean-Charles. "Eléments idéologiques et revendications dans *Le Roman de la rose.*" *Littérature et société au moyen âge.* Actes du Colloque des 5 et 6 mai d'Amiens 1978. Ed. Danielle Buschinger. Amiens: Université de Picardie, 1979. 285–304.

———. "L'art d'aimer chez Guillaume de Lorris." *Études sur "Le Roman de la rose" de Guillaume de Lorris.* Ed. Jean Dufournet. Geneva: Slatkine, 1984. 105–44.

———. "*Le Roman de la rose* et la notion de carrefour idéologique." *Romanistische Zeitschrift für Literaturgeschichte* 1 (1977): 193–203.

Pearsall, Derek. *The Life of Geoffrey Chaucer: A Critical Biography.* Cambridge, Mass.: Blackwell, 1992.

Peck, Russell. *Kingship and Common Profit in Gower's "Confessio Amantis."* Carbondale: Southern Illinois University Press, 1978.

———. "Love, Politics, and Plot in the *Parlement of Foules.*" *Chaucer Review* 24 (1990): 290–305.

Pelen, Marc. *Latin Poetic Irony in the "Roman de la Rose."* Liverpool, U.K.: Francis Cairns, 1987.

Pigg, Daniel F. "With Hym Ther Was a Plowman, Was His Brother." Lambdin and Lambdin 263–70.

Poiron, Daniel. "Alain de Lille et Jean de Meun." Roussel and Suard 135–51.

———. "Jean de Meun et la querelle de l'université de Paris: Du libelle au livre." *Traditions polémiques.* Cahiers V. L. Saulnier. Paris: Centre V. L. Saulnier, Université de Paris-Sorbonne, 1984. 9–19.

Putnam, Bertha. *The Enforcement of the Statute of Labourers: During the First Decade after the*

Black Death, 1349–1359. Studies in History, Economics, and Public Law 32. 1908. New York: AMS Press, 1970.

Radshall, Hastings. *The Universities of Europe in the Middle Ages.* Ed. F. M. Powicke and A. B. Emden. New ed. Oxford, U.K.: Oxford University Press, 1936.

Ramsey, Susan. "État présent du *Roman de la rose.*" *Chimères* 4 (Summer 1975): 14–28.

Rand, E. K. "The Metamorphosis of Ovid in *Le Roman de la rose.*" *Studies in the History of Culture.* Ed. Percy W. Long. 1942. Freeport, N.Y.: Books for Libraries, 1969. 103–21.

Renoir, Alan. "Criseyde's Two Half Lovers." *Orbis Litterarum* 16 (1961): 239–55.

Rhonheimer, Martin. "The Concept of the Natural Law in Thomas Aquinas." *Natural Law and Practical Reason: A Thomist View of Moral Autonomy.* Trans. Gerald Malsbary. New York: Fordham University Press, 2000. 58–175.

Richards, Earl Jeffrey. "Reflections on Oiseuse's Mirror: Iconographic Tradition, Luxuria and the *Roman de la Rose.*" *Zeitschrift für Romanische Philologie* 98 (1982): 296–311.

———. "The Tradition of 'otium litteratum' and Oiseuse in *Le Roman de la rose.*" *Studi francesi* 32 (1988): 271–73.

Robathan, D. M. "Ovid in the Middle Ages." Binns 191–209.

Robertson, D. W., Jr. *A Preface to Chaucer.* Princeton, N.J.: Princeton University Press, 1962.

———. "The Subject of the *De Amore* of Andreas Capellanus." *Modern Philology* 50 (1952–53): 145–61.

Rouche, Michel. "Une révolution mentale du Haut Moyen Age: Loisir et travail." *Horizons marins, itinéraires spirituels (Vᵉ–XVIIIᵉ siècles).* Ed. Henri Dubois et al. 2 vols. Paris: Publications de la Sorbonne, 1987. 1.233–37.

Roussel, Henri, and F. Suard, eds. *Alain de Lille, Gautier de Chatillon, Jakemart Gielee et leur temps.* Lille: Presses Universitaires de Lille, 1979.

Rowe, Donald W. *O Love! O Charite!: Contraries Harmonized in Chaucer's "Troilus."* Carbondale: Southern Illinois University Press, 1976.

Roy, Bruno. "A la recherche des lecteurs médiévaux du 'De amore' d'André le Chapelain." *Revue de l'université d'Ottawa* 55.1 (1985): 45–73.

Sadlek, Gregory M. "Bakhtin, the Novel, and Chaucer's *Troilus and Criseyde.*" *Chaucer Yearbook: A Journal of Late Medieval Studies* 3 (1996): 87–101.

———. "Interpreting Guillaume de Lorris' Oiseuse: Geoffrey Chaucer as Witness." *South Central Review* 10.1 (1993): 22–37.

———. "John Gower's *Confessio Amantis,* Ideology, and the 'Labor' of 'Love's Labor.'" *Re-Visioning Gower.* Ed. R. F. Yeager. Asheville, N.C.: Pegasus Press, 1998. 147–58.

———. "Love, Labor, and Sloth in Chaucer's *Troilus and Criseyde.*" *Chaucer Review* 26 (1992): 350–68.

Salter, Elizabeth. "*Troilus and Criseyde:* A Reconsideration." *Patterns of Love and Courtesy: Essays in Memory of C. S. Lewis.* Ed. John Lawlor. London: Edward Arnold, 1966. 86–106.

Sasaki, Shigemi. "Sur le personnage d'Oiseuse." *Études de langue et littérature* 32 (March 1978): 1–24.

Scanlon, Larry. "The Unspeakable Pleasures: Alain de Lille, Sexual Regulation and the Priesthood of Genius." *Romanic Review* 86.2 (1995): 213–42.

Scattergood, John. "The 'Bisynesse' of Love in Chaucer's Dawn-Songs." *Essays in Criticism* 37 (1987): 110–20.

Schmitz, Götz. "Gower, Chaucer and the Classics: Back to the Textual Evidence." Yeager, *Recent Readings*, 95–111.

Shannon, Edgar F. *Chaucer and the Roman Poets.* 1929. New York: Russell & Russell, 1957.

Sharrock, Alison. *Seduction and Repetition in Ovid's "Ars Amatoria 2."* Oxford, U.K.: Clarendon Press, 1994.

Simpson, James. "Ironic Incongruence in the Prologue and Book I of Gower's *Confessio Amantis.*" *Neophilologus* 72 (1988): 617–32.

Soble, Alan. *The Philosophy of Sex and Love.* St. Paul, Minn.: Paragon House, 1998.

Spearing, A. C. "Al This Mene I Be Love." *Studies in the Age of Chaucer: The Yearbook of the New Chaucer Society. Proceedings* 2 (1986): 169–77.

Stakel, Susan. *False Roses: Structures of Duality and Deceit in Jean de Meun's "Romance of the Rose."* Saratoga, N.Y.: ANMA Libri, 1991.

Stasko, Nicolette. "The Tale of Iphis." Beidler, *John Gower* 33–36.

Steinle, Eric M. "Anti-Narcissus: Guillaume de Lorris as a Reader of Ovid." *Classical and Modern Literature* 6 (1986): 251–59.

Stock, Brian. "Activity, Contemplation, Work, and Leisure between the Eleventh and the Thirteenth Centuries." *Arbeit, Musse, Meditation: Betrachtungen zur "Vita Activa" und "Vita Contemplativa."* Ed. Brian Vickers. Zürich: Verlag der Fachvereine, 1985. 87–108.

Stone, Lawrence. "Passionate Attachments in the West in Historical Perspective." Gaylin and Person 15–26.

Strohm, Paul. *Social Chaucer.* Cambridge, Mass.: Harvard University Press, 1989.

Szittya, Penn R. *The Antifraternal Tradition in Medieval Literature.* Princeton, N.J.: Princeton University Press, 1986.

Thomas, Keith. "Work and Leisure in Pre-Industrial Society." *Past and Present* 29 (December 1964): 50–66.

Tinkle, Theresa. *Medieval Venuses and Cupids: Sexuality, Hermeneutics, and English Poetry.* Stanford, Calif.: Stanford University Press, 1996.

Todd, Margo. "Work, Wealth and Welfare." *Christian Humanism and the Puritan Social Order.* Cambridge, U.K.: Cambridge University Press, 1987. 118–75.

Travis, Peter. "Chaucer's Chronographiae, the Confounded Reader, and Fourteenth-Century Measurements of Time." *Disputatio* 2 (1997): 1–34.

Trout, J. M. *The Voyage of Prudence: The World View of Alan of Lille.* Washington, D.C.: University Press of America, 1979.

van den Hoven, Birgit. *Work in Ancient and Medieval Thought.* Amsterdam: J. C. Gieben, 1996.

Veyne, Paul. *The Roman Empire.* Trans. Arthur Goldhammer. Cambridge, Mass.: Belknap Press of Harvard University Press, 1997.

Viederman, Milton. "The Nature of Passionate Love." Gaylin and Person 1–14.

Wack, Mary. *Lovesickness in the Middle Ages: The Viaticum and Its Commentaries.* Philadelphia: University of Pennsylvania Press, 1990.

———. "Lovesickness in *Troilus.*" *Pacific Coast Philology* 19 (1984): 55–61.

Wallace, David. *Chaucerian Polity: Absolutist Lineages and Associational Forms in England and Italy.* Stanford, Calif.: Stanford University Press, 1997.

Weber, Max. *The Protestant Work Ethic and the Spirit of Capitalism.* Trans. Talcott Parsons. 1930. New York: Charles Scribner's Sons, 1956.

Webster, James Carson. *The Labors of the Months in Antique and Medieval Art.* Princeton, N.J.: Princeton University Press, 1936.

Wenin, Christian. "Saint Bonaventure et le travail manuel." Hamesse and Muraille-Samaran 141–55.

Wenzel, Siegfried. "Acedia, 700–1200." *Traditio* 22 (1966): 72–102.

———. "Notes on the Parson's Tale." *Chaucer Review* 16 (1982): 248–51.

———. *The Sin of Sloth: Acedia in Medieval Thought and Literature.* Chapel Hill: University of North Carolina Press, 1967.

Wetherbee, Winthrop. *Chaucer and the Poets: An Essay on "Troilus and Criseyde."* Ithaca, N.Y.: Cornell University Press, 1984.

———. "The Function of Poetry in the 'De Planctu Naturae' of Alain de Lille." *Traditio* 25 (1969): 87–125.

———. "The Literal and the Allegorical: Jean de Meun and the *De Planctu Naturae*." *Medieval Studies* 33 (1971): 264–91.

———. *Platonism and Poetry in the Twelfth Century: The Literary Influence of the School of Chartres.* Princeton, N.J.: Princeton University Press, 1972.

White, Hugh. "Division and Failure in Gower's *Confessio Amantis*." *Neophilologus* 72 (1988): 600–616.

Wilkinson, L. P. Introduction. *The Georgics.* Trans. L. P. Wilkinson. New York: Penguin Books, 1982. 11–49.

———. *Ovid Recalled.* Cambridge, U.K.: Cambridge University Press, 1955.

Williams, Raymond. *Marxism and Literature.* Oxford, U.K.: Oxford University Press, 1977.

Windeatt, Barry. *Oxford Guides to Chaucer: "Troilus and Criseyde."* Oxford, U.K: Clarendon Press, 1992.

Workman, Herbert. *John Wyclif: A Study of the English Medieval Church.* 1926. Hamden, Conn.: Archon Books, 1966.

Yeager, R. F. "English, Latin, and the Text as 'Other': The Page as Sign in the Work of John Gower." *Text* 3 (1987): 251–67.

———, ed. *John Gower: Recent Readings.* Kalamazoo, Mich.: Medieval Institute, 1989.

———. *John Gower's Poetic: The Search for a New Arion.* Cambridge, U.K.: D. S. Brewer, 1990.

Yunck, John A. *The Lineage of Lady Meed: The Development of Mediaeval Venality Satire.* South Bend, Ind.: University of Notre Dame Press, 1963.

Zumthor, Paul. "Narrative and Anti-Narrative: *Le Roman de la rose*." *Yale French Studies* 51 (1974): 185–204.

Subject Index

aristocracy *(continued)*
 Amantis, 169, 189, 192, 203; in *De amore,*
 72, 74, 76–89, 108, 120, 260–61; medieval,
 58–60, 147; in *Mirour de l'Omme,* 188; in *Remedia amoris,* 111; Roman, 28–29, 31–32;
 in *Roman de la rose,* 118, 121–26, 129, 131,
 148–50, 159, 163, 165, 262; in *Troilus and
 Criseyde,* 237, 239, 255
army of love, 56, 76–78, 83, 86, 160
ars, 47–49, 65–66, 87, 117
Ars amatoria (Ovid), 13, 22, 24–54, 233, 264;
 compared to *Confessio Amantis,* 167, 169;
 compared to *De planctu naturae,* 90–91,
 101–2, 108, 110–12, 169; compared to *Roman de la rose,* 117–18, 121, 127–28,
 130–31, 150, 153, 165; compared to *Troilus
 and Criseyde,* 231n42, 251, 255; influence
 on *De amore,* 55–58, 71, 77–78, 87–88;
 love's labor in, 7, 114, 155–57, 218, 243,
 246. *See also* Ovid
ars erotica, 7n22, 169, 260, 263
Ars Poetica (Geoffrey of Vinsauf), 246
art, 1–2, 9, 27, 39–40, 47, 146–47, 153,
 164–65. *See also* liberal arts; mechanical
 arts
Art *(Roman de la rose),* 165
artifex, 35, 48, 65–66, 87, 98, 103. *See also*
 homo artifex
artisans, 64, 89, 91, 98–100, 175, 261, 265. *See
 also* craftsmen
art of love, 13–14, 209, 219; in *Ars amatoria,*
 47, 51; in *Confessio Amantis,* 167, 199–200;
 in *De amore,* 57n6, 77–78, 87; in *Roman de
 la rose,* 117, 147, 151–52, 154, 157, 164n102
*Art of Love: Amatory Fiction from Ovid to "The
 Romance of the Rose," The* (Allen), 12–13
As You Like It (Shakespeare), 259
Augustine, St., 60n18, 62–65, 80, 93, 135, 137,
 140n60, 143, 175, 185, 215, 230
Aurelius, 63
authors, 11–17, 23. *See also* poets
Automedon, 47–48
autonomous individual, 11n33
avarice, 132

Bailly, Harry *(Canterbury Tales). See* Host
 (Canterbury Tales)
Bayard *(Troilus and Criseyde),* 237
begging, 9–10, 133–39, 143–45, 184
behavior, of lovers, 13, 77–79, 83–85, 111,
 233n51, 266

bellum. See war
Benedict, St., 9, 71, 132, 173
Benedict's *Rule,* 92–97, 100–101, 103–104,
 113, 175–76
benefacta. See deeds, good
besoing. See needs
bestiality, 102
Bible, 56, 60–63, 135, 175. *See also individual
 Books*
birds of prey *(Parlement of Foules),* 220–24,
 237, 263–64
bisig, 190
bisischipe, 189–91
Black Knight *(Book of the Duchess),* 217n18
Black Plague, 10, 174
blacksmiths. *See* smiths
Boccaccio, Giovanni, 236, 237n66, 242–43,
 258
Boethius (Anicius Manlius Severinus
 Boethius), 101, 115
Bonaventure, St., 135, 139–43, 147, 162,
 202–3
Book of Vices and Virtues (Lorens), 173
bourgeoisie, 11n33, 262, 265; in Chaucer's
 amatory fiction, 209n2, 210, 212, 216,
 217n16, 222, 224, 232, 258; in *De amore,*
 84n72; in *De planctu naturae,* 98–99; in *Roman de la rose,* 126–27, 129, 149, 154, 165;
 in *Troilus and Criseyde,* 256
Bromyard, John, 183
business, 64, 88, 99, 195
bysynesse, 22, 45, 173, 189–93, 198–99, 204,
 206; in Chaucer's amatory fiction, 208–58,
 265

Cadmus, 203
Caesar Augustus, 22. *See also* Age of Augus-
 tus
Calva, Domenico, of Pisa, 181
Canon Yeoman's Tale *(Canterbury Tales),* 218
Canterbury Tales (Chaucer), 171, 180, 214–18,
 225–29
Capellanus, Andreas. *See* Andreas Capellanus
capitalists, 28, 94–95
Carmen ad Robertum regem (Adalbéron),
 66–71, 81–83
Carmente, 203
carpe diem motif, 155, 200–201
Carthusians, 95, 106
Cathar heresy, 5
Cato the Elder, 30, 33–34, 38n44

Index to Authors Cited

.

Idleness Working: The Discourse of Love's Labor from Ovid through Chaucer and Gower was designed and composed in Monotype Dante with Monotype Centaur display type by Kachergis Book Design, Pittsboro, North Carolina; and printed on 60-pound Glatfelter Natural and bound by Edwards Brothers, Inc., Lillington, North Carolina.